THE DEVIL'S SANDBOX

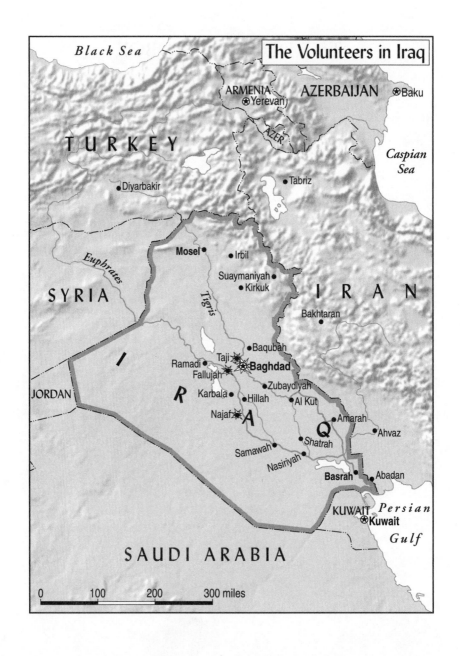

The Volunteers in Iraq

Black Sea

ARMENIA
⊛Yerevan
AZERBAIJAN
⊛Baku

AZER.

TURKEY

Caspian
Sea

•Diyarbakir

•Tabriz

Euphrates

SYRIA

Mosel •
•Irbil
Suaymaniyah •
• Kirkuk

I R A N

Tigris

Bakhtaran
•

•Baqubah

Ramadi •
Fallujah •
Taji ✴
✴Baghdad

JORDAN

I
R

Karbala •
• Hillah
•Zubaydiyah
• Al Kut

Najaf ✴
A
Q
• Amarah
• Ahvaz

Samawah •
• Shatrah
Nasiriyah •

Basrah • Abadan

KUWAIT
⊛Kuwait

Persian
Gulf

SAUDI ARABIA

0   100   200   300 miles

THE
DEVIL'S
SANDBOX

WITH THE 2ND BATTALION, 162ND INFANTRY
AT WAR IN IRAQ

JOHN R. BRUNING

ZENITH PRESS

DEDICATION

To the entire 2-162 Family: courage is your legacy.

First published in 2006 by Zenith Press, an imprint of MBI Publishing Company,
Galtier Plaza, Suite 200, 380 Jackson Street, St. Paul, MN 55101-3885 USA

Zenith Press titles are also available at discounts in bulk quantity for industrial or sales-promotional use.
For details write to Special Sales Manager at MBI Publishing Company, Galtier Plaza, Suite 200,
380 Jackson Street, St. Paul, MN 55101-3885 USA.

Library of Congress Cataloging-in-Publication Data

Bruning, John R.
  The devil's sandbox : with the 2nd Battalion, 162nd Infantry at war in
Iraq / John Bruning.
     p. cm.
  Includes index.
  ISBN-13: 978-0-7603-2394-6 (hardbound w/ jacket)
  ISBN-10: 0-7603-2394-1 (hardbound w/ jacket)
  1. Iraq War, 2003—-Commando operations. 2. United States. Army.
Infantry Regiment, 162nd. Battalion, 2nd. I. Title.
DS79.76.B78 2006
956.7044'3092—dc22
[B]
                              2006022064

All photographs are from author's collection except as noted.

On the front cover:
A Charlie Company soldier mans his machine gun inside the turret of a Humvee during the August 6, 2004
battle in Northeast Baghdad.

On the spine:
Sergeant First Class Ezelle on patrol in Baghdad. *Courtesy of Rebekah-mae Bruns*

ISBN-13: 978-0-7603-2394-6
ISBN-10: 0-7603-2394-1

Cover by Tom Heffron

Printed in the United States of America

CONTENTS

AUTHOR'S NOTE

Hello, and welcome! Come on in, we've got meat on the grill and enough beer to last us all night. Don't be shy; have a seat out back. The view of our valley is fabulous. All our guests remark on it. We've got every shade of green you can imagine. The lush grass, the tall firs stippling the hills . . . well, nothing beats it in my book.

You've got to know up front that our valley isn't the Silicon Valley. We don't drive Beamers and Benzes to work. We're an SUV and pickup kind of place—the bigger the better. Out here, we've got the bedrock types who built this country and made it great. We are Middle America, the heartland in our chunk of Oregon. We're old school. We don't judge by job or vehicle. We look into each other's eyes and measure the man by the content of his character.

Relax—kick your shoes off. I've got much to tell you, but first I need to introduce you to my neighbors. Sure, you've probably seen them before. Vinni Jacques was on CNN. So was Pete Wood. Chris Bailey made the front page of the *New York Times*. Sean Davis and Ray Byrne were interviewed on *60 Minutes*. Luke Wilson made the cover of *Field and Stream* in November '05. Matt Zedwick has his own action figure now. Jim MacMillan's photo of Shad Thomas won a Pulitzer Prize. In one memorable issue, Pete Salerno's narrow mug graced the cover of the *National Enquirer*. You can't buy that kind of love.

If you've been watching the news a lot, you probably saw some of my neighbors die.

Yes, I'm sure you've seen them before, but now I want you to really get to know them. Tonight, I'm going to fill you in on a bunch of guys, and one woman, who happened to be the most ribald, feral, loyal, and dedicated humans I've ever encountered. I love them like I love my own kin.

They're a deceptive bunch. Head into the Wal-Mart, or one of the mills around here, and you'll find them hard at work. Drop by the HP printer factory a ways down the road in Corvallis. You'll find a handful of them there in button-down shirts stuffed away in cubical land. They look like any other nine-to-five Joe just trying to make ends meet. They don't stand out, not at first glance, anyway. They pass through their days in average obscurity, raising their families and doing the best they can in this crazy world.

Truth be told, they are a different breed of cat. Once a month and two weeks out of every summer, they strap on their gear and go learn how to kill people. My neighbors, you see, are citizen-soldiers. They call themselves "Joes" or "Pot-bellied steely-eyed killers." They say the latter half in jest. While some of them are a bit saggy around the midsection, most could make any Bowflex ad look good. They are the infantrymen—Joes—of the 2nd Battalion, 162nd Infantry, Oregon National Guard.

Fate threw them into the middle of the most important battles in the Iraq War during 2004–05, a period the army refers to as Operation Iraqi Freedom (OIF), Part II. Now, as we sit on this porch, the army's up to its fifth sequel and some of my pals are heading back into the fight. You see, they are a committed bunch. They love this country. They've seen our enemies firsthand and know the ruthless evil that resides in their cause. They know that should we falter in Iraq, the War on Terror will surely be lost.

During OIF II, the Iraq War morphed into something greater than itself. It became a titanic test of wills between America and the forces of Islamic fascism. The battlefields in Iraq became our generation's Guadalcanal and Stalingrad. Both sides have invested everything they've got. Now, the battle has outgrown its strategic significance into something larger: a crucible of resolve.

My neighbors saw this transformation firsthand. And, if you'll pardon the bragging, they helped shape it during their time in the Sandbox. These average work-a-day stiffs helped beat down the two Al Sadr uprisings. They fought the Battle of Najaf. They fought the Battle of Fallujah. They called the Sunni Triangle home.

When they returned to a hero's welcome here in Oregon, they discovered the marines had hogged their glory. Every book, every documentary on the History Channel failed to recognize their achievements. They even got dissed by the local politicos, who during their demobilization ceremony extolled their service without a clue of their accomplishments.

You're on my back porch tonight to fix all that. Please, sit back and take this in. I'll tell you about their goofy humor and ridiculous pranks. I can't help that; I've been victimized by their devious plots. You've got to watch these neighbors of mine. They'll tie you to your cot quicker than you can say, "Buddy Fucker."

We'll have some fun, and I'll use foul language. It is their language, and to discard it for propriety's sake does them an injustice. I want you to get to know them, not some sanitized image the faint of heart can handle. Friend, if you can't handle the f-bomb, then my porch is not for you tonight. If you can, stick around; we're going to have a hell of a ride.

Just don't let the goofy stuff take your eye off the ball. There is a larger, more poignant story beneath their antics that you'll hear in my tale tonight. That aspect of these men (and one woman) deserves your attention. They earned that with the blood they spilled and the brothers they buried.

In many ways, the National Guard has eaten a shit sandwich since the Battle of Bunker Hill. The Continental soldiers looked down their noses at the Min-

utemen and their militia brethren. They remarked on all of their defeats and celebrated none of their victories. But who has fought and won America's wars?
Our citizen-soldiers.

Take the Civil War. The regular army was too small and too fractured to win
that war on its own. No, the regulars didn't win it, the farm boys and city folk
who flocked to Lincoln's call for militia levies won that one. And when the flood
of volunteers dried up after the bloodbaths of Antietam and Gettysburg, the
draftees finished the job in the Wilderness, Atlanta, and Petersburg.

What's that? Okay, sure, that's just one example, but the militia gave birth
to the National Guard. The Guard units formed the cornerstone of America's
war effort in World War I. In World War II, Guard divisions fought side by side
with the regular divisions. These weekend warriors had their moments of glory:
Tennessee's 30th Division became *the* elite infantry outfit in western Europe. The
"Blue and Gray" Division from Virginia, Maryland, and Washington, D.C.,
stormed Omaha Beach. Oregon's Sunsetters served as MacArthur's mailed fist
for his island-hopping campaign back to the Philippines.

The National Guard has always been there in the thick of the fight. At key
moments, it has changed the course of history. They've protected all that we find
of value in our two-hundred-year experiment in freedom and democracy.

Nobody remembers that. Instead, they remember the slipshod units, the
elected officers, the weekends of drill that were little more than an excuse to
binge drink with the boys. Kent State? Yeah, that's remembered. But who recalls
Biak or Palawan or the Crossing of the Roer? Since its inception, the Guard has
been stigmatized as "Big Army's" raggedy-assed, attention-deficit cousin. That
bias led to the Guard's general exclusion from the Gulf War. Vietnam gave it a
twist: join the Guard to stay out of the fight. For years, public perception of the
Guard was little more than a disorganized rabble of slackers and draft dodgers.

All of this has kernels of truth, but only kernels. The Guard has been painted
with the brush of its extremes. If the U.S. Army were judged solely on Bull Run,
Kasserine Pass, and Korea in 1950, it would look pretty incompetent as well.

Tonight, on this porch, we're going to change that. I'm going to tell you the
story of one National Guard unit that did it right. They went into a dirty fight
and waged it with honor. They emerged victorious and left Iraq confident that
it was a better place for their efforts. Sure, they rolled up their sleeves, bought
nonstandard gear, and loved to poke Big Army in the eye once in a while. If you
want to call that undisciplined, so be it. That said, there are plenty of times where
they faced a decision: shoot first or risk their own lives. Many times, they chose
to risk their own lives, unsure of who was downrange. They saved a lot of civilians with their actions.

Enough of this chatter. Here's another beer, my friend. Let's get started. I'm
not afraid to say it: these friends and neighbors of mine are the finest people I've
ever met. I've found it impossible not to love them a little.

Or a lot.

Now, let me introduce you . . .

INTRODUCTION

THE SANDBOX

August 12, 2004
Day One of the Battle of Najaf

Second Platoon led the way. Rolling from Forward Operating Base (FOB) Duke south of Najaf, the American column headed east into the inky blackness of the southern Iraqi desert. After a pause to test fire weapons, the vehicles pressed on with Second Platoon's HMMWVs (Humvees) out in front, the 2-7 Cav's Bradley fighting vehicles trailing behind. In the predawn hours of August 12, 2004, this hybrid formation of regular army armor and National Guard light infantry drove toward the coming battle. Weapons locked and loaded, sights zeroed, the fight would soon begin.

The Americans came to an intersection. To the right, the asphalt road led to Kuwait, and ultimately, to home. To the left, the hard ball fed straight into the southern end of Najaf, one of the most holy sites in the Muslim world. In recent days, the fanatical street army controlled by Muqtada Al Sadr had taken over the city. With their HQ at the Imam Ali Mosque, Sadr's men, known as theMahdi Militia, had unleashed a reign of terror on the city's inhabitants. After months of dickering, pointless negotiations, enough was enough. Al Sadr's Muslim brownshirts would soon face the full wrath of the U.S. Army.

The moment of contact would soon come. The Humvees backed off and let a platoon of Bradleys take lead position. Their armor and deadly effective weaponry would blaze a trail into the city that the Humvee-mounted infantry would try to exploit.

The column rumbled north, putting the path to home to its rear. To the east, daybreak cast an incandescent, almost eerie red-orange glow across the desert floor. Silhouetted by the rising sun, Iraqi civilians led donkey carts full of their possessions away from their city. They had fled on foot in the dead of night in search of safety in the desert's broad expanse. Unsure of what would happen to their homes and businesses, they would wait out the storm on the edges of the battlefield.

Up ahead, the Americans could see the city in the distance. It stretched before them, laid out atop an escarpment and plateau. They'd have to fight their way uphill to get into Najaf.

The column paused. Somewhere in the middle of it, Specialist Spike Olsen hunkered down in his turret. Only a few months before, he'd been a student at Western Oregon University. Now, eight thousand miles removed from his home in tiny Monmouth, he served as a Humvee gunner who covered the flanks of his fellow Bulldogs of Bravo Company, 2nd Battalion, 2-162 Infantry, Oregon National Guard. Almost always smiling, even in the middle of a fight, Spike represented the typical Bravo enlisted man: smart, cagey, and endlessly resourceful. A large proportion of the enlisted men had joined the company to pay their way through college. It gave this otherwise gritty and lowbrow bunch of light infantrymen an ethereal, almost erudite quality at times. The platoon loved to argue politics, religion, abortion, or anything else controversial. Their freewheeling debates appeared more appropriate for the tweedy environs of a 400-level seminar than a squad bay, a fact which bemused their hard-core, Ranger-qualified NCOs.

On this morning, there were no political arguments, no treatises on philosophy. Spike remained silent in his turret and listened to the Humvee's radio, which had been tuned to the battalion frequency. He knew his platoon would soon face the full fury of a house-to-house city battle. He understood what that meant. During advanced infantry training the previous summer, he had read the army's urban warfare combat manual. In cold terms, the book said to expect 70 percent losses in any such fight. That 70 percent would be made up of men like him and his brother infantrymen of Bravo Company. Of the twenty-eight men in 2nd Platoon, the book said fewer than ten would come out of Najaf alive and unharmed. They'd already lost one man in June. That was hard enough to take. Looking at two-thirds of the platoon dead or maimed, well, that level of despair and grief just could not be fathomed.

The column lurched forward. With the Bradleys on point, the column's speed plummeted. Used to buzzing through Iraq at 50 mph in their Humvees, 2nd Platoon's men fidgeted and grew anxious. They were out of their element at these speeds, and it contributed to their discomfort. Five, ten miles an hour, they plodded along. Second Platoon could only wait, carried along by the column's inertia straight into the teeth of the waiting enemy.

Hell broke loose only moments later. To the west, Charlie 3-8's tanks and infantry ran headlong into a swarm of Sadrist RPG teams, mortar positions, snipers, and machine-gun nests. Over the battalion net, Charlie 3-8's pugnacious commander, Captain Pete Glass, reported that an RPG team had already disabled one of his M1 Abrams. They were only minutes into the engagement and Captain Glass needed some direction.

Not that Glass needed much direction. While driving into Iraq from Kuwait four months before, his convoy came under fire. He had two of his Abrams drive right off their tank-carrier trucks and counterattack directly into the ambush. Nicknamed "Captain Chaos," Glass had already been decorated twice for valor.

After Glass finished his report, the battalion commander, Lieutenant Colonel Jim Rainey, came over the radio. Knowing that at least half his battalion would be listening to his response, he picked his words carefully. Here at first contact in what would be a long fight, he wanted to set the tone and inspire his men.

Inside the 2nd Platoon Humvees, Rainey's calm voice came through the radio, "Okay Pete, stay within the ROE [rules of engagement]. If they're shooting at you, I want you to kill them. Keep killing them. Kill them all. As long as you are killing them, you are meeting my intent."

"Roger that, sir!"

Big grins lit up the faces of the light infantrymen from Oregon. Rainey was a *leader*.

Up ahead, Spike could see his own column getting into the fight. Explosions marred the skyline. Plumes of smoke towered over the low-slung buildings of Najaf. Helicopters buzzed here and there, unleashing rocket salvos. The sharp *crack-crack-crack* of AK-47s rattled across the desert, followed by the deep bark of American M2 heavy machine guns.

Stuck in dream-like slow motion, the road seemed like a conveyor belt dragging them inexorably into the growing furnace of shrapnel and steel.

Spike Olsen stared at the growing conflagration and struggled to get his mind around the idea that *he* and all his buddies from Oregon would soon be thrown into the midst of it. A year ago, they were just college kids, drinking and raising hell. Their weeks were full of classes, girls, cheap beer, and pranks: *Animal House* in the new millennium.

And for Spike there was Mandy Ferguson, his fiancée. She had just taken a job as a teacher while Spike's civilian life was put in stasis when he went off to war.

That seemed a lifetime ago. Just college kids no longer. Iraq had turned them all into trigger-pullers.

It was time to give battle. The asphalt conveyer belt carried them headlong into the raging firefight. Spike charged his M240 and searched for targets as the battle engulfed him.

Part I

BONDS

ONE

JULY 2003

Throughout 2-162 territory the rumors flew.

In Eugene, the scout platoon picked up tidbits here and there at the armory across from the University of Oregon's football stadium. Staff Sergeant Kevin Maries, the senior sniper in the platoon, overheard some of the chatter and went home to prepare his wife.

The AGR (Active Duty Guard and Reserve—full-time soldiers) network went into overdrive. With ties throughout the brigade, these veteran noncommissioned officers had served together in Oregon for years, sometimes decades. As close as family, they swapped stories and rumors on a regular basis. Their network hummed all week. Something big was definitely afoot.

The wives and families of 2-162's soldiers shared their own grapevine. Phone lines lit up all over the Willamette Valley and down the coast to Coos Bay as their network spun up to report every crumb of info falling out of the Oregon Military Department in Salem.

With all the talking, the fact was nobody really knew what the army had in store for 2-162. The rumors hinted at a new deployment in support of the War on Terror. Within the brigade, two of the three infantry battalions had already been sent to foreign shores. In southern Oregon, 1-186 territory, families had said good-bye to their soldiers in 2002 when the battalion deployed to the Sinai for a year. Earlier in 2003, the 1-162, centered in Portland and Salem, had departed for Kuwait in the wake of Operation Iraqi Freedom.

For 2-162, that assignment seemed to have been swiped out from under them at the last minute, a fact that remained a sore point within the battalion. At the beginning of 2003, the 41st Brigade had alerted 2-162's leadership for deployment overseas. The battalion made frenzied preparations. Then 1-162 landed the assignment. The Volunteers, as the battalion calls itself, stood down. Thoroughly disappointed, the men of 2-162 called it "Operation Just Kidding."

This time, the hard news broke just before annual training that summer. Delta Company's Sergeant First Class Kerry Boggs, an MDAY (part-time) Guardsman with twenty years' experience in Oregon's 41st Infantry Brigade, was perhaps one of the first to receive it. A Lane County sheriff in his civilian life, he had gone up into the forested coastal range in search of a stolen car. While out there amid the Douglas firs, his cell phone rang. It was an old friend, one of the AGRs at the battalion's headquarters company.

"Kerry, just want to give you a heads-up. We're going to Iraq."

"Ah, *fuck*. How am I going to tell my wife?"

Turns out, thanks to the wives' network, she already knew.

As the summer's two-week annual training (AT) began that year, the official alert order reached the Oregon Guard's headquarters in Salem. It percolated through the chain of command until Major Dan Hendrickson, 2-162's battalion commander (BC), received it on July 13, 2003. He had been standing in the battalion Tactical Operations Center (TOC) when a sergeant from the 91st Division's training staff approached him.

"Sir, General Byrne wants you to call him as soon as possible."

The sergeant handed Hendrickson a phone, which the BC used to dial General Byrne's number. The general broke the news: the Volunteers were going to Iraq.

Hendrickson made a living as a tough, no-nonsense officer who emphasized accountability, discipline, and the standards set by the army. He drove his men hard and expected them to be disciplined professionals at all times. He demanded that they always do the right thing. Now, the training and values he set for the battalion would be put to the test of combat.

At least the news came at the right time. The battalion had just congregated at Camp Rilea for its two weeks of summer training. Set on the coast just south of Astoria, its red-roofed buildings and rolling green hills make for a picturesque scene. Clean and well tended, the base looked more like a historical landmark than a typical infantry training site.

Hendrickson decided to brief his command immediately. After lunch, he called his staff officers and company commanders into the battalion's TOC.

At 2:00 p.m. that afternoon, the officers streamed in and took their seats around an L-shaped series of tables. Captain Demian San Miguel, a Eugene police officer and the battalion's scout platoon leader, took one look at the officers assembled in the room and thought something bad had already happened.

Oh man, somebody must have already lost a sensitive item. We're going to get bitched out over our accountability, and we haven't even been here a day yet.

San Miguel sat down next to the Delta Company commander, Captain Chris Graves.

"What's going on?"

Graves shrugged, "No idea."

Major Hendrickson stepped into the room and took station in front of the group. He looked around the room, his eyes intense and focused.

"What is leadership? What is good quality leadership?"

San Miguel sat silent as a few officers offered up their opinions. This seemed like a prelude to the mother of all bitching-out sessions.

Then, the BC dropped the bombshell.

"Men, sometime around August or September we will be mobilized. . . . Sometime in October, we will move to Fort Hood, Texas. And sometime in March, we will be attached to the 1st Cavalry Division and will begin combat operations inside Iraq. We should be in country for six months."

Not a man stirred. Not a sound was made. The TOC seemed bathed in crypt-like silence.

San Miguel reeled from the news. He'd recently gotten married to another Eugene cop. They had a kid on the way. Now he was heading to Iraq? It was the last thing he expected, especially since 1-162 was still deployed. Like some of the other men in the unit, he assumed that 2-162 wouldn't go until well after 1st Battalion came home.

Major Hendrickson let the news sink in before he continued.

"We're going to Pause Ex for the next three hours. Go back and get your men in formation. Tell your company, then give them some time to call their families. The local news will be broadcasting it tonight. I don't want your families finding out from the television."

The meeting ended. The officers filed out to brief their men. After they left, the BC reached for his phone. He had calls of his own to make now.

Alpha Company's readiness NCO, Sergeant First Class Vince "Vinni" Jacques, walked into the TOC just after the meeting disbanded. As he stepped through the door, one of the army reserve training NCOs from the 91st Division told Jacques the news.

"Hey man, you guys are going to Iraq!" he exclaimed.

Jacques had served in the first Gulf War with the world's only airborne 155mm artillery battalion. Assigned to the 82nd Airborne for Desert Storm, he had already been through one alert order and overseas deployment. He'd seen how some of the men in his unit had cheered at the news. He later noticed that those who cheered ended up being the first ones weeded out and sent stateside. He wondered if the same thing would happen this time.

Then the professional NCO in him kicked in. He returned to his company area. There would be much to do to get the boys ready for the ordeal ahead.

Captain San Miguel stood before his command. Normally in charge of the Scout Platoon, for this (AT) San Miguel had been tasked with commanding "Ack" Company. Both Charlie and Alpha companies were seriously under strength, so the BC had combined them into one composite unit under San Miguel for the AT. Never big on formal, dramatic speeches, San Miguel broke the news in his typical low-key manner.

"Hey guys, here's the deal," he began, "I just got back from meeting with the BC. He told us that we've been mobilized for service in Operation Iraqi Freedom and that we'll be serving with the 1st Cavalry Division."

As Jacques had experienced in 1990, a small ripple of cheers went through the composite company. But at the same time, San Miguel detected shock and surprise on the faces of some of the men. Others stood stoic, watching him intently.

Somebody shouted out, "Sir, what sort of combat patch are we gonna get?"

A wave of laughter swept across the company. Then the serious questions came.

Someone asked if AT would be canceled. That sounded good to a few of the men. They wanted to head back and be with their families.

Patiently, San Miguel answered each one in turn. Finally, he announced, "Okay, go use your cell phones or the pay phones and call your families because the news is going to air on TV tonight. Be back by 1700, and we'll get to work."

The men of Ack didn't have much privacy to call their families. They spread out as much as they could, each man in his own little cell phone bubble a few feet from his comrades. Some leaned against nearby trees, others stared at the ground as they made their calls.

San Miguel moved to one side to make his own calls. All around him, Charlie and Alpha's soldiers were talking to their families. Some were low key. Others were already getting heated as their wives or girlfriends reacted to the news. Some of the wives broke down. But for the most part, the vast majority of them took the news with stoic determination to get through it.

Not far from Captain San Miguel, Sergeant First Class Alan "E. Z." Ezelle stood in the parking lot talking on his cell phone with the mother of his son. Though they had never married and were now broken up, she did not take the news well. In fact, she grew hysterical as the conversation progressed. Tears flowed, and Ezelle wasn't quite sure how to handle it. He had called his mother first, and she'd taken the news very calmly. His son Chuck had listened carefully and had been solid.

Hysteria was not an emotive response that Ezelle really understood. Rugged, blunt, and loud, Ezelle had long since become one of those lug nut NCOs who holds his unit together. He carried that responsibility as effortlessly as someone else would carry a wallet. It was instinctive, and that's what made him such an outstanding leader.

Ezelle was a legend within the battalion. With wide, steel blue, slightly bugged-out eyes, E. Z. looked like a man perpetually in a rage. Even his most friendly looks could scare a civilian into incontinence. When he grinned, he looked even scarier, like somebody just gave him a grenade launcher and a hundred rounds of ammo and told him to go have fun on a Military Operations in Urban Terrain (MOUT) range.

Another guts-and-gristle NCO once quipped, "E. Z. looks like he's been fed a steady diet of lizards and small children."

He lived to be a soldier. He'd spent his life marinating in testosterone. He tested himself in every imaginable manner. He'd served in the regular army in the 1980s as a kid fresh out of high school. After he separated with the service and moved to Oregon, he took a job as a bouncer at a strip club. He'd had his share of brawls there, and he relied on his wits and knuckles to win those battles. He never lost.

Later, he joined the Oregon Guard and served as an MDAY infantryman with Charlie Company.

He could handle almost anything thrown his way, but when his ex collapsed into tears at the deployment news, he simply did not know what to think. They hung up and Ezelle stuck his phone back in his pocket. He smothered his puzzlement by focusing on the task at hand. He headed off to find his close friend, Sergeant First Class Jacques. They had a lot of work to do.

Up the road from Ack Company, the Bulldogs of Bravo learned the news behind Rilea's freshly built multimedia center.

As usual, Bravo was almost at full strength. This was a company with such a good reputation that it attracted all manner of prior service types still looking for a challenge. The NCOs were particularly hard core. In the process, they had formed an esprit de corps that few units ever achieve.

First Sergeant Brunk Conley, a high-school science teacher and football coach in his civilian life, gathered the company around him. Though not very tall, Conley cut an impressive figure with his solid build and strong command presence. In the 1980s, he had just joined the 2nd Ranger Battalion when it got spun up for Grenada. He missed that fight to his lasting regret.

With two decades of experience, Conley was another of the battalion's grizzled and well-seasoned noncommissioned officers. Unlike Ezelle, he had a conversational voice and a teacher's talent for reading a crowd. Conley was a second generation 162nd Infantry NCO. His father had served in the unit in the 1980s and '90s, and his son ultimately would follow his father and grandfather into the unit.

Looking at the faces around him, First Sergeant Conley began, "Men, we've been alerted for service in Iraq."

That got everyone's attention. In the back of the crowd, Sergeant Matt Zedwick ("Z") did a double take. All he heard was the final part of that sentence: *Iraq.*

What the . . . ?

"What did he just say about Iraq?"

"Dude, we're going there!" came the whispered reply.

Holy crap.

The scene seemed surreal. The news percolated through Zedwick's mind; he struggled to grasp the consequences, as he knew them to be huge.

As with Ack Company, some of the Bulldogs cheered. Somebody piped up, "Right on! We get to go to war!"

"Fuckin' A, we get to play with guns and shoot people!"

A few questions were thrown Conley's way, then he dismissed the men so they could call their families.

While Matt Zedwick called his wife of three months, his best friend Ron Clement stayed close by and dialed home as well. Matt and Ron had been inseparable for years. Now they would go to war together.

Their friendship started when they were kids growing up in Corvallis. Zedwick and Clement had gone to high school together and had joined Bravo Company at the same time—before they had even graduated. In college, they rented a dilapidated house not far from the Oregon State campus. It became the nexus of all Bulldog activity in Corvallis.

Dubbed "the Greenhouse," the place was not for the weak or easily offended during the weekends. Drinking—serious projectile-vomiting, puking-dog, stagger-around-then-pass-out-in-a-puddle-of-your-own-piss drinking—was mandatory at the Greenhouse. Soldier humor mainly involves a lot of body fluids, drinking, and frequent public nudity. All could be found in ample quantities at the Greenhouse. On any given drill weekend, the place would be defended by almost a full platoon of happy, drunken college-student-soldiers who would finally crash in all sorts of interesting places at the end of their ribald evenings. On the pool table was a prime location. Under the pool table was considered choice as well. The back porch, the closets, and the sagging garage sale sofas would all usually be called on long before dusk on drill weekends.

As Ron and Z entered their twenties, things changed for them. Zedwick got married in 2003 and had his own family responsibilities. Ron soon followed. The day before AT, Ron had proposed to his girlfriend, Kelly, up in the hills overlooking Corvallis. He'd been old-fashioned about it, having first asked Kelly's dad for permission to marry his daughter.

Now, as he dialed Kelly's number, he was filled with conflicting emotions. Part of him was excited to learn that they'd be going overseas. He'd trained for years for war, and now he'd have the opportunity to put all that experience to the test. And with the United States at war, it was about time he and his fellow Bulldogs got into the game.

The phone rang on the other end. Ron broke the news, trying not to sound too excited. Kelly, who was a few years older than Ron, reacted as calmly as she could. She tried to sound encouraging and tried to be happy for him, but she knew the separation and threat of loss would hang over them for months to come.

Not far from Ron and Z, Sergeant Ryan Howell reacted stoically to the news. As some around him celebrated, he wondered what his girlfriend, Julie, would think of this development.

He broke the news to her as she lay on the bed in their Corvallis townhouse. Tall and slender, with expressive eyes and a tremendous sense of humor, Julie did her best to conceal her shock and fear.

Though they'd known each other for more than a year, this phone call was a seminal moment in their relationship, as it was for every couple in 2nd Battalion. It was the first signal that their relationships would be tested to the limits.

What sort of stuff are we truly made of? Can we make this work?

The deployment would answer both questions decisively. They exchanged "I love yous" and hung up. Julie lay on the bed and stared at the ceiling. Ryan went to find his brother, Sergeant First Class Jacques. They found each other not far from the media center.

"Well, Ryan, what do you think?" Vinni asked.

Ryan shrugged, "Well, it looks like the real deal this time." Vinni nodded. Both them sensed this would not be a repeat of Operation Just Kidding.

Vinni blurted out, "Well, maybe you'll get lucky and get to make a canoe out of somebody's head."

The two howled with laughter.

"You crazy little bastard!"

"Hey bro, we'll take it one day at a time."

The heart and soul of Bravo Company could be found embedded in the wiry, muscular frame of Sergeant First Class Pete Salerno, the Bulldogs' Readiness NCO and platoon sergeant for 2nd Platoon. A prior service paratrooper and cavalry scout, Salerno embodied the best aspects of the National Guard: diversity of experience and excellent small-unit leadership.

His experience was invaluable. Though he'd never seen combat, his career with the army stretched back to the Carter era. He'd enlisted for the first time before some of his soldiers had even been born. At thirty-eight, he went to Ranger school and graduated with the AUSA Leadership Award. He'd smoked guys almost half his age in one of the most intensive training programs in the world.

And the battalion's deployment had just complicated his own life to a degree unique in 2-162. His wife, Major Trudy Salerno, served as a veterinarian for the 364th Civil Affairs Brigade, a reserve outfit based in Portland. Her unit was scheduled to leave for Afghanistan that fall. With both parents deployed, Pete's mom would have to come from Florida and take care of their two boys.

Pete called Trudy and broke the news. After AT, they'd have some serious family logistics to work through.

Two

SYNERGY

Al Ezelle, Pete Salerno, and Vinni Jacques never let conventional thinking get in the way of training their boys for war. Dan Hendrickson and his executive officer, Major Tanguy, shared the same rebel spirit. In the summer of 2003, the deployment may have come as a shock to some of the men, but the battalion had been prepared months in advance, thanks to these leaders.

In the wake of Operation Just Kidding, Salerno studied what a potential war in Iraq would mean to a light infantry unit like Bravo Company. For more than two decades, the Guard had prepared to fight the Russians in Europe in wooded, hilly terrain. The training plans focused on conventional battles against a uniformed and disciplined modern army.

The coming war in Iraq didn't fit that bill at all. Pete huddled with his NCOs and Captain Ben Long, Bravo's cheerful, soldier-focused commander. Together, they crafted a remarkable training exercise designed to duplicate a security-and-stability operation in the Middle East. It took weeks to plan, and even incorporated civilians on the battlefield. Real civilians couldn't be used, but Sergeant First Class Everett Horvath, the Corvallis recruiter, dragooned the Oregon State ROTC cadets for that role.

Pete worked through the details with full OpSec (operational security). If anyone at brigade or their reserve training unit, the 91st Division, got wind that Bravo was getting a bit maverick again, Salerno was sure their plan would have been smacked down. Long ago, he learned that it was far better to plead forgiveness than ask permission.

Nevertheless, Major Tanguy learned of the plan. He gave Salerno a call and asked him about it. After listening to his aggressive NCO explain what he had in mind, Major Tanguy told him to drive on. Tanguy saw the exercise's value.

That drill weekend at Dunn Forest became Pete's crowning achievement as the Readiness NCO. For two days, the company maneuvered through almost a mini–Joint Readiness Training Center (JRTC) operation where every man was tested to his professional limits.

On day one, Ben Long maneuvered the company into contact with the opposing force (OPFOR). Horvath appeared right in the middle of the battle. Dressed as "Mr. Mohammad," a leader of an Islamic relief agency, Horvath caused all sorts of trouble. Finally, Ben Long stormed over to Pete shouting, "I don't think this Mr. Mohammad is any innocent bystander! I think he's working for the other side!"

Pete took great pride in achieving that level of realism. To do it during a drill weekend was a rare accomplishment.

After sunset, the entire company launched a night assault, something that Bravo had never attempted during a weekend drill. The maneuver platoons crept within twenty meters of their assigned objective before the OPFOR even noticed them.

The next day, two platoons advanced to secure a four-way intersection. As they approached it, Pete's platoon ran into a contingent of ROTC cadets dressed as farmers. The cadets demanded that the soldiers pay them a bribe for the right to cross their fields. Negotiations grew tense. Suddenly, a farmer grabbed at a soldier's weapon, which prompted a hail of simulated gunfire. Pete's platoon smoked every last civilian. They later called it the "Mini-Mogadishu" incident.

That was a great lesson for the after-action review.

By the end of the weekend, the company surged with confidence. The real-world exercises challenged the men. The men performed superbly, the exercises were real-world-based and multifaceted, and the company emerged all the better for it. Even the chow, prepared by Bravo's longest-tenured soldier, Sergeant Bill Woodke, was outstanding. And all of this was done in-house, without any support from battalion.

In the wake of Salerno's mini-JRTC weekend, planning began for the coming summer AT. The list of standard drills and maneuvers looked out of date to Jacques, Ezelle, Pete, and Sergeant Jeff Miotke. Their men needed realistic training that would prepare them for the War on Terror. When the invasion of Iraq began, the men watched *Fox News* and could see that the tried-and-true stuff wasn't going to work on the mean streets of the Middle East; the battalion needed urban warfare training, and lots of it.

They approached Major Hendrickson and outlined some new ideas. The two weeks of AT would be divided into a week of marksmanship and a week of MOUT training. To satisfy the conventional wisdom, they'd run a few battle drills in the woods, but the focus of the final week would be short-range, close-quarters combat. Hendrickson appreciated their initiative and gave them the green light to develop a plan.

For three months, the NCOs fleshed out their ideas. Jacques found an excellent site for a short-range marksmanship range at Rilea. When Vinni discussed constructing it with the range control officer there, he just stared at Jacques like he'd taken leave of his senses. Vinni was prepared for that. He had poured over the army short-range marksmanship (SRM) manual and knew the procedures almost verbatim. When he demonstrated the knowledge, the range control officer relented.

It took two more trips to Rilea to complete the range. Nothing like this had ever been done in the 41st Brigade, and the drills Jacques planned for it were nothing short of controversial.

In short-range battlefield environments, a soldier needs to know how to bring his weapon to bear and shoot accurately while in motion. The SRM range would simulate this, which presented an array of safety issues. Typically, the Guard practiced marksmahip prone and stationary, as it was the safest way to use live ammunition. Moving and firing standing up would be a radical departure.

The NCOs had even more radical ideas in mind for that summer. Nobody in the battalion had ever used their laser sights at night on a range. Jacques planned a night drill on the SRM range with the lasers. Rilea's officers had kittens over the safety issues. It seemed a tailor-made situation for an accidental discharge and injuries. Nevertheless, 2-162 intended to do it.

Meanwhile, Salerno and First Sergeant Conley created a new live fire maneuver drill. In it, the battalion's infantry squads would move through the range with the teams supporting each other by fire. Again, this involved a lot of motion with loaded weapons, which caused controversy. Brunk and Pete didn't care. Their men needed to know how to do this with real ammunition.

In week two, the battalion would move over to the MOUT range. Military operations in urban terrain was not a new aspect to warfare, but how the army conducted it had changed since the invasion of Panama in 1989. The house-to-house battles in western Europe during World War II and Hue City during Vietnam formed only one component to the broader concept of city-fighting in the modern army. The men needed to learn the other aspects more suited for stability-and-support operations; these included raids, cordons, searches, traffic, and crowd control techniques.

As the AT approached, the companies spent their drill weekends rehearsing some of the new exercises they would go through at Rilea. Using the drill floors, the NCOs taught them the procedures and safety rules so they'd be thoroughly prepared.

By July, the battalion was prepped and ready for what was sure to be an interesting AT. In the process, the NCOs had ensured that the training plan would be exactly what the unit needed to practice after the alert order arrived. It was one of those moments of true serendipity, where plans made months ahead of time meshed perfectly with a sudden development—like going to war.

During the first afternoon of AT, the battalion's leadership reviewed the training plan. A few tweaks were made, but for the most part it reflected the real-world situation the battalion would soon experience. They just needed to execute and hope the men would be motivated.

That wasn't a problem. That first week on the marksmanship ranges, the men absorbed every lesson thrown their way. Sergeant Ezelle ran a machine-gun range that gave the men ample opportunity to shoot live rounds with the M2 .50-cals and the M240 Bravos.

During every National Guard AT, the army sends observers and controllers (OCs) to ensure that the citizen-soldiers train to meet the prescribed standards. In 2-162's case, the 91st Division provided the OCs. The 91st was full of conventional thinkers, and some of them immediately clashed with the battalion over the innovations set forth for the AT.

Conley and Salerno's squad live fire maneuver range appalled the 91st controllers. Pete saw one enraged sergeant major throw a conniption fit over it. "How do we validate this?" he shouted. "This isn't even in the mission training plan!"

They ignored him and ran the range their way. Each squad maneuvered, fired, and worked out the tactical details that in combat would become of vital importance. After each squad finished the range, they discussed those issues and crafted solutions. The soldiers took great strides forward.

At the end of the day, Pete and Brunk conducted an oral after-action report for the range. As they talked, the 91st Division sergeant major interrupted, "Okay, did we teach this to standard?" The sergeant major decided to demonstrate one aspect of by-the-book technique called the "Bunny Hop." The men gaped as the sergeant major went through the drill using an M16. "Now, that's the proper way to do it."

That was great, except the Volunteers carried M4s. The procedures were different. Pete and Brunk looked over at each other and rolled their eyes.

Vinni Jacques also caught flak from the 91st. When he turned in a training report, a female major from the division's transportation section lit him up.

"What the hell are you doing? You're not training to your MTOE [official, published standard]! This is outrageous! You guys think you can do whatever you want, but this doesn't meet the requirements of what you're supposed to be doing this year. This is wrong, and I'm pushing this with my chain of command."

Jacques stood through her tirade. Her outburst was extremely unprofessional, but as an NCO, he could only listen and stifle his rage. The fact that she was a transportation type made him that much more indignant. When she finally shut up, Vinni walked away muttering, "You need to go watch the news you fucking retard. We're not fighting the Germans again."

If the 91st had a problem with the way the AT was being run, Major Hendrickson loved it. During the SRM drills that first week, he came out to observe. He watched for quite a while, then walked over to Vinni Jacques.

"Sergeant Jacques, this is absolutely amazing what you've done here. Good job."

Vinni beamed. Praise from the BC meant a lot. Hendrickson was not a man of many words. When he spoke, he spoke with blunt sincerity, good or bad. That tended to put off some people, who thought him colorless and unapproachable. Those who understood him respected and admired his style.

Later that week, thanks to the BC's support, Jacques ran night laser drill on the SRM range. It went off without a hitch, though thanks to the Rilea range controller, the men fired from the prone position instead of standing up. Some compromises couldn't be avoided.

The men loved the training. They worked their tails off and absorbed everything the NCOs threw their way. The battalion always trained hard; the NCOs, the BC, and Major Tanguy made sure of that. But the alert order had given them all a sense of urgency. In a matter of months, their lives would depend on their infantry skills. They honed them to a fine edge.

Every battalion, be it regular, reserve, or National Guard, carries on its books a few slackers and malcontents. The 2-162 was no different in that regard, though its slackers were probably a bit more colorful than their active-duty counterparts. That July became a turning point in their careers. Going into a combat zone had a way of changing attitudes, and the NCOs noticed that development right away.

Nowhere was it more evident than in Specialist Eric McKinley, one of Bravo Company's ne'er-do-wells.

McKinley had shown up at the Corvallis armory in the late 1990s looking for extra money and a challenge. Staff Sergeant Tommy Houston, one of the Corvallis recruiters at the time, recalled how McKinley walked in the door with spiked hair. He looked like he'd just been electrocuted.

Eric McKinley embodied the culture of the disaffected. He'd stumble into the armory during drill weekend with purple, green, or sometimes flaming red hair. He was the antithesis of the poster-boy soldier with his spiked leather jacket, outrageous hairstyles, tattoos, and body piercings.

Underneath the punk-rock gargoyle exterior, McKinley possessed a keen intellect. He loved to debate current events. Unlike most of his fellow soldiers, he was an unabashed liberal. It gave him a distinctive voice within the company and made him a contrarian. He reveled in that role.

Pete Salerno's combination of butt-kicker and "platoon daddy" persona usually brought the young soldiers around quite quickly, but Eric resisted. Through his first years with the company, he never took soldiering seriously.

During Operation Just Kidding, McKinley took Salerno aside. Piercings were not allowed while on active duty, and Eric had just acquired another one.

"Uh, Sergeant, I have a small problem."

"What's that Eric?"

"I've got a titanium ring in my taint."

Salerno, who had gone to special forces (SF) medic school while serving in Big Army, knew that this was slang for the perineum, the space between the anus and the testicles.

"Oh Jesus, why me, God?" came Salerno's response.

McKinley grinned and waited for Salerno's response.

He got both barrels. "Okay, Eric, you better figure out how to get rid of it or I'll take a pair of bolt cutters and do it myself!"

As the readiness NCO, Salerno had seen soldiers like Eric come in off the street and grow up to be team and squad leaders. In between, he got to know them like his own kids. They shared their problems, shared their successes, and sought council from him. McKinley was no different. He'd left home in his teens and ended up on the street. Once, when he failed to show up for drill, Pete called the phone number he had provided only to discover it was a pay phone at the local mini-mart.

In recent months, McKinley started to change his life. He'd found some direction and had gone back to school. Now, those positive developments took root in his soldiering.

On the SRM range, Vinni noticed McKinley's transformation during a ready-up drill designed to teach the men how to swing their M4s to a firing position in a swift, fluid motion. Bringing their weapons to bear quickly could mean life or death in a close combat environment, and this skill demanded smooth precision. Vinni watched McKinley as he repeatedly executed the drill better than anyone else on the range.

Jacques was so impressed that he took McKinley aside and said, "Fucking goddamned McKinley . . . born again! How about that? You're doing an outstanding job!"

The kid lit up. Vinni continued, "I'd like you to come out here and give me a hand getting these guys squared away."

McKinley's jaw dropped. He'd never had any sort of responsibility before, and now Sergeant Jacques wanted him to be his assistant instructor. This was new terrain for him.

"You're shitting me, Sergeant!"

"No, I'm not shitting you, Eric. You're the fastest sonofabitch out here. Show them how you do it."

"Roger that, Sergeant!"

Full of enthusiasm, McKinley went to work.

Later that day, McKinley drew Salerno's attention. During a snap-shooting drill on the SRM range, Eric put twenty rounds in a three-inch pattern into his target. Snap-shooting that well took real talent.

"Jesus Christ, Eric!" Salerno shouted. "Where the hell was all this three years ago?"

McKinley grinned. "Well, Sergeant, I never took it seriously before now."

Pete rolled his eyes. "What the hell did you think we were doing all this time?"

During the second week at Rilea, the battalion switched to maneuver exercises. Each company cycled through the MOUT range in a three-day round robin.

Jacques and Ezelle ran the range and introduced all sorts of new material to the Volunteers. In days past, MOUT operations were driven by firepower. If a unit assaulted a city, it would do so with massive artillery and air support. Resistance would be crushed by sheer volume of fire.

There would still be a place for that kind of fight, but precision operations dominated the scene in Iraq. For example, if a unit located an insurgent cell in a building in Baghdad, the army could not blast it with artillery or air strikes without killing innocent civilians and doing damage that the coalition authorities would ultimately have to fix.

Instead of brute force, the army in Iraq relied on tactics similar to what domestic SWAT teams employed. A platoon or company would seal off the target building, then kick the door in and start a systematic room-to-room search.

To avoid close-quarters firefights, the trick with this sort of cordon and search operation lay in violence of action. If the assaulting squads breached the building with weapons ready, chances were anyone inside would be too surprised and terrified to put up any opposition.

The battalion had never done cordon and searches. They went right to work and learned many lessons in the process. Once, a Bravo Company squad entered a building and took simulated casualties. They called in a medevac. A few minutes later, an ambulance came roaring to the building. The medics charged inside, ready to give assistance.

Pete Salerno and Vinni exchanged knowing looks.

"Should we do it?" asked Jacques.

"Hell yeah!"

They sauntered over to the ambulance and drove it off.

When the medics came out carrying the wounded on stretchers, they looked around in puzzlement. Their ambulance had been pinched. This is what the NCOs called a "classic training moment."

Vinni and Pete returned and explained to the medics that in an urban setting, anything left unguarded would likely be stolen. That was particularly true in Baghdad.

From that point on, the boys made sure to secure their vehicles. One or two men always remained with their rigs. It was a lesson always employed on every mission in Iraq in the months to come.

As the companies cycled through the MOUT range, the 91st OCs remained displeased. Pete Salerno butted heads with them again. Once, while at Tactical Assembly Area Black (TAAB) near the MOUT range, Pete had taken his platoon and established a perimeter in some light woods. Some engineers showed up. Pete put them in the middle of his perimeter and told them to stay put.

A 91st OC walked up. He saw the engineers and lectured Pete over their correct doctrinal placement. Salerno explained that he didn't know these engineers and didn't want them up on the perimeter until he knew he could trust them.

As if on cue, the OPFOR launched a probing attack. Pete's guys deftly handled the situation, but the engineers reacted in all the wrong ways.

Pete looked over at the 91st OC and gave him a royal *I told you so* alpha-dog eye-fucking. The OC made himself scarce.

During the AT's final event, Bravo Company executed a night raid on the MOUT range. Hunkered down just outside of the town, Salerno intended to launch a surprise attack with 2nd Platoon.

The 91st OC on hand objected to that. "According to doctrine, you need to lay down fire with your machine guns."

Pete goggled, "What? It's two in the morning out here! Firing will just wake them up. What kind of sense does that make?"

"Do it."

Weary of arguing, Salerno did it. His M240s swept the MOUT range. When his platoon jumped off, they ran into a hail of fire from the alerted OPFOR. After that, Salerno wanted to lynch every last damn member of the 91st. On the other hand, the incident underscored Pete's conviction that doctrine should serve only as a guideline. Knowledge, experience, and the real-world situation should always drive tactics. Lesson learned.

The AT ended with a morale boosting, male-bonding event known as the Celtic Games. With careful attention to detail, Vinni Jacques formally requested persmission to hold the Celtic Games on the last night of AT. The BC was always a stickler for details, and Sergeant First Class Jacques did not disappoint him. He outlined his plan, wrote up a safety report that was somewhat tongue-in-cheek, and submitted it to the BC. Major Hendrickson approved it with the stipulation that alcohol consumption remained under control.

Every good unit shares a common tradition that helps create bonds between the men. With the Volunteers, the Celtic Games became that tradition. Started by Vinni Jacques, Brunk Conley, Sergeant Michael Di Guistino, and Sergeant Paul Warnock during an AT in 1997, the Celtic Games served as the post-training party that punctuated every subsequent AT.

The Puck of the battalion, Jacques had served in nearly every company of 2-162 during his decade in the Guard. Everyone knew Jacques, and everyone in the battalion cherished their own Vinni stories. He'd pulled off some legendary pranks that years later still kept the men in stitches. Once, he stuffed a live nutria in Sergeant Ezelle's gym bag. He later put the rodent on a leash and took it for walks down the hallways at the Eugene armory. Another time, legend had it that he instigated switching a training video with a porno flick called, *Chicks with Dicks.* That stunt got a very unpopular major chewed out by a general.

Dead things were his specialty. He once stashed a dessicated rodent in another NCO's file cabinet after the man messed up his Class-A uniform. When discovered, it was so pungent and maggoty the NCO hurled his lunch.

Plumper-porn was another Jacques weapon. He'd go out and find photos of absurdly obese women in all sorts of obscene poses, cut them out of magazines, and slip them into his officers' notebooks. This usually caused great gales of laughter.

Pranks aside, Vinni Jacques was a superb noncommissioned officer. A natural teacher, his base of knowledge and his fatherly approach made him ideally suited for his role within the battalion. He also possessed just enough feral, crazy knuckle-dragger in him to keep the battalion laughing. He had long since become the bellwether for the 2-162's morale and had a knack for knowing when to stop pushing the men and get them engaged in some screwball misadventure.

Staff Sergeant Kevin Maries put it best: "Vince Jacques was the best small-unit leader in the 2-162, but he was wilder than a pet 'coon. I sometimes wondered if he didn't get hit in the head during the Gulf War."

On the last night at Rilea, Vinni emerged from the barracks dressed like a crazed Scottish warrior. With his face and chest painted blue, he had stripped

17

down to nothing but a BDU (battledress uniform) top wrapped around his waist. The lack of underwear was startlingly apparent.

He went off into the woods in search of a good log for the caber toss.

At dusk, Major Hendrickson had his hands full. Surrounded by some unhappy officers from the 91st, plus a bunch of 2-162 wives who had materialized earlier, he was trying to diplomatically get everyone away from his battalion. The last night of summer AT belonged to the men. It was their chance to kick back and bond with each other. Having wives and brass around made that impossible.

Vinni picked that moment to hike by with a log across one shoulder. He spotted the BC surrounded by concentric circles of interlopers and simply said, "HUAW, sir!"

Jaws dropped. Eyebrows arched. The group gaped as Vinni strutted away, a big, mischievous grin on his face.

Hendrickson closed his eyes and suppressed a smile. He really wished Jacques had been wearing underwear.

The games began. From all over Rilea, the battalion gathered to toss cabers, smash fruit with a tent mallet, throw rocks, and wrestle one another in chest-thumping, beer-fueled matches. It was great fun, and the men showed up wearing all sorts of wacky apparel. Some had copied Sergeant First Class Jacques' BDU kilt. Others had wrapped their whoobee (a camouflaged blanket that also serves as a poncho liner) around their hips, which made them look more like homoerotic hula dancers than Scottish berserkers. Still others had used towels or jock straps. Their pale, sun-deprived Oregon bodies fairly glowed like ghosts in the summer night.

The officers did not participate. They grabbed chairs and hooted from the sidelines while nursing their beers.

The next morning, the battalion held its final formation to give out awards. To Salerno's delight, Staff Sergeant Sean Davis and his men took top honors as the best squad in the battalion. Davis was another old-school, Bravo Company NCO. Tall and broad shouldered, Davis possessed dark, piercing eyes and an uncharacteristically soft voice for the infantry.

As the BC handed out the remaining awards, Jacques and Ezelle stood side by side in the ranks with Ack Company. Somewhere in front of them, a soldier blurted out, "Hey, what about Sergeant Ezelle and Sergeant Jacques? Don't they get anything?"

Ezelle flipped a quick grin Jacques' way. Vinni leaned forward and tapped the Joe on the shoulder. "Hey, did you get some good training?"

"Hell, yes!"

"Then that's all the reward we need."

THREE

MANPOWER PLUS BRUNS

No National Guard unit is ever at full strength. Soldiers are always on detached duty, there are injuries within the companies, or there is dead weight left on the roster to make their numbers look better than they actually are. After returning from Rilea, the Volunteers needed serious reinforcements.

The worst shortages had resulted from the brigade's prior deployments. Significant chunks of Alpha Company, Charlie and Bravo, had volunteered to serve with the 1-186 and 1-162 overseas. Thus raided, the 2-162 roster looked pretty thin in places.

Major Tanguy concluded that the battalion possessed only 370 deployable soldiers. The battalion needed about seven hundred to function in Iraq.

The only solution was to pull men in from other units within the 41st Brigade. At first, a call for volunteers went out. Hundreds came forward to offer their services. Eighty came from the 2-218th Field Artillery, including a thirty-five-man fire support element led by Major Mike Warrington.

Captain Scott Hildebrandt learned of the deployment after returning from a tour in Washington, D.C. with the National Guard Bureau. He'd been working in the operations office at state as a full-time officer. Scott's army career dated back to 1988 when he had served with the 3rd Infantry in Washington, D.C. He'd been in the National Guard for more than a decade. Since January 2003, he also commanded E Troop, 82nd Cavalry. Based just south of Portland in Woodburn, E Troop had yet to deploy. Hildebrandt decided to test the waters.

At the end of the August drill weekend, he gathered his troopers and called for volunteers to go with 2-162. Nearly everyone volunteered.

Encouraged by his troop's response, Captain Hildebrandt advocated a role for his men in the coming deployment. E Troop got the job. Later that month, the unit was activated for duty in Iraq. Ultimately, sixty of E Troop's one hundred men qualified as deployable. That gave Major Hendrickson a significant infusion of manpower.

The BC folded the troopers into Delta Company. The BC kept one original platoon of Delta soldiers and broke the rest of the company up to serve as replacements for Charlie and Bravo. One of the senior NCOs in Delta, Sergeant First Class Kerry Boggs, handpicked the men who would stay behind with Hildebrandt's troopers. An experienced and able NCO, he knew every man in Delta Company like his own children. Boggs assembled a hard-core platoon whose men had long since become family. They were solid, tough, and referred to one another by first name regardless of rank.

Hildebrandt took command of the hybrid. It turned out that the troopers and the original Delta soldiers worked well together. The two groups shared a camaraderie that grew through the deployment. The Cav troopers were generally younger than the original Delta soldiers, so inevitably they hassled them about their age. They called Boggs' men the "Old Man platoon," but only behind their backs.

Unlike the other line companies, the original Delta was not straight-leg infantry. It served as the mounted anti-armor force for the battalion. As a result, Kerry Boggs' men had plenty of experience in TOW missile-armed Humvees. The Cav Scouts shared a similar background. They drove Humvees armed with grenade launchers and heavy machine guns. In the weeks to come, that collective experience would prove invaluable to the battalion.

In Eugene, a veritable skeleton crew ran Alpha Company. With so few men left, Major Hendrickson broke up the unit and used the men to plus-up Bravo and Charlie.

Vinni Jacques joined Bravo Company along with Alpha's first sergeant, Paul Warnock. Warnock, who worked as a software engineer at the Hewlett-Packard printer facility in Corvallis, took over as Bravo's first sergeant after the BC selected Brunk Conley as the new battalion sergeant major.

Though the infusion of Alpha and Delta refugees helped flesh out the ranks in Bravo and Charlie, the battalion still needed an Alpha Company. Down in Southern Oregon, the call for volunteers reached Charlie 1-186 Infantry where about thirty-five men stepped forward. Most were young soldiers who had not gone on the Sinai deployment. Sergeant First Class Shannon Compton saw the volunteers and realized they would need steady leadership. He signed up to go with them.

Like Pete Salerno, Sergeant "C" had long since become a father-figure inside his company. Muscular and built like a bulldog, Compton exuded confidence and command ability. Born in Roseburg, he was a native Oregonian. He had served ten years in the regular army before returning to Oregon in '95, where he joined the Guard and found work with a local steel company and lumber mill. Four years later, he became a full-time AGR Guardsman and joined Charlie 1-186 in his hometown of Roseburg.

When Compton threw his hat into the ring, many of the company's other NCOs followed suit. This included Staff Sergeant Phil Disney. Disney was a case study in what the National Guard can do for a young man. A high-school dropout, he'd drifted around partying and doing drugs. One day, he woke up and realized he hated what he had become. He joined the Guard and grew into a proud and confident man with newfound self-respect. In the years that followed, he owed much of what he had become to the Guard, and his loyalty to it never wavered. When the Iraq deployment came up in the summer of '03, there was no way he would be left behind. Sergeant C would need somebody to watch his back.

Charlie Company sent almost forty soldiers to the Volunteers. Major Hendrickson formed them into 1st Platoon, Alpha Company.

Down in the Medford and Klamath Falls area, volunteers from Alpha Company 1-186 formed their own platoon for the 2-162. At their head was a no-nonsense, extreme type-A personality in the form of Second Lieutenant Cory Jones.

Jones hailed from Illinois and had only recently seen the light and emmigrated to Oregon with his fiancée, Suzanne. Cory had graduated from Illinois State in June 2003. Suzanne, a very independent, self-starting type-A personality in her own right, held a master's degree in biology. She came west to work for the State Parks Commission. They settled in southern Oregon where Cory joined Alpha Company 1-186 in the summer of '03.

His platoon included a cache of outstanding NCOs, such as Staff Sergeant Doug Jackson. Jackson hailed from hardy stock. A fiery, aggressive Native American, warrior blood ran in his veins. His great-great grandfather was Captain Jack, the Modoc Indian leader who had held off the U.S. Army in the southern Oregon lava fields for months in 1873 in one of the epic sieges in Old West history. Captain Jack also earned notoriety after he killed General Edward Canby with a shovel during peace negotiations with the army.

Devoted to his tribe and active in his community, Doug Jackson's competence and natural leadership impressed Lieutenant Jones. Later, Jackson became Jones' platoon sergeant, despite being a staff sergeant.

After they joined the Volunteers, Lieutenant Jones' men became 2nd Platoon, Alpha Company.

The final pieces came from Bravo and Delta Companies, 1-186. Thirteen of the men in this contingent had served in the Sinai. They knew each other like brothers. These men formed Alpha Company's 3rd Platoon with Sergeant First Class Phil Larson as their platoon sergeant. Larson joined the Guard in '91 after seven years of active duty service. He spent the next twelve years with 1-186 and served with the unit in the Sinai.

To Larson's initial disgust, Staff Sergeant John Neibert joined 3rd Platoon. Neibert had been a captain in the Guard and had deployed to Saudi Arabia in '99. While a company commander overseas, a paperwork snafu back in Oregon hopelessly snarled his career as an officer. Disgusted, he left the Guard in '02. But soldiering ran in his blood. He returned to the 41st Brigade in January 2003 as an E-5 sergeant, where he worked in the brigade operation's office. He volunteered for the Iraq deployment and found himself in Larson's platoon.

Larson did not like the idea of having a former officer-turned-E-5 in his ranks. At first, he gave Neibert the cold shoulder. But Neibert never let his former career get in the way of his current job. Larson warmed to him, and the two formed a tight friendship.

At the head of this newly formed Alpha Company stood Captain Scott Granger, a rigid, no-nonsense officer with good instincts and an excellent grasp of tactics. In his civilian life, Granger was an Oregon State trooper. In '02, he took a company to the Sinai with 1-186. In Egypt, his men respected Granger's abilities, but his lack of people skills caused considerable friction. As a result, Granger already had a history with some of his men in Alpha.

*   *   *

Charlie Company needed men as well. Almost a platoon of Charlie had gone with 1-162 to Iraq earlier in 2003. Now, the battalion's rear detachment returned the favor and sent Charlie some soldiers who had stayed behind. These men volunteered under the condition that they would go as an integrated platoon and would not be broken up and scattered through the battalion. General Byrne agreed. Led by Sergeant First Class James Ferrel, these men became Charlie Company's 3rd Platoon.

Bravo Company was also down a platoon. It had sent about forty men off with the 1-162 and needed a platoon's worth of replacements.

The Bulldogs received all manner of volunteers. Clerks, helicopter crew chiefs, truck drivers, mechanics, a scattering of computer geeks, and medics flowed into the Corvallis armory. Salerno put them all in 3rd Platoon, where Platoon Sergeant Vinni Jacques rode herd on them. To help Vinni out, Pete Salerno gave him some of the company's best team and squad leaders.

Nevertheless, the first day Vinni saw his platoon formed on the armory lawn, he knew he had his work cut out for him. He had six months to turn them into meat-eating knuckle-draggers. It would be a challenging task.

Fortunately, these men had tons of heart, which made Vinni's job much easier. Sergeant Bill Stout embodied the motivation that drove the platoon. Bill had been a marine back in the '80s, long before he joined the National Guard. A tire salesman for seven years, by the summer of 2003 Stout had landed a civilian job working with the 1042nd Medical Company in Salem, where he also served as an MDAY crew chief on Blackhawk helicopters. He spent much of his time flying around the Cascades rescuing lost hikers.

Bill was the kind of guy who'd give a Joe his last cigarette. Bill's can-do attitude made him an outstanding team leader despite the fact that he'd last been a rifle-carrying grunt when Reagan was in the White House.

Vinni gave Bill two other volunteers to flesh out his team, Kenny Leisten and Ken Kaiser. Bill grew to love both kids like an overprotective father. Just before leaving for Iraq, he told them that he'd never ask them to go through a door first. Bill would lead the way. "I've lived my life," he said, "yours is just beginning."

Ken Leisten did not look like a typical infantryman. He'd been a clerk at Rilea doing computer work before he volunteered. Feisty, rebellious, and smart, Kenny soon demonstrated a natural talent for soldiering. He learned things faster and did things better than most of the other Joes. They worked harder to keep up with him.

And then there was the battalion's beloved anomaly, Staff Sergeant Rebekah-mae Bruns. Although women are not usually posted to infantry battalions, Bruns had transferred from a reserve psychological warfare unit into the Guard in 2000. She became the platoon sergeant for the battalion's transportation platoon.

Bruns had grown up in rural poverty in Illinois during the '80s. During her third year of college, she joined the army as an act of rebellion against her adopted family. She ended up in the 10th Mountain Division serving as a truck driver in Haiti during the '94 deployment. She later returned to school and graduated with a B.S. in sociology. She started another degree in photo journalism. One class shy of her second degree, she took a job with the *Cottage Grove Sentinel.*

Tough and experienced, Bruns understood that her presence in an infantry battalion would not be appreciated by some of the men. She decided to set the tone right away. During her first drill, she settled into her new desk, where she discovered a *Playboy* magazine. Inspiration flashed, and she pulled out the centerfold and taped it the wall behind her. Then, she called in her NCOs for a meeting.

With her back to the centerfold, she introduced herself and explained, "Okay, this is what we've got to get done this weekend." As she ticked off her list, she stole quick glances at the NCOs. All looked dreadfully uncomfortable. She continued. Their discomfort grew. The NCOs began whispering to one another.

"Who the fuck put that on the wall?"

"I don't know, but we're screwed."

Bruns stifled a smile and blithely carried on. When she finished, she said, "Let's go knock this stuff out."

The NCOs were slow to leave. They looked like somebody had just kicked their dog. Bruns decided it was time to let them off the hook.

She half-turned and pointed at the centerfold, "Oh, by the way guys, ain't she great?"

Stunned, they froze. Visions of sexual harassment claims danced before their eyes. This was the new army, and this stuff just was not acceptable anymore. The NCOs waited for the coming storm.

Bruns grinned and burst out, "Jeez, I put it up there, you guys."

A wave of relieved laughter swept through the room.

That broke the ice nicely.

Of course, the men had to retaliate. During that summer's AT, Bruns showed up at a battalion staff meeting. When one of the officers asked her a question, she opened her leader's book to check on a date.

Staring at her was a seventy-something naked woman, boobs down to her knees, legs spread, and a lascivious smile on her overdone lips.

Bruns slapped the book closed. An officer next to her had caught a glimpse, and asked, "What the hell was *that*?"

She took it as a sign that she'd been accepted by her Joes. The old lady porn made the rounds in (HHC) for the next two years. It became a running joke. It ended up in wall lockers during company inspections, in offices, more books, and in other assorted places. Ongoing pranks like these helped build bonds and overcome differences.

In '02, Bruns went to the Sinai with 1-186 as photographer and public affairs NCO for the battalion. During the deployment, she met Captain Granger and many of the NCOs who would subsequently join the Volunteers as part of Alpha Company in '03.

When she returned from Egypt, Bruns needed to clear her head. Though she was always up for pranks, she was a deeply spiritual person. Out of high school, she had considered becoming a nun. After the Sinai deployment, that thought crept up again.

She flew to Spain and walked the El Camino de Santiago, the Way of St. James. One of the most spiritual pilgrimages in the Christian world, the El Camino de Santiago stretches from the Franco-Spanish border five hundred miles to the coast. Rebekah searched for guidance among ancient churches and holy sites. She lived as a Spartan and carried only what she needed to get her through the next day. She spent her nights in convents. Every day, she prayed for guidance.

Bruns rarely revealed this spiritual side. To some, it would have been a complete contradiction to her playful curiosity, which had landed her in such places as punk bars, underground shows . . . and an infantry battalion. Her urge to explore propelled her into some strange corners of the world. Yet, those journeys only reinforced her spirituality and convinced her that everything had a purpose.

Through her deliberations in Spain, the answers came to her. She would not become a nun; somewhere in her current life, she still had work to do. She returned from Spain puzzled and frustrated. She still did not know her path.

That afternoon, her phone rang. "Sergeant Bruns, I wanted to let you know that 2-162 is going to Iraq." It was Major Arnold Strong, one of the brigade public affairs officers (PAO). "Do you want to go?"

Her course had suddenly become crystal clear. "Hell, yes," she replied.

She understood now. There *was* work yet to be done.

Four

THE FIRST GOODBYES

In mid-August, Pete Salerno called Ron Clement and broke some bad news. "Ron, it looks like we're going to be gone eighteen months. Six months in training, a year in Iraq."

Ron and Kelly talked over this new development and decided to get married. Throughout Volunteer country, the soldiers with serious girlfriends wrestled with the same issue. Eric McKinley and his long-time girlfriend, Coventry, elected not to get married. Others did as well. There seemed no harm in waiting.

At the same time, plenty of Joes married their sweethearts before they left. Specialist Marty Theurer, a heavyset Bulldog who was a civilian paramedic, was one of the first to marry his fiancée that fall.

Ron and Kelly Clement tied the knot next. In less than two weeks, Kelly threw together a terrific ceremony that included Matt Zedwick as Ron's best man.

Ryan Howell and Julie married at the end of September. Vinni served as his brother's best man. With time running out before the battalion left, they postponed their honeymoon until after the deployment.

Throughout Oregon, the families made final preparations for the months ahead. At the Salerno household, Pete's wife, Trudy, departed for her predeployment training. Pete's mom moved in and ran the household. In the meantime, Pete worked long hours with the other Bulldog NCOs as they tried to complete the mountain of paperwork required to get the unit overseas.

The basic logistics of an eighteen-month absence proved particularly rough on the single soldiers. Without a wife or partner to run their households while they were gone, many gave up their apartments and put their belongings in storage. Others, who were single but owned a house, had to find somebody to take care of their property. The mundane aspects of life would not change while they fought in Iraq. Bills had to be paid and lawns needed mowing. Orchestrating these things took time and energy. For some, it would become an enduring problem throughout their time overseas.

The end of the summer became a time to sever the threads that bound their civilian lives together. Like Cortez burning his boats before marching on the Aztecs, there would be no turning back. With their civilian lives in storage and lacking a permanent address, the deployment cast them adrift and made some feel rootless. It would be a hard thing to return and face following a year of combat in Iraq.

For the family men, these final weeks grew tense. With the battalion's departure looming, a raft of emotions came into play. Stress, anger, fear, and love all converged on these families and interacted in different ways. In some cases, it destabilized the household and harkened to difficult days ahead. In others, the families drew closer and held on to every moment they could share together.

To the Volunteers, it came as a shock that their beloved and feral Sergeant Jacques had actually found somebody who would marry him. He seemed too untamed for the domestic passivity of marital bliss. In fact, some of his men couldn't fathom a woman enduring Vinni's penchant for dead things, public nudity, and occasional barroom brawls.

This made Rhonda Henderson all the more a cipher when she first came in contact with the Volunteers. Vinni had met Rhonda at an Albany tavern soon after she graduated from Western Oregon University. They'd been brought together by mutual friends, and Rhonda was taken by Vinni's life-of-the-party persona. When he and Ryan walked into the tavern that first night, the entire place lit up. Strangers clustered around them. Stories flowed and beer was quaffed.

They couldn't have been more different on the surface. Vinni's hair-on-fire personality contrasted with Rhonda's quiet and shy demeanor. She tiptoed through life. Vinni assaulted it. He overwhelmed her, pushed her far from her comfort zone, and to her surprise she found she liked it.

They began to date. When Vinni took Rhonda to one of the company's dining out events, she overheard two of Vinni's soldiers arguing about her.

"That's the woman with Sergeant Jacques."

"No way."

"Go ask her."

"Screw that, you ask her."

Finally, one came over and said, "Is it true you're actually here with Sergeant Jacques?" When she nodded, the young Joe shook his head in wonder as if Vinni finding a nice girl was a sure sign of the apocalypse.

Such encounters made Rhonda wonder what she'd gotten into with Vinni. But about a month into their relationship, she discovered the fun-loving, goofball side to him cloaked a much more significant human being.

One night, while she was driving home before meeting Vinni and Ryan, a drunk driver slammed head-on into her Toyota. The collision broke bones and left her unable to get out of the car. Paramedics rushed her to the local hospital. As she reached the emergency room, she saw her father and asked him to call Vinni.

An hour later, Vinni reached her. He stayed by her bed through those first terrible hours. The gesture signaled the depth of Vinni's sense of loyalty.

The accident turned Rhonda into an invalid for almost three months. She couldn't walk on her own, couldn't dress herself, and relied on her mom's help for such basic things as taking a shower. Her whole world had been rocked by the accident; she'd gone from a freshly independent college graduate to totally dependent on her parents again. Depressed and frustrated, she tried to push Vinni away.

He always came back. For months, he'd come and just sit with her at her folks' house. Her injuries prevented them from doing little but talking. These long visits showed her a side of Vinni most people never saw. Concealed beneath Vinni's Cro-Magnon exterior lay a family man struggling to get out.

As she regained her strength and began walking again, they picked up where they left off. Two years into their relationship, Vinni proposed to her at the beach one night. He picked his birthday to do it, so he'd never forget their anniversary.

Married five months later in January 2001, Rhonda became his center of gravity, the force who brought balance into his life. He orbited around her, still the loud and brash knuckle-dragger whose idea of a barbecue was meat, meat, meat, and beer . . . side dishes be damned.

In June 2002, their son Gabe entered the world. Vinni reveled in his new role as a father. He loved his son with ferocious intensity and talked about all the things he would show him how to do. Shooting and fishing were at the top of his list.

Then the deployment came, and Vinni's departure became imminent. His entire family rallied around him and Ryan. They'd been through this before when their dad deployed to Vietnam as a special forces medic. The Jacques clan had a warrior tradition, and the family had long since learned how to support its men when they went overseas.

But leaving Rhonda and Gabe was new ground for Vinni. When he'd gone off to the Gulf in 1990, he was a young Joe with no family of his own. This time around, he knew leaving would be exponentially more difficult.

Preparing a will underscored that point. In August, Vinni broached the subject with Rhonda, but she refused to talk about it. The possibility he would die in Iraq was something she didn't want to face. Vinni let the matter rest for a few weeks.

As his departure grew near, he spent as much time as he could with Gabe and Rhonda. They went to the coast, shared time together on the beach again, and tried not to look too far ahead. Whenever they did, both became unsettled as if something deep down inside them sensed that bad times were coming. They huddled together and tried their best to ignore the coming storm.

In October, they sat down and prepared the will.

In the final weeks before leaving for Texas, a surprising development took place within many 2-162 families that would have profound implications on everyone touched by the battalion's coming service overseas.

Politics.

Most of the soldiers assumed that their extended families and friends would support them while they were in Iraq. Most, at least initially, backed the soldiers 100 percent. But in the late summer of '03, the first divisions appeared. Usually, it began with a family member who voiced opposition to the war. Sometimes, avoiding the subject, or respectful disagreement held the family together. However, with emotions already heightened, often this division caused significant family trauma and left the soldiers feeling angry, hurt, and puzzled.

Nobody was immune. Almost every family had to deal with this issue, and it became one of the lingering effects of the deployment that continues to drive some family dynamics to this very day.

Nowhere was this more clearly illustrated than in Major Hendrickson's family. The BC looked forward to the deployment. He'd trained for this mission all his professional life. He'd married the daughter of an army brigadier general. He had relatives who'd been at Pearl Harbor, and his father had flown F-86 Sabrejets over MiG Alley during the Korean War. He came from a family of warriors, and now it was time for him to take men into battle.

His father, who had opposed the invasion of Iraq, erupted when he learned his son would soon be going to Baghdad. Over the phone, he launched into long diatribes about the war. When they failed to have any other effect than anger the BC, his dad switched tactics and called Suzanne, Major Hendrickson's wife. The situation got out of hand, and the BC's father broke off contact with the Hendricksons. The family schism opened deep wounds long before the BC's boots hit Iraqi soil.

Friendships began to waver as well. When the MDAY soldiers prepared to leave, they discovered that some of their civilian friends had never understood the role they played in the National Guard. They could not relate, and in some cases their behavior unwittingly caused damage to their friendships.

In other cases, the damage inflicted turned out to be politically motivated, deliberate, and premeditated. One young soldier who'd been a student at Oregon State University discovered that his college friends had collectively decided to sever ties with him in protest over his involvement in the war. He'd been cast adrift, a political sacrifice by people he had counted on for support.

In October, the soldiers gathered at their local armories and prepared to move to Hood. The noninfantry volunteers went through quick infantry training to get them MOS (military occupation specialty) qualified. Others faced intense days of Common Task Training (CTT). The CTTs were the elemental soldiering skills that every Joe needed to have before going into combat. Everyone had to be certified in a wide range of these basic tasks, such as cleaning a weapon, assembling a tent, or operating a radio. Altogether, there were more than seventy CTTs. The box-checking frenzy began, and the men spent long hours getting certified.

Meanwhile, Sergeant Bruns embraced her new role and saw herself as the battalion's chronicler. She intended to document its history. When the battalion stood up for its pre-deployment marathon in Oregon, Bruns circulated through the ranks and interviewed some of the soldiers. She found idealists in every nook and cranny, including in the Headquarters Company (HHC), where she met Specialist David Johnson.

Johnson was a cook. He understood that it was probably the most thankless position in the battalion. He didn't care. His grandfather had served in the 5th Armored Division during World War II, and after he died his mother shared with him the ribbons, medals, and photographs of his wartime career. They made a lasting impression on Johnson, and he joined the Guard in 2000 to be a part of something larger than himself.

He volunteered to go on the deployment and transferred to HHC from the 218th Field Artillery Battalion. As he sat and spoke with Rebekah-Mae, she detected a wellspring of motivation that seemed unusual for one in such an anonymous position.

"I know I'll be helping soldiers perform their duty at a high level," he explained. "The army moves on its stomach. And morale is composed of the three Ms: mail, money, and meals." He would go to Iraq and support the soldiers in the field by keeping them well fed.

When the conversation turned to the cause in Iraq, Johnson never hesitated. "Will it be worth it?" he mused. "I've heard the way people are treated over there, and it is deplorable to me. If we can change that, it'll be worth it."

Bruns found another idealist in Sergeant Ric Spitler, a fireplug of a man with an easy grin and a grandfatherly air to him. He was, in fact, a grandfather. At age fifty-one, Spitler counted himself one of the oldest in the battalion. Back in the mid-'70s, he had served in the Marine Corps. He left in 1985 with eleven years under his belt. In November 2001, he joined the Guard in the wake of 9/11, feeling he needed to do something for his country. That something, for him anyway, was to serve in the infantry with Bravo Company.

When Bruns finished her pre-deployment tour through the battalion, she came away with profound respect for the men. The chance to operate freely allowed her to take the battalion's pulse. She found the men motivated and earnest to make a positive impact on the Iraqi people.

At the end of the month the Volunteers congregated at the county fairgrounds in Eugene for the official activation ceremony. It was the first time Hendrickson's new, polyglot battalion had come together in one place. The core of the old 2-162 remained in Bravo and Charlie companies, but almost half the battalion had come from elsewhere in the brigade. They had different expectations and procedures from 2-162. Integrating them into the battalion's way of doing things would take time. Time was the one thing the battalion lacked.

At the activation ceremony, Oregon governor Ted Kulongoski addressed the Volunteers. A former marine, the governor had made a point of attending every activation and demobilization ceremony of Oregon Guard units. Kulongoski was a Democrat with deep misgivings toward the Iraq War, and his speech reflected his respect for the soldiers without supporting the cause.

"I understand the sacrifice you're making and the patriotic duty you're performing.... As a country, we will continue to debate the merits of this war. That is what free people do. But there will never be any doubt about your courage and professionalism."

The governor finished his speech, "You are Oregon's finest. Along with your families, I will await your safe return knowing you are standing up for your country."

When the BC stepped forward to address his men for the first time, he reminded them of the pride and traditions of the 2-162. The battalion had fought in some of the fiercest, though little-known, engagements of the Pacific war, and the history of the unit stretched back to the pioneer era. Major Hendrickson made it clear that they were all now going to be a part of that long and noble history. That afternoon, the BC released the battalion so the men could spend a few final hours with their families.

Rhonda and Vinni Jacques drove back home to spend a few last hours together. Vinni fussed about the house, fixing a few things he'd meant to get to before he left. Rhonda was touched that he would do this for her and Gabe during his last evening in Oregon.

Gabe, all of a year and a half, sensed something wasn't right. As the evening progressed, he grew uneasy. So did Rhonda. She felt like she'd been locked in a cave with a ticking clock echoing through the darkness. Every second grew oppressive. Every second meant one fewer with Vinni. Finally, time ran out.

Late that night, they drove back down to Eugene with Ryan and Julie. On the way, Gabe snapped. Unsure of what was happening, but knowing it was bad, the little guy burst into tears. The car stopped, Vinni and Ryan climbed out. One last good-bye, a kiss, and they were gone. The drive home for Rhonda and Julie was nothing short of torment.

The next morning, the Volunteers left for Texas.

FIVE

TEXAS

Day one at Hood the nightmare began.

It started with the living conditions and went downhill from there. The battalion's move into barracks vacated by the 4th Infantry Division when it left for Iraq. The buildings had been slated for demolition and replacement with new construction while the division was deployed overseas. With the sudden influx of fighting units at Hood, the barracks gained a new lease on life. The Oregonians must have drawn the short straw.

Broken windows, overflowing toilets filled with feces and garbage, rotting food, and mildew-covered walls greeted the Volunteers as they walked into their new homes.

Bravo Company moved into their wing to find the rooms were freezing cold. The heat didn't function, and there was no hot water in the building. They couldn't even find basic items such as toilet paper and soap. It was as if nobody had even expected them and their arrival had caught the base unawares.

Over in the D Company barracks, the men found a decomposing rat in the trash. Mold covered the walls, and the foul stench inside turned stomachs. It made the men indignant. This was how they were going to be treated before going to war?

In Charlie Company's area, the mold became a serious problem. Ezelle found it in the ductworks. When the soldiers turned on the heat, it blew mold spores all over the barracks and caused many Joes to fall ill with vomiting and fevers.

And this was the good part.

As the executive officer, Major Ed Tanguy's primary duties included running the day-to-day operations of the battalion. When they first got to Hood, doing his job posed a challenge. Obviously, the barracks needed to be cleaned up and new equipment purchased, but getting that accomplished required going through three separate chains of command. The 4th Infantry Division (ID) owned the barracks, the battalion was now attached to the 39th Brigade (Arkansas), but the 7th Infantry Division was supposed to ensure the Volunteers received their predeployment validations. Thrown into the mix was the 75th Training Support Brigade, which was tasked with supervising 2-162's training, and the 1st Cavalry Division, which the battalion would ultimately work for in Iraq.

The 4th ID didn't want to pay for improvements in the barracks because it planned to tear them down as soon as the battalion departed. Simultaneously, the 39th Brigade, the 7th ID, and 1st Cav ended up in a tug-of-war over who controlled each aspect of the battalion's training and operations at Hood.

To add more trouble, when the 2-162 departed for Texas, the battalion's computers, office supplies, and other installation gear remained behind as property of the Oregon National Guard. The Oregon Military Department took the stance that with the battalion now federalized, anything it needed should come from Big Army. Major Tanguy and Sergeant Major Conley discovered that buying replacement equipment was almost impossible. Stuck among the 1st Cav, the 7th ID, the 39th Brigade, and the State of Oregon, the 2-162 could not even get a unit code assigned to it. Without a code, the battalion could not get a credit card to purchase even basic items.

Tanguy and Conley fought through the layers of red tape. Initially, the progress they made was glacial. While they found most everyone had the best intentions, there were just too many fingers in the pie. They did find that help arrived from a variety of places, including the 7th ID and the 39th Brigade, but the basic structural issues were not going to be resolved during this deployment.

Some of the problems should have been expected. It took tremendous planning to move thousands of men from various parts of the country into one place. Things go awry, that's just life. The battalion staff worked with the 39th Brigade, which was largely in the same boat, to fix it while the NCOs told the men to get over it and drive on.

In fact, most of the NCOs didn't think the conditions were all that appalling. Ezelle concluded that the barracks were better than sleeping in the mud, something he'd done plenty of over the course of his career.

Some of the men did not react well to the change of lifestyle. As civilians, they were used to functional, basic housing and decent food. As Sergeant Major Conley put it, "One day they were driving forklifts, the next they were carrying rifles. There was no transition period."

Had it been left to Conley, he would have given the men three weeks to work into the military mindset where they would have done nothing but physical fitness drills to get into shape. The transition was so abrupt that it magnified their indignation at finding their new home a shambles. It quickly became political.

One of the men in Delta Company had a connection within Congresswoman Darlene Hooley's office. A few phone calls were made in hopes that she might be able to do something about the mess at Hood. Darlene Hooley and the rest of the Oregon congressional delegation descended on Hood to personally see the living conditions. In Oregon, the press covered their visit and ran stories highlighting the lack of equipment and battlefield gear the battalion needed for Iraq. The battalion had not been outfitted for Iraq yet, but the press failed to notice this nuance.

In fact, the coverage distorted the truth. The media alleged that the regular army was treating the Volunteers like second-class citizens and giving them second-rate gear as a result. That wasn't true. The Oregonians possessed better weapons, helmets, and other equipment than the regular army units at Fort Hood.

When all the dust settled, the press coverage and congressional visits had little effect on the battalion. Many of the NCOs were embarrassed by the whole affair. The battalion could solve its own problems. Besides, the interlaced command structures lay at the root of most of the issues. That was something the lawmakers could not fix. The Volunteers had to make do largely on their own. They went to work.

It started with the barracks. Using their own pocket money, the soldiers bought cleaning supplies. They mopped out the barracks, boarded up broken windows, and scrubbed away the mold.

Actually, the chaos in Texas could not have been better for the battalion. The Volunteers started from scratch with nothing but the gear they packed into Hood with them. It forced the staff and NCOs to set the tone and drive forward. It made them self-reliant. They learned to improvise, get around roadblocks, and work through issues on their own. They learned to problem-solve.

It was a lonely way to start the mobilization, but in the end it paid off. The chaos may not have been a planned method of training the Oregonians, but it served better than anything at Hood to ensure they would land on their feet once inside Baghdad a few months later.

The 1st Cavalry Division is one of those storied, tradition-soaked units with its own special esprit de corps. The 1st Cav battled the Sioux and Cheyenne on the Plains during the 1870s and '80s. In World War II, it fought alongside the 41st Infantry Division as MacArthur's sledgehammer. In Vietnam, the 1st Cav fought the first pivotal battles of the war during the Ie Drang Valley Campaign. It was the unit of Custer and Hal Moore, of such movie fame as *They Died With Their Boots On*, *Apocalypse Now,* and *We Were Soldiers*.

A National Guard battalion joining such a legendary division could have been a very tricky thing to successfully engineer. Historically, there has usually been a bias against citizen-soldiers by the regular army. It dates back to the Revolutionary War when Washington struggled to integrate the local militias with his Continental Army. During World Wars I and II, the National Guard division earned a reputation within the regular army for being second rate. This was largely unfounded. At times, the Guard units performed brilliantly, such as the 29th Division at Omaha Beach and the 30th Division during the Normandy Breakout and the Bulge. In some instances, a Guard unit's lack of training or experience caused serious problems, as was the case during the Battle of New Georgia during the Solomons Campaign in 1943. The 43rd Infantry Division, a National Guard outfit from the New England states, performed very poorly. Thrown into the fight against the Japanese without any jungle training, they suffered heavy losses. Such incidents reinforced the regular army's sense that the Guard units were of questionable value.

The Guard remained largely at home during Vietnam and the Gulf War. But in the '90s, when budget cuts reduced the army's size by 30 percent, the subsequent manpower shortage made the National Guard an integral part of any overseas operation. Should war break out, every regular division would have its strength enhanced by one brigade of National Guardsmen.

This represented a departure from World Wars I and II, when the Guard units formed their own divisions. Now, they would be plugged into a regular division to create a hybrid, integrated force.

With Iraq destabilized by a growing insurgency, it was time to put this new plan into effect. The 1st Cavalry Division became one of the early test cases for this new approach. It absorbed the 39th Enhanced Brigade from the Arkansas National Guard as its citizen-soldier component. When the 39th got ready to deploy, it was short an infantry battalion. The 2-162 was pulled from Oregon to fill that hole.

Such a situation could have easily failed if the relationship between the regulars and the Guard wasn't managed well. Fortunately, the 1st Cav commander, Major General Peter Chiarelli, set the tone right away.

During the first week at Fort Hood, Chiarelli hosted a commander's call for all the company-level officers. At the start of the meeting, the general asked for all the National Guardsmen to stand up.

Chiarelli addressed them: "I want you to know I appreciate you being here. We could not do this without you."

The general continued, "You are the heroes here today. You've left your jobs and families, and I appreciate that. I want you to know that there will be no difference between you and the men sitting down."

With one short speech, Chiarelli established the standard for his division. The Guardsmen would be treated as equals. Welcome to the 1st Cav. For the Volunteers, it was the warmest greeting they could have imagined. It earned Chiarelli their instant loyalty and respect.

SIX

LIGHT INFANTRY ON WHEELS

Light infantry is the arterial blood of the army. Trained to fight on foot in any conditions from urban terrain to snow-capped mountains, light infantrymen go where the tanks and mech infantry in their Bradleys cannot: jungles, thick forests, and narrow back alleys.

When the Volunteers reached Fort Hood, they discovered they would ride into battle mounted in Humvees. From light infantry they had suddenly morphed into motorized infantry. What a difference a word makes.

Motorized infantry in the army had gone extinct after the first Gulf War, so there was no model for the battalion to emulate. This presented an array of challenges.

Humvees hold five soldiers. One drives, one functions as the truck commander (TC), another mans the gun, and two men in the rear seats serve as dismounts. This limitation clashed with the organization of the battalion's nine-man rifle squads. A light infantry squad is formed around a balance of firepower and flexibility. Shoehorning that balance into a Humvee forced the Volunteers to rethink how they would go to war.

When Charlie Company received its Humvees, they came with no information on task organization, battle drills, basic tactics, formations, and weapons load-outs. The NCOs played around with different configurations to find the right balance. They decided to spread the SAW (squad automatic weapon) gunners through the vehicles and did the same with the grenadiers. Then they worked out a set of tactics that ensured 360-degree protection while on the road.

As they experimented, the Volunteers found themselves hampered by a shortage of vehicles and a lack of time to train on them. They also faced problems with the 75th Training Support Brigade, the unit assigned to train them. Composed of reserve medics, artillerists, and transportation specialists, few of the 75th TSB's trainers had any combat experience. Almost none held an infantry MOS. Without practical infantry experience, the trainers relied on the field manuals for their information.

Since the battalion had converted to motorized operations, field manuals didn't exist for their new role. That left the 75th groping in the dark.

The relationship with the 75th created little but frustration. During the first week of training, Sergeant First Class Ezelle found medics assigned to teach his men how to sandbag positions. His squad was full of infantrymen with years of collective experience. They knew how to fill sandbags; they didn't need medics to show them how to do it.

The scout platoon faced similar problems. Sergeant Andy Hellman, a quiet butcher in his civilian life, showed up for a class on infantry tactics to find a female master-sergeant with a transportation MOS teaching it. She had no idea how infantry squads functioned.

During another class, a training officer told the scout platoon, "Okay, this isn't the way you're going to do business in Iraq, but we need to check this box off, so listen up." Comments like that only ratcheted up the frustration level.

Pete Salerno experienced plenty of angst with the 75th. The instructors frequently argued with him and his men over how they did business. This couldn't have been more maddening; the Bravo Company soldiers had light years of experience and knowledge over their training OCs. To be told by a truck driver that he and his men had assaulted a building incorrectly seemed the essence of stupidity. If chiding his platoon aggravated him, the OCs became counterproductive at times when they argued among themselves in front of the men. During a Humvee exercise in which his men were supposed to react to an improvised explosive device (IED), he watched as two captains from the 75th got into an argument over tactics. Both had read the same manual, but had interpreted it differently. The issue went unresolved.

To be fair, some of the training had value. For the cavalry troopers in Delta Company, the short-range marksmanship ranges and the close-quarters-combat drills proved particularly useful. The men learned to fire their weapons while squared to the enemy to maximize the protection their body armor offered. They also learned how to engage targets with their M4s while walking, a skill that takes practice to master. Not used to fighting as dismounted infantry, Delta Company's men needed these lanes.

For the rest of the battalion, individual marksmanship also had value. But getting time to do it became yet another nightmare. With so many units vying for range time, scheduling even a few hours was difficult. Worse, the Volunteers frequently showed up at their specified range at the proper time only to find it occupied. They burned hours waiting around for their chance to shoot.

The 75th's organizational issues caused the 2-162's officers fits. Captain San Miguel discovered the 75th routinely lost his paperwork. The 75th would order San Miguel to send his men back through lanes they had already completed. When he protested and stated that he personally saw them attend those classes and complete those lanes, they refused to accept it. That the 75th would not take the word of a fellow officer rankled San Miguel and only made dealing with the OCs that much more difficult.

The other company commanders discovered the same thing. Sign-in sheets disappeared, the paperwork sent in showing who had completed the CCTs back in Oregon vanished, and the men were forced to redo much of the training they'd already finished. The early weeks at Hood had everyone going in circles.

*　*　*

As the training wore on, the men wore out. They worked seven days a week without any respite. The box-checking fest became a daily exercise in frustration-management from the BC on down to the newest private.

Between Thanksgiving and Christmas, the men received tactical training based on reports coming from Iraq. The platoons mounted up in their Humvees and practiced IED reaction drills and setting up snap traffic control points. They sat through classes in cultural sensitivity training, IED construction, and insurgent tactics.

All of this was remarkable for its inaccuracy. During one traffic control drill, an Iraqi veteran from a different unit happened to be observing. Pete Salerno walked over to him and asked, "Did you use these over in Iraq?"

The vet replied, "No, we never really did it that way."

The IED construction classes showed the men what they would probably experience over in Iraq. For the most part, the instructors showed them small homemade bombs built to look like soda cans. Some reports from Iraq indicated that the insurgents stuffed IEDs inside dead animals. The Oregonians were warned about getting too close to roadkill. One class showed how insurgents had modified an old 105mm artillery shell. That was the largest IED the battalion saw at Hood.

By the end of 2003, most of the U.S. casualties incurred in Iraq came from IED attacks. Learning how to avoid them, or react effectively to them once engaged, became of paramount importance to the Volunteers.

At Hood, the 75th TSB taught them to get out of the kill zone during the react-to-IED drills. Should an IED disable a vehicle, the other Humvees were to clear the area and stop several hundred meters from the stricken rig. There, the gunners were to lay down a base of fire while the dismounts re-entered the kill zone to conduct CASEVAC (casualty evacuation). Others would dismount and sweep along either side of the road.

In some cases, the OCs taught the men to blow through the kill zone by simply stomping on the accelerator. That's how Sergeant First Class Compton's 1st Platoon, Alpha Company, received its instruction. But other OCs taught the Joes to split up their platoon. If a Humvee in the middle of the patrol took an IED hit, the vehicles ahead of it would drive forward out of the kill zone, while the ones behind would back up and get out of it in reverse.

Unknown to the Oregonians, the tactical situation in Iraq changed daily. The insurgents, eminently adaptable, modified their attacks in response to American tactics. The constant evolution between enemy tactics, techniques, and procedures (TTPs) and American countermethods created a dynamic that was patently impossible to train for back home. By the time the TTPs filtered back to Hood, the situation on the streets of Baghdad had changed because the insurgents had developed new ones. The situation was just too fluid to accurately portray stateside.

At best, the training should have emphasized flexibility. It should have taught the men to react as the tactical situation demanded. The 75th didn't have that knowledge base so they couldn't teach it.

On their own, Pete Salerno, E. Z., and Sergeant Compton worked hard to institutionalize flexibility in their platoons and squads. They stressed that doctrine was nothing more than a guideline, not gospel.

Compton worked especially hard to train his men to think on their feet. He did not want robots; he wanted men who could adapt and be mentally tough. On its own initiative, his platoon practiced ready-up drills, ran room-clearing exercises in their barracks, and worked out tactics for vehicular searches. They developed methods for close-quarters combat and practiced quick change-outs of magazines for their weapons.

Compton was not alone in this. All around the battalion, the companies and platoons trained on their own. The soldiers cross-trained on their crew-served weapons. They taught one another how to drive Humvees. Some of the men read books about Iraq and passed along nuggets of knowledge. The Volunteers were self-motivated. When the army failed them, they trained themselves.

At Hood, 2-162's companies developed their own identities. Bravo Company for years had been known as the "Ranger Company" for the number of Rangers in its ranks. The Bulldogs proudly considered themselves the best unit in the Oregon Guard. The BC reinforced this when he selected Bravo Company to be the 1st Cavalry Division's rapid reaction force. This meant Bravo would be the fire brigade, moving to assist other units in need or peril. It also meant the men needed to be fast-rope qualified.

Fast-rope training is not for the meek. The idea behind it is to get men out of a helicopter without the bird actually touching the ground. This makes air assault missions possible in areas with no landing zones, such as in the middle of a city. To be effective, the men have to get out of the helicopter and down onto the ground in a matter of seconds. A hovering helicopter is an easy target, and the longer it takes the men to descend, the more the bird is at risk.

Bravo Company's soldiers loved the fast-rope training. They started on the tower, learning how to slide down the ropes using their feet to control their rate of descent. Then they practiced with the helicopters, throwing the ropes overboard, then going down them one at a time. After they mastered that, they began group descents from fifty feet. By the time they had finished the program, they could get an entire nine-man squad out of a Blackhawk in a matter of seconds.

There were some injuries, but the trainers were surprised at how few men got hurt, especially since this was the first time a National Guard unit had received such training. Usually, only special forces and the 101st Airborne learned fast-rope techniques.

Between its original Ranger persona and the pride the company took in the fast-rope training, Bravo Company saw itself as the high-speed unit of the battalion. They were good, and they were proud of it.

If Bravo was the elite company, Charlie was the battalion's Rock of Gibraltar. Never flashy, they executed without fanfare. They were the blue-collar company, the throwbacks who formed the battalion's spine and gristle. Their NCOs, like Ezelle and Sergeant First Class Tim Bloom, knew their men like their own sons. They knew their strengths, they understood their limitations. They never asked them to do more than what they knew they could handle. That balance helped offset some of the frustrations at Hood, and it helped bond at least the original part of the company even further together.

Meanwhile, trouble brewed in Alpha Company. Captain Granger ran his command with an iron fist. He demanded more from his men and showed less sympathy for them than any other company commander in the battalion.

For example, he often briefed his subordinates late at night after returning from the evening battalion staff meetings. Though sometimes the information he shared with his leaders might have waited until morning to be passed on to the men, he usually ordered his NCOs to wake up their Joes and brief them. The soldiers, exhausted from the day's training, resented this.

Other times, the soldiers would be enjoying some rare down time, only to have Captain Granger appear and order them to do some seemingly meaning-less task. Once, during a precious day off, some of the 3rd Platoon Joes and NCOs were playing video games on a LAN network they'd set up. Captain Granger showed up, saw what the men were doing, and ordered them outside to carry out a laborious chore.

Such things may have appeared pointless to the soldiers, but Granger's style made the men hard. It got them used to changes of schedule and routines. It made them able to better adapt. They worked harder than almost everyone else, and it forged platoon unity. They didn't like it, they called him all manner of names, but in the end he made them better soldiers. Better soldiers have a better chance of staying alive in combat. That was Granger's greatest accomplishment.

At the same time, Alpha had its share of problems with battalion. Captain Granger and the BC never developed a good rapport. This struck some of the staff officers as odd, because they were both police officers and Granger had been one of the BC's ROTC cadets back in the '90s when Hendrickson taught mili-tary science at Oregon State. They expected Granger to be the fair-haired boy. It didn't work out that way.

Because of this, Alpha Company felt like the black sheep of the battalion. "We were the red-headed stepchildren of 2-162" several of the Alpha's NCOs later explained. The fact that the BC and the original elements of 2-162 had their own way of doing things with which Alpha was not familiar reinforced that sense of isolation. It later morphed into an us-against-the-world mentality. In some ways this was good. It forged unity within the company and gave the men their own esprit de corps. They saw themselves as the outcasts who could do no right anyway, so they'd go out and do things their own way.

At the same time, it led to problems. Nearly everything the battalion staff did became an affront or slight to Alpha Company. The men thought they received the worst assignments, the least amount of equipment, and the least amount of support.

Captain Eric Riley, working as the assistant S-3, knew better. He had been to the Sinai with the 1-186 and knew most of the men in Alpha Company. He also had an insider's perspective on how the battalion staff conducted business. To his friends in Alpha, he tried to explain that nobody was punishing the company—the battalion simply had limited resources. Most of his explanations fell on deaf ears. The men of Alpha remained outcasts, at least in their own mind.

Delta Company, the other "outsiders" in the battalion, established its identity in a remarkable manner. As cavalry troopers, Delta's men proudly stood apart from their straight-legged, light infantrymen brethren. What could have been a very divisive difference became a strength that knitted the company tightly into the rest of the battalion.

It started when General Chiarelli released a memo that authorized his troopers to wear their old-style cavalry Stetsons. This really was meant for the regular battalions in the 1st Cav, but Hildebrandt decided it applied to his company as well. He did it to get a rise out of the BC, but also to help forge the company's identity.

The first Friday came around and his men proudly wore their Stetsons. The BC saw this, raised an eyebrow, and had a talk with Scott Hildebrandt. When he brought up the matter, Hildebrandt grinned, pulled out the memo, and showed it to the BC.

Hildebrandt liked messing with the BC. Part of this was his natural character, but part of him also saw that his commanding officer was under a huge strain at Hood. The man needed a little levity; he needed to loosen up a little bit.

The cav guys went to work on the BC. E Troop, 82nd Cav, stickers started to appear in various places around the battalion, including on the BC's Humvee. Later, Hildebrandt and a few of his men purchased a cavalry license plate, signed it, and mounted it over the BC's desk in his office.

Such pranks seemed harmless enough, but they actually performed a valuable function: they turned what could have been a weakness into an asset. Hildebrandt's approach created unit pride and built a good working relationship with Major Hendrickson. In retrospect, it couldn't have been handled any better.

SEVEN

STRAINS OF COMMAND

Major Hendrickson faced many challenges at Hood. Unsnarling the supply situation took time and energy. Fighting with the layers of command to get his men the training they needed proved frustrating. He advocated for his soldiers, and at times took stands that angered his superiors. He did this because it was the right thing to do. He made hard choices and learned that command can be a lonely thing.

In December, the staff organized a battalion run. The men needed some PT, and this was the first chance to get the entire unit together for some exercise. As the run began, CSM Conley noticed that Bravo Company lagged behind. When he went to investigate, he found the men had slowed down to stay with Captain Long. Ben Long was not in shape, and later he fell out. The incident highlighted Captain Long's physical fitness and raised questions about his ability to function in Iraq.

The BC assessed the situation. Captain Long was a good company commander. His men loved him and would follow him anywhere. They knew him, understood him, and the company worked well with him in charge. Long was a good man, an able officer, and an asset to the battalion. But Long hadn't met the standards. He later failed a PT test. In the harsh desert of Iraq, how would he lead from the front? Physical conditioning was essential for the infantry and even more so for an officer. The company could not afford to have its commander go down to heat prostration in the middle of a fight.

The BC relieved Captain Long. It was a difficult decision, and a fairly rare one as well in the National Guard, where officers do not get relieved nearly as often as in the regular army. Bravo took it very hard, but most of the men understood. The move devastated Ben and did lasting damage to his career.

After such a stunning blow, everyone assumed he would not want to remain in the battalion, but that's just what he did. He became the liaison officer between the 39th Brigade and 2-162. Bravo Company's Joes thought it took a lot of guts and character to stick around.

The BC gave Bravo Company to Captain Demian San Miguel. That lessened the impact of Captain Long's departure. San Miguel had earned a good reputation with the scout platoon. He joined the Guard as an enlisted man at age seventeen, so he understood the perspective of the Joes. He also loved adventure and challenges. As a kid, he spent his summer weekends leaping off a four-story cliff into the waters of Drina Lake and jumping from covered bridges. When he grew old enough, he set out to explore the world. By 1996, he'd explored thirty-six countries on three continents.

San Miguel's transfer opened up a slot in the scout platoon. Lieutenant Ross Boyce took the job. A mech infantry officer, he had been an aide to General Keen at Fort Hood when the slot had opened up. Keen knew Boyce wanted an assignment with the troops, so the general sent him to the Volunteers. General Keen wanted his aide to go with a good unit, and he had come to respect 2-162, Major Hendrickson, and Command Sergeant Major Conley. Boyce joined the Volunteers, the only regular army officer to deploy with the battalion.

In January, with a month left in Texas, the battalion received its last infusion of manpower as members of the battalion trickled in from various other training assignments.

The second lieutenants fresh from Infantry Officers Basic Course (IOBC) formed the largest group of arrivals. Among them were Lieutenants Pete Wood, Brandon Ditto, Keelan Rogers, and Chris Boeholt.

Ditto initially received a platoon in Delta Company. Not long after he arrived, the BC reorganized the company. From five sixteen-man platoons they reformed into three with about thirty to thirty-five men in each one. Later, a platoon of New York National Guard infantry under Lieutenant Dave Williams joined Delta, giving it four platoons.

The reorg left Ditto jobless. He landed on the battalion staff serving in the future plans section under Captain Riley.

Keelan Rogers went back to Alpha Company. He'd been an enlisted man in the unit since '99, but in June he graduated from Oregon State and the ROTC program. He received his commission that summer and went off to infantry officer basic course (IOBC). When he rejoined the battalion, he took command of 3rd Platoon, Alpha. He didn't know a soul, even though he had been in the platoon the previous spring. Fortunately, Rogers and Sergeant First Class Larson formed a solid working relationship. Keelan gave his platoon sergeant a long leash while he worked hard to manage platoon within Captain Granger's demanding framework.

Chris Boeholt, a tall and dedicated young officer, received the battalion's 81mm mortar platoon. It would be a very difficult assignment. In Iraq, the rules of engagement virtually prohibited the use of indirect fire weapons, which left the mortarmen thoroughly frustrated.

Pete Wood landed in Bravo Company, where he took over 1st Platoon from Sergeant First Class Ken Jackola. Jackola, one of the most impressive NCOs in the battalion, became Wood's platoon sergeant. Wood was exceptionally fortunate having Jackola as his platoon sergeant.

If Pete Salerno was revered and Vinni beloved, then Sergeant First Class Ken Jackola set the standard for excellence within the company. The entire battalion respected Ken Jackola, who had jumped into Panama with the 82nd Airborne in December 1989. At six-foot-four, he possessed a commanding presence.

It was battalion policy to fit the new lieutenants with exceptional platoon sergeants. The NCOs were expected to teach the young lieutenants the basics of leadership and soldiering. Unfortunately, there just wasn't much time left to do that.

Later that month, the battalion's prodigal sons returned. This included the ever-smiling Corporal Shane Ward. He missed the first months of the deployment while at air assault school at Fort Benning, but he'd long since become one of Bravo Company's enduring characters. When he and his brother, Brian, joined the company in the late '90s, they showed up for their first drill straight from a high-school baseball game still wearing their uniforms and cleats. They never quite lived that down and had endured years of light-hearted teasing.

Shane and Brian grew up in tiny Alsea, Oregon, a logging town tucked up in the coast range near Corvallis. It's a wide spot in the road with a tradition of military service. After 9/11, the Alsea boys gained statewide fame through a series of articles in the *Oregonian* and other papers. Bravo had a deep Alsea connection thanks to the Wards and one other pair of brothers, Sergeant Gabe Sapp of 1st Platoon and his younger brother Jesse who served in 3rd Platoon.

Shane arrived back with Bravo Company at the same time Specialist Spike Olsen returned. Pete Salerno grabbed both of them and stuck them in 2nd Platoon. Shane had always been an outstanding soldier, and Spike soon impressed everyone with his skill and competence.

In his most honest moments, Spike would admit he joined the National Guard not out of any altruistic sense of duty, but because he was bored. At the time, he and Gabe Sapp roomed together while going to school at Western Oregon University. Though Spike also pole-vaulted for the track team, he yearned for a bigger challenge. One night, Gabe introduced him to Bravo Company, and after a few more wild evenings on the town with the Joes, Spike signed up. Little did he know that in his quest to escape boredom he'd endure some of the dullest moments of his life.

Shortly after joining the Guard in 2002, he met Mandy Ferguson at a bar in Independence. Mandy worked at the circulation desk of the school library where her arresting beauty had earned her local fame among the male population. She and Spike began to date, and by early 2003 they were an exclusive couple. Their story differed little from thousands of other college-born romances that ultimately led to something more serious.

Then came the deployment. Spike went to basic and advanced infantry training that summer, then moved on to airborne school. Mandy missed him dearly while he was gone, but they managed the long-distance relationship well. Their time together became episodic. Spike returned briefly in the fall for a few days, then he went to airborne school. When he returned home to Mandy in December, she had finished school and was working as a sex education teacher in Portland. After checking in at the armory, Spike learned he'd be going to Iraq.

He drove to Portland and broke the news to Mandy. They hugged each other and cried. Mandy's world had been turned upside down. Her college love affair had just collided head-on with the real world. Life had arrived, and now they faced a terrible challenge to make it work. Exactly how difficult it would be neither knew or even sensed.

Before he left for Hood, Spike took Mandy to the park where they'd gone on their first date. It was snowing that day, a very unusual thing in the valley, and the park looked lovely covered in virgin snow. At a bridge over a small stream, Spike got down on his knees and proposed. Somehow, they would muddle through the months ahead. When he came home they would be married.

Spike left a few days later, Mandy now his fiancée.

Second Platoon envied Spike and Mandy. During the last weeks at Hood, she wrote him almost every day. Packages arrived, letters came. She e-mailed him. They talked on the phone. The level of support she gave Spike bordered on superhuman. He took a lot of razzing from his fellow Joes over the mushy stuff, but Mandy had resolved to make this work. Besides, she missed him terribly; writing to him made her feel connected. The letters became signposts of their trail together as they struggled to survive and keep their relationship intact.

Sergeant Jacques and the Bravo Joes just couldn't hold it in anymore. Hood had pushed everyone to the threshold of hell. Between the seven-day work weeks, the missions taught by trainers totally inferior to their own abilities, the loss of Captain Long, the food, the living conditions, and the myriad red tape they faced every day, Bravo had reached the breaking point. Vinni sensed the time had come to either vent steam with some good clean fun or face a serious morale crisis.

At dusk on January 12, Vinni organized a mini–Celtic Game event. In the Bravo barracks, beer arrived in quantity and the men soaked their capillaries with it. The Celtic hammer, the tent mallet used in the original games in '97, materialized and the boys set to work smashing things, including one of the many faulty refrigerators they inherited from the 4th ID.

Then Captain Insano, Matt Zedwick's alter ego, arrived. Zedwick, dressed in nothing but a Speedo and a recognition panel wrapped around his shoulders like a cape, bounded out of his room to much fanfare. Captain Insano sallied forth on a streaking expedition through Charlie Company's barracks. The Charlie Joes tried to catch him, but Z was just too fast. He returned safely, a triumphant grin on his face. Meanwhile, Chris Johnson snatched up a pair of clippers and attacked people with them. He nailed Shane Ward and cut a four-inch bald spot out of Shane's otherwise immaculately coiffed hair. Minutes later, CJ stumbled over to VanLeuven and went to work on him. VanLeuven was perhaps the hairiest man in the battalion. He'd long since been nicknamed "Chewbacca" by his fellow Joes. Johnson gave him what could only be described as a "full body mohawk" from his forehead to the small of his back.

Vinni decided Charlie Company needed to join in the fun. The C Company barracks stretched out along the far end of a small grassy quad. Nearly naked, Vinni stood on a balcony and shouted, "Hey, you bastards! Come drink with us!"

He received no response. He tried again, "Hey E. Z., come drink whiskey with us!" The C Company guys didn't seem interested. Vinni grew puzzled. He'd never known Charlie's Joes to turn down a drink.

Bravo Company concluded they needed some encouragement. Sergeant

Lucas Smith showed up in Chris Johnson's room with a giant slingshot made from a signal panel and surgical tubing.

Initial tests proved quite effective. The device launched fruit clear across the quad into a nearby warehouse. As the Joes trained up on their new weapon, some of the other men went off to find ammunition. They returned with all manner of goodies, which soon splattered the side of Charlie Company's barracks.

They peppered Charlie Company with pudding cups, which exploded on impact in a very satisfactory manner. They ran out and switched to half-pint cartons of milk. The C Company men scurried for cover as they dodged showers of incoming moo juice.

Other items followed until the Joes hit upon the ultimate weapon: wet toilet paper rolls. Those sailed across the quad and detonated like mini-mortar shells. Soggy shrapnel flew everywhere, sticking to walls and trees after every volley.

Charlie Company called the MPs, who arrived just as another barrage swooshed overhead. When the Bravo Joes spotted the MPs in the quad, Tommy Houston recalled, "We scattered like cockroaches." Everyone dashed to their rooms to hide. Not that they could, the halls were full of victimized appliances, beer, more beer, and leftover ammunition for the slingshot.

Vinni made first contact. He somehow made it down the stairs and met the MPs in the quad. The trees were festooned with toilet paper. Broken milk cartons, pudding streaks, and smashed fruit littered the quad. The MPs asked for the senior man present. Vinni, swaying slightly, bellowed, "I am, and I'm going to get to the bottom of this."

Somehow, everyone avoided jail.

The next morning, E. Z. Ezelle stood before Charlie Company and demanded to know who had ratted out Vinni. Nobody stepped forward. Ezelle had been off post that night. Had he been there, though, the fruit projectiles would have flown in both directions.

At the end of January, the battalion packed up and left Fort Hood. They did so with few regrets. The training they'd received had been a terrible disappointment. During the interlude between Hood and moving on to JRTC at Fort Polk, Louisiana, one of the battalion's rising stars, First Lieutenant Erik McCrae, married his fiancée, Heather. Most of the battalion staff and many of the junior officers attended the wedding. It became one of the great bonding experiences between the officers prior to the deployment. In fact, it was one of the few chances the officers had to socialize before going to Iraq. It could not have been a better setting. Erik McCrae came from a Guard family. His brother served in the 1-186 and had gone to Egypt in '02. His father, Colonel Scott McCrae, had spent almost forty years in the Oregon Guard.

Everyone admired Lieutenant McCrae. Devout, he prayed at every meal. He treated his soldiers with an easy formality that underscored his respect for them. When he took over Boggs' Old Man platoon in Delta Company, Kerry could not help but be impressed with his new platoon leader.

McCrae had a natural ability to grasp complex subjects, perhaps in part because he'd been a double science major at Linfield College, where he'd graduated in only three years. Ultimately, McCrae intended to apply to NASA and join the civilian astronaut training program.

At the wedding, the officers toasted McCrae and his new bride, whom Erik called "Chika." Few men had ever been so in love as Erik obviously was with his new wife. He represented the best of them, proof that the National Guard attracted brilliant minds and outstanding leaders. In the months to come, he would prove that he had courage to match as well.

EIGHT

FINISHING SCHOOL

At Fort Polk, the battalion was put to a final series of tests at JRTC. For a month, they lived in FOBs and conducted real-world missions complete with Iraqi civilians on the battlefield.

Bravo Company worked with the 1st Cav's aviation brigade and carried on air assault operations. The other companies ran convoy escorts, patrols, cordon and searches, and other operations using new tactics the OCs shared with them. The observing OCs generally possessed considerable experience and offered excellent advice. Some of them had been to Iraq, and their combat experience helped the battalion fine-tune the way it did business.

Polk turned out to be everything Fort Hood should have been. For a month, the battalion honed their skills, refined procedures, and worked to put the finishing touches on their ability to fight a three-block war.

Major Tanguy especially appreciated the time at Polk because it gave the battalion its first opportunity to work closely with the 1st Cav Division as a complete battalion. This gave the staff a chance to iron out issues and find its battle rhythm under the tutelage of some very good OCs. The final exam came on the Shuckart-Gordon Range. This marvelous training facility allowed the companies to conduct MOUT operations with live ammunition.

The Volunteers threw themselves into the exercise with passion, using tactical creativity and violence of action. At times, this caused some trouble. Bravo Company went out and Captain San Miguel's Joes assaulted multiple buildings simultaneously. This was not what the OCs expected: they wanted Bravo to be methodical and seize one building at a time. Salerno and San Miguel didn't see the sense in that, and they set up a different plan. The company swarmed into the mock cityscape and captured all its objectives simultaneously. The OCs gave them all sorts of grief for the way they carried it out, but the fact remained—their plan had worked.

On the range that day, Vinni Jacques' platoon came of age. They'd come a long way since that first day Vinni had seen them on the armory lawn, as green as the grass under their boots. They had worked together for almost six months and had trained on their own with every spare moment.

The company started the range at a staging area in some nearby woods. San Miguel put everyone in a firing line, where the M240 gunners laid down suppressing fire. Under the chatter of the machine guns, the platoons attacked into the cityscape, covering one another as they moved. Third Platoon reached a building and Bill Stout's team climbed into it through a window. Sergeant Jeremy Turner, the chemistry student from Oregon State, directed the squad to clear the first floor and move upstairs. Bill, closely followed by Kenny Leisten and Ron Bates, romped upstairs tossing live flash-bangs as they went. When they got back downstairs, Specialist Marty Theurer, a paramedic from Philomath, hunkered down behind a desk with his SAW to cover the first floor doorways and windows. Meanwhile, Bates handed Kenny a flash-bang and told him to throw it down the basement stairs. The squad stacked up in the hallway around a corner from the stairwell, and Leisten reached around to chuck the flash-bang.

The flash-bang didn't bang. It popped. Thinking it must have been a dud, Bates pushed Leisten and yelled, "GO! GO! GO! GO! GO!" Kenny turned the corner and reached the top of the stairwell just as the flash-bang detonated. Marty saw Leisten silhouetted by brilliant white-light. Kenny had just taken the full effect of the flash-bang. It left him loopy. Nonetheless, he staggered down the stairs with Bates, John Rosander, and Bill Stout hard on his heels.

They reached the basement and spotted a dummy with an AK-47. Bates swung his shotgun to the ready and pulled the trigger. The other Joes came on line and unleashed a torrent of M4 fire right into the dummy. They didn't let up. Bates kept pumping the 12-gauge. Rosander, Stout, and Leisten peppered it with their M4s. Finally, another shotgun blast sent the dummy spinning off its mounting rack. It hit the floor, where even more bullets slammed into it. The boys emptied their magazines, changed them out, and kept firing. The dummy shook and rattled as the gunfire blew it fifteen feet across the floor.

Upstairs, Marty and Jeremy Turner heard the firing and wondered what was going on. Jeremy bolted down the stairs and found his men still blazing away, big grins on their faces.

"Cease fire, cease fire, Goddamnit," Turner shouted.

The din ebbed away. Smoke curled up from Bates' shotgun barrel. Turner looked them over.

"What the hell are you doing?" demanded Turner.

Bill Stout replied, "Killing the shit out of the enemy!"

Later that day during the after-action review, the OCs were shocked by the video of the incident. They showed it to a lieutenant colonel, who told Sergeant Jacques, "Your men are going over to conduct social operations," the colonel said, "They're overly aggressive, and you've got to control them."

"Sir," said Jacques, "we're going to war. I'd rather have to rein them in than boot them in the ass."

Vinni had spent months training them to be aggressive and violent. He'd pushed them, demanded much of them. At times, the platoon resented him because he worked them so hard. But Vinni had been to war before, and he knew that if he didn't push them, they wouldn't be ready. After the colonel lectured him, he watched the film himself. He burst out laughing as his men drilled the dummy over and over again. This was what he wanted: men who wouldn't hesitate to pull the trigger. He wouldn't need to worry about these guys. What they did in the basement ranked as the single most violent thing he'd ever seen in training. He liked that. Liked it a lot.

Later, the OCs' critique reached the squad. When told they needed to tone it down, Bill looked over at Kenny and said, "Tone it down? Shit, we're going to war here. We're not going over there to be pussies. Besides, Sergeant Jacques always says if you're going to make a mistake, make an aggressive one."

Vinni sought them out at the end of the day. When he found the squad, he growled out, "You motherfuckers! My God! You're my hell hounds!" Far from being upset, Vinni was proud of them. Clerks and mechanics no more, Vinni's boys were knuckle-draggers to the core.

Charlie Company's Joes loved their commander, Captain Aaron Noteboom. A University of Oregon law student, Noteboom had served as the XO for years before going to battalion staff. When he came up for company command, he specifically wanted C Company. He returned to his beloved unit, which welcomed him with affection and loyalty.

For years, the company had been known as "Team Charlie." Noteboom sat down with E. Z. one day and asked him, "Is this 'Team Charlie' stuff a World War II thing, or is it some gay '70s–'80s thing?"

Ezelle replied, "I think it's pretty much a gay '80s thing, sir."

"Well, we're going to change it."

Charlie became Caesar Company, and a gladiator with his sword raised over the words *Oregon Is the Light* became the company's symbol. The Joes embraced the new identity and ran with it. Soon, during company formations, when the men came to attention they'd shout in unison, "All hail Caesar." At Fort Polk, somebody stuck a sign outside the company tent that read, "Upon entering the C Co AO, all outsiders must yell, 'All Hail Caesar.'" Outsiders did indeed do this, and in return the Charlie Company soldiers would shout back, "Toga!"

Noteboom was intimately connected to the company's identity and the way it did business. The men showed great affection for him. At Polk, they lost him.

During a combative drill, Noteboom suffered a serious knee injury that required surgery and months of rehabilitation. Eventually, he would make it to Baghdad, but not as a company commander. It was a bitter blow.

Lieutenant Colonel Hendrickson gave the company to Lieutenant Wyatt Welch, who had only recently joined the Oregon Guard. Initially, the transition was a rough one on the company. Welch was not a warm and cuddly officer, he was a disciplinarian who demanded much from his NCOs.

Wyatt Welch was perhaps the most distinctive officer in the battalion, if for no other reason than his accent. Born in North Carolina, he'd been raised in Mississippi, Louisiana, and Alabama and carried his unfettered southern accent throughout his military career. His had the only rich southern drawl in the entire battalion.

In those final days at Fort Polk, Welch couldn't change how the company did business. There just wasn't time. He did get a sense of where Charlie Company's strengths and weaknesses lay. Welch also learned the character of each platoon. First platoon were his planners; they took pride in their detail-oriented approach. Second platoon knew how to handle fluid situations and react on the fly; they were his improvisers. Third platoon, comprised of 1-162 boys under Sergeant First Class James Terrell, served as Wyatt's bruisers. Ham-fisted and blunt, they loved a good scrap.

Just before going into Iraq, Welch received his captain's bars. The company was his, and in Iraq he would help mold it into the rock-steady and reliable back-bone of 2-162.

By the end of JRTC, Lieutenant Colonel Hendrickson now had two new company commanders in Welch and Captain San Miguel. Two more, Captains Granger and Hildebrandt, came from outside 2-162 and had not worked with him prior to Fort Hood. This was not an optimal situation, but the battalion would have to make it work.

NINE

ONE MORE LAST GOODBYE

The 1st Cavalry Division's deployment to Iraq signaled the beginning of the army's largest relief-in-place operation since World War II. Starting in March, more than one hundred thousand fresh troops reached southwest Asia as the veteran units pulled out. It was a tricky operation that demanded tremendous planning and enormous air support. Originally, the Volunteers had been told they would get a weekend off at Polk to say good-bye to their loved ones before flying to Kuwait. Families, already stretched financially by the deployment, scrapped together the cash for airfare from Oregon to Louisiana. Then the battalion learned that its departure had been pushed back two weeks. As a result, the Volunteers received a fourteen-day leave.

The men welcomed the news, but discovered it was too late to cancel the tickets their wives and families had purchased to Louisiana. They ended up with two last goodbyes. After the weekend with their families in Louisiana, most of the men returned to Oregon.

That two-week break before heading into combat left the men in limbo: no longer part of their old lives, not yet started in their new lives in Iraq. It was odd and unsettling, a situation made worse in some households by the opposition of a few family members to the war itself.

One young scout platoon NCO went home to spend his leave with his mom and grandparents down in California. It turned out to be a mistake. His grandmother made no effort to conceal her opposition to the war, or to his role in it. It made him feel uncomfortable at a time when he was mentally preparing himself for war. By the end of the leave, he'd left his grandparents house and moved to a motel to escape the situation.

Pete Salerno returned to his farm south of Corvallis and paced like a caged jaguar. He wanted to just get on with it, and this two-week lull seemed to kill all the momentum gained at Polk. Trudy had already left for Afghanistan, so his mother was running the household and taking care of the boys. Still, lots of little things needed to be addressed around the farm. That irritated him. He was about to go to war, and he found himself doing odd jobs back at home. It seemed incongruous and made him moody. He was not good company. In retrospect, he decided he should not have gone home.

Doug Jackson, the Modoc from Alpha Company arrived back in Southern Oregon to be with his girlfriend, who had recently broken the news that Doug was going to be a father. The prospect of being a dad delighted him. He spent his two weeks with her, as well as elk hunting and partying with the boys. When it came time to leave, forty people, friends and family, saw him off at the airport. For him, there'd be no lack of support.

Spike and Mandy spent the leave clinging to each other in the face of a coming storm. They'd gotten good at these episodic moments together. At first, they put the future out of their minds and focused on the moment. They went to the coast, ate out, and started planning their wedding.

The last two days were hell. The future could not be denied; it loomed over them and colored every moment. The clock ticked, time together ebbed away. The morning came, and as they prepared to say good-bye, Spike's stomach twisted into knots and made him nauseous. Mandy sobbed. They kissed one last time, then left her apartment. Mandy had to go to work, so this was it.

They climbed in separate cars and followed each other onto Interstate-5. Spike pulled up alongside Mandy, and they drove side by side as they talked on their cell phones. They reached Mandy's off-ramp. She merged onto I-205 and looked over her shoulder as Spike's truck drove out of sight. It struck her that this could be the last glimpse she'd ever have of him.

Vinni and Rhonda Jacques both had a bad feeling about this good-bye. At the airport with Julie and Ryan, they said their last goodbyes. Gabe burst into tears again, and the sight of his little boy crying just about broke Vinni's heart. He wanted to reach out to the boy and never let him go, to tell him everything would be okay. But he couldn't do that. In his heart, he sensed that this was the last time he'd see his little boy.

Ryan had a bad feeling as well. Something was going to happen to his tight-knit family; it overshadowed his good-bye with Julie. She felt it, too. She hugged him fiercely and told him to come back to her.

The brothers grabbed their gear and headed for the gate, Gabe's crying lingering in their ears. When Rhonda returned to her car, she turned on the radio. Toby Keith's "American Soldier" came on.

You've got to be kidding me.

That song could have been written about Vinni, or Ryan, or any of the men she knew from the battalion. There in the parking garage at the Portland airport, PDX, she leaned back in the driver's seat and wept.

In Eugene, Al Ezelle struggled with his good-bye. A man of action, a warrior, a proud father to be sure, Al Ezelle handled all with confidence and skill. Now, he struggled to understand the conflictiong emotions at odds inside him that night. He didn't *do* emotional. Now, the moment had come to say good-bye to his son. He entered his room and sat down on the side of his bed. E. Z. was the kind of man who could face bullets without flinching, but on this night he couldn't bring himself to look at his son. If he had, those emotions he so little understood would have gotten the best of him.

"You're thirteen now, Chuck," Ezelle began. "You're old enough now to know that everything I'm going to teach you, I've already taught you. You just don't know it all yet."

Struggling, he continued, "You listen to your mother. Be strong. Hope for the best but expect the worst."

Steel does not bleed. Nor does it cry. But a man does; Ezelle, after all, was human. Tears squeezed through his self-control and blurred his eyes.

"What's my job, son?"

"To make me a man and get me ready for when you're not here."

"Good. What's the definition of a strong man?"

"Doing what's right even when nobody is looking."

Ezelle left early the next morning.

Part II

ROAD WARRIORS

TEN

THE CARDBOARD COFFINS

The battalion awoke to the cradle of civilization. A bloated sun lurched over the horizon, and the red-orange hue it cast across the miles of sand around their tents made it look like the Volunteers had landed on Mars, not Kuwait. Not a tree stood in view. Nothing green, not even a weed, grew. For men used to the verdant Willamette Valley, this was alien landscape.

The smells were different as well. Getting off the plane the night before, the sweet, sickly stench of Kuwait reminded Major Tanguy of his tour in Korea in '88. Others not used to foreign smells gagged at the undertones of sewage and rot.

Long before dawn, buses had dumped them at Camp New York, an ugly, tent city in the middle of nowhere. Now in the new sun's light, Ed Tanguy regarded the vast nothingness and wondered if he'd see T. E. Lawrence come dashing over the horizon.

First mission: get acclimated. Vinni awoke and told his men to get outside and do some PT. They resented this, but having been here before, Vinni knew that the quickest way to get used to the heat was to get into it.

Tent flaps opened, and the blowtorch morning winds struck pale faces. It wasn't just heat. It was a searing presence that sucked the hydration out of a man and made every motion an act of will. In Oregon, 80-degree summer days were considered barely tolerable. Here, at daybreak, the thermometer touched 120. Throats parched in minutes, the sand burned, metal became a danger to touch. To avoid heat prostration, the men carried camelbacks (backpacks with a bladder full of water) and sucked them dry from a long tube as the day wore on. Canteens emptied and emptied again. The men drank liters of water and needed still more.

Some became dizzy, lightheaded, and rummy. Those were the first signs of heat prostration. More water would do only so much good. Without electrolytes, they'd keel over. The men carried beef jerky and potato chips and munched on them between shots from their camelbacks. That kept them upright.

That night, Bravo Company pulled out of Camp New York and said goodbye to the rest of 2-162. Bused to Camp Udari, they arrived exhausted from their travels. At first, they thought they would be assigned to the 1st Cavalry's aviation brigade. That was the plan back in the States when the Bulldogs had landed the Division Rapid Reaction Force (DRRF) mission. They'd stay at Taji with the helicopters while the rest of the Volunteers moved into Baghdad.

Captain San Miguel staggered into a tent and could not wait until his head hit a pillow. But before he could catch some sleep, Lieutenant Colonel Charles Fourshee came through the tent flaps and introduced himself. He was the commander of 2-7 Cav, and he explained to Demian that the Bulldogs had been assigned to his unit.

The news dispirited Captain San Miguel. He asked, "Sir, does this mean we won't be doing the DRRF mission?"

Fourshee, who had been genial only seconds before, snapped angrily, "No, you won't be doing DRRF."

The sudden mood change left Demian uneasy. He wanted to fight for that mission, but he knew to pick his battles, especially when first meeting his new boss.

The news that their DRRF mission had been taken from them angered the Bulldogs. Before leaving the States, General Chiarelli had come to visit them and had told the Oregonians that they were his boys, and he'd personally selected them to be the reaction force. It had been a source of enormous pride. Now, they were just another line unit again. It stung.

For two weeks, Bravo stayed at Udari as 2-7 Cav prepared to move into Iraq. Vinni wanted to test fire his machine guns and have his men zero their weapons, but he ran into roadblocks. There was no live ammunition, so the men were forced to zero their M4s with blue, plastic-tipped training rounds. Ballistically, they behave differently than live ammunition, so zeroing their M4s with these rounds didn't make sense. Vinni also couldn't get his M2 .50-caliber machine guns test fired. Notoriously fussy weapons—they were sixty years old—he decided to keep them stored away until they reached Taji.

At Camp New York, the rest of the Volunteers fell into a routine of PT and preparation for the road march into Iraq. There was only so much they could do, because their vehicles had yet to show up.

Delta Company was the only unit in the battalion that had its own Humvees. They'd been packed and put aboard a ship a few weeks before Delta left Louisiana. These Humvees were twenty years old and had spent most of their existence on the Oregon coast. The salt air had not been kind to them, and many were rusted with turret rings that would barely traverse. Sergeant Boggs knew these vehicles intimately, and he picked out six of the best for the Old Man platoon.

Even with those twenty, the company still came up short. To haul everyone into Iraq, Delta needed five more Humvees. The Cav guys waited just like everyone else.

And waited.

Finally, with only a few days to go before their scheduled departure, they received their rigs. It was a puzzling, crazy-quilt collection of pickups and turtle-backs, two-doors and four-doors. Most had seen better days. They'd been ridden hard by other units and recycled to the 39th. Mixed in were a few, precious M1114s, brand-new armored Humvees with ballistic glass and the ability to withstand rocket-propelled grenades.

When Lieutenant Colonel Hendrickson took a look at the arriving Humvees, he went to see 39th Brigade commander Brigadier General Ronald S. Chastain.

"This isn't what we were supposed to get," he told the general. The Volunteers had trained on turtleback Humvees with turrets mounted on the roof. They'd been given mostly M998 pickups and precious few turtlebacks. The pickup variant lacked a turret, and most of them had only two doors. Chastain agreed, but he couldn't do anything about it.

"This is unacceptable," argued the BC.

Chastain nodded. It was unacceptable. But this was it. Either they drove the 998s or they walked into Iraq.

In the months since the 1st Cav entered the fight, the American media has raised many questions about the Humvees being used in Iraq. Some of the articles and television pieces accused the regular army of dumping the worst Humvees on the National Guard and reserve units. The press triggered a congressional response, and the whole issue became political. A year later, the Pentagon released a study that concluded no favoritism had been shown. The reserve components shared the best equipment equally with the regular army. The media scoffed. Politicians hinted at a whitewash and blew off the report.

The fact is, within the 1st Cav Division, the report was accurate. General Chiarelli divided up the available vehicles fairly and took care of his 39th Brigade Guardsmen as well as he could. The problem was not a reserve versus regular issue. It was an army-wide problem. There simply were not enough M1114 armored Humvees to go around.

The root of the issue lay in the nature of the war in Iraq. When the insurgency flared in the wake of the U.S. invasion, it caught the military by surprise. The available units in Iraq were soon stretched thin as they patrolled vast amounts of battlespace. To do it required motorizing the army. It also required converting units into roles for which they had never trained. Artillery battalions suddenly found themselves on wheels carrying out infantry patrols or working the streets of Baghdad as provisional MPs. All of these units now needed armed Humvees. There just weren't enough to go around, and it would take time to gear up production to build new ones. In the meantime, the soldiers would have to make do.

Modern warfare evolves so quickly that weapons procurement always lags behind. It takes time, occasionally years, to make up that deficit. And as it happened, the Volunteers went to war right in the middle of this transitional phase. It was the luck of the draw, one that many American soldiers have faced before. Knowing this didn't make it any easier. The leadership in both the 39th and 2-162 faced some tough choices. Who would get the armored Humvees?

Hendrickson decided he wasn't going to take one. He didn't want his men to think he wouldn't share their risks, but Sergeant Major Conley wouldn't hear of it. "Sir," he rejoined, "we cannot afford to lose you. And if the men are mad, let them be mad at me. But you need to take an eleven-fourteen."

Hendrickson resisted. He refused to concede. "Bullshit, sir. You've got to take one. It has the better commo, and if you go down, we all go down."

Major Tanguy agreed. Reluctantly, the BC took an M1114.

In each company, that decision played out all the way down to the platoon levels. The Volunteers received enough new 1114s that each platoon could have two. The other six vehicles per platoon would be a mix of turtlebacks and pickups.

The 1114s should have gone to the leaders in each company, mainly because they had the Blue Force Tracker (BFT) system installed, along with better communication gear. The BFT was a computer system designed to show where all friendly units were in Iraq at any given moment. It also showed the vehicle's exact location, the road network, and engaged enemy units.

Some of the leaders refused to take armored Humvees. In Alpha Company's 1st Platoon, both Sergeant First Class Compton and Lieutenant Dewayne Jones gave the 1114s to their men. Both men took 998 unarmored pickups. In 3rd Platoon, Sergeant First Class Larson and Lieutenant Keelen Rogers received three 1114s. Rogers took one, and the other two went to the men who would take point and trail positions in the convoy during the road march into Iraq. Sergeant Larson took a well-abused 998 as his own rig. Sergeant John Neibert, the officer-turned-NCO, received a turtleback M1025 with no armor on it at all.

In Charlie Company, Captain Welch spotted a beat-up older M1114. He took it and gave the new ones the company received to his platoon leaders. Wyatt picked the older 1114 in part because it didn't have the armor protection of the new ones, and the fact that it had obviously been IEDed several times and rebuilt. There was a sentimental reason as well; he found stenciled on the front bumper "Blackjack 22" and knew right away this Humvee would be his. Welch loved history and read voraciously. He counted General John J. "Blackjack" Pershing among his heroes. As a young enlisted man, he'd driven a TOW antitank Humvee with the number 22. Not surprisingly, it seemed serendipitous to Wyatt that he'd run across the number associated with his hero's nickname, like fate had conspired to throw man and vehicle together.

Over at Camp Udari, Bravo Company faced the same issues. When 3rd Platoon's trucks arrived, Vinni looked them over and wondered what the hell he was supposed to do with the 998s.

The answer was plywood.

The men built double-layered plywood boxes around the pickup beds of the 998s. For added protection, the soldiers placed sandbags between the layers of plywood.

This was not an optimal solution. The company scroungers went off in search of anything that could be used as extra armor. Vinni, Ron Bates, and Christopher Clark drove all over Udari scoring bits of steel plates from various sources. They returned to shove them down inside the plywood layers. Other squads acquired 300-pound armored door kits and mounted those on their rigs. At least they offered some side protection.

At Camp New York, Charlie Company operated the same way. The men searched for extra armor, laid sandbags on the floors of their Humvees, and stole whatever they could find that would help them out.

Sergeant Brian Hambright, a former University of Oregon football player and Gulf War veteran, inherited two 998s for his squad. His men built the plywood boxes, but discovered the sandbags added so much weight Hambright thought they'd break their rear axles. Most of the sandbags came out. Other platoons discovered the same thing: the sandbags made the Humvees so heavy they bottomed out. The men were faced with a choice: protection or functionality. Most everyone chose the latter.

With the boxes mounted, the platoons needed a way to defend themselves. Unfortunately, machine-gun mounts were in short supply. In Salerno's platoon, Spike Olsen couldn't get a mount for his M240. He had to strap it to the cab roof of his 998. Others did the same thing. Major Tanguy drew a 998 with a soft canvas top. His driver mounted Kevlar doors on it, painted them brown to look like the more meaty, 300-pound armored kits, and then took a piece of plywood and strapped it to the canvas top. That served as the bipod mount for Tanguy's gunner, who had only an M249 SAW. These Rube Goldberg solutions allowed minimal fields of fire, a serious problem if the insurgents hit them on the way to Baghdad.

Alpha Company probably had it the worst. They drew their vehicles last and found themselves at the back of the lines at the assembly area. When Compton's 1st Platoon finally got through the line, the base had run out of plywood. Sergeant Cs men pinched enough to build boxes on four of their five 998s, but the other one was left bare. Whoever gunned in that truck would be thoroughly exposed.

In the scout platoon, Lieutenant Boyce sent Andy Hellman and a few other drivers down to a marshalling yard in Kuwait City to pick up their trucks. When Andy got down there, he found four factory-fresh M1114 armored Humvees waiting. They still had that new car smell and plastic covering the seats. Andy's eyes lit up. These rigs were nice. They had air-conditioning and a turret with an armored shield to protect the gunner. Seeing them got his hopes up. Perhaps he'd get one.

No luck. He delivered them to New York and the 39th Brigade took ownership of them. The scout platoon received only one of the new 1114s along with a collection of broken-down rigs that barely functioned.

Andy Hellman received the worst vehicle in the battalion. Battered and used like a middle-aged whore, it lacked armor, ballistic glass, and rear passenger doors. It didn't even have a roof over the cab, just a soft canvas top and a pickup bed in back. It would have been an eye-catching ride back home at the beach, but to drive into battle with a convertible four-door that had only two doors, well, that seemed just a tad west of crazy.

Andy embraced the craziness and grew to love his vehicle. The platoon nicknamed it the "Rat Rig." Andy bolted armored door kits onto the driver and passenger sides, but the rear seats remained exposed.

And then there was Sergeant Bruns. Rebekah-mae didn't even get a Humvee. Assigned a five-ton truck, she drew an ancient and very nervous 39th

Brigade mechanic as her driver. Private Max Corrigan from Alpha Company's 1st Platoon would be her gunner. In a twist of irony, the five-tons had better turrets than many of the Humvees. The men mounted .50-cals on them.

The battalion made do with what they received. As Sergeant Major Conley put it, "You go to war with what you're given. Rumsfeld was right."

Little did they know that even as they prepared to drive into battle, the very nature of the war in Iraq had suddenly changed. They'd be driving right into the middle of Moqtada Al Sadr's Shia uprising.

ELEVEN

MUSLIM BROWNSHIRTS

One look at Muqtada Al Sadr's recessed eyes, chubby face, and rotting teeth and most Westerners would conclude he was little more than a creepy, petty criminal. They'd be wrong: he's a brilliantly successful criminal.

The son of a well-known scholarly Arab family, Al Sadr's father was a beloved Shiite religious leader whom Saddam Hussein assassinated in the late '90s.

Muqtada never became the religious scholar his father was, but he did his best to claim that mantle. Once his father died, he took over his dad's religious institutions and used them to line his pockets.

To the world, Al Sadr presented himself as the embodiment of Islam; behind closed doors, he maneuvered for power and cynically used the faith of his followers for his own self-interests. He spoke Arabic with a rough, colloquial street accent, and it was from the streets he gained his power. Al Sadr appealed to the poorest of his people. Teenage boys, twenty-something men with no prospects and no hope rallied to him. He used them as a ragtag band of operatives to carry out his bidding. When Hussein's regime collapsed, he made a grab for power.

In April 2003, U.S. forces captured Najaf and its holy site, the Imam Ali Shrine, which is the final resting place of Muhammad's son-in-law. Shortly afterward, Imam Abdul Majiel al Khoei arrived in Najaf. Khoei was a pro-West exiled Iraqi Imam who the United States hoped would help lead Iraq into the post-Saddam era.

Muqtada's thugs beat him to death a few blocks from the Imam Ali Shrine. It was the start of a reign of terror that ultimately stretched from Basra to Baghdad. Moqtada's thugs later tried to assassinate Sistani, perhaps the most beloved Shia Arab religious leader. Al Sadr wanted control of the income-producing religious sites and organizations Sistani controlled. Later, other assassinations took place as Muqtada used his ruffians to eliminate his competitors.

In the spring of 2003, Al Sadr denounced the U.S. invasion. His fiery Friday sermons burned with hate for the West and Jews. Imams all over southern Iraq joined him. They preached that Americans had invaded Iraq not to get rid of Hussein, but to kill the great Messiah of Islam, the Mahdi, who it is said will appear in the final days of the world.

Most Shiites ignored him. Al Sadr's popularity in '03 remained confined to a tiny proportion of the Iraqi population. But his Islamist messages did strike a chord with some. Sadr City in northeast Baghdad became his most loyal base of support. Through its slums and sewage-soaked streets, his message took root. In the summer of 2003, he started to recruit young men for his new "Mahdi militia." The poor and dispossessed in Sadr City flocked to join up. The Coalition Provisional Authority (CPA) did nothing to stop this.

As his street army grew, Al Sadr positioned himself as the great savior of Islam who would cleanse Iraq and purify their religion. His followers referred to him as the "son of Mahdi." Others implied that he may be the savior himself.

Funding his Mahdi militia never posed a problem, thanks to the Iranians. They funneled money and support to him, and he developed close ties with Iranian intelligence operatives. With a private army at his disposal, Al Sadr unleashed a wave of terror. In Basra, his militiamen attacked a group of college students having a picnic. According to his spokesmen, they did it to stop the students from dancing and wearing sexy clothing. One said, "We beat them because we are authorized by Allah to do so."

Bands of militiamen attacked merchants selling pornographic DVDs, burned liquor stores, and destroyed buildings used for any form of vice. His men established their own kangaroo courts and prisons for those they "arrested." Hundreds disappeared and were later found murdered.

In southern Iraq, citizens of Qawliya, a gypsy town known for its tolerance of gambling, drove out a small force of Mahdi militiamen only to face Al Sadr's full wrath. His street army returned, killed or drove out the entire population, at least a thousand people, then bulldozed every building and home. Before departing, they set fire to the ruins. In one swoop, a town ceased to exist. The CPA did nothing in response. Without check, Al Sadr had become a Shiite fascist with his own brownshirts. Like Hitler's street army of the 1920s, the Mahdi militia would be wielded against a nascent republic.

Encouraged by the CPA's lack of response, Al Sadr created his own "shadow government" in the fall of '03. It fizzled from lack of general support. His street army gave him power and leverage, but he needed to reach out to other Shiites to widen his power. He declared himself an ally of Sistani, acting on his behalf. This was nonsense; Sistani despised him and knew Al Sadr had tried to kill him. Nevertheless, some Shiites believed it.

Following Sistani's opposition to the CPA's plan for drafting a constitution, Al Sadr made inroads with other radical Shiite groups. In March 2004, Al Sadr sent a representative to England to take part in the operational planning of a joint uprising against the coalition.

Held in an Islamic center in London, the meeting cloaked its motives under the innocuous title, "Islamic Movement and Iraq Conference."

Behind closed doors, Al Sadr's representative met with Syrian and Iranian intelligence agents, members of Lebanese Hezbollah and Al-Qaeda. Sunni Jihadists also attended the meeting, and participants gathered from Europe, Iraq, Syria, Iran, the Gulf states, and Saudi Arabia.

Together, they planned to extend and unite the insurgency in Iraq under one Islamic umbrella. They knew that the Sunni nationalists battling the coalition in the Anbar province could not beat the United States alone. If the Sunni and Shia militias could unite, the balance of power would shift. The Americans could be overwhelmed and defeated.

This conference, held in the capital of America's most loyal ally, signified the first effort to create a national opposition to the coalition's occupation of Iraq. The meeting concluded with a detailed planning session designed to bring the Shia into the war in one massive uprising. According to Yusef Bodansky's book, *The Secret History of the Iraq War,* that plan included significant support from Syria and Iran. Al-Qaeda and Hezbollah would provide leadership, support, and experience while Iranian intelligence coordinated the operation. News of the conference leaked out in April, and while it made headlines in Europe, the American media hardly noticed.

A few weeks later, Sunni insurgents formed the Patriotic Front for the Liberation of Iraq (PFLI). Designed to serve as the umbrella organization that would unite the Sunni and Shiites into one Nationalist-Islamist revolutionary force, the PFLI signaled a radical new development in the Iraqi insurgency.

On March 31, 2004, Sunni insurgents killed four American contractors near Fallujah. The insurgents hung their burned and defiled bodies from a bridge, where an Associated Press stringer photographed them dangling from ropes like burned hunks of meat. The incident served as the flashpoint for the first Battle of Fallujah.

The following Friday, The CPA closed down Al Sadr's inflammatory magazine *Al Hawza.* That served as the pretext for the Shia uprising. On April 3, thousands of Mahdi militiamen streamed into Baghdad as Al Sadr called for rebellion. All over southern Iraq, prepositioned Shiite insurgents rose up against the coalition. The attacks came as such a shock that for a time the Mahdi militia gained control of most of the key Shiite cities in the south. They'd done so without a major fight. The coalition units, including the Spanish troops in Najaf, withdrew to their compounds or pulled out of town altogether.

The Shia uprising had begun.

TWELVE

THE ELEPHANT

The Oregonians drove headlong into the Shia uprising. On April 4, 2004, the 2-7 Cav and Bravo Company streamed out of Camp Udari in several serials bound for the Iraqi frontier. Each serial, or convoy, consisted of a mix of Humvees, flatbed trucks called Hemmits carrying Bradley IFVs, fuel trucks, and five-tons stuffed full of supplies. After a night at the border, the columns pushed into Southern Iraq along a narrow gravel road. Buzzing along at 50 mph, the vehicles kicked up huge plumes of white, powdery dust that obscured vision and coated every weapon. After an hour, the Bulldogs looked like they'd been rolling in talcum powder. Only the flesh under their tinted goggles had escaped the dust. The drivers could hardly see through it, yet they kept their speed up and just prayed they wouldn't hit anything.

It was a spooky sensation for the men, made even spookier by the skeletalized Soviet tanks lying derelict on the roadside. Pete Salerno and the other Bravo Company Joes stared as they passed them by, their minds heavy with the thought that they were now on the battlefield. Spike Olsen stayed on his gun and stared out at the barren countryside. He found it remarkable anybody could live in this place. Occasionally, they drove past kids selling gas or begging for money. Where they lived was anyone's guess. The desert stretched to the horizons.

The Oregonians grew weary at their posts, alertness levels dropped. The longer the road march continued, the more wrapped around the axles some of the serial's leaders became. Seeing this led to an epiphany for Pete. There was no way his men could be on their triggers 24/7. They needed to be aware, but hyperalertness was counterproductive.

That night they stopped at Convoy Support Center (CSC) Scania, which was little more than a gigantic military truck stop out in the desert south of Baghdad. There, the units stayed lined up in their serials while the men performed maintenance and caught some sleep.

The next morning, Bravo rolled north. As the day unfolded, both the serial directly ahead of them and the one directly behind them got ambushed. In one fight, Captain Glass drove his M1 Abrams right off a hemmit and counterattacked into the ambush. His men followed, and the tanks crushed the opposition. After that, Glass was nicknamed "Captain Chaos."

2-7 had seen the elephant.

Later that day, the Bulldogs rolled through Baghdad. For Bill Stout it was a strange feeling seeing the place that had been on the nightly news so often back home. Spike Olsen couldn't believe the number of people. They were everywhere among the bullet-scarred buildings, burning trash piles, and open fields where goats grazed and feral dogs roamed.

The stench got to everybody; it was unlike anything they'd ever experienced stateside. Sewage was the first odor they detected. Diesel fumes permeated their nostrils next, followed by the acrid reek of burning plastic. Rotting garbage provided the icing on the cake. It was a veritable cornucopia of putridity. The men held their noses and hoped that Taji wouldn't be as bad.

They got through Baghdad and up Route Senators toward Taji. That's when they hit the dump. Bill Stout looked out in shock at the vast field of garbage piled out in the open. It stretched for miles. No landfill here. The sanitation crews just dropped the garbage and left. People moved among the trash. The Bulldogs suddenly realized that they weren't working there, they were *living* in it. They'd built pathetic huts from Baghdad's refuse. They hunted among the debris for food, clothing, and pieces of metal for their garbage hooches.

A half hour later, they reached the south gate at Camp Cooke, Taji. The serial slowed to a halt, and as the men waited to get in, they waved at passing cars and people on the street. Then the 4th ID showed up. Humvees beaten and abused, dust-covered gunners with grim faces and a *no bullshit* posture behind their weapons, they stood in stark contrast to the Guardsmen happily greeting the passing Iraqis.

Inside the gate, Bravo discovered there were no quarters for them yet. They dismounted at an Iraqi air force warehouse and bedded down for the night.

The next morning, word arrived that B Company could move into their living quarters. In 1st Platoon, Ken Jackola organized his men. He put Sergeant Spitler, Ryan Howell, and Alvin Bemis on duffel detail. The three Joes walked over to a Humvee, loaded the platoon's duffel bags into it, and headed over to their assigned living area. Ryan and Alvin had to walk as no space was left inside the Humvee.

About a hundred and fifty meters away from the rest of the company, Ryan and Alvin came to a chainlink fence. They found a hole in it and pushed through. In the distance, both men heard a whooshing sound.

"Well, I guess we're lighting up somebody," Ryan said to Bemis.

Back at the rest of the vehicles, Ken Jackola heard a distant explosion. Somebody nearby said, "Oh, that's a controlled detonation; they're blowing up old ordnance."

Ryan and Bemis got through the hole in the fence. Seconds later, they heard another explosion.

"Boy, we're *really* lighting somebody up!" Ryan said.

Over at the company's new living area, Vinni busied himself with assigning trailers to his men. He heard one of the explosions and thought somebody had just slammed a trailer door. Ken Jackola looked over his Humvee just in time to see an explosion mushroom up out of a field to the east. Controlled detonation, hell, they were taking incoming. Other men from the company had seen the blast, but they seemed puzzled, unsure what was going on.

Someone shouted "Incoming!" and that broke the spell. The Bulldogs scrambled for a nearby Iraqi bomb shelter. As the men ran for cover, Ken Jackola threw his IBA (Interceptor body armor) over his shoulder, stuck a cigar in his mouth, and strolled for the bomb shelter. Another explosion erupted, this one only a few hundred meters away. To the men, Ken appeared the picture of a warrior under fire.

"Jesus Christ," he shouted, "You fuckers act like you've never been mortared before!"

Another round exploded, and the area around Bravo Company rocked and shook from the impact. Then it was over. The NCOs checked on their men.

Minutes later, Sergeant Keller, a devout and well-respected member of the company's mortar section, drove a Humvee up to the trailers. As he rolled to a stop, he spotted Vinni and shouted, "Sergeant Jacques!"

"Yeah?"

"We just got mortared," Keller began as he walked up to Vinni. "Your brother was where the mortars landed, and I don't know if he's okay or not."

Vinni reeled. They'd been at Taji less than fourteen hours.

"Here, take my Humvee and go find your brother."

Vinni and Bill Stout climbed into the rig and drove off in a cloud of dust.

They drove to the impact site. Vinni asked around about his brother. Somebody told him, "One guy got killed. One's severely wounded. One other guy got wounded, too."

Nobody could tell him if Ryan was dead or alive. One Joe said, "I think your brother got hurt pretty bad."

Getting desperate, Vinni and Bill sped to the battalion aid station.

Please God, let my brother be alive. If he's wounded, let him be wounded just bad enough to be sent home so I don't have to worry about him anymore.

They reached the aid station. Vinni flew out of the truck and searched for his brother. Inside, he ran into Ken Jackola.

"Vince, Ryan is okay. He's back over at the company area." Relief flooded through Vinni. His boat had been thoroughly rocked.

As he and Bill headed back to the company area, they encountered Sergeant Spitler. Beneath that grandfatherly exterior beat a heart of iron. At fifty-one, he'd completed the fast-rope training at Hood, something so physically demanding that many men in their twenties couldn't do it.

Spitler took Vinni aside and explained what had happened. As the rounds walked across the outskirts of the company area, Ryan and Bemis realized a hair too late they'd been caught in the open in the middle of an indirect fire attack. A rocket landed a few meters away. Ryan felt a sledgehammer blow to his arm. When he looked down, he saw a hunk of shrapnel sizzling in it. Blood coursed from the wound to soak his BDUs.

He tried to pull the piece out, but it burned his hand.

"Bemis, get down! Incoming," he warned.

They rode out the rest of the attack prone in the dirt. When it ended, Spitler drove up and found the two Joes and asked, "Are you guys okay?"

Ryan mentioned off-handedly, "I got hit."

Spitler reacted at once. He sprang out of the Humvee and yelled at Ryan to lie down.

"It's okay, just a scratch."

"Get down!"

Spitler checked him out. A medic arrived, and they took him to the aid station. While Ryan received a couple of stitches for his wound, Ken Jackola showed up. Ken and Ric watched as another group of medics worked frantically on an NCO from the 39th Brigade. He'd been hit in the chest and legs while standing less than fifty meters from Ryan.

When Spitler finished explaining all this to Vinni, they returned to the company area. He spotted his little brother right away, standing a full head taller than most of the other Joes from 1st Platoon. As he moved to him, Vinni saw a burn mark on his bloody BDUs. It was too much. Vinni couldn't restrain his emotions anymore. He reached his brother and engulfed him in a fierce bear hug.

"Don't you ever scare me like that again, you crazy bastard."

The rest of the company looked on silently. It had been a close call. Sergeant Lafferty, a soldier with Echo 151, 39th Brigade, died of his wounds later that day.

Back in Oregon, word reached the battalion's rear detachment (det) that Ryan Howell had been wounded. No details followed, but at first the rear det soldiers expected the worst. Sergeant Jeff Miotke drove to Ryan's mother's house and parked nearby, waiting for word on Ryan's condition. Jeff, a type-A, hard-charger knew Vinni well and specifically requested the assignment.

He sat in the car and waited for further news, wondering if he would have to tell Ryan's mom her son was dead. Details reached him a short time later. Not today. He called Ryan's mom, then dialed Julie Howell's number.

Julie had spent the day with her folks, who were visiting from California. When the phone rang, she picked it up and heard Jeff's voice.

"Julie, Ryan's been involved in an altercation," he began.

Julie thought that very strange. Vinni was the brawler of the family. It wasn't like Ryan to get into a fight.

"He's okay, though," Jeff continued, "He's been returned to duty and I'm sure you'll hear from him soon. If it had been more serious, somebody would have come to your door."

Suddenly it hit her. Altercation? Ryan had been wounded in action. She hadn't even known he was in Iraq yet. Last she'd heard, they were preparing to leave Kuwait. She hung up the phone, shaking with emotion. Tears flooded her cheeks. As the gravity of the situation sank in, it overwhelmed her. Thank God her parents were there.

That night, Julie and Rhonda talked on the phone. They drew strength from each other. Both had plenty of steel in them, but this incident shook them to the core. Day one, and already their family had been scarred by the war.

"How are we going to do this, Rhonda? This is only day one. How are we going to deal with three hundred and sixty-four more of these?"

Rhonda ached for Vinni. She cried for him, knowing what it must have been like to find his little brother bloodied after that first attack. Here she was safe. She got to see Gabe grow up every day. Vinni was thousands of miles from home. Now people were shooting at him and trying to blow his Joes up. She knew it would be pretty selfish to feel sorry for herself. Every day would bring more uncertainty, more dread. A ringing phone, a car passing in the street would bring sudden stabs of anxiety: *Are they going to tell me Vinni's been hurt?*

Through her tears, Julie wondered again, "How are we going to get through this?"

Rhonda gave her the same answer Vinni gave Ryan back at Rilea: one day at a time. That's the best they could do.

THIRTEEN

THE JED CLAMPETTS
GO TO WAR

Sergeant Luke Wilson was one of those bulletproof NCOs who had spent his entire military career chasing a fight. He joined the Guard in eastern Oregon his junior year in high school and went to basic training before he'd even graduated. Later, after he turned eighteen, he went regular army and served in the 2nd Ranger Battalion. For three years at Fort Lewis, he waited for his chance to go to war. He'd been built for combat; as a little boy he'd seen men in uniform around his hometown of Hermiston and would call them "GI Joeses." He wanted to be one. He wanted his war.

He used to joke that he rejoined the Guard to get into the fight. After getting out of Big Army, he returned home and re-enlisted in the Guard. When the 2-162 deployment came up, he volunteered for it out of the 218th Field Artillery. He landed in Alpha Company, where he became 1st Platoon's forward observer (FO).

The day 2-162 rolled out of Camp New York, Luke clambered into the back of Lieutenant Dewayne Jones' 998 "Jed Clampett" along with Specialist Steven Baldwin and Private First Class Andres Molero. Baldwin mounted his M240 on the 998's cab roof.

Throughout Camp New York, the rest of the battalion prepared to depart. With Major Bill Edwards in Iraq with the advanced detachment, Captain Riley had functioned as the S-3. He put together the road march plan along with the S-3 from the 39th Brigade.

The plan divided the Volunteers into eight serials. The Oregonians would escort the more vulnerable vehicles from the brigade's rear echelons. The BC and Riley would ride with Serial Three. Hildebrandt would lead out, and Major Tanguy would bring up the rear.

A special mission awaited Sergeant Ezelle and Sergeant Hambright: they would lead the battalion into Iraq.

On April 6, 2004, the battalion moved up to Navistar, a base on the Kuwaiti border. The next morning, with the battalion staged and ready to go, the scout platoon sortied out ahead to reconnoiter the road to the border. Ezelle and Hambright rolled next with their four rigs. They moved across the frontier, where Hambright's squad secured the first checkpoint into Iraq. Ezelle drove to the second one and secured it. Both had been the scene of IED attacks only a day before, so the mission made the men tense. E. Z. and Hambright kept them alert and vigilant.

All was quiet. They reported back to the BC, and the Volunteers streamed out of Navistar bound for Scania. Like Bravo Company, the drive into Iraq left everyone "puckered tight." The gunners sweated behind their weapons; the dismounts scanned the sides of the road.

The detritus of war attracted much attention. The same skeletalized tanks Bravo had seen evoked similar emotions among the rest of the battalion. But later they came to a fresh IED site. A huge crater marred the talcum powder road. Lying nearby Luke Wilson spotted the gnarled remains of a Humvee's grill. Somebody had been hit hard.

The trailing serials ran into trouble. Some of the 39th Brigade's vehicles suffered mechanical problems and could not keep pace with the rest of the convoys. The serials lagged behind. Sergeant Major Conley heard about that loudly and often from Major Tanguy, who worried that they'd still be on the road at dusk.

A five-ton truck blew a tire and halted the last serial. Tanguy watched as his Joes swapped out the tire. It grew dark. Finally, with the flat fixed, Serial Eight drove into Scania without further incident.

Not long after the Volunteers arrived, a southbound convoy drove in from Baghdad. Bullet holes pockmarked the sides of the vehicles, and they saw at least one RPG strike on an eighteen-wheeler. Things got very real in a hurry at that point.

That night, Luke Wilson developed a very bad feeling about what lay ahead. He lay in his cot next to Lieutenant Jones' Jed Clampett and thought of home. His mom worked for the Corps of Engineers as a civilian, but hadn't wanted him to join the military way back in '97. He and his dad had convinced her to sign the papers that allowed him to join at seventeen. He had spent his last leave with them at home, spending time with his seven-year-old daughter, Corrine, and his girlfriend, Tonya. His dad was a state trooper, and while home he had picked up a murder case. Somebody had tipped off the police as to the location of the body. Luke's last time with his dad was spent driving around eastern Oregon, digging holes in search of a corpse. It made for a good story when he got back to Polk.

Now he wondered if he would see his family again.

Rebekah-mae Bruns felt the same way. Something inside her told her tomorrow would bring a fight. She had prepared herself as best she could. Before leaving Kuwait, she familiarized herself with every weapon in the battalion, including the M240, the Mark 19 (MK19) and the M249 SAW. Sergeant Maries, the sniper section leader in the scout platoon, even showed her how to use the .50-caliber sniper rifle. Though she was ready, Private Max Corrigan, her twenty-three-year-old gunner, was not. Since leaving Navistar, he'd been vomiting. He also had diarrhea. Bruns knew she'd need him come morning, so she rounded up some medicine for him.

"Max," she said, "We're going to hit the shit tomorrow, and I need you to be ready." She gave him the medicine and hoped he'd be healthy by morning.

The next morning, Captain Riley sat down for a briefing at 0800. A lieutenant colonel from the 1st Cav Division showed up and announced, "Gentleman, you are no longer doing a tactical road march. You are conducting a movement to contact. The enemy is out there, and you will find him today."

Around noon, the serials hit the road. As they closed on Baghdad, the terrain changed. The day before, they'd seen little but open desert. Today, the road was studded with little towns and villages. They saw trees again, tall palms with big bushy tops that swayed in the desert breeze.

Toward mid-afternoon, Serial One entered the outskirts of Baghdad, where it was supposed to link up with a platoon of Bradleys from the 1-36 Armored. Before the serial reached the rendezvous point, the lead vehicles encountered an IED. Three artillery rounds wrapped together dangled from a tree not far from a small village. Nearby, the men discovered a dead dog lying on the right shoulder of the road. Wires protruded from its mouth. That drew grave concern, as the men flashed back on their IED training at Hood where they'd been warned about bombs stuffed in roadkill.

Serial One lurched to a halt. The scouts wanted to use their sniper rifles and detonate the IEDs, but their request was denied. The serial waited for an explosive ordnance detachment (EOD) team to come take care of the bombs.

The scouts dismounted. The other serials stacked up on the highway behind them. The delay snarled five serials, almost a hundred and fifty vehicles, and left them strung out for miles south of Baghdad. Everyone grew nervous. The longer they sat, the higher their chances of getting attacked. The gunners tried to stay hypervigilant, but the heat wore them down. In every serial, the readiness posture diminished.

Hours passed without any sign of the EOD team. In Scania, Serials Six through Eight had yet to leave. By 1630 that afternoon, Major Tanguy decided to hold the final serials for a day. Tanguy did not want his men driving through Baghdad in the dark.

In Serial One, some of the scouts fell ill. They vomited over the sides of their Humvees. Hours passed, the sun and the heat cooked them. Some of the men started to doze. But then, a mortar shell woke everyone up. It landed out in the distance some eight hundred meters southwest of Serial One. A second one followed. The insurgents had found them.

In Serial Two, Lieutenant McCrae and Sergeant First Class Boggs began to take small-arms fire. McCrae kicked Boggs out onto a hill with another sergeant first class to see if they could locate the shooters. They searched the area with their optics but could not find the insurgents. As they started back for their Humvee, the mortar round spotted by Serial One exploded around the platoon's trailing three rigs. Boggs remounted. The platoon's gunners searched for targets as the rattle of AK-47s hammered the silence between mortar rounds.

Back in Serial Three, the BC decided to investigate the incoming and the delay. His driver swung out of the column and drove north on the right shoulder. At the tail end of Serial Two, the insurgents lit up the Old Man platoon. Bullets cracked and whizzed overhead. Where were the insurgents? Boggs finally caught sight of a couple off to the right. He shouted out their location. His other truck commanders, Sergeant Bobb Fleming and Sergeant Al Carle, relayed the information to their gunners. In seconds, Boggs' men brought their weapons to bear. As they prepared to fire, a Humvee scooted past and obscured their field of fire. Lonnie and Josh Harrison, brothers gunning for Sergeants Fleming and Carle, cursed loudly and eased off their triggers.

It was the BC, who hadn't known the serial was under small-arms fire attack.

As the action unfolded behind them, A Polish EOD team appeared and defused the IEDs. Hildebrandt ordered the serial forward, and the vehicles moved about a kilometer up the road, where they found the Bradley platoon waiting for them.

The serial stopped. Hildebrandt and Lieutenant Boyce hopped out to meet with the Bradley platoon leader to coordinate the drive through Baghdad. Tyson Bumgardner, one of the scouts, dismounted and walked over toward the tracks. The Brads had seen a lot of action. Their sides were blackened with grime and grease. The armor looked scorched in places from RPG strikes. As he stood in his brand-new DCUs (desert combat uniforms) regarding the Bradleys, the turret hatch suddenly opened and a filthy E-7 climbed out. He hit the pavement next to Tyson, who stared at the NCO and his grease-stained face and hands. Unshaven, hair askew, he had a wild look in his eyes. The veteran barely glanced at Tyson before lighting a cigarette. He drew quick, almost birdlike drags from it every few seconds, which reminded Tyson of a nervous tick.

Jesus, this is something right out of Platoon. *This guy looks crazy.*

The veteran asked, "What held you guys up?"

Bumgardner explained the situation.

The E-7 took another drag on his smoke. As he exhaled, he asked, "Why didn't you shoot the IED off the road?"

Tyson shrugged, "Maybe our leadership was a little reluctant to open fire."

"Well, they better get over that." With a jerk, he pointed over across the road at a bullet-riddled car lying in a ditch. Inside, Tyson could see an Iraqi slumped in the driver's seat, a ragged bullet hole in his throat.

"We took that guy out as he was trying to sneak up on you," the veteran explained.

Right then, the Bradley's gunner popped out of his hatch. He looked even wilder than the track commander with his dirty DCUs and hollow gaze. Tyson began to wonder what he'd just gotten into. Would he look like them in a year?

While Serial One halted to coordinate the next phase of movement, Serial Two crept about a kilometer forward and came to a stop. Behind them, Serial Three drove right into the ambush zone that Boggs and his trucks had just vacated. The men dismounted and the BC told everyone to stay alert.

At the rear of Serial Three, Sergeant Phil Larson dismounted and watched as Serial Four came into view to the south. They parked a good kilometer down the road. Suddenly, an army mail truck bounced along the shoulder past Serial Four and approached Larson's Humvees. A sergeant climbed out and asked, "Hey, can I hook in with you guys to get through Baghdad?"

That astonished Phil, who replied, "What are you talking about?"

"Well, we got hit back there, and we lost one of our trucks. We got all the mail into this one and I've got to get north to Taji."

"Well, yeah, move in right in front of me," Phil replied.

A mortar shell exploded about fifty meters from the center of the column. The fight was on again.

At the head of Serial Three, John Neibert ran for his Humvee. Tracers zipped through the convoy. A hundred and fifty meters away on the left side, a group of insurgents blazed away at them from behind a dirt berm. The Volunteers swung into action. The gunners unleashed a torrent of return fire. Incoming mortar shells walked toward the convoy. Suddenly, a rocket-propelled grenade sizzled toward the Americans. It passed right over the BC's gunner. Seconds later, another one narrowly missed his Humvee.

Inside the BC's 1114, Lieutenant Colonel Hendrickson didn't hear the initial mortar attack. He had on a set of headphones that were connected to his radio, and combined with the noise of the engine—a Humvee is extremely loud—they prevented him from hearing the first explosions. Then one mushroomed up right outside his door. At the same moment, tracers laced past and bullets skipped off the pavement. Above him, his gunner yelled, "Contact!" and returned fire. The BC got on the radio and relayed the situation to the 1-36.

They needed to get out of the kill zone. Serial Three included several five-thousand-gallon fuel tankers, medical trucks, and other highly vulnerable targets. His gunners had only a few hundred rounds of ammunition, and his Joes carried only three magazines each for their M4s. That's all they had been given; it was enough to defend themselves and roll through any attack, but totally deficient if they needed to stand and fight.

In the rear of the column, Phil Larson couldn't see the enemy; the sun was in his eyes. He wanted to shoot but had no targets. Bullets bounced off the asphalt, kicking up sparks and zinging past. Phil turned to his medic and shouted, "Doc! Holy crap? This is real!"

Not far from the BC's rig, Eric Riley looked up to see the Humvee in front of his backing up into him. Over the radio, he heard Lieutenant Marshall shout, "IED! IED!" He'd spotted a sandbag with wires protruding from it. Riley's driver backed up too. Mortar rounds exploded nearby, and a streak of red tracers cut between the vehicles. Riley noted that the insurgents used red tracers, just like the Americans. He'd always assumed they would use a different color, maybe green.

In the front of the serial, Neibert peeled his lead gun trucks out of the column to counterattack. They'd rehearsed this maneuver several times, and now as he executed, the BC called him back. They needed to get through the kill zone and keep the soft vehicles safe.

A 39th Brigade mechanic manning a Mark 19 spotted the insurgent mortar team. They were dug in near a small pond surrounded by reeds and cattails. The mechanic swung the turret to the right rear and sent two grenades downrange. The mortar pit disappeared in a shower of dirt and smoke. He fired six more in quick succession.

Neibert couldn't believe it. Earlier that morning, that same mechanic had asked him how to load the Mark 19. He had never fired one before, so Neibert gave him a quick lesson on the weapon. He obviously had the heart of a warrior.

Three minutes into the firefight and the column started to roll. Neibert's Humvee led the way. A few hundred meters later, he spotted four Bradleys near an overpass. He dismounted and ran over to them.

"Hey, Sergeant," he called to the track commander, "We've got more serials coming down this road. Do you think you can take your Brads down either side and clear the area out?"

The sergeant's RTO (radio telephone operator) called it up. Moments later, the four Bradleys sprang forward. Two drove right over a concrete divider, swung across the southbound lanes, and charged off road. Their 25mm guns raked the berm to the west. Meanwhile, the other two rumbled down east of the convoy running across an open field. Their guns peppered the insurgents around the pond.

Serial Three pulled clear of the ambush but split into two groups. In the middle of the column, a 39th truck suffered mechanical problems. The head of the column broke off and went on ahead. The trailing half took a wrong turn and got snarled in heavy traffic in downtown Baghdad. Long after dark, the two elements linked back up and reached Taji late that night.

The fighting did not end with Serial Three's engagement. It was just beginning.

Serial Four drove forward into the fight just after sunset. Doug Jackson and a couple of trucks from 2nd Platoon, Alpha Company, brought up the rear of the column. Captain Granger commanded the serial. As they approached the original ambush point, Jackson heard a female soldier come over the radio, "I hear gunfire," she reported. Doug looked around and didn't see anything. He blew off the report.

Whatever.

Suddenly, the early evening sky lit up with crisscrossing tracers. It seemed impossible to drive through them without getting hit, but somehow Jackson's rig didn't get a scratch. His .50-caliber machine gunner opened fire. Nearby, an insurgent RPG (rocket propelled grenade) gunner and his loader popped up and fired a rocket. It streaked through the night just as Jackson's gunner unloaded on the insurgents. They died in a hail of .50-cal fire.

The rocket skipped across the pavement, sailed into the air, and exploded right next to Jackson's Humvee. The blast rocked them, but the men kept firing.

How long did it last? A minute, maybe two at most, but it seemed like forever. With agonizing slowness, the column dragged itself forward and out of the kill zone. As they left, Lieutenant Cory Jones lit a cigar and smiled. If this is how it is going to be, bring it on. He puffed on that stogie all the way through Baghdad.

A kilometer behind Jackson's rig, Luke Wilson in Serial Five could see the firefight through his night vision goggles. He would finally taste battle. He checked his M4 and prepared himself.

In the Humvee behind Wilson, Specialist Chris Bent stared at his first sight of combat from behind the wheel. His truck commander, Sergeant Neilson, shouted, "Who's got their battle dip?" Bent reached into his pocket, pulled out his chewing tobacco, and stuck a wad in his mouth. The other men did the same thing.

"We're ready now!" Bent shouted.

Neilson smiled, "That a boy, Bent!"

Sergeant Neilson uttered a prayer, "Yea, though I walk through the valley of the shadow of death, I will fear no evil because we are the baddest motherfuckers in the valley."

And then, it was Serial Five's turn.

Fourteen

SERIAL FIVE

Rebekah-mae Bruns worried about her gunner, Max Corrigan. Max still felt woozy and weak from his illness the day before. Throughout the day, he nodded off inside the five-ton's turret. Bruns, in the passenger side, sat next to Max's feet. Whenever she noticed him dozing, she tugged his pants and called, "Come on now, Max, I need you." Despite his illness, he refused to leave the turret and stayed up there for hours without relief.

Now, as Serial Four got hit, Bruns felt a calmness sweep into her. It did not seem warranted. Without armor or even a roof, her truck would not survive an RPG hit. In Kuwait, she had scrounged a Vietnam-era flak vest, which she hung on her passenger-side door. It was the sum total of her protection.

The column ahead started to move. Serial Four had cleared the way. Bruns gripped her M4 and waited for the showdown sure to come.

At the head of Serial Five, Lieutenant Jones' rigs lurched forward into the night. As they reached the ambush point, the lead rigs drove through without any contact. Perhaps the Brads had killed all the bad guys. The middle of the serial reached the kill zone. A scattering of AK-47s barked, and tracers shot toward the Americans. The convoy never slowed and escaped unscathed.

The journey continued into southern Baghdad. Running up Route Tampa, the plan was to turn onto Route Irish to go through Baghdad, then catch Route Senators for Taji. They came to the interchange, and the lead elements drove onto an overpass near two derelict buildings.

This time, the sky seemed to explode with tracers and lightning-quick streaks of rocket propelled grenades. Serial Five had just been hit by more than a hundred enemy fighters. In the convoy's van, the insurgents detonated an IED alongside the lead Bradley from the 1-36. The blast sent it rocking on its tracks. It ground to a halt even as the turret traversed right and returned fire. An instant later, a second Bradley took an RPG right in the turret. The serial stacked up behind the stricken Bradleys. More RPGs whirred overhead. All around them, civilian vehicles raced for safety. The enemy shot them up.

At the rear of Serial Five, Staff Sergeant Brock Kelly looked out his window just in time to see an RPG lanced straight for him. It whizzed past and blew apart a nearby civilian BMW. Another RPG struck the Beamer. The civilian car erupted in flames even as a third RPG came out of the night. This one looked sure to hit Kelly's Humvee, but at the last second it veered sharply away and struck a Bradley right behind them.

More RPGs sizzled into the convoy. In the middle of it, Rebekah-mae Bruns stuck her M4 out the window and shot back. Corrigan stood above her, coolly snapping out bursts with his .50-cal. Bruns banged away with her M4, changed magazines, and kept firing. Nearby, an insurgent snaked up to the convoy and jumped to his feet at the base of the right shoulder. He shouldered an RPG launcher and pulled the trigger just as a 39th Brigade gunner cut him to pieces. The rocket skipped off the pavement and ricocheted into the air next to Bruns' five-ton. It exploded less than five feet from her rig. The five-ton shuddered and bucked from the concussion, which sent her 39th Brigade mechanic-turned-driver into an uncontrollable panic. He grabbed the radio, keyed the microphone, and screamed, "We're in the fucking kill zone! We're in the fucking kill zone."

At the rear of Serial Five, Sergeant Compton spotted an insurgent with an AK standing on a balcony. He killed him with his M4. An instant later, several rockets zipped over and around his 998. Bullets smacked the asphalt and ricocheted under his rig. Shannon could see more rockets coming at them from the right side and rear. To the left, AK-47s and RPKs stitched the convoy with tracers. Compton kept firing. From another building an insurgent sprayed AK fire at his Humvee. He shot him, then shot another one seconds later. He changed out magazines, blew through another thirty rounds, and grabbed his final magazine.

In an MP Humvee in front of Compton, a Mark 19 gunner targeted a van in an alleyway. Shannon could see a group of insurgents clustered around the vehicle as others unloaded RPGs from it.

With his first volley, the Mark 19 gunner blitzed the van and blew it apart, sending insurgents sprawling in all directions. Then he went to work on one of the buildings even as the column's .50-cal gunners raked the balconies. The fire proved so effective that the entire front wall of the building collapsed. Insurgents tumbled to the ground amid the rubble.

The fight continued.

Just in front of Sergeant Bruns and her five-ton, a five-thousand-gallon fuel tanker became an RPG magnet. Rockets sailed over it, skipped under it, and zipped past on either side. If it got hit, the explosion would have engulfed multiple vehicles. The insurgents tried furiously to blow it up.

"We're in the fucking kill zone! We're in the fucking kill zone!" Bruns' driver was still screaming hysterically over the radio. She'd had enough. She stopped firing, turned, and said to him, "Calm down, it's going to be okay."

With the radio mike still keyed, he shouted back, "Okay? No, it won't be okay! Don't you get it? They're trying to fucking kill me!"

Okay, this guy is a lost cause.

"Get off the radio. Now!"

He ignored her order and ranted on. Suddenly, the whole scene seemed utterly absurd. She started to laugh and shouted up to Corrigan, "Hey, Max?"

"Yeah, Sergeant Bruns?"

"You're earning your combat patch tonight!"

"Maybe I am, but I think I'm going to shit myself!"

Bruns thought he meant he was scared. Max meant he was still violently ill with diarrhea and nausea and was desperately trying to hold himself together.

"Bullshit, Max, you're doing great! Just keep rocking!"

Max's M2 barked. Hot brass fell out of the turret and landed on Bruns' neck. Some of the casings ended up inside her DCUs. She called out a target at eleven o'clock. Max cut him down. She spotted another and called the location. Max swung the .50-cal and hammered the insurgent. He was a rock that night, preternaturally calm and totally professional. His short bursts struck the enemy with deadly accuracy.

Bruns sent more rounds downrange. At one point, she was trying to shoot out to her one o'clock. She pulled the trigger and walked her fire right through the five-ton's side mirror. It shattered on the bullet's impact. After that, some of the men called her "Mirror-Shot Bruns." Later, rumors flew about the incident, and some in the battalion who were not there that night retold the story to suggest she'd seen herself in the mirror, gotten scared, and shot her own reflection. That was nonsense, but the rumor never died.

The fact is, unlike Jessica Lynch, Rebekah-mae returned fire that night. In the heat of combat, she conducted herself with professionalism and aggressively fought back against a well-placed enemy. In short, she became a combat veteran on day two in Iraq.

All around them, civilian vehicles rolled to a stop and Iraqis piled out and tried to flee on foot. Some died in a hail of incoming AK fire. One man defied the odds and sauntered right through the middle of the engagement as if taking a stroll in a park. He walked the length of the convoy and escaped to its rear.

In Lieutenant Jones' 998, Sergeant Luke Wilson finally got his life's dream: he was leading men in battle. Baldwin, his gunner, blazed away on the M240 while Molero used his M4. To Luke, the sound of that M240 rocking was nothing but sweet music. He stood up and exposed himself as he scanned for targets. Then he threw a pillow down and knelt on it. He went to work with his M4.

Luke had gone through about half his magazine when he spotted a black-clad, RPG-toting insurgent in the alley between the two enemy buildings. The enemy leveled his launcher right at Luke's rig. Luke drew a bead on him. Just before he pulled the trigger, he saw a puff of white smoke sprout from the rocket launcher. Then everything went white. All he knew was pain.

The RPG glanced off a nearby Bradley and careened into the back of Lieutenant Jones' Jed Clampett. The plywood, the sandbags, and all the stored gear in back failed to stop it; the rocket pierced all with ease. It tore off Luke's leg.

As soon as his senses returned, he knew he'd lost his leg. He couldn't kneel or stand. He refused to look at it. Instead, he checked on Baldwin and Molero. The impact had sent them flying, and Molero had been hit by shrapnel, but both were already scrambling for their weapons.

Luke reached for his rifle. Struggling to get back into a firing position, he leaned forward and climbed onto his rucksack. He brought his M4 to his shoulder. This was his fight. It was his moment. He pulled the trigger. And pulled. And pulled. And pulled again. Never mind the blood pouring from his wound. Never mind he'd have to relearn to walk. Never mind his first five minutes in combat just turned him into what he swore he'd never endure: an amputee.

He stayed in the fight. Around him, Baldwin returned to action with his M240. Molero banged away with his M4. Luke said nothing about his wound. He wanted them on their weapons, not treating him.

Luke fired until he drained his magazine. Before he could reload, the Bradleys began moving again, and his stricken Jed Clampett surged north and out of the kill zone.

Exactly who shot at them that night was not clear. Intel suggested they were Syrian Jihadists. Whoever they were, they suffered heavy losses for wounding Luke. An MP patrol later happened upon the scene and found between fifty and sixty insurgent corpses sprawled around the buildings.

Once out of the ambush, Luke laid back and let his helmet slide off. Now came the hard part. He needed Baldwin and Molero to save his life.

"Hey guys, I'm hit," he told them in such a matter of fact way that they didn't think they heard him quite right.

"Guys, my fucking leg is gone."

"What?" It was Baldwin.

"My fucking leg is gone." Luke sounded like he'd just lost five bucks in a penny ante poker game and was mildly disappointed.

They looked at the remains of his leg and the gravity of the situation struck them. Luke's calm voice seemed totally divorced from the reality of the situation. It unnerved them. In the cab, Lieutenant Jones heard a commotion. Baldwin and Molero shouted something about a broken leg. Jones couldn't understand why a broken leg would cause such a ruckus.

"You don't understand, sir, his leg is *gone.*"

Jones grabbed the radio and tried to call the situation up to the serial commander, but Bruns' driver was still screaming "They're trying to fucking kill me!" over the net. He had his hands full just getting the information reported.

In the back, Luke grabbed Baldwin and pulled him close. He needed to calm down his gunner.

"Luke," he started, his voice choked with emotion, "I love you."

Baldwin hugged him close.

"Okay, Steve. Let's get this done real fast then." Baldwin put a tourniquet on Luke's leg while Molero, who'd been one of Luke's combat lifesaver students back in Oregon, prepared to give him an IV.

"Just do it like we did in class," Luke told him.

The rocket had taken most of Luke's leg off at the calf. Baldwin examined it and reported, "I've got good news and bad news."

"What?"

"Well, the good news is the RPG cauterized everything it went through."

"What's the bad news?" Luke asked a little impatiently.

"Well, except for the major artery."

"Oh. Okay, thanks."

Baldwin finished the tourniquet and studied the wound. The artery was still bleeding. He stuck two fingers into it, hoping to stem the flow.

The moment his fingers touched his wound, a tidal wave of pain swept up Luke's thigh. Luke grabbed Baldwin again, "What the hell are you doing?"

"I'm just making sure the bleeding is stopped."

"Well look at it, don't fucking touch it!"

Luke leaned back into a sea of pain. Suddenly, he felt totally parched.

"Hey guys, can you find me some water?"

Both Molero and Baldwin glanced around. No water in sight. They dug through all the gear in back. Stuff was flying, they were cursing, and finally Baldwin found one of the Cokes they'd bought in Kuwait. He cracked it and passed it over to Luke. He took a sip, then another. Then Luke realized Coke has caffeine in it. Caffeine restricts arteries. He didn't need that to happen right now. He dumped the Coke over the side.

"Guys, I can't drink that. I need water." A full-on scramble ensued. Finally, Molero produced his two-quart canteen. He'd last filled it back in Oregon. He handed it Luke, who took a swig and gagged. Six months in the canteen, and it had gone foul. He drank it anyway.

Minutes later, the convoy rolled to the gates of FOB Provider. As they waited at the gate, Baldwin and Molero grew impatient. What was taking so long? They needed to get to the aid station right away.

A Humvee emerged from the gate. As it rumbled by, Baldwin reached out and grabbed the gunner. He latched onto him so fiercely that he almost got dragged right out of the 998.

"Hey, we need to get this guy inside now!" he shouted to the gunner.

The gunner disappeared inside his Humvee. An instant later, he popped back into the turret and yelled, "Follow us."

Jones' driver pulled out of the convoy and slid behind the Humvee. As they went through the gate, they bounced over a couple of rows of sandbags designed to slow everyone down. The Humvee slammed up, then down, hammering Luke with unbelievable pain.

They reached the aid station. Between all the gear in the back and a 2 x 4 bracing the plywood box, it took some engineering to get Luke out. Baldwin kicked the 2 x 4. Molero did too. It gave way so suddenly that Baldwin fell forward right onto the remains of Luke's leg. Luke went rigid with agony. Gingerly, they lifted him clear of the Humvee. It was time to say good-bye.

Luke threw an arm over Baldwin and gave him a peck on the cheek. "You take care of yourself, okay?"

He then turned to Molero, who looked utterly stricken. Ever since they first met last fall, Luke had called Molero "His Boy." Molero called him "Pappy" in return.

"Hey take care of yourself, Boy. I'll see you soon." He tapped Molero's head.

Then, his buddies were gone as the medics rushed him through the doors to the aid station. As they moved, Luke said to a medic, "Well, I guess I won't be doing any three-legged races anymore."

Inside, the ER erupted in a flurry of activity. Nurses moved about while doctors examined his wound. Minutes later, the ER staff called in a chaplain. Luke had lost six pints of blood in fifteen minutes. They expected him to die. The chaplain slipped into the room and gently took Luke's hand.

"Would you like to chat?" he asked softly.

Through a haze of pain, Luke looked at the chaplain, then to all the activity buzzing around him.

"I'm a little fucking busy, sir!" he growled. The chaplain made himself scarce.

A nurse moved over and started to cut his gear off. She cut off his IBA, then started on his Under Armour shirt. That roused him to a fury. He'd paid for some of this gear out of his own pocket, and the nurse was destroying it.

"What the hell are you doing?" he demanded.

"We have to cut everything off," she explained.

"Hey! It's my leg that's hurt, not my shirt." His complaints fell on deaf ears.

A captain showed up next. He was a doctor but he appeared nervous and ill-at-ease. He examined the wound. When he finished, he timidly approached Luke. Almost in tears, he told him that they'd have to amputate his leg.

By now, the pain roared through him like a freight train. To him, the captain's comment seemed so obvious it was absurd. It only angered him more. He sat up on one elbow and speared the doctor with his fiercest NCO gaze, "Well, what gave you the first fucking clue, the RPG through it?"

The captain reacted with complete surprise. After a minute, he composed himself and told the staff to get Luke ready for a medevac flight to the Green Zone hospital.

Standard procedure for a medevac flight included catheterizing the patient. Luke recoiled at this.

"Excuse me?"

One of the nurses replied, "We have to put a catheter in before we get you on the Blackhawk."

"I'm not going to piss in your fucking chopper."

The staff persisted; he had no choice. A nurse went to work, but couldn't get it in and succeeded only in stabbing Luke in the genitals and inflicting even more pain.

The tough NCO raged.

Finally, they abandoned the whole catheter idea. They put him on a Blackhawk. Two minutes later, he landed at the Green Zone Combat Support Hospital (CSH). Rushed into the ER, he found himself engulfed by a small platoon of nurses and doctors. Again, as all this activity swarmed around him, a chaplain appeared.

"Would you like to talk?"

"No, but could you get me a cheeseburger and a Coke?" The chaplain vanished.

Another doc showed up, turned Luke on his side, and began to examine his rear end for further injuries. Luke had suffered all manner of indignities that night. He could either go insane or ratchet up his smart-assness a notch. He chose the latter. He pooched out one hip and remarked, "Hey Doc? I don't swing that way."

The work continued. Luke asked for water, but they refused. He cajoled them. It did no good. He tried to pull rank. It didn't work. Finally, they pushed him into an elevator and took him upstairs into a waiting room next to surgery. A nurse told him he was next in line.

Stretched on the gurney, the throbbing in his leg grew worse. The pain tormented him. He lay there with a pretty nurse for company. He said little. She said nothing. What could be said? His leg was gone, his life scarred forever by this night. What does anyone say to that?

At last, his system reached overload. It began to shut down. His eyes grew heavy; he fought for consciousness. It ebbed away. The last thing he saw was the pretty nurse sitting across the room, staring at him with red-rimmed eyes, a tear on her cheek.

FIFTEEN

WAITING: THE OTHER AGONY

At 3:00 a.m., the phone rang at the Wilson household back in Hermiston. Luke's mom had been unable to sleep. She had spent the night in her den unable to shake the feeling that something was wrong. When the phone rang, it didn't come as a big surprise.

"Hello," she said.

"Mom? Are you there?" It was Luke. He always called her "Ma" not "Mom." Something must have happened.

"Where are you, Luke?"

"Well . . . I'm in country."

"Where are you?" she demanded.

"Mom . . . I'm in Baghdad."

In the background, Luke's mom could hear a nurse talking.

"Are you in a hospital?" Her voice grew anxious.

"Yeah, kind of." Then it dawned on him that the army had not yet contacted his parents. They didn't know. His mom started to sob.

His dad took the phone, "Luke, what's happened?"

"It's just my left leg. I'm fine. Gotta go." Click.

Luke couldn't handle breaking the news to his parents. He needed them strong for him, not shocked and scared. He'd wait until the army filled them in to call them again.

In the meantime, he lay in the recovery room next to an Iraqi insurgent who only hours ago had fired at his convoy. An American patrol had found him wounded on the side of the road. Now the insurgent lay next to one of the Americans he'd tried to kill.

In Oregon, the wait began. The minutes ticked by with interminable slowness. The first hour passed. Luke's parents could hardly stand it. Dawn broke, and finally Luke's dad couldn't take it anymore. Angry and frightened, he stormed out of the house to repair a fence.

At seven, Luke's mom called the Oregon Military Department in Salem. They had no idea Luke had been wounded. Fortunately, Colonel Douglas Pritt, a dedicated officer, happened to be in his office. He promised Luke's mom he'd get to the bottom of the situation.

She settled down for more waiting, left alone with her ranging imagination.

An hour later, the phone rang. Colonel Pritt's gentle voice asked, "Mrs. Wilson, is your husband with you? Are you sitting down?"

Luke's mom called to her husband, who joined her.

Colonel Pritt told them, "Your son's convoy was attacked and your son was injured. We don't know how badly yet, but a contact team should be there to see you by two o'clock."

Five more hours of waiting lay ahead. The Wilsons lived through that morning in a limbo of concern and dread. Hermiston is a small community. When people around town heard the news that Luke had been wounded, they showed up at the Wilson house. One or two at a time, they arrived on the front porch to offer support and food. Nobody left. They stayed with Luke's folks, helped take care of his little girl, and refused to let the family wait alone.

The contact team didn't show up at two. It didn't show up at three. All afternoon, the Wilson family waited and suffered. Long after dark, when the contact team finally arrived at their front door, it was greeted by Luke's frantic parents and *sixty* of their closest friends.

SIXTEEN

FIRST DAYS OF WORK

Sergeant Ed Hoeffliger of 1st Platoon, Bravo Company, opened the Port-a-John's door and stared in disgust. Flies buzzed around a toilet seat covered with human feces. The desert heat had turned the Port-a-John into a sweat box. The stench of well-cooked urine hit him full force. He stood in the doorway and wondered, *What the hell are those hillbillies from the 39th thinking with this?* Later, he found out the Iraqi contractors on the base had done this to the latrines. Instead of sitting on the toilet seats, they stood over them and squatted. It was Ed's first taste of culture shock.

Taji was supposed to be a paradise—quiet, nice, and well maintained. At least that's what 2nd Platoon's Lieutenant Christopher Kent had told Ed. If the latrine was any indication, they were in for a rude awakening.

On April 8, 2004, there were an awful lot of *supposed to's* running through Bravo Company. Quiet? Hell, in two days at Taji they'd already been mortared. A paradise? Camp Cooke resembled a gigantic scrap yard. Acres of leftover Soviet-era trucks, tanks, and aircraft lay rusting in vast boneyards. Skeletalized French attack helicopters sat amid Soviet T-54 and T-62 tanks. Piles of random military junk dotted the landscape. It was a redneck paradise, like Saddam had gone rural and left his army up on blocks in the back forty.

Of course, it became a soldier's playground, and the Bulldogs combed through the ruins of Iraq's former military glory to pinch souvenirs and spray tanks with graffiti. They left one T-54 with its tank barrel reading, "Property of Rhonda Jacques." Wonder who did that.

The army housed the men in groups of trailers. The Joes dubbed these "hooches" and the groupings were called "pods." Bravo Company received a pod surrounded by 39th Brigade units, a lone island of Oregon surrounded by "y'alling" Arkansans.

The fence protecting the base had fallen into disrepair. Holes in the barbed wire allowed access from the outside—a fact insurgents and Iraqi thieves soon discovered. The thieves would try to penetrate the base to filch from the boneyards. The insurgents did it to try and cause casualties. Delta Company killed two insurgents trying to sneak through the wire only a few days after reaching Taji.

On April 9, 2004, Bravo Company and the 39th Brigade went to work. Their mission: stop the indirect fire attacks. The new Joes were supposed to get some time with the vets in right-seat rides. This way, the old hands could show the greenhorns the area of operation (AO) and give them tactical tips. That would not happen now.

Things moved so fast that in 2nd Platoon, Lieutenant Kent and Pete Salerno did not even receive an OPORDER for the first patrol. They had no graphics or maps of their assigned area either. Then a 2-7 officer announced, "There is a hundred percent chance of contact today."

Salerno protested to Captain San Miguel. Without any information, 2-7 expected them to go out beyond the wire and drive around until somebody shot at them. San Miguel's hands were tied: this was what the battalion commander, Lieutenant Colonel Fourshee, had ordered. They *had* to execute.

Shortly before leaving, Captain San Miguel gave Salerno the best map available. It didn't show all the roads, and the scale was huge, but at least it was something. Kent and Pete took it and drew up hasty contingency plans in case they got hit, then they climbed aboard their cardboard coffins and went to war.

They drove out the south gate and rolled down the main supply road (MSR), dubbed Route Senators. Shortly after leaving the wire, the battalion TOC radioed Kent to tell him a FRAGO (fragmentary order) had just been released with a new rule of engagement. "You will now shoot anyone wearing black. No questions asked."

Pete Salerno heard this just as they passed through a neighborhood where practically everyone was wearing black. He shook his head in frustration and wondered, *Does the person who wrote that order understand how many people in Iraq wear black? What the fuck?* The actual order issued had been to shoot anyone wearing black with green or yellow arm- or headbands, which was the pseudo-uniform of the Mahdi militia. That part didn't reach 2nd Platoon. Pete called over the platoon radio net and told the men to ignore the order. "We're not shooting everyone in black."

Confusion ruled the day. Luckily, Bravo Company did not get engaged, but the 39th did. A patrol from Echo Troop, 151 Cav, ran into a complex ambush initiated by an IED. Small-arms fire and RPGs tore into the column before help could arrive. The attack killed Sergeant Felix Del Greco and wounded two other men.

The next day, Lieutenant Pete Wood took 1st Platoon on a patrol down to the Tigris River. The day before, the platoon had covered the same route. They'd passed through villages full of people and kids had run out into the street to wave as they passed.

On the 10th, as the platoon rolled through the first village, the Joes saw few people in the streets. It didn't look right. They went through a second village. Again, the platoon found few people in the streets. Their unease ratcheted up a notch. In Sergeant Sapp's 998, Ryan Howell caught sight of two Iraqis crossing their hands at them. Was it a warning?

They broke into open country. Fields and orchards dotted the area. The road followed a canal. In the lead rig, Sergeant Ed Hoeffliger worried that his driver, Specialist Campbell, was too close to the right shoulder. He opened his mouth to say something, when two insurgents detonated an IED on Ed's 998.

A blast, a boom. Black smoke shrouded the Humvee.

"Contact! IED! IED!" Ed shouted into the radio. He looked left. Campbell was slumped against his door, his windshield shattered. He called to Anthony Alabe, his gunner. No answer. He called to Ron Clement. No answer.

Jesus Christ. My whole squad is dead.

Behind them, the platoon skidded to a stop. The IED kicked up an enormous cloud of dust and smoke, which swirled across the road and obscured their view. What had happened to Hoeffliger's truck?

Lieutenant Wood grabbed his radio and called for a situation report (SITREP). He tried to get battle roster numbers for the men in Ed's Humvee, then reported the situation to the 2-7 TOC. But other voices came over the radio, shouting over each other. In the trail vehicle, Sergeant First Class Ken Jackola listened to the snarl over the radio and grew impatient at the paralysis. He couldn't leave his men by themselves on the other side of the smoke cloud.

He grabbed his medic, Specialist "Doc" Miller, and dismounted. They sprinted forward past Lieutenant Wood's rig.

Ryan Howell, in the 998 directly behind Hoeffliger's, looked out at the billowing smoke cloud and heard Gabe Sapp shout, "Back up! Back up! Back up!" This was standard procedure in the Fort Hood IED drills.

Before Sapp's driver could do anything, Ken Jackola jumped on to the back of the 998, Doc Miller at his side. "Sergeant Sapp," Jackola called out, "Drive forward and get us through the kill zone so we can support Sergeant Hoeffliger!"

"Roger that, Sergeant!" The 998 rolled forward. Inside the stricken Humvee, Ed Hoeffliger's hearing returned. Beside him, Campbell moved.

"Campbell, you okay?" Ed yelled.

"Yeah."

"Then go!"

Campbell threw the Humvee in gear and hit the accelerator. It pushed through the smoke cloud and emerged on the east side. Alone, in unfamiliar and hostile territory, Ed hoped the rest of the platoon would not leave him hanging.

The men dismounted while Alabe covered them with his M240. Other than their hearing, nobody was hurt. Behind them, a staccato burst of gunfire rang out. Ron Clement said, "Okay, this is it boys. Get ready." Weapons leveled, they waited for a fight.

"Sergeant Howell," Ken Jackola shouted as Sapp's Humvee closed on the smoke cloud, "Open up on any suspected enemy positions, okay?"

Howell and Sapp's gunner, Private Second Class Werner, swung their weapons to the right. Along the shoulder ran the canal. On the other side stretched another road with a berm alongside it. A shack stood behind the berm near an orchard.

Ryan and Werner opened fire. Ryan emptied his magazine at the shack and the berm. Werner laced both with his M240.

They plunged into the smoke.

Ed Hoeffliger stared intently back to the west, trying to divine the meaning of the gunfire. Suddenly, Sapp's rig roared out of the smoke and skidded to a halt. Ken Jackola jumped off the back, ran around the side, and linked up with

Ed. Hoeffliger was relieved to see him.

They didn't leave us hanging.

Doc Miller climbed up into the Humvee to treat Alabe. The IED had ruptured his eardrums.

As the confusion of the initial attack evaporated, the rest of the platoon dismounted on Lieutenant Wood's orders and swept the area on either side of the road. Second Platoon showed up a short time later, driving in from the East. Lieutenant Kent and Pete Salerno set up security on the far side of the ambush and helped sweep the area.

Their search uncovered a wire running from the IED site across the canal and up the other side. Ken Jackola and Gabe Sapp waded through chest-deep sewer water in the canal to trace the wire back to a car battery emplaced behind the berm. Next to it lay a brand new AK-47 with a spare ammo magazine.

Ken realized that the insurgent could not possibly have seen the road. He was well behind the berm with no view to the north. He must have had an accomplice. A sweep of the area revealed an observation point about sixty feet from the car battery, where another insurgent had dropped his AK-47 and a spare magazine.

The insurgent observer had watched 1st Platoon's vehicles come up the road, and as the lead vehicle passed next to the IED, he had shouted down to his comrade behind the berm. He then touched the wires to the car battery, which sent an electrical charge into three 122mm rockets separately emplaced alongside. Two of them detonated, the other did not. As fate would have it, Hoeffliger's Humvee was between two of the rockets when they went off.

This initial IED incident taught the Oregonians several very valuable lessons. First, they needed to forget the tactics taught at Fort Hood. Had they reacted as trained, Hoeffliger's vehicle would have remained isolated on the east side of the IED impact while the rest of the platoon backed up the appropriate three hundred meters to get out of the kill zone. Doing it by the book would have left Hoeffliger's squad at the mercy of the insurgents, and would have been lethal had they run into a complex ambush complete with machine guns and RPG teams.

Second, the discovery of the AK-47s showed they had intended to shoot at the patrol. What made them run away? Werner and Howell? When they lit up the area around their positions, the insurgents panicked and fled through the orchard. This critical piece of the puzzle convinced the entire company that when engaged, the gunners needed to open up and establish fire superiority. Some later dubbed it the "breathing dragon" or the "mad minute." Bang . . . IED goes off . . . all the gunners traverse and shoot. This became their standard tactic, and it worked well in the sparsely inhabited rural areas around Taji.

Ken Jackola provided the last lesson of the day. By running forward, jumping on the back of Gabe Sapp's rig, and driving through the kill zone, he demonstrated to every man in the platoon his commitment to them. Cool under fire, capable of making split-second decisions and leading the men, the confidence level in their towering platoon sergeant soared. Ken Jackola would not leave them hanging.

SEVENTEEN

THE 91ST PSALM

It was time to go outside the wire again. For almost a week, Bravo Company had been patrolling as full platoons. Now, though, they broke into sections. The platoon sergeant took one-half of the men, the platoon leader took the other half. The insurgency had fragmented the American army so thoroughly that at the tip of the spear stood fifteen to twenty men. If World War II was a theater commander's war, and Vietnam a company commander's war, Iraq had become a section leader's war. It was a clash between cells and squad leaders. Twenty men, four rigs. That was Bravo's basic patrol element.

On the night of April 14, 2004, Vinni Jacques gathered his men for one final pep talk before heading out. Not long before, one of his men had come to Vinni and suggested he read the 91st Psalm before every patrol. Legend had it that during WWI, the Oregonians of the 91st Division had recited that psalm before going into battle and did not lose a man. Vinni liked the idea, and it became part of the platoon routine to read it before every patrol.

He withdrew from his pocket a small, laminated card that Joel "Stiney" Stinemann's church had sent to every member of the platoon. On it was the 91st Psalm. Vinni began to read.

He shall call upon me, and I will answer him: I will be with him in trouble; I will deliver him, and honour him.

With my long life will I satisfy him, and shew him my salvation.

The final words uttered, Jacques and his men saddled up in their cardboard coffins and rolled for the gate. Tonight, they'd patrol Route Senators.

The mission started uneventfully. The drivers kept up their speed in order to present a more difficult target in case they got ambushed. They hummed along at forty-five to fifty miles an hour, slowing down only when they came through the small villages in the area. Other units didn't bother to reduce speed in the villages, a fact that angered the locals and sometimes caused civilian casualties. On an earlier patrol, Vinni met an Iraqi policeman who reported that an American convoy roared through his town and killed a boy. As they boy lay in the road, the American convoy had not even stopped to check on him. The incident enraged the population and made the Oregonians sick to hear about it. After that, Vinni's section always slowed down in the small villages, accepting the risk in order to avoid a similar tragedy.

The night grew long; the men grew weary. It looked like the patrol would end on a boring note until a Kiowa helicopter spotted a group of Iraqi males huddled together on a remote stretch of Route Redleg. The Kiowa crew tracked the Iraqis back to a pair of cars, which took off together and headed for a nearby town.

The Kiowa shadowed the vehicles while the pilot called for ground forces to give chase. The task fell to 3rd Platoon. Guided by the Kiowa crew, Vinni led his section in pursuit. The Iraqi cars reached a village and parked next to a house. The men entered it. The Kiowa crew did not see them leave.

Back at Rilea, 3rd Platoon had trained for this exact scenario. Roll up, establish an outer cordon while part of the platoon covers the house, then send the dismounts in to nail the bad guys. It all sounded easy, but this would be 3rd Platoon's first cordon and search in country. They didn't know the town and had no idea what the target house looked like. Back in the States, they always trained to do it as a full platoon.

They reached the village. The drivers maneuvered into position, the gunners swung out their machine guns. In the shadows around them scurried dozens of people. They darted between buildings, slithered through alleys, and peeped from rooftops at the Americans. It gave Vinni's men a *Dawn of the Dead* sort of vibe. It was creepy and subtly hostile. This was not a town that welcomed Americans.

Vinni climbed out of his rig and went over to his Hell Hounds, Stout, Kaiser, and Leisten. Altogether, he had four dismounts available to hit the house. He didn't consider that enough. He didn't want them to rush in and be overwhelmed by superior numbers. They also had no chance of achieving surprise, not with the Kiowa overhead spot-lighting the house. The Kiowa crew grew impatient. The pilot called down to Vinni and told him to get inside the house. Vinni wouldn't do it. He needed more men.

"Get in that house now!" shouted the Kiowa pilot.

"I do not have enough men."

Not with four guys. Forget it.

"Get in the house!"

The 2-7 TOC had been listening to this exchange. The battle captain came over the net. "Can you get into the house? Can you execute?" Vinni explained the situation. He didn't have the dismounts to go into the building. He needed backup.

The 2-7 TOC sent him the battalion quick reaction force (QRF) platoon. Within minutes, a column of cav troopers rolled into the town; Vinni was amazed at the speed of their arrival.

The platoon leader, a young lieutenant, climbed out of his rig and went over to talk with Vinni. The two leaders conferred, and the lieutenant agreed to hit the building together. One of the lieutenant's squads would go in first to secure the first floor. As they moved in, Vinni and his boys would follow and clear the second floor and roof. Meanwhile the rest of the cav platoon set blocking positions around the house. A sniper team moved to cover the rear.

Specialist Marty Theurer stood behind an M240 Bravo and watched the raid unfold. The troopers kicked in the door and stormed inside. Chaos erupted; voices shouted in fear, women screamed. The lieutenant gave the all clear signal. Bill Stout led the Hell Hounds through the doorway.

Inside, Bill found the cav guys amid at least fifteen men and another five or ten women and children. The sight of the heavily armed Americans created hysteria. The first floor was anything but secure. Bill led his men up the stairs with Vinni in the rear to give support. Right then, two Iraqi males bolted from the house through a rear exit.

The cav snipers opened fire. Halfway up the stairwell, Vinni heard the shots ring out. He shouted, "Keep your friggin' heads down!" He had no commo with the QRF platoon and feared a fratricide incident.

Unsure of who was shooting, they continued up the stairs. Vinni heard the first shot strike home. It made a wet, meaty sound like a watermelon being smashed. The second shot missed. The third shot produced another hit. The two fleeing Iraqis tumbled to the weeds, dead. The Hell Hounds reached the roof. They cleared it, and Bill looked down to see the field behind the house now teaming with Iraqis.

Where had they come from?

The locals dragged the two bodies away before the Americans had a chance to search them.

Vinni returned to the first floor and found the cav troopers struggling to control the situation. They had zip-cuffed the men and were separating the women and children from them, which caused howls of protest and panic from all the Iraqis.

At his blocking position, Marty Theurer had heard two of the shots. He couldn't see who was shooting, but it made him extra alert. Suddenly, a car flew out of a back alley, its engine over-revved and tached out. It was the sound of a vehicle being abused, like the driver had hit forty while still in first gear.

The car drove right into one of 3rd Platoon's blocking positions. At the last second, the driver hit the brakes and the car shuddered to a stop.

Marty heard somebody yell, "Medic!"

Back inside the house, Vinni had just started to leave when he saw Specialist Josh "Doc" Smith run past the front entryway.

"Doc, where the fuck are you going?" Vinni called out.

Doc replied, "We have a civilian hit."

Oh fuck. Vinni took off after his medic.

Doc Smith looked twenty-eight but was actually a nineteen-year-old college student who'd left school to volunteer for the deployment. His deep voice, profound intellect, and thoughtful observations all made him appear wise beyond his years. He reached the car, Vinni right behind him. They took one look at the tragedy inside and shouted for Marty Theurer.

Marty had no idea what Doc needed, but he swapped out of the gunner position, hit the pavement, and grabbed his combat lifesaver bag. He ran for the car. Doc Smith was half in and half out of the car. He saw Marty and said, "I think I have a pulse."

In the back seat, a woman lay slumped on her side. She was heavyset, middle-aged, about five-four and two hundred pounds. Her sobbing husband and her father stood to one side.

Doc Smith and Marty eased her out of the car and onto the road. Marty felt for a pulse but didn't find one. Doc cried, "She's not breathing."

What was wrong?

Marty saw that her stomach looked distended. He searched for a wound. Her abdomen felt soft and mushy, like she was bleeding internally. But where was the wound? He cut open her cotton dress, but the injury eluded him.

"I'm not seeing anything. Doc. Let's roll her over." Together, they gently moved her on her side and found a single, pencil-thin entry wound on her flank. They checked her pulse. No pulse. They checked her breathing again. No breathing. She was slipping away.

Through his interpreter, Vinni learned the family included four children. Two of them, both boys, cautiously came out of the alley and approached their mother. Their grandfather shooed them away, but they'd already seen too much.

As Vinni looked at the dying woman and her family, all Vinni could think of was Gabe and Rhonda. Right then he knew without a doubt, no matter how feral he was once in his life, he was nothing but a family man now. His devotion to Rhonda, his love for Gabe, his profound sense of loss and loneliness from missing them all swirled together. Here he was five thousand miles from home watching another family much like his own suffer an unbearable tragedy. He could not help but empathize. And it hurt; God, how it hurt.

"How are we looking here, Doc?" Vinni asked.

Before Smith could answer him, the 2-7 Cav lieutenant appeared and glanced down at the mother. "Sergeant, it looks like she's dead. These guys probably have AKs in their house. You got the situation covered, okay? I'm going to go back to the house." He turned around and vanished, leaving Vinni to deal with everything.

What the fuck? That was seriously fucked up.

Tough, always ready for a fight, and prepared to kill anyone who threatened his boys, Vinni also possessed a compassionate heart. He knew what it meant to have a family. And here a mother was dying in front of hers. It shook him to the core. Instinctively, he knew he had to handle it as a human being, not as a soldier. He must face this Iraqi family as a fellow husband and a father. It was the only thing he could do.

I have tried all my life to be a good human. I did not mean to hurt anybody.

Marty touched Doc's arm. "It's no use. We can't do anything for her. We need to stop."

Doc Smith, his face a mask of grief, turned to Vinni, "Sergeant Jacques, she's gone. It's over."

The interpreter heard this and said to the woman's father, "Your daughter is dead." It was blunt and harsh, and it made things worse. The husband wailed in anguish.

Jacques could not believe the callousness the interpreter had just displayed. He grabbed him by the collar and shook him hard, "You keep your fucking mouth shut you sonofabitch!"

After a pause, Vinni approached the grieving father. Man to man, human to human, father to father, they stood together, eyes locked. The Iraqi was an old man, whose creased face belied much hardship. Later, they found out he was the Imam of the village.

"Sir, I don't even know what to say," Vinni began, his voice choked with raw emotion. Vinni made the interpreter translate word for word. "We did not come here for this to happen. We're here to protect you. I don't even know what to say. I am so sorry. We did not mean to hurt anyone."

The father listened carefully to the interpreter. Vinni feared his reaction. If this had been his own family, Vinni knew he'd simply want to kill those who had killed his wife. He expected no less now.

The old man took a step forward and embraced Vinni. He hugged him hard, backed off, and then gingerly touched the sergeant's cheeks with his hands. The intimate gesture astonished Vinni and sent his heart spiraling. This was almost worse than a violent reaction. They made eye contact again. Vinni held his gaze, the old man's hollowed eyes a window to his despair. Yet with a steady voice he comforted Vinni, "My son, I know why you are here. And I am glad you are here."

The veteran, burly sergeant choked up. He embraced the Imam again and replied, "I want to help you. What can we do?"

"Help me get my daughter to the car, and we will take care of the rest. This was God's will."

The woman's husband remained inconsolable. Tears streaked his face as he cradled his dead wife. The old man stepped away from Jacques, bent down, pulled his son-in-law to his feet, and hugged him fiercely. "We must take care of the children," he told him. Speaking a few more words in Arabic, he held him until the husband regained control of himself. The Americans remained silent, every moment of the scene a torture.

Finally, they laid the woman carefully back inside the car. Vinni watched them drive off, his vision blurred by the tears in his own eyes.

A family just like ours. Just like any American family, maybe closer than most of ours.

Vinni turned away, overcome by emotion. This had been the worst day of his life, and nothing could ever undo it. Though he hadn't pulled the trigger, though his men had not fired a shot, he felt responsibility for what had happened. Proud and honorable, a man who always tried to do the right thing, Vinni was powerless to right this wrong.

And yet, the old man had given him absolution. Despite his own pain, he had told him not to carry this burden. It was simply God's will. Three shots. Two hit their targets. The third went astray and hit a woman standing on a porch, kids underfoot, husband and father at her side. Maybe, just maybe, the Imam was right. But that didn't take the ache away.

"You okay, Sergeant Jacques?" It was Kenny Leisten, manning the gun on a near-by Humvee. Vinni looked up at him. Leisten was a great kid, always squared away, always eager to help. Vinni had become especially fond of him, as had Bill Stout.

"I'm always good when I'm with my boys, Kenny."

They loaded up and rolled. Tomorrow, reading the 91st Psalm would take on an entirely new meaning.

EIGHTEEN

THE ROCKETS OF TAJI

One morning outside the PX, Bill Stout leaned against his Humvee reading *Cycle World* magazine when three rockets sizzled over and hit the dirt not forty feet away. Spaced about ten feet apart, they stippled the hard ground like overgrown child's toys. Bill could hear one fizzing. Smoke curled up over their fins.

"Holy Shit!"

Bill scrambled to the other side of the Humvee and took cover. The rockets had landed right in front of two Joes from the aviation brigade. They'd been sunning themselves in lawn chairs, but now they bolted into their nearby hooch. They emerged with their IBAs, then grabbed their lawn chairs and pulled them clear of the rockets.

What are the chances that three rockets would malfunction simultaneously? If any one of them had detonated, three men would have either died or suffered grievous wounds. It was enough to give a man religion in a big hurry.

Taji in the spring of 2004 was nothing short of the Wild West. Lawlessness reigned, and the cavalry was having a tough time finding the Indians. Outside the wire, the local population, composed mainly of those Sunnis who profited most from the Saddam regime, remained generally hostile to the Americans. They gave aid and comfort to the insurgents.

That spring, these insurgents launched indirect fire attacks on Camp Cooke every day. Sometimes, they'd explode in a remote section of the base. Occasionally, they got lucky and walked their fire right through the living pods. The sheer randomness of indirect fire made the Americans fatalistic. *If you're gonna die, you're gonna die. No use worrying about it.*

On April 24, men did die. That morning, Vinni and his roommate Specialist Josh "Doc" Smith were still in bed, half asleep. Their section had been given the day off, and they intended to sleep late. *Thud. Thud, Thud.* In the distance, mortar shells left insurgent tubes. A minute later, the early morning resounded with multiple explosions.

Vinni got up, checked on his Joes, and returned to the hooch. A minute later, inbound rockets scorched the dark sky. These were close. Damn close. They landed in the pods, prompting a mad dash to the bunkers. Doc Smith grabbed his aid bag and his IBA. Together, he and Vinni sprinted into the darkness wearing only body armor and boxer shorts.

The scene was chaotic. People ran everywhere; they could hear screaming in the distance. "Hey, is everyone okay in here?" Sergeant Jacques' voice bellowed through the first bunker they reached. Next to him, Doc Smith scanned the darkness to see if anyone had been hit. In the distance, the sizzle and *boom* of more incoming could be heard.

They ran to another bunker. Inside, they found no wounded. Vinni and Doc charged to the next one, checked on the men inside, and kept moving. The barrage continued.

They came to a 39th bunker. As they peered into it, the babble of dozens of voices rose out of the darkness. Vinni tried to ask if anyone was hurt, but the din was just too loud. That pissed him off. He shouted, "Unless you're wounded, shut the fuck up!"

Everyone went silent. The two Oregonians continued on. They spent the next ten minutes trying without luck to find wounded men. Later, Spike Olsen emerged from a bunker and saw some Arkansans policing up body parts. A rocket had landed right at the entrance to a bunker while a 39th unit held accountability. Four Arkansans died in an eyeblink, blown to fragments by a one-in-a-million impact.

The 39th redoubled its efforts to find the mortar and rocket cells. Stopping the attacks proved to be a significant challenge. At times, when the point of origin (POO) of the attacks could be identified, the 206th Field Artillery Battalion would lay down counterbattery fire, but it rarely proved effective. The insurgents had a knack for shooting and scooting.

The 2-7 conducted numerous raids to capture the cells, and these had some good results. Bravo Company took part in a raid that netted a former Republican Guard artillery officer. The major had been dubbed "the rocket man" by the Bulldogs, who were all too glad to put him behind bars.

Gradually, the efforts to counter the indirect fire attacks paid off. By early summer, the number of attacks diminished and the incoming never posed the threat it had in the spring. Yet, even at the end of the deployment, the insurgents still launched occasional waves of indirect fire attacks, a symbol that in an insurgency rarely is any operation truly decisive.

NINETEEN

THE FINE ART OF COMMAND

At times, military operations can unfold with all the precision of a pit crew at a NASCAR race. At other times, they devolve into a mess with all the sense and reason of a party in an insane asylum. Excellent leaders keep the friction to a minimum. Poor ones can create bedlam.

Colonel Fourshee, the 2-7 Cav BC, fancied himself a bold dragoon. He rolled out of Taji on patrols with a cavalry saber strapped to his Bradley's turret. His sense of history pervaded every battalion operation. During one multi-unit briefing for an air assault mission dubbed Operation Yellowstone, he interrupted his staff and postponed the mission for twenty-four hours because they had not named the phase lines after events related to the Plains Indian Wars. He wanted everything to be connected to the 7th Cav's past. Except, of course, for Little Big Horn.

Fourshee's seat-of-the-pants style of leadership created a comedy of errors that nobody found funny.

It began with Operation Medicine Arrow, Bravo's first air assault mission. The men looked forward to riding in Blackhawks again, but as their leaders showed them the landing zone, puzzled faces abounded. It was right on the other side of the south wall. What was the point in air assaulting into a field within slingshot range of the base?

Orders were orders. The men mounted up. They made history that day in what must have been the shortest air assault mission ever. The Blackhawks spent about thirty seconds in flight before reaching the landing zone (LZ). The men jumped out only to find the 2-7 sergeant major and a sniper team waiting for them. Pete Salerno climbed off his bird and gaped at the sergeant major. What were they doing in the LZ before the Blackhawks even got there?

The helicopters had dropped two platoons from Bravo Company into a field about a hundred meters north of a house targeted for a raid by a Macedonian special forces outfit. In effect, they'd been landed right between the south wall and the potential bad guys. Exactly how they were supposed to be an outer cordon in that situation was clear only to the 2-7 commander. The Bulldogs were confused and angry.

The Macedonian SF team hit the target house and found nothing. Then the mission expanded. Fourshee ordered Lieutenant Kent to sweep eastward. The sergeant major micromanaged the platoon the entire way. They walked through the fields and orchards. They waded across a canal and kept going east. This did not make much sense to anyone. Not too far in front of them, the Bulldogs could see a road with Bradleys parked on it. Fourshee was in that group. Their BC had ordered them to sweep right into friendly forces. Salerno quipped, "If there are any bad guys within five miles of us, I'd be fucking stunned."

In the lead squad, Corporal Shane Ward simmered. The 2-7 sergeant major came over and positioned his men along a wall running east-west. Shane looked around. He had friendlies in front of him, friendlies to the rear, and friendlies to the right. And to the left? A wall they could not see over. When Pete Salerno came over to check on the squad, Ward vented, "This is fucked up!"

Pete stormed off. His boiling point had been reached.

Lieutenant Kent's radio crackled. Fourshee ordered them to move north into a nearby palm grove and look for a "possible RPG team."

Salerno snapped. He erupted in a rage and shouted, "There ain't no god-damn RPG team. We're out here maneuvering just because Fourshee can make us maneuver. This guy is fucking crazy." He turned around to find the 2-7 sergeant major scowling at him.

Uh-oh.

The command sergeant major stormed up to Pete and poked his IBA with an index finger, "I will see you back at Taji, Sergeant. You and me, we're gonna have words."

Pete said, "Roger that, Sergeant Major."

The mission accomplished nothing. It was a case study on how not to run a raid.

Bravo's relationship with Colonel Fourshee deteriorated after Medicine Arrow. The Bulldogs sometimes entered the TOC and found Fourshee brow-beating his staff officers. Shouting is one thing. Every officer and Joe in the army is used to that, but Fourshee would attack his officers personally and challenge their manhood in public. At least one Bulldog heard Fourshee call an officer a "stupid fucker"!

He did not limit his tirades to his staff officers; at one time or another most of the Bulldogs saw or felt his wrath as well. In the field, he would scream at soldiers for not wearing their uniforms correctly. He chewed Captain San Miguel raw one day after his RTO failed to use the word *out* to end his radio transmissions.

And yet, at times Fourshee appeared friendly and concerned about the men. After Ryan Howell got hit, Fourshee checked on him and talked with Vinni. Some of the men had high hopes for him after meeting him in Kuwait. But once in country, they saw their commander turn into a Jeckyl and Hyde. Beyond the wire, he micromanaged his men. At times, he went so far as to reposition indi-vidual soldiers in the middle of operations, making him the highest paid team leader in the army. In the field, he surrounded himself with his personal secu-rity detail (PSD). The detail stayed in a tight cluster around him, and the Bull-dogs joked they were Fourshee's human shields. Sergeant Tommy Houston saw this one day and thought this very dangerous; they made an excellent target massed together like that.

Colonel Fourshee's behavior dramatically affected how the 2-7 Cav functioned in those first weeks at Taji. Captain San Miguel found the battalion staff in a state of near paralysis. Anything they did would likely get them yelled at, so they were afraid to make decisions.

Bravo Company grew to despise Fourshee and miss Lieutenant Colonel Hendrickson's steady hand and leadership. Some, including Pete Salerno, thought Fourshee would get them all killed. The situation quickly reached a climax. During a townwide cordon and search operation in one of the nearby communities, Fourshee's sergeant major caught sight of some kids approaching a Bravo Company blocking position.

Fourshee had just climbed out of his vehicle some fifteen meters away when the sergeant major pulled out his 9mm pistol, pointed it at the kids, and told one of the Bravo Company FOs to shoot the kids if they got any closer. Matt Zedwick was standing next to the FO when the sergeant major gave the order. The two Oregonians stared at each other. No way were they going to murder children.

To be fair, reports had emerged from southern Iraq that suggested the insurgents were paying children to throw grenades at American vehicles. There was a good military reason to keep the kids away. But Zedwick and the FO weren't going to shoot them when they clearly posed no threat.

Later that day, 2nd Platoon was tasked to clear a house. As the entry team moved to the front door, Eric McKinley covered them with his M240. Colonel Fourshee suddenly appeared and barked at McKinley to roll his sleeve cuffs back down. He'd been out in 120 degree weather and the young Oregonian had rolled up his cuffs to try and cool off.

Now, as the entry team continued with the mission, the men lost their security as McKinley got off his gun to adjust his uniform. Matt Zedwick watched this in a fury. The aftermath of that raid caused great turmoil in the 2-7. First, the FO reported the sergeant major's order to the brigade's JAG (judge advocate general—army lawyer) office. That triggered an investigation that infuriated Colonel Fourshee. He attempted to get both First Sergeant Warnock and Captain San Miguel relieved. General Chiarelli relieved Fourshee instead. He stayed in theater in another position for a while, but eventually retired from the army and now works in private industry.

In any organization, especially large ones, there will be bad apples and poor managers. That's just a fact of life. To the army's extreme credit, it took less than seven weeks of combat operations to remove Fourshee from command. The system worked.

Lieutenant Colonel James "Jim" Rainey took over the 2-7 Cav. Rainey grew up in a middle-class Ohio home and became an athlete in high school. He later attended Eastern Kentucky University, where he earned a three-year ROTC scholarship. During eighteen years in uniform, Jim Rainey never had a bad day. Some seriously grim hours, yes, but he loved the army and loved leading his men from the front.

The 2-7 and Bravo discovered that General Chiarelli had sent them a real gem in Jim Rainey. Dynamic, charismatic, and highly intelligent, Rainey transformed the atmosphere in the 2-7. He gave his staff officers the latitude they needed to thrive. He never micromanaged, and when he rolled outside the wire, he did so in an unarmored 1025 Humvee, the worst rig the 2-7 owned. He set an example right away with his willingness to share the risks his soldiers faced every day.

A fresh infusion of leadership was all that the 2-7 needed. The battalion's sergeant major was subsequently reassigned and returned to the States. Rainey brought in a new XO, Major Scott Jackson, and a new S-3, Major Tim Karcher. Together, they studied how the 2-7 had operated. They patrolled with every platoon and learned its capabilities. Afterward, Rainey concluded that he had an exceptional battalion full of outstanding officers and NCOs. His company commanders particularly impressed him, as did the Bulldog platoon sergeants.

Next, Jim and his staff worked out a new vision for operations around Taji. Intelligence became a high priority, and he tripled the size of the S-2 department. He put an end to townwide cordon and searches. The 2-7 under Fourshee had been heavy-handed in its approach with the locals. Now, Rainey intended to be more focused. Instead of raiding entire villages, the 2-7 would acquire accurate intel and target only houses harboring insurgent cells. It was a more precise, intel-driven approach. And it was exactly what the area needed.

Rainey's AO included 685 square kilometers of countryside and 26 kilometers of the MSR. All of it needed patrolling, while at the same time, the 2-7 had to provide security for Camp Cooke and escorts for vehiclar convoys. Doing these things absorbed much of his combat power.

Then there was the enemy. The Taji area was home to a particularly sophisticated group of cells. In nearby Taramiya, Saddam's intelligence service had built a major base. Many of those intel types had now turned terrorist. They were well trained, well led, and disciplined.

Many of their marching orders came from the local sheiks and Imams. The mosques served as communication hubs for the insurgency. The middle-class former Baathists living in the area served as the insurgency's financiers, funneling foreign money and weapons to the locals. They also cooperated with the foreign volunteers who had flocked to Iraq.

In this sort of environment, Rainey assessed the threats in each section of the AO and deployed his forces accordingly. He gave MSR patrols to the wheeled units in the battalion, including Bravo Company. Route Senators was a paved highway, one that the insurgents would have a hard time placing IEDs under its roadbed. Those were the most deadly bombs, and Rainey wanted to keep his wheeled elements away from such threats if possible. Meanwhile, his Brads and Abrams would cover the dirt roads and the more dangerous sections of the AO.

In early June, Bravo Company witnessed firsthand the sophistication and ruthlessness of the enemy they faced. Early on the morning of June 9, local Iraqi contractors lined up at Camp Cooke's north gate for another day's work inside the wire. These locals had been hired to build sidewalks and buildings on the base. They were average Iraqis just trying to make a living in the middle of chaos. The chaos came to them.

An insurgent cell drove two car bombs into the waiting lines of people and vehicles. The explosions caused gruesome devastation. Lieutenant Kent's section of 2nd Platoon had been guarding the bridge over the Tigris River on the MSR. They had just been relieved, so Kent took them north to help out.

The scene was nothing any of these young college-kids-turned-soldiers could have ever imagined. Body parts lay scattered everywhere. Spike Olsen looked around in shock and horror at the ghastly sight. Disembodied arms, legs, hands, partial torsos, and entrails all littered the road and the shoulders. Dead Iraqis bled out inside their vehicles. Some of the dead had already been piled to one side of the road by other U.S. troops. At ground zero, the vehicle-borne IED (VBIED) had blown an eight-foot hole some four feet deep in the roadway.

The drivers eased around the body parts and continued north to the second VBIED site in front of an Iraqi national guard compound.

Another scene of horror greeted the men. Bodies lay burned in wrecked vehicles. They dismounted and established security as the smell of charred humans assaulted them. It was a pregnant, heavy stench intermingled with the reek of diesel fuel and singed hair. No matter that the wind was blowing that day. The smell did not dissipate, and breathing became an act of will.

Spike sat on the gun, staring down at what was left of an overweight, middle-aged Iraqi male. He'd been torn open from his groin to his sternum and was still burning. Yellow fat bubbled and popped, and the man's face had been partially burned away, exposing buck teeth. Spike had never seen a corpse. His stomach heaved. Everyone's did. He struggled to get a handle on the moment.

Okay, what are my options here? Throw up? Cry? Break down?

Somebody suddenly quipped, "Hey, that guy looks like the wood rat from *Shrek!*" A ripple of laughter spread through the Joes. Black humor saved them all. Spike laughed. It was a valuable lesson for the platoon, and from that point on, even in the worst of it they would be able to find humor in their predicament.

More than two dozen people died in the twin VBIED attacks at the front gate of Camp Cooke. Al-Qaeda later took credit for the operation. At day's end, Jim Rainey and every Bulldog who witnessed the aftermath had a new understanding of who they faced. The ever-elusive enemy would stop at nothing to inflict chaos and harm. Here, to break the growing bond between the locals and the Americans at Taji, they had deliberately targeted Iraqi civilians. It was chillingly ruthless.

And, it was only the beginning.

Part III

CONTACT

TWENTY

RIGHT SEAT INTO RPGs

While Bravo Company saw action immediately, the rest of 2-162 was split between FOB Provider and Taji. Provider would be the battalion's home, but with the 1st Armored Division still in the area and the Shia uprising in full bloom, it would take time to get 2-162 up and running there.

In the meantime, some of the battalion's leaders went down to Fire Base Melody in Baghdad to get right-seat rides with the veteran 1-36 Armored. The ride-alongs taught Captain Welch some valuable lessons. Shortly after their arrival at Melody, Welch, Hildebrandt, and several of the Charlie and Delta NCOs joined a 1-36 patrol down Route Wild into the edges of the the oldest slums in Baghdad, known as the Sheik Umar District. Normally, the area did not see much action, and Captain Chris Ayres of B Co, 1-36 intended to show the Volunteers their new area on a routine familiarization patrol.

Four Bradleys and two M1 Abrams tanks rumbled out of Melody that night with Welch and Hildebrandt in their Humvees. For a routine patrol, the Spartans of 1-36 had brought along a lot of firepower.

The patrol began peacefully. Ayres got on the radio and gave a commentary on the area, acting almost as a tour guide. On the right, they went by an abandoned girls' school. Up ahead, on the other side of the road, a propane factory came into view. Out in front of the building stood row after row of trailer trucks with hundreds of propane tanks stacked on them.

So far so good. The only problem had been Captain Welch's Humvee. He had left Blackjack 22 behind at Melody and climbed into Lieutenant Becerra's rig. For some reason, whenever they turned to the right, the truck would stall. The driver, Sergeant Little, had to restart it every time.

The trailing M1 went past the girls' school. Seconds later, a bright streak of fire lit up the column crossing from right to left and passing up its length. Something exploded off to the left. Wyatt twisted around in his seat just in time to see another flash and another explosion. RPGs!

Whoosh! An RPG skimmed past Hildebrandt's gunner and exploded right next to his door. Hildebrandt's gunner returned fire at small knots of insurgents using the rooftops for cover. Hildebrandt felt odd. He seemed outside of himself, disembodied, like he was an observer at somebody else's battle.

The Bradleys swung out their turrets and spit 25mm rounds back at the insurgents. The 25 mike-mike is a deadly effective urban weapon, and the

Bradley fighting vehicles (BFVs) wrought total havoc to the neighborhood that night. That did not stop the insurgents from shooting back. AK rounds zinged off the pavement.

Sergeant Terrel, Welch's 3rd Platoon leader, stood on the gun that night with just his shoulders and head exposed out of the turret. In front of him a SAW gunner in a PSYOP (psychological operations) Humvee turned around to spray the girls' school with 5.6mm bullets. That would normally have been a good thing, except this time the SAW gunner had to shoot directly over Terrel's head. Terrel and Welch were not happy with that development. *Hadn't anyone taught this guy about fields of fire?*

The Bradleys never slowed down, and soon the column shot beyond the propane plant into a quiet area. At that point, the 1-36 battalion commander ordered Captain Ayres to turn around and go kill the insurgents. The column pulled a U-turn and drove right back into the kill zone.

This time, small-arms fire rattled the length of the column from both sides of the road. Welch's Humvee rolled slowly past the propane factory again. Wyatt could smell the gas in the air. If something detonated it, the entire factory might go up, along with half the neighborhood.

Behind Hildebrandt, the tanks unleashed their main guns at point blank range into a building. The huge cannon shells laid waste to the structures and killed numerous insurgents. Meanwhile, the column moved forward to an intersection and came to a stop next to the abandoned girls' school, the propane factory now to the rear. Sporadic small arms continued. Ahead of Wyatt, the trunk monkeys in the Bradleys dismounted.

A burst of gunfire came from the back of the column. A shattered BMW glided past Wyatt's Humvee, the driver slumped against the window. Dead. He was the first of many corpses Wyatt saw in Iraq.

A moment later, some of the Bradley dismounts walked over, gave the dead man a cursory glance, then turned away. The professional in Welch watched them and wondered why they didn't check the trunk. He made a mental note to make sure his men were more thorough when they conducted searches. The private, human part of Welch wondered if the poor bastard wasn't just trying to get home and got caught in the wrong place at the wrong time.

The Bradleys opened up again, this time sending their 25mm shells into an apartment complex on the other side of the intersection. Several insurgents with AK-47s fired back from the roof. Wyatt turned from the dead man in the BMW and watched the Brads stitch the apartment. The 1-36 guys sure were laying into the neighborhood. It seemed like overkill, and Welch thought, *Surely there are kids in that apartment building.* Then again, these 1-36 guys were veterans. They knew the score. Who was he, a captain in country for less than a month, to judge?

The firing continued. Welch glanced at the BMW again. Blood trickled down from the door to form a puddle under the car. Later, he found out the BMW had raced straight for the back of the column. Warning shots had failed to dissuade the driver. He came right at the Americans. The 1-36 had seen too many car-bombs and VBIEDs during their tour in country. They machine-gunned the BMW and killed the driver.

Another car approached the intersection from the right. Warning shots turned it away, but seconds later it swung around and sped for the column. This was not an innocent man trying to get home. The Bradleys took out the vehicle. Moments later, a third showed up, but warning shots drove it away.

The din ebbed away. The firing stopped. Only the idling engines of the American vehicles broke the silence. The column continued with the patrol. The rest of the night was uneventful.

When they returned to FOB Melody, Captain Ayres apologized to Hildebrandt for getting into such a big scrap on his first night out. Later, Scott learned that they'd been hit by another Syrian cell and the column's return fire had killed more than two dozen of these foreign fighters.

At Melody, Welch noticed that the men did not celebrate. There was no revelry. The soldiers finished their tasks and disappeared. Wyatt remained behind, alone with his thoughts. *They'd been shooting at me. Me.*

It was hard to come to grips with the thought that people out there wanted to see him dead. Wyatt finished up his own work, then headed to the Internet café to write Gina, his wife, and tell her all about it.

TWENTY-ONE

DUMPED IN BAGHDAD

It had happened again. By the end of April, the battalion minus Bravo Company reunited down at FOB Provider only to find a lack of living space. Those barracks that existed were already being used by a support battalion from 1st AD, so no bunks awaited the Oregonians. They racked out in a gravel parking lot and explored some of the other buildings on the base, trying to find a creative place to grab some shut-eye.

Provider had been build around the old Iraqi Olympic training compound. The men found some interesting things, including Uday Hussein's mangled Ferrari and the grubby room he used to torture Iraq's soccer team.

Here and there, some of the units found places to sleep indoors. The scouts got tired of the parking lot and made their way inside the aquatic training facility. They claimed the shower and locker rooms. Part of Delta staked out the drained Olympic-sized swimming pool.

Not long after moving in, the support battalion packed up and left. The 1st AD Joes were supposed to go home, and they had promised Lieutenant Colonel Hendrickson that they would leave most of their furnishings behind. Then their tour got extended by ninety days, thanks to the Shia uprising. Bitter and angry, they took everything with them. *Everything* meant they tore out walls in the barracks, packed up cubicle dividers, interior doors, computers, air-conditioners, chairs, cots, mattresses, generators, and swamp coolers. They stripped down the base to the ice cube trays in the refrigerators, then took the trays, and the fridges as well.

Once again, the Volunteers would start from scratch with little power, fixtures, or functionality. Fortunately, Fort Hood had taught them how to be proactive and work through their problems. And few were more proactive than Captain Hildebrandt and Delta Company.

Delta took over the sports medicine building and created its own mini-FOB. They scored an ancient generator, which provided them steady power. They bought, borrowed, or pinched everything else they needed. By the end of April, Delta had the sweetest setup in the battalion. Their mini-FOB included a horseshoe pit, a weight-lifting room, a volleyball court, and indoor plumbing so the men could use the urinals inside. The men also built a small library and in a common area set up Xboxes, which were later used to run Madden NFL football tournaments.

The BC came and checked things out and gave the thumbs up. Delta scored some points with their initiative. The rest of the battalion moved into their new barracks and did what they could to make them more livable. Without air-conditioning, that was a tall order. Power became a serious headache right away. Without enough generators, the battalion connected the base to the Baghdad power grid. That helped the situation a little bit, but the Volunteers still suffered long blackouts. Fortunately, the National Guard's secret weapon is the versatility of its men. First Sergeant Forrester was an electrician in his civilian life, and the BC put him on the power problem. He eventually got the problems sorted out.

On April 25, FOB Provider officially became Patrol Base Volunteer. The leaders at Melody returned, the men unpacked their conex boxes, and then they performed maintenance miracles on their polyglot fleet of Humvees. Vehicles prepped, weapons cleaned, Lieutenant Colonel Hendrickson's men were ready to meet the neighbors.

TWENTY-TWO

A GLIMPSE OF WHAT COULD BE

Sheik Majeid refused to give up on the Americans. In 2003, he had welcomed the fall of Saddam Hussein and saw the occupation as a new beginning for his people. And his people needed a new beginning. Majeid lived in the Sheik Umar neighborhood of Rusapha (Old Baghdad), perhaps the worst slum in the country. Basic essentials: water, power, access to schools and hospitals; these were virtually unobtainable in Sheik Umar. As the occupation developed, gangs took over much of the neighborhood. They terrorized the locals and fought pitched battles with the Americans. No help reached this desperate community. The Americans, having arrived with so much promise, had failed to deliver.

Majeid refused to be bitter. When the Coalition created the neighborhood and district advisory councils (NACs and DACs), he joined. The NACs and DACs were supposed to give the Baghdad neighborhoods their own experience with grass-roots democracy while serving as the liaison between the people and the coalition military forces. For his efforts, the same artillery unit featured in the movie *Gunner Palace* kicked in Majeid's door and arrested him as a suspected insurgent. After his release, he returned to Sheik Umar and continued his work.

Sergeant First Class Brian Hess, leader of a human intelligence team later attached to the 2-162, first met Sheik Majeid at one of the local NAC meetings. Majeid intrigued the American because whenever he spoke, he spoke only on behalf of his people in the Sheik Umar. Many of the NACs and DACs had been taken over by men serving only to line their own pockets. Majeid appeared willing to bridge long-held tribal grudges and bring his people together. And his neighborhood was one of the most diverse in Baghdad. Sunni and Shia lived cheek to jowl, interacting every day. Elsewhere in Rusapha, small Jewish and Christian communities flourished. Hess regarded Majeid and saw a potential diamond.

He struck up a conversation with Majeid. One talk followed another and a friendship bloomed. One day, Hess asked Majeid, "What will it take for the people of Sheik Umar to stop shooting at coalition forces?"

Majeid answered, "What will it take for the coalition to see the people of Sheik Umar as people, not as savages?"

Touché. Hess hoped Majeid might get a second chance with the Americans. The Oregonians became that second chance. When the Volunteers took to the streets of their new AO, the locals noticed a difference. The men with the setting sun patch on their left shoulders grinned and waved as they patrolled Rusapha. They greeted children, they showed a willingness to be a part of the community.

Majeid saw this as a good sign. He'd recently become the vice chairman of the Rusapha DAC, and in that capacity he visited Patrol Base Volunteer. Major Mike Warrington, the battalion's fire support officer, sat down with Majeid along with Brian Hess. They listened to Majeid outline the problems in his community. When he finished, Major Warrington nodded and grinned. This was exactly the sort of thing he had come to Iraq to fix. He saw Majeid's plight as a golden opportunity to win the hearts and minds of the Sheik Umar community. Hess agreed, and knew he'd found the right unit to help restore Majeid's faith in Americans.

The Americans promised to help. Majeid offered to take them on a tour of his neighborhood. The Volunteers readily accepted.

Not long after the meeting, Charlie Company escorted Major Warrington and Sergeant First Class Hess into the Sheik Umar district, where they met with Majeid and a throng of onlookers. The Volunteers discovered that they were the first American soldiers to go into the neighborhood. Other than to shoot into it, the Americans had essentially ignored the place.

Sergeant Ezelle's squad took point. Initially, as he pushed through the crowd of onlookers, he was as "nervous as a whore in church." If shooting erupted, they'd be trapped in the narrow streets with little cover. The men scanned the nearby buildings, watched the crowd, and tried not to step on the kids running underfoot. They proceeded into the heart of Sheik Umar, leaving their Humvees behind when the street became too narrow for them.

The trip became a descent into the hell of Third World poverty. Piles of trash overflowed the broken sidewalks and filled the streets. In parts, garbage had stopped up the primitive drainage and sewer systems. Raw sewage puddled on the streets. The stench made the men gag.

Behind Sergeant Ezelle's squad, Captain Welch, Major Warrington, and Hess studied the scene. Wyatt had gained the neighborhood as his main area of operation, so he wanted to see it firsthand. The patrol reached a dental clinic. Major Warrington and a civil affairs team entered the clinic to conduct an assessment. The facility lacked most everything, including power.

Later, Majeid led the Americans back out into the street. As they walked to a school, Captain Welch sensed an upswell of excitement in the crowd. Earlier, some of the adults had been standoffish and had stared at the Americans from a distance. Now, they saw that the soldiers meant well. That gave them hope, a scarce commodity in this neighborhood.

Sheik Majeid pointed out a broken water line. A small fountain of water emerged from cracked concrete. He explained to Major Warrington that this was the sole source of water for an entire section of Sheik Umar. Horrified, Warrington took photos of the water and of the sewage pools nearby.

Mike Warrington looked around and saw potential, lots of potential. These people had nothing. If the battalion could bring some basic services to them, Sheik Umar could become the coalition's biggest bastion of support.

They reached the school. Broken desks, broken blackboards, feces in the corners, and a building ready to fall apart greeted the Americans. Sheik Majeid turned to Captain Welch and through their translator said, "The children of Sheik Umar need money for their education so they don't have to live in poverty for the rest of their lives."

As the patrol came to an end and Ezelle's squad led the way back to the Humvees at the dental clinic, the people around them could no longer contain their enthusiasm. They began to chant "Our blood for Sheik Majeid."

The Americans left that day with grins on their faces. They'd already brought hope to an abandoned community. Ask any of the Joes, and they'd say they went to Iraq hoping to do some good and make a difference in the lives of these proud people. What better place to start than Sheik Umar?

Majeid received what he needed most: a second chance.

TWENTY-THREE

OPERATION OSCAR

Major Williams stared hard at the garbage men standing in ranks before him. The Rusapha sanitation engineers had long since ceased to function as an effective community asset. Instead, the men drew a public paycheck every week, then picked up trash only in the neighborhoods that offered them bribes. After hours, they kept their trucks and used them as personal vehicles or taxis to further supplement their incomes. The triple-dipping was about to stop.

Williams began his speech. "In a recent public health survey of two hundred major cities, Baghdad ranked two-hundredth in public sanitation." He paused, then pointed straight at the assembly of garbage men, "And that's your fault!" The Iraqis reacted as if slapped. The speech hit a nerve. Arabic pride was at stake.

Williams continued, "But we're going to help you fix that. We've got ID cards for you, we've developed routes for you, and from now on any garbage truck seen outside its assigned route will be recorded and the driver will be fired."

And so began Operation Oscar. Put together by Captain Eric Riley, the BC and Major Tanguy, Oscar formed the main effort of 2-162's public works program. The garbage in Sheik Umar needed to be removed. This was the first step toward rehabilitating that neighborhood.

Staff Sergeant Bruns showed up for the inaugural day of Operation Oscar. It seemed like a perfect story the army would want released to the world. She kept an eye on Oscar's progress. The battalion hired contractors to build trash bins in the sections of Sheik Omar too narrow for the garbage trucks to reach. The drifts of filth shrank. It looked like an outstanding success, so Bruns wrote an article about it. The 1st Cavalry Division's public affairs office censored it. Rebekah-mae was puzzled. Here was tangible progress, a piece of good, noncombat news in the middle of a flow of bad press. The Cav's public affairs office refused to release it because it revealed corruption among the public employees in Baghdad.

The reception Alpha Company received on the streets of Rusapha surprised Sergeant Phil Disney. At first, sending six hundred Oregonians to patrol a section of Baghdad that included about 1.2 million Iraqis seemed a bit risky. But out on the streets, the vast majority of the people Disney met welcomed the new Americans. People would clap when they walked by. Other times, strangers would approach them and kiss their cheeks. Once, later in the year, an old man threw himself on his knees and thanked Disney for coming to help his people.

113

Lieutenant Erik McCrae and his platoon sergeant, Kerry Boggs, encountered the same reaction wherever Delta's Old Man platoon went. During May, McCrae's men carried out a number of mosque-monitoring missions where they would park and listen to the Friday sermons. The interpreters would tell them if the mosque's leaders were urging their followers to attack the coalition. Usually, in Rusapha, that was not the case. The locals would approach their rigs and chat amicably with the soldiers.

Lieutenant Colonel Hendrickson made it a priority for the battalion to get to know the neighborhoods. Being a law enforcement officer in his civilian life, he believed in community policing. In Rusapha, it paid dividends.

One afternoon, Sergeant Ezelle's platoon had set up a snap traffic control point. The heat beat down on the men, and they quaffed water and suffered in the sun. An ancient Iraqi gentleman—he had to be at least ninety—emerged from his house with tea for Ezelle's men. Ezelle thanked him and walked him back to his house. A short time later, they brought him several cases of MREs and water. The elderly man was so touched by the gesture he broke down in tears.

This was not the Baghdad of CNN and the *New York Times*. That disconnect bothered Major Warrington, who had picked up the added responsibility of battalion information officer just before leaving for Baghdad. In that role, he tried hard to engage the media outlets and show them the good things going on in Rusapha. Nobody seemed interested.

Frustrated, Mike and Staff Sergeant Bruns sat down with Kevin Flower, CNN's Baghdad bureau chief. The Rusapha district included the riverfront hotels across from the green zone where most of the Western press corps lived and worked. In fact, one company of Oregonians was always assigned to "hotel duty," guarding the hotels and the reporters inside. Flower and the rest of the press corps were no strangers to the Volunteers or their efforts. Major Warrington asked Flower to cover the good things happening in the battalion AO.

Flowers stressed that violence sells, and that's what CNN was going to cover. Warrington pointed out that this distorted what was happening in Iraq for the people back home. Flowers agreed that there was probably not balanced coverage of everything happening in Baghdad, but told Warrington that it wasn't going to change. CNN would cover the "bleeding and burning" stories. The rest would be virtually ignored. Warrington left, thoroughly disappointed.

The school playground was nothing but an empty lot with garbage strewn across it. Rebekah-mae Bruns looked it over and her heart ached for these children who attended Sister Benina Hurmez Shukuana's Catholic school. She thought of her pilgrimage in Spain and wondered if she'd really made the right decision with her life.

She'd come here with a patrol of Oregonians to conduct an assessment of the school. Inside, the Volunteers heard Sister Benina leading a prayer. The interpreter told them they were praying for the safety of the coalition soldiers.

Later, as the Volunteers made plans to build a soccer field and playground for the school, the kids mobbed them. They asked for autographs, and some of the soldiers felt like rock stars as they scribbled their signatures. The men handed out T-shirts. Some of the more crafty kids got in line three or four times and hid the extra shirts by stuffing them down their pants. Grinning, they'd flash the Joes, show them their booty, and run away laughing.

The Oregonians loved it.

Rebekah-mae and Sister Benina struck up a conversation, and Bruns discovered a kindred soul. They chatted like long-lost friends and Rebekah-Mae opened up to her. She mentioned that she had considered the life of a nun. Sister Benina smiled and told her she could do more good wearing the uniform she had on. Rebekah-mae was deeply touched.

Throughout Rusapha, the Oregonians made contact with other schools. When the men saw the deplorable conditions as well as the lack of paper, pens, and other supplies, they took it upon themselves to get the kids the things they needed. Sergeant Major Conley asked the families back home to donate backpacks, pens, and pencils. A veritable flood of goodies arrived at Patrol Base Volunteer. For the rest of the year, the men would visit the schools and take backpacks for the children. Inside each one was a standard package of pens, pencils, paper, a T-shirt, and sometimes even shoes. The look on the faces of these young and innocent Iraqis was thanks enough.

When Staff Sergeant Randy Mitts learned he'd be going to Iraq back at Rilea in '03, he envisioned himself an avenging crusader. A fundamentalist Christian, Mitts looked upon the war in Iraq as a battle of religious ideologies. He was anxious to participate and do his part to destroy Islamo-fascism. After 9/11, he despised the Muslim world. Then he arrived in Baghdad. Mitts, a strapping, tall computer programmer and former marine served with the scout platoon. When the scouts moved out of the shower rooms into their permanent barracks, the scouts ended up sharing a building with a platoon of Iraqi soldiers.

When soldiers share a communal living area, they are bound to bond no matter what their nationality. And so it was with the scouts and these Iraqi Joes. The men got to know and respect each other. They played video games and soccer and taught one another English and Arabic. They patrolled the streets of Baghdad and shared their knowledge and experience.

Randy resisted befriending these Iraqis at first. But as he got to know them, he came to respect their commitment. The Iraqi army's pay system was a mess, and frequently these soldiers didn't receive their wages. They showed up every day, strapped on their gear, and patrolled anyway. They believed in what they were doing—believed in democracy. They believed enough to risk their lives to bring a better future to Iraq.

Ayad was one of those soldiers. Full of energy, his natural charisma completely won Randy over. Before the fall of the regime, he'd been a BMP (Soviet mechanized infantry vehicle) driver. Now, Ayad and Randy patrolled side by side outside the wire. They raided houses together, went through doorways together. Randy trusted the Iraqi with his life.

One day, Mitts asked Ayad to clear an alleyway for him. Ayad charged into it and disappeared. When Randy came back to check on him, he found Ayad presiding over fifteen suspected insurgents. He'd captured them all himself, ordered them on their stomachs, and zip-tied them all in a matter of minutes. Randy hadn't even known there were people down there.

Another favorite of the scouts was Corporal Waleed Falah Hassan. Loyal and devoted to his men, Hassan's passion impressed everyone. He took Randy under his wing and taught him Arabic. They shared the same Humvee on many patrols and came to rely on each other as brothers-in-arms.

Then, Mahdi militiamen captured Hassan's brother. They hung him in a traffic circle as a warning to Waleed and the rest of his family. Randy saw him the day after it happened. Waleed had been very close to his brother. His murder had left him in utter despair. Because it took place outside the AO, the Volunteers could do nothing to help. Walleed chose to leave the army and move his family away. He did not want to lose another loved one to the depredations of Al Sadr's brownshirts.

Randy's friendship with Ayad and Waleed opened his heart to the suffering of the Iraqi people. Before he went overseas, he saw terrorism as a Muslim-Christian issue. Now he saw that Americans were not the only ones to suffer from terrorism. Perhaps this wasn't a war of religious ideology after all.

TWENTY-FOUR

THE EDGE OF SADR CITY

Through the spring, while Rusapha remained relatively quiet, fighting raged across the Canal Road (Route Pluto) in Sadr City. Al Sadr's militia carried out daily attacks against American troops sent into the Shia slums to establish order.

To the south, the Shia uprising failed to attract widespread support, yet still succeeded in destabilizing the entire area from Najaf to Basra. The 1st Armored Division and other units fought pitched battles with the Mahdi militia, inflicting heavy casualties on the ill-trained, but fanatically brave, Al Sadr loyalists.

The turning point came in May. Thanks to substantial support from the local Iraqis, the coalition captured or killed many of the Mahdi leaders. As the fighting continued, Al Sadr ran low on martyrs. His gambit to create a national uprising had failed. Hundreds and probably thousands of Iraqis lay dead in its wake.

But Sadr City remained a mess. There at the nexus of the Shia uprising, the militia fought on with ferocious intensity, if little actual skill. In early June, the other Shia militias agreed to disband. Not the Mahdi, however. Al Sadr's fighters launched a new offensive against the Iraqi police (IP) stations in Sadr City. The IP stations had served as a source of ammunition and weapons for the insurgents in the past. Usually, the IPs would not stand and fight; they'd run away and let the Mahdi take whatever they wanted. Occasionally, they actively helped out and provided guns and ammo to the insurgents. This time, Al Sadr's brownshirts were in for a battle.

Captain David Beveridge's Bravo Battery, 3-112 Field Artillery, had just received Sadr City as its new AO. His unit had been in Iraq since February, serving as provisional MPs and renamed Charlie Company, 75th Military Police for the deployment. Their job was to get the IPs trained and functional.

For three days straight, Beveridge's men absorbed the Mahdi attacks as they defended eight of the sixteen police stations in Sadr City. It was a formidable assignment for these 184 New Jersey National Guardsmen.

At the Al Carama Police Station, Beveridge's men fought a furious battle with Mahdi militiamen who attacked them with RPGs and mortars. The station sustained heavy damage, and then was destroyed by militiamen using satchel charges. Fortunately, none of Beveridge's men died in the attacks.

Low on food and water, Captain Beveridge launched his QRF platoon to bring supplies to his men. Three uparmored turtleback Humvees rolled out of the MP base at Camp Cuervo. They turned onto Route Pluto and sped northward for Sadr City. Meanwhile, Beveridge headed south on Pluto with his section, bound for Cuervo.

The QRF force sped past Martyr's Monument, the gigantic reminder of the Iran-Iraq war. The MPs had reached the eastern side of AO Volunteer. They pressed on for Sadr City.

That afternoon, four brothers prepared to earn their pay. Muhamad Hashim Sharif and his siblings Umar, Becka, and Balal had teamed up with family friend, Ahmad Abdul Hassan, to make a quick buck. They had been a poor family living in a slum just north of Sadr City in what the U.S. Army called Zone 22. Earlier that spring, neighbors noticed the Sharifs had suddenly come into money. They brought home new consumer goods they'd never been able to afford. The Sharifs had made a deal. In return for attacking the Americans, a foreign financier would make sure a steady flow of cash reached their pockets. They weren't nationalists. They weren't Sadrists. They weren't even idealists. They were mercenaries in their own country.

The Sharif cell led another team of insurgents, possibly Mahdi militiamen, to the outskirts of Sadr City that day. With professional help, they had acquired and planted three IEDs along a stretch of Route Pluto near a footbridge overpass. On a nearby street in Sadr City, the Sharifs and their cohorts milled around, carrying their RPGs and AK-47s as locals watched them. Three photojournalists joined them. Two of them, Hussein Malla and Karim Kadim, worked as stringers for the Associated Press, an American news corporation. The other one, Cerwaan Aziz, toted a video camera and provided footage for London-based Reuters. They began to photograph and film the scene.

The insurgents took cover less than a hundred meters from two of the IEDs the cell had planted on Route Pluto. Hunkered down among some buildings east of the northbound lanes, they waited to spring their trap. The 3-112 QRF column came into sight. Kadim snapped a photo of it as it approached. The attack would soon be launched.

A sudden flash, a tremendous *boom,* and the New Jersians went down. The shock wave resonated all the way to Patrol Base Volunteer. It shook all of eastern Rusapha. The Sharifs had detonated the first IED.

It was a sophisticated bomb, similar to what the Israelis saw from Lebanese Hezbollah cells. Packed in front of the explosives were hundreds of tiny ball bearings. When the IED went off, it sprayed the ball bearings right into the QRF's lead Humvee. Like super powerful shotgun pellets, they ripped through its vulnerable, unarmored flanks. Disabled, the Humvee coasted to a stop.

The Sharifs and their allies unleashed a torrent of AK-47 fire onto the stationary Humvee. The RPG teams sighted in and let fly with their rockets.

The Humvee took four RPG hits in quick succession. One hit the radiator and the other three struck the right side, blasting through the uparmored doors. The truck commander, Sergeant Frank Carvill, suffered a catastrophic amputation of his leg. A fifty-one-year-old Irish-American, Carvill had survived two brushes with terrorists before Iraq. As a civilian, he had worked in the World Trade Center.

Behind Carvill, Christopher Duffy went down, probably from the initial IED blast. The rig began to burn. To the east, the Sharifs kept up a steady fire even as the remaining two Humvees stopped behind Carvill's. The Americans returned fire. The skirmish raged.

Inside the burning Humvee, driver Specialist Carl Oliver knew he had to get his buddies out. In a feat of both desperation and tremendous courage, Oliver pulled Carvill and Duffy clear. Moments later, the second truck in the column pulled up. The men knew Carvill needed immediate medical attention. They placed him on the hood and sped north for the Al Jazeera police station.

Duffy could not be helped. And now, with only one Humvee running, the New Jersians lacked the firepower to drive off the insurgents. The Guardsmen dismounted and fought back desperately, but they needed help.

TWENTY-FIVE

THE FIRST HEROES

"I have a Humvee burning."

Lieutenant Erik McCrae looked across the highway at the unfolding battle. He and his three Humvees from Delta's Old Man platoon had been patrolling nearby when the blast rattled their rigs. McCrae went to investigate and discovered the MPs were in a jam.

McCrae knew the Americans needed help. He told his men they were going in. He radioed Kerry Boggs and told him to bring his section into the engagement from the north side. He'd take the south.

Boggs and his men had been only a few blocks from Pluto on a mosque-monitoring mission. They jumped into their three rigs and headed for the nearest overpass. Both sections crossed over Pluto simultaneously. Boggs turned into traffic and sped down an exit ramp the wrong way to get into the northbound lanes. Meanwhile, McCrae's men rolled up from behind.

In the trail rig of McCrae's section, Sergeant Bill Thompson could see the MP gunner on the remaining Humvee engaging east into Sadr City. He spotted one other dismounted MP returning fire with his rifle. But as they rolled up, the Oregonians could not see any targets. They held their fire.

North of the engagement site, Boggs also saw the MPs firing. One was shooting across the hood of the undamaged Humvee. He and his men searched for targets, but the footbridge overpass obscured their view of the Sharif brothers' cell.

Lieutenant McCrae's rig rolled to a stop. He dismounted as Bill Thompson climbed out of his rig some fifty meters to the south. Nate Melton covered them from the turret on McCrae's Humvee. McCrae told Thompson to provide security while he went forward to help. Thompson nodded and turned to head back to his truck. McCrae grabbed his two combat lifesavers, Specialist Justin Linden and Justin Eyerly. Together, the three Oregonians ran forward.

They ran across 250 meters of open terrain. Terribly exposed, the three Oregonians ran to the rescue of total strangers. They did so in the middle of an ongoing firefight without any thought for their own safety. They reached the intact MP Humvee, where McCrae found Specialist Timothy Brosnan. Linden and Eyerly, known as the "two Justins," continued on toward Duffy's unmoving body lying next to the flaming Humvee.

Boggs, on the north side of the footbridge, caught sight of two men running for the casualty lying in the road. It looked bad.

Back at the south side of the ambush, Thompson was almost back to his own rig when another MP column drove up. This was Captain Beveridge and his men. Beveridge opened his door and called out, "Sergeant, get with your lieutenant and find out whose burning rig that is."

"Yes, Sir," Thompson replied.

He looked over his shoulder. He could see McCrae about two football fields away. He thought about running to him, but something seemed wrong, somehow off. It gave him a bad feeling. He hesitated, then walked over to to his truck. He'd call McCrae on the radio.

Meanwhile, Brosnan explained the situation to McCrae. The two talked as Captain Beveridge's patrol moved toward them. That's when the Sharif brothers detonated a second IED.

A Humvee-sized fireball unfurled across the Americans. Kerry Boggs saw the two running figures collapse as the blast engulfed them. Then the shock wave hit his section with such power that it shattered windows on every Humvee. A spinning ball bearing struck Kerry's windshield at eye level.

The shock wave reached Thompson and the rest of McCrae's section a split-second later. It knocked some of the men down and twisted Bill Thompson's head to one side with incredible force. As it struck him, Bill caught a glimpse of McCrae at ground zero. He saw his lieutenant stagger, take two steps, and fall.

Oh my God. Erik.

Bill Thompson had joined the Oregon Guard in 1983. His first platoon leader had been Lieutenant Scott McCrae, Erik's father. During the unit's Christmas party that year, Bill had met Erik for the first time. He was six years old. The veteran sergeant had watched the boy grow into a man. He took enormous pride in serving with two generations of McCraes. Now, the boy he knew when Reagan was president needed him.

Thompson and Nate Melton, who had been wounded by the second IED, ran forward. Nearby, Sergeant Carle pulled a litter out from his Humvee and joined them. Together they reached the wounded men. Tim Brosnan lay beside Lieutenant McCrae, his legs peppered with wounds. Bill Thompson reached him. Brosnan waved him off.

"Work on the lieutenant first. He's worse off than I am."

Bill looked at Brosnan's bloody legs and marveled at the man's selflessness. Brosnan repeated himself. Bill turned away and joined Carle and Melton, who had knelt beside their fallen leader.

Erik looked up at Bill and asked about his guys. Were the two Justins okay?

The men went to work on the lieutenant. He asked for water. Carle shook his head. Bad idea. Erik asked for water again. Bill trickled a bit on his lips. The sun beat down on them. It was well over a hundred degrees. Bill and Nate put a cold compress on Erik's face and dabbed water on him to keep him cool. Then Bill saw a hole in McCrae's arm. He and Melton started to bandage it. They worked to get a tourniquet on him while trying to start an IV.

Carle put the litter on the ground and the three soldiers eased their lieutenant onto it. Erik sat up and asked to be cut free from his body armor. Bill didn't think that was a good idea. How many more IEDs were in the area? They cut his webbing and the rest of his gear loose, but left his IBA on in case of further attacks. As they did this, they found a finger-sized hole in the back of his shoulder. It was an exit wound from one of the ball bearings.

Bill flashed to a scene back in the States a few months before. It was the last time he'd seen Colonel McCrae, Erik's dad. The colonel had taken Bill aside and they had talked. "Bill, take good care of the men. Take good care of my boy."

Bill worked to patch up the wound in Erik's shoulder. Then they eased him on his side. As they turned him, Bill cradled Erik's head.

"Hey, Lieutenant, who's gotcha?"

"You do, Sergeant T."

"Good. You're still with me."

Kerry Boggs looked through his shattered windshield and watched the IED's fireball boil skyward and dissipate. He'd just kicked his dismounts out and they were sweeping for more IEDs on either side of the road when the shock wave struck them.

He ordered everyone into the rigs, and they backed up about fifty meters. Moments later, the remaining MP Humvee limped toward the Oregonians. It drifted alongside and two men tumbled out onto the asphalt. A third lay slumped in the turret.

Three wounded MPs. They needed immediate help. Fortunately, Boggs had a medic with him, plus one of his truck commanders, Chris Harrington, was a paramedic in his civilian life. Josh Harrison was also an EMT. He ordered them to treat the wounded MPs.

Meanwhile, the other dismounts swept the shoulders again. Kerry heard somebody say, "We've got another IED. It's right behind you Sergeant Boggs."

Boggs took a look. A 122mm artillery shell encased in a concrete pipe sat in the grass only a few feet away. Kerry told the trailing two trucks to back up to the nearest overpass and put Josh's brother, Lonnie, in charge of them. As they executed, Kerry got into his truck and repositioned it between the wounded MPs and the IED to afford them some protection.

When he finished, he called over to Lieutenant McCrae's section and asked for a status report. Sergeant Carle answered, "The lieutenant's down. I don't know how bad he is."

Kerry steeled himself, called it into the battalion TOC, and requested ambulances. In minutes, they had arrived and the MPs were loaded aboard.

Scott Hildebrandt came over the radio and told Kerry to move south and link up with 1st Platoon, which he had launched to support them.

That meant driving through the kill zone.

Kerry climbed behind the wheel of his Humvee and threw it in gear. The truck inched forward under the footbridge. Ahead, Carvill's Humvee still burned. Scattered around it were three bodies. Kerry carefully weaved around them and drove to McCrae's rigs on the south side of the kill zone.

It was there he learned that Lieutenant McCrae had just been evacuated by an ambulance and taken to the Green Zone hospital with part of 1st Platoon as escort. When 1st Platoon arrived, the Sharifs had engaged the men again. They medevaced McCrae while under fire.

Specialist Hunt, the medic who had helped treat the three MP casualties near Boggs' rig, asked Kerry if he could go back to the ambush scene. Kerry nodded and then worked to reposition his trucks.

A few minutes later, Hunt returned to hand Kerry two sets of dog tags. Confused, Boggs demanded, "What's this?"

The medic choked out, "Linden and Eyerly."

"What the hell do you mean 'Linden and Eyerly?' "

"They're dead."

Kerry reeled. With a shock it struck him that two of the bodies he'd weaved around had been his men. He hadn't known. He made it to his Humvee and sat down inside; he needed to collect himself.

A breath. Another. Questions shot through his mind in a confluence with pain, shock, and loss. Another breath.

I've got nineteen other guys who need me right now. We'll take care of all this later.

The professional in him returned. Another breath. He was ready. He stood up and went back to work taking care of his men.

TWENTY-SIX

SIXTY YEARS OF
SHATTERED PEACE

Sergeant Major Brunk Conley stood at the threshold of the battalion aid station and braced himself. Nate Melton was inside undergoing treatment for shrapnel wounds to his neck. Brunk knew his duty. He had to go inside and be with his soldier.

In April, a patrol from the battalion mortar platoon had hit an IED. A soldier named Private First Class Charles Feldman had taken a sliver of shrapnel to the hand. The wound resulted in a loss of one of his fingers, and Feldman became the second Volunteer to be evacuated home. While he was at the aid station, Brunk and Sergeant Major Di Giustino had gone to see him. Di Giustino went through the door. Brunk had not. He couldn't do it and couldn't figure out why. Later, that ate at him. He realized if he were to do his job right, he needed to get over whatever it was that had held him back that day.

On June 4, he paused in the doorway for only an instant. He pressed on and went inside. Melton was in good hands and would be returned to duty. Brunk stood and talked with his soldier while the medics finished up with him.

The field ambulance arrived with the two Justins inside on stretchers. Brunk said good-bye to Melton and went outside to meet the ambulance. With Specialist Joe Fleischman, Brunk carried the body bags to the morgue.

Brunk had to do it; he felt it was his duty. And in the process, that moment became a turning point in his life. Every step of the way was sheer anguish. By the time they finished, the task had torn him up so badly he needed a moment alone.

He found some privacy. His men needed to see a stalwart sergeant major, not one who'd lost his composure. He had to set the example and maintain it. He wrapped his steel will around his emotions and squeezed tight. In control again, he went to be with his men.

Lieutenant Colonel Hendrickson had been out with the scout platoon when the ambush took place. He and the scouts had pulled security north of Kerry Boggs on both sides of Pluto. While there, the MP Humvee that had gone into the Al Jazeera police station came through their blocking position. Frank Carvill was dead. The grief-stricken MPs paused briefly while the BC talked to them, then vanished into the city bound for Camp Cuervo.

As they returned to Volunteer, the BC kept a firm clamp on his emotions. Self-discipline and self-control had been the hallmarks of his career. Under it, he seethed with rage and pain. They'd killed two of his men.

He went to see them. Alone in the morgue, the BC stood beside them, these first Oregon Guardsmen to be killed in action since the Philippines campaign fifty-nine years before. His iron composure cracked.

"I'm sorry. I'm sorry I couldn't bring you home."

He said a few final words. A silent moment followed. And then he said good-bye.

He left the morgue. Few of the Volunteers even knew he'd been there.

In the D Company motorpool area, Scott Hildebrandt broke the news to his 3rd Platoon. Sergeant Brian Zacher's men had been particularly close to them. They stood together in small groups, consoling each other.

The BC walked in. Scott looked up and saw Hendrickson in tears.

"Scott, Erik didn't make it. He died on the operating table."

In their fight to save him, the doctors had given Lieutenant McCrae forty-two pints of blood. The news crushed Scott. The two officers embraced and wept unashamed. They grieved together, two proud warriors struggling to understand why such fine men had to die.

There are no words for moments such as these. *Grief?* Doesn't even come close. *Despair? Helplessness? Rage.* Fury at a people they'd come so far to help, only to be shot at by them. All of these things and more weaved together, formed an interlaced emotion nobody has invented a term for yet.

Word of Erik McCrae's death spread through the battalion and devastated the officers and men. It was a body blow to the unit's soul. Losing Linden and Eyerley was terrible enough, but McCrae was supposed to live. They'd gotten him out in an ambulance. He'd been talking to them to the last, coherent and resolutely more concerned with his men than himself. His death pushed the Volunteers to the far end of despondent.

That night, they sought solace among friends. The BC sat with Brunk Conley in his office. The two senior leaders had few people to turn to in such a moment. Command is always a lonely responsibility, especially at times like these.

Brunk thought he was perhaps the only man who could see the BC's true emotions. He had come to trust Lieutenant Colonel Hendrickson long ago. They'd shared an outstanding professional relationship, but now, in this moment, Brunk felt a bond grow between them on another level. It was a human one, and intensely personal.

Warriors are trained to be bulletproof. They are trained to stifle emotion and act. Within infantry platoons, emotion is seen as weakness. The men try to hide it, deny it. They expose themselves only with great care and to a select few they come to trust. Sometimes it is their wives. On nights like this one, it is one another.

Brunk came to love the BC that night. Respect, pride, devotion, they formed the bedrock of that connection. And with Brunk, it took root when he realized why the day had left the BC so brokenhearted. Lieutenant Colonel Hendrickson didn't care what people thought of him. He didn't care for accolades or promotions.

He had only one goal for this deployment: take them all home to their families. Four brothers and their cohorts had robbed him of that, and the consequences would linger in Oregon for decades to come.

Later, alone, the BC picked up the telephone and dialed the phone—to Oregon. One by one, he called the families. It was the most difficult thing he ever had to do.

As he finished, Sergeant Bruns happened to walk by his office. She looked in on the BC and saw him lost in thought, eyes red. He looked desperately lonely at that moment, and Rebekah-mae felt a rush of sympathy for him. She wanted to offer words of solace, but there were none. She moved silently through her office and into the corridor, the BC behind her consumed by grief.

From that point on, Rebekah-mae would always defend the BC to his critics. She'd seen beneath the façade and knew he was not just a fine officer, but a fine human being. That's what it took to be a leader in Baghdad.

The officers gathered in Major Tanguy's office, where they abandoned military convention for the evening. Captain Welch came in. Scott Hildebrandt followed. Without enough chairs, they sat on the floor, leaned against the walls, or perched atop the furniture. As it got dark, they kept the lights off. They talked about Erik McCrae, his family and his dad. The BC came in briefly to check on his officers. He leaned against the wall near the door and shared a few words. Major Warrington realized that in a way, this tragedy had brought them together like nothing else had. Their shared grief became the first key experience that would weld them together.

While the officers talked, Kerry Boggs stayed with his men over at Delta's mini-FOB. At one point, he walked past Justin Eyerly's room, where he found Nate Melton in the darkness sitting on Justin's bed. Gently, he led him from his friend's room. Nate would not be alone that night anymore. In fact, Kerry decided that the only way to get through this ordeal was as a platoon. For the next two weeks, he made sure they did everything together. Nobody would be alone. They'd buddy up or sortie as one group. Their grief would be shared. It would bind them together as nothing else could.

But late at night, alone in their racks, the mind played havoc with a soldier's soul.

The next evening, Captain Welch sat down to write his wife, Gina. Writing had long since become a key outlet in Wyatt's life. At sixteen, he had left home to live with his grandmother. A lack of supervision there gave him plenty of opportunities to get into trouble. But he bucked the odds and avoided the teenage traps of drugs and alcohol. He steered through the worst of it with plenty of help from the two pillars of his life: his faith and his writing. His faith gave him hope for the future, guidance during the rough times, and comfort in the face of grief. In his most emotional moments, he wrote poetry and at times had considered a life as an Episcopal priest.

Welch's two earliest memories directed where his life would ultimately go. The first was a fragment of a day spent in his backyard low-crawling with his dad's assault pack slung on his back. The other snippet was of a Sunday morning when he climbed into the pulpit at his home church back in Mississippi. Both memories gave him comfort and direction. When time came to choose the life of a soldier or the life of a priest, he took the former. He became a warrior with a heart.

On June 5, he sat at his desk and wrote:

Gina,

This letter is going to be a somber one. I told you already that three guys from Delta Co. were killed yesterday. . . . Two of the guys killed were recently married. Lt. McCrae just got married while we were at Polk. Gina, this guy was one of the good ones! He loved getting out there with his guys and doing the do. I feel terrible for his family and wife. His death is a terrible loss to the unit and his family.

This morning I talked to CPT Scott Hildebrandt and as I told him this my voice cracked and it was tough to get out, "I'd like to extend Charlie Co's deepest sympathy to D Co." He put out his hand as if to shake mine, or I mistook it for that and it turned into a hug. At that time I was on my way out of the wire for a recon of some additional areas I pick up tomorrow. He gave me, and I him, a "half man hug" if you can imagine what that looks like, and he said, "get outta here, be safe. I'll see you when you get back." I think from this the company commanders are getting a bit closer. This is a good thing.

This event has given me pause, and forced me into the position of telling you something that is extremely important to me. I don't like writing this any more than you reading it. I want you to SWEAR to me should I not make it back to your loving arms you'll LIVE your life, continue it as you should, raise our son to be a good man. I don't want you to shut yourself out from the world, SWEAR to me you'll live on. I'll love you always and as soon as I get a chance I'll be right there with you, always. Well I need to get in the rack, I love you Ladybugg!

Faithfully,
Wyatt

TWENTY-SEVEN

TOBY KEITH INTERLUDE

The day Erik McCrae, Justin Linden, and Justin Eyerly died, Toby Keith and Ted Nugent arrived at Taji to perform for the troops. After hearing the news from Baghdad, Vinni Jacques decided his men needed a diversion. Losing three men from the battalion had hit everyone in Bravo Company. Vinni, ever vigilant of morale in his platoon, bent some rules to get his men a bit of R & R.

But as they arrived to see the show, they looked in dismay at the line to get into the concert. Vinni and his platoon stood behind hundreds of POGs (personnel other than grunts), REMFs (rear echelon motherfuckers), and FOBbits (FOB bitches). These were all very unfriendly names for the men and women who remained inside the wire full-time as part of the logistical tail supporting the combat units. Somehow, the guys who'd been fighting the war had been left out of this event, a fact that angered 3rd Platoon.

Vinni refused to give up. He talked to a couple of people, and the next thing 3rd Platoon knew, they were ushered inside. The concert turned out to be an absolute blast, and the support Ted Nugent and Toby Keith showed for the troops was a much needed sign that they had not been forgotten back home.

Afterward, Vinni and some of 3rd Platoon talked their way backstage and met both Keith and Nugent. Vinni shook Toby Keith's hand and told him how appreciative he was that this country star had come so far to perform for them. Then he mentioned how much his guys needed this. "Our battalion lost three men today." Keith appeared genuinely saddened by the news.

Not long afterward, Keith, Nugent, and their bands flew back down to Baghdad to catch a flight to Kuwait. As they climbed aboard their C-130, Keith saw a flag-draped coffin sitting in the cargo bay.

It was Erik McCrae on his way home.

They sat nearby the young lieutenant for an hour and a half and hardly said a word to each other. Keith later recalled in an interview with *Country Music Weekly*, "It was a great honor for me to be with him on that plane. I will never forget that."

Keith never did. Upon returning to the United States, he contacted Colonel McCrae and told him of his experience. The two men formed a unique bond and still remain in touch. In January 2006, Toby Keith came to Oregon and performed at the Rose Garden Arena in Portland. Much of 3rd Platoon was in attendance again, as was Colonel McCrae and his family.

Toby Keith dedicated the night to Erik McCrae.

Twenty-Eight

JUSTICE: SWIFT AND RIGHTEOUS

The moment the Sharif brothers detonated the IED on Captain Beveridge's men, the clock ticked down their demise.

Barely had the smoke cleared when 2-162's Human Intelligence team descended on the neighborhood to gather leads. They noticed that most of the windows had been covered or taped over to protect those inside from flying glass. The neighborhood had been warned in advance of the attack. They picked up a couple of clues. One witness told them some of the insurgents had escaped on a red scooter. It was a thin lead, but thanks to Staff Sergeant Rebekah-mae Bruns, an important one.

Bruns happened to be at Volunteer when the Old Man platoon returned from Pluto. As they came in, somebody told her they'd seen reporters taking photos of them. She hurried to a computer and discovered the photos that Hussein Malla and Karim Kadim had taken were already posted on the Associated Press website. She also found screen captures from Cerwaan Aziz's footage. She showed them to Major Warrington. Warrington studied the photos and asked Rebekah-mae to put together a full report.

Bruns threw herself into the work. She downloaded all the photos and screen grabs of the attack she could find. She built a file of photographs that Malla and Kadim had taken in recent months and discovered a pattern. These two men had access to sensitive areas of the Green Zone. One of them had photographed senior American generals, including Lieutenant General Kemmit. Malla had photographed Secretary of State Colin Powell only a few weeks before when Powell visited Jordan.

They'd also spent a lot of time embedded with the Mahdi militia. This troubled Bruns. As a journalist herself, she knew that reporters were under siege in Baghdad. The Western journalists lived in the hotels the 2-162 guarded down on the riverfront. The insurgents frequently attacked them with rockets, mortars, and small-arms fire. Journalists, Western and Arab, moving on the streets had long since become targets for assassination or kidnapping.

Why did the Mahdi militia give these three stringers access to their operations?

Bruns wrote up her report and passed it to Warrington. Lieutenant Gilman, the intelligence officer, and the HUMINT (human intelligence) team studied the photos and found several clues. For one thing, few of the men in them had bothered to hide their faces. They just needed to ID them. And, in one of the photos, the scooter the informant in Sadr City had mentioned could be seen.

Gilman and the HUMINT team went to work. Through informants they learned of the Sharif brothers. A highly educated Iraqi operative volunteered to find the brothers' house in Zone 22. It was a dangerous assignment. If he got caught, the insurgents would surely kill him.

The Volunteers gave him a GPS locator and a set of night vision goggles. As he drove up to Zone 22, he hit an Iraqi police (IP) checkpoint. They searched his car, discovered the equipment, and concluded they'd just found an insurgent. They beat him raw and called the 2-162 TOC. The intel team had to go get him. At least the IPs were doing their job.

Despite his bruises, the operative sortied out again. This time, he located the house. From his car, he watched the brothers come and go. At one point, the Iraqi patriot took an extraordinary risk: he walked to the Sharif brothers' front gate, pulled out his GPS system, and got an exact position for the Volunteers.

In the darkness, the Oregonians rolled for justice. They reached Zone 22, found the correct street, and sealed it off. A Bradley rolled over the front gate of the target house, and Staff Sergeant Randy Mitts' squad burst into the yard with Tyson Bumgardner in the lead. They placed a quarter-pound C-4 charge on the door, wired it, and pulled back. Seconds later, it exploded. When the smoke cleared, the door looked as if it hadn't been touched. Their demolition expert, an EOD team member from outside 2-162, rushed forward and this time put a half-pound charge on it. That did the trick. The next thing the scouts knew, the door sailed over their head and clattered to the road behind them. The entire front of the house had been blown out.

Tyson led the way inside, crunching over broken glass that now littered the area. They established a foothold and found a family sound asleep inside. They'd slept through the arrival of the Bradleys and Humvees and two attempts to blow their door off. The scouts couldn't believe it. They woke the family up and moved them outside. To keep one of the little girls from cutting herself on the glass, Sergeant Paul carried her gingerly to the street. Randy Mitts carried another little girl to the street as well.

Meanwhile, Tyson led a team upstairs and onto the roof. As they came up, two men on a rooftop to the north opened fire on them with AK-47s. Tyson saw them through his night vision goggles and brought his M4 to bear. He lased them with his PEQ-42 and pulled the trigger. Both men ducked and scampered away into the darkness. Simultaneously, a burst of gunfire erupted behind Tyson. Specialist Trevor Ward, one of the scouts, was down at a blocking position when an Iraqi opened a window and unloaded an AK at him. He took cover behind a wall just as some of the Iraqi soldiers showed up and returned fire. For several heart-pumping minutes, Ward found himself trapped between warring Iraqis rocking and rolling on their AK-47s.

The scouts discovered they had hit the wrong house. This was not the Sharif family at all. In fact, the house they'd just partially demolished belonged to an

Iraqi soldier and his family. Later, Major Williams and a civil affairs team would compensate the family and repair the damage. But that was for later. Right now, the Sharifs' house needed to be found.

Randy and the rest of his squad moved to the roof, where Tyson was still shooting into the night. Randy climbed over a low wall to the next house over. Wrong house, and remarkably that family, too, was still asleep.

The fire slackened and stopped. The scouts moved over one more house and again entered from the roof. Jackpot. They found the Sharifs, incredibly, still asleep. In minutes, the brothers lay face down, zip-cuffed and caught red-handed. The scooter sat nearby. Andy Hellman climbed onto it and someone clicked a photo of the moment. A subsequent search of the house revealed IED-making equipment and weapons. The scouts also found a completed IED in the trunk of a car in the front yard. The Sharif brothers were toast. Abu Ghraib would be their next stop.

The scouts prodded the four murderers into the street. Behind them, the wives and children of this family sobbed. One woman cried to Lieutenant Boyce, "What am I going to do? What am I going to do?"

The Americans had little sympathy. The Sharif brothers looked like Luddite, hard-core killers. They glowered at their captors. Boyce thought they wanted to spit at his scouts. Tyson and his team came down to guard them. As he stood regarding the captives, Tyson noticed one steadily gazing at him with a look that bordered on vicious. Hate burned in his eyes. These guys may have been merce-naries, they may have been killing for spending money, but they also despised Americans.

The scouts loaded the killers into a vehicle. Randy Mitts climbed into his rig. The mission had been a tremendous success, despite the initial mistakes. They had the men responsible for June 4; they would lay no more IEDs.

Yet, the last thing Randy saw as the Volunteers packed up and left was a lit-tle boy. He belonged to one of the Sharifs, and he stood stoically in the street watching the scouts take his father away. Then, he turned and walked back into the house. No tears, no panic. He just went inside to face a life without his dad. That image was burned into Randy's memory, and as the Volunteers drove away that night, he kept thinking, *Well, there's our future terrorist right there.*

TWENTY-NINE

THE IMAGES AT HOME

Thanks to Cerwaan Aziz, all of Oregon saw the deaths of Linden, Eyerly, McCrae, and Duffy on the evening news. Only minutes after the firefight on Route Pluto ended, Aziz and his two photojournalist colleagues, Karim Kadim and Hussein Malla, uploaded their images into the Reuters and Associated Press news chain. The images were sent throughout the world. They ended up in dozens of papers, foreign and American. Some would be recycled and appeared again long after the event. One photo showing Linden, Eyerly, and Duffy dead on the ground showed up a year later in the *Philadelphia Enquirer*. Some are still on Al Jazeera's website.

In the immediate aftermath of the attack, the local TV news in Oregon aired clips of Aziz's footage. In homes all over the state, jaws dropped in horror. Families of 2-162 glimpsed the chaos their men experienced that day. Rhonda Jacques sat through it, and at the end Aziz had filmed a crowd celebrating the ambush. She exploded with rage.

How dare they! How dare they do this when we are trying to help them, to make their lives better.

Vinni called later that night. Rhonda was all tears and steel. "Vinni, I am so angry. I am so *angry*. You and your men are risking your lives and these people are trying to kill you." She paused, then managed, "I saw them cheering."

Vinni remained silent. He hadn't known that. Fury boiled in him.

Rhonda's voice grew strong. Never one to use profanity, she burst out, "Vinni, you kill every one of those fuckers. Do you hear me? Every one. I don't care. You just come home to me, okay?"

Darcy Woodke, the 2-162 family support coordinator sat with Kerry Boggs' wife, Laura, at Justin Linden's funeral. This had been an extraordinarily traumatic week for everyone. The families of the men killed on June 4 had seen their lives transformed overnight. The grief and loss and pain would never vanish. It would stay with them and mark their lives forever.

In the middle of the funeral service, an officer tapped Darcy and took her aside.

"Darcy, one of the soldiers from Bravo Company has been killed near Taji. We don't know who right now."

The news stunned her. Her husband, Bill, was Captain San Miguel's gunner. He'd been in Bravo longer than any other man in the unit.

And now, it would be her turn to wait. Was Bill alive? Whose family would the

contact team visit next? Tormented, she returned to Justin Linden's funeral. As she sat through it, she wondered if she'd be sitting through her own husband's next.

Later that night, Shane and Brian Ward's mom received a phone call from Alice Tallmadge, a female reporter working for the *Oregonian* newspaper.

"Have you heard from your boys today?" she asked.

Cindy Ward said no.

"Well, did you know an Oregon National Guard soldier from Bravo Company was killed today?"

This fishing expedition infuriated Cindy Ward. She lit into the reporter, who hung up and cold-called another family and tried the same approach. Coming on the heels of the funerals for McCrae, Linden, and Eyerly, she wrought havoc with her duplicity. When word reached Salem of what she was doing, the Oregon Military Department reacted with outrage. Cindy Ward and others later filed formal complaints. But the damage had been done.

Across Bulldog country, the wives, fathers, and mothers prayed that they would not see a uniform at their front door.

THIRTY

THE ONE WHO HAD TO DIE

The early morning hours of June 13, 2004, found Lieutenant Kent's section of 2nd Platoon, Bravo Company, lounging by its vehicles waiting for the word to roll for the Wild West. Eric McKinley sat quietly in the back of Staff Sergeant Sean Davis' cardboard coffin. Normally, the Joes could count on McKinley for some color and a bit of humor. Not today. He was in a funk.

Shane Ward stood nearby, clicking photos of McKinley's rig with a digital camera. Perhaps if somebody saw the battered rig back home, something could be done. After almost three months, Davis' 998 looked ready for a boneyard, not another combat mission. The plywood had begun to bulge. The sandbags were leaking, and only by wrapping towropes around the entire mess were they able to keep the makeshift armored box from coming completely apart.

This seriously pissed Shane Ward off, especially since parked nearby was a beautiful new 1114. That one was off-limits. It belonged to an officer in the 39th Brigade and rarely, if ever, left the base. The 1114s were well regarded by the POGs, as they came equipped with air-conditioning, something the other Humvees did not have. Ward looked over at that 1114 and thought, *Somebody is going to have to die to get those things to us.*

For now, he documented the piece-of-crap cardboard coffin his Joes were forced to use.

Meanwhile, Shane noticed something was up with McKinley. Usually, by this point, he'd have his sleeves rolled up and one side of his boney hat folded up like an Aussie bush hat, as if to dare a sharpshooting officer or NCO to give him grief. Not this morning.

McKinley looked around at the sagging plywood box and said almost to himself, "I'm going to die back here." His buddies tried to buck him up, but Shane noticed a strange look in Eric's eyes. Part resignation, part fear, McKinley looked haunted, like fate was chasing him down and he didn't have the strength to run anymore.

Later that morning, it was time to roll. As they left Camp Cooke, Kent led the way with his Blue Force Tracker–equipped 1114, followed by the two coffins. Shane's turtleback brought up the rear with Spike Olsen in the turret.

The four-vehicle patrol sped north of Camp Cooke, heading for a pair of dirt roads that ran east-west off Route Senators, which followed both sides of a dry canal. The plan was to establish snap checkpoints on both roads right near a suspicious house. Earlier in the day, they'd been briefed that a Syrian arms

dealer used the house as his base of operations. Somehow, he had been able to steal some jet engines, which he was smuggling into Syria in exchange for weapons and ammunition. The checkpoints cloaked the patrol's true purpose: scoping out the Syrian's hideout.

When 2nd Platoon reached the area, they saw the plan would not work. The house lay concealed inside a palm grove and little useful intelligence could be gathered from the dirt roads. As a result, Lieutenant Kent went looking for another vantage point that might give the door-kickers some decent intel.

They drove around the neighborhood for a while. As they came back up on Route Senators, Shane Ward heard Lieutenant Kent's voice come over the radio, "I have one of the MP's Humvees on the Blue Force Tracker."

Not long before this patrol, Bravo Company had been briefed that several 1114s had been stolen from an MP unit in Baghdad. The men were told to be on the lookout for these Humvees. The same information had been passed throughout the area; Lieutenant Ditto received the news while operating as the 2-162's battle captain in the TOC at Volunteer. He had briefed the BC on the subject. Exactly how the vehicles were stolen, and by whom, remained a mystery to the Oregonians. But the fact was they had gone missing along with at least one Blue Force Tracker, the most sensitive item inside a Humvee.

And now a section from 2d Platoon, Bravo, had just stumbled across at least the missing BFT, if not one of the MP rigs. Every American vehicle has a transponder attached to it so that it will appear on the Blue Force Tracker computer screen. The vehicle has a unit ID number attached to it that can be seen on the BFT's screen. Lieutenant Kent had seen the ID number for the stolen MP Humvees pop up on his screen.

"Either it is one of the stolen vehicles, or I've got a computer glitch." Kent told his men. They assumed it wasn't a glitch. Kent turned the column around about two hundred meters south of an asphalt and cement factory that was set back from the east side of the road. They sped north to investigate.

It was a trap. An insurgent cell had flicked on the captured BFT to draw Kent's patrol into a carefully prepared ambush. At the same time, the Blue Force Tracker gave them unbelievable real-time battlefield intelligence. They knew exactly where every American wheeled vehicle was in Iraq at any given moment just by scrolling around on the BFT's screen.

Up ahead, Shane Ward could see open terrain on the left. To the right, he could see another open field, broken by a berm that ran parallel to the cement factory.

Lieutenant Kent came over the radio, "Okay, it should be right around here."

Everyone became extra vigilant, searching either side of the road.

"I think I see something over to the right," called Sean Davis. McKinley trained his M240 over toward the factory.

"Okay, let's check it out," Ward replied.

Kent and Matt McCreary's Humvee slowed down as Davis turned off on a side road that skirted the south side of the factory. Shane's rig followed. Together, they drove past the berm, a small pond, and a few shacks until they reached a parking lot. Eric and Spike both spotted a number of Iraqis looking out of windows along the factory's main building. More sullenness. More subdued hostility. Spike began to get a bad feeling.

They reached an area filthy with tar slicks and other industrial waste. The rigs turned around. They came up alongside each other and Spike called out to Eric. "See anything?"

Eric replied, "No. But those guys didn't look friendly."

"Yeah, I kinda got a bad vibe from them. Hey, watch out for the tar!"

And then they were past each other, falling into trail formation again.

Inside McKinley's cardboard coffin, Matt Zedwick drove carefully around the tar slicks as he made for the MSR. Kent and Matt McCreary's Humvees waited for them on the main road. Zedwick hit the MSR, turned, and started to catch up to the rest of the column. Nearby, on the right shoulder sat a Toyota 4Runner, white with orange doors and fenders. Its hood was up, but nobody was around. Apparently, it had broken down right alongside a drainage ditch that ran along the road. A concrete culvert stuck out of the east side of the ditch not far from the Toyota.

Kent drove around it. So did McCreary. But something didn't feel right. Kent keyed his mic and radioed back to Staff Sergeant Davis, "Go wide around that vehicle."

Matt started to turn the wheel. That's when a massive explosion vaporized the Toyota. The blast wave spun Davis' Humvee 180 degrees. It swung to a stop on the shoulder facing south.

Smoke filled the cab. Zedwick looked over at Davis. He was slumped over. Dead? Unconscious? He couldn't tell. Suddenly, a bullet pinged off his door. He looked out his side window and saw flames licking the glass from the outside.

Oh my God. We're on fire.

To the rear, Shane Ward's turtleback had just hit pavement again when Sean Davis's coffin vanished in a boiling mix of smoke, flames, and dirt. Spike happened to be looking right at it and saw the 4Runner explode, leaving only its rear axle behind.

An instant later, the concussion wave slammed into Spike and bent him over backward in the turret. It pinned him in place as the sound of a thousand freight trains thundered past. The sheer, raw power of the explosion, the inundation of every sense, left him utterly overwhelmed.

Spike fell forward across his gun. As he sat back up, he glimpsed Davis' 998. It looked like a shoebox somebody had crushed. Then the swirling smoke and dust obscured it from view. Shane's driver, John Michael, hit the brakes. Hardly had the rig stopped when they all heard the bark of AK-47s. Spike recovered with remarkable speed. He sat up, trained his gun to the east, and pulled the trigger. His M240 stitched the berm and tore apart one of the shacks sitting beside the pond.

"Contact right side!" he shouted.

Shane returned fire from the right seat of the Humvee, getting off five shots before his M4 jammed. The AK fire continued. The insurgents concentrated on Davis' ruined vehicle.

Shane flung open his door, unjammed his weapon, and ran around the back of his Humvee, ducking as he went just to make sure Spike didn't take his head off by accident with a burst from the M240. At the same time, Shad Thomas jumped out of the rear left side of the turtleback and threw four boxes of ammo up onto the roof for Spike's M240. Then he shouldered his M4 and came out fighting. He swung to the right, laid his M4 over the hood, and opened up.

Shane turned past the Humvee's left rear fender and shouted, "Where's the CLSB [Combat Lifesaver Bag]?"

"In back," yelled Thomas as John Michael jumped out of the driver's side to add his M4 to the fusillade.

Shane reached inside the Humvee and found the glorified first aid kit.

"Shad, vehicle's in your control." Thomas nodded to him, then Shane dashed forward, his only thought to help Davis and his men. Inside the burning Humvee, Davis regained consciousness. Z heard him mumble a few words and knew he was alive. Then he passed out again. Matt could feel the heat of the fire on his back now. Bullets still clanged off his door. He could either sit inside and burn to death, or chance the insurgent AKs.

"Eric? Eric, are you okay?"

Z's call elicited no response. Matt figured he'd been knocked unconscious as well. He yelled for McKinley one more time. No response.

I've got to get out of this thing.

He swung the door open and sprang from the Humvee. He emerged on the engaged side of the vehicle, bullets cracking past him, flames singeing his uniform. He ran for McKinley. The blast had blown the plywood box to pieces. An entire section was gone, disintegrated by the blast.

Eric McKinley lay draped over the splintered wreckage, hanging half in and half out of the remains of the box. Matt, who had served with Eric for six years, knew his friend was dead.

Stricken by the sight, Z stopped short for a split-second as his mind brushed against the enormity of the moment. Then he thought of Sean still inside, still alive, and he knew he had to act. He ran around to the other side of the vehicle and yanked open the door. Sean, a towering NCO, still lingered in the twilight of consciousness. Zedwick was a shorter man, wiry and strong. Pulling Davis out of the rig took tremendous effort, but he got him out and laid him to the asphalt with the door open to provide them cover.

He looked around as he shielded Davis' body with his own. Through the smoke and dust, he could see Shane beating feet his way, running across a terribly exposed stretch of road to get to him. At the same time, Lieutenant Kent and Matt McCreary's rigs had turned around and had come back for him. Kent's 1114 rolled to a stop about fifteen meters away. The lieutenant jumped out and, using his door for cover, returned fire with his M4. Patrick Eldred, one of Major Warrington's forward observers, hopped out of the back of Kent's rig and started for

Matt and Sean Davis, a combat lifesaver bag (CLSB) in hand. Help was coming.

To cover all the men exposed on the road, Spike lit up the berm with short, disciplined bursts from his M240. He reloaded and went back to work, strafing the area furiously.

To Shane, everything seemed to happen in slow motion. He ran as if in a nightmare: legs pumping but his destination remained distant, somehow unreachable. And then, something swept him into the air and flung him across the road.

Spike glanced up just as a second IED hidden in the concrete culvert blew up. Built from a 155mm artillery shell, the EOD team later told them it had a kill radius of one hundred meters. Shane was running less than ten meters from the culvert when it went off.

Once again, the blast freight-trained into Spike and slammed him against the back of the turret. Shrapnel scythed through the air, striking Shane's Humvee with dull, metallic thuds. One jagged piece penetrated the windshield to strike the inside of the turret ring. It ricocheted through Spike's M4 before embedding itself in his left arm. Shrapnel thunked into Davis' burning rig as well. Some of it struck the open passenger-side door. Matt used his body to shield Sean from the worst of it. A sharp pain in his left arm made him glance down. Right under his watch band sizzled a sliver of shrapnel. It burned his flesh. Zedwick plucked it out and tossed it aside.

Just to the north of Davis and Zedwick, Lieutenant Kent took the brunt of the shock wave. It knocked him into the doorframe and he fell to the ground, his eardrums damaged by the enormous roar of the explosion. But he picked himself up, leveled his M4, and went back to laying suppressive fire.

An insurgent broke cover near the pond. Spike spotted him as he fled toward the factory. The Oregonian brought his M240 to bear and squeezed off a twenty-round burst. The terrorist went down.

Two more men emerged from the weeds, but Matt McCreary's gunner laced both of them. He sawed one practically in half with a long, furious burst. Later, some morbid soul counted more than seventy-two bullet wounds in the two halves of the insurgent's corpse.

Spike eased up on the trigger after he saw his target drop. He looked north and saw Shane lying in one of the southbound lanes flat on his back. He wasn't moving.

Come on Shane. Get up.

The fickle wind blew the smoke clear of Davis' burning Humvee. Spike's eyes flicked up. He saw McKinley. With dawning horror he realized Eric didn't have a head.

Eldred reached Davis. Together, he and Z dragged Sean over to Kent's 1114. As they did, Caulkins sprinted forward to help Shane, who had regained consciousness and was kicking his legs like an overturned beetle. Dazed and weak, Shane tried to get up, but fell back onto the asphalt. As bullets streaked overhead, he stared up at a crystal blue sky.

This is it. I'm done. I'm going to die.

As Shane lay on the road, Zedwick ran back to his burning Humvee. He grabbed the radio and as many weapons as he could and returned to Kent's rig. Then he turned back for McKinley. He needed to get McKinley out before the flames reached him.

Right then, Z heard an explosion. Off to the right, near the side road leading to the concrete factory, a plume of dirt and smoke erupted. Another one followed. They were being mortared.

Zedwick ignored the new explosions and reached his Humvee again. He tried to get to McKinley, but the flames touched off the ammunition in the back. He heard a dull *whump* as an M203 grenade detonated. Then another. A white phosphorous grenade exploded. Z made a final effort to get to his friend, but the fire proved too intense. He retreated back to Kent's 1114 as additional explosions consumed his Humvee.

Kneeling next to Sean Davis, Matt checked on his squad leader. Sean's arm had obviously been fractured. Together, Z and Eldred put it in a sling.

"How bad, Z?" groaned Sean.

"You're fine, man. Doing good."

"Leg's hurt."

Z cut his pantleg off. He could see burns and bruise marks. The blast had fractured it in two places, though Z had no way of knowing that. Another grenade exploded inside the 998.

A few meters away, the muffled thuds of the grenades were lost to Shane Ward, whose hearing had yet to return. As he tried to shake off the haze clouding his head, he realized that perhaps he wasn't going to die after all. He kicked his legs and discovered he could move.

"Shit, I'm hit. I'm hit," Ward called. He tried to get up, but they were still under small-arms fire. Dimly, he realized that and flopped back down onto the pavement.

Caulkins reached him, pulled him to his feet, and half-supported, half-carried him back to Kent's Humvee. At first, Ward thought he had gotten lucky. The blast had knocked him out and had made him groggy. He could hardly move his right arm. His back hurt, but he didn't seem to be bleeding much, so he told Eldred to work on Sean's injured leg.

As he waited his turn, Shane got on his knees behind Lieutenant Kent's Humvee next to Sean. Sean looked dazed and was clearly in considerable pain. Zedwick appeared in front of him. He put one hand behind Shane's head and the two soldiers touched foreheads.

"Eric's gone, man—he's gone."

"I know, man—I know. It'll be okay."

But Shane knew it would be a long time before they were all okay after this. And at that moment, the same thought must have hit Z as well. Brutal, raw anguish writhed across his face. And then, it was gone, replaced by the soldier's stoic façade. Z went back to work on Sean Davis.

The mortar fire continued. The men got Shane and Sean into the armored Humvee to give them a little better protection in case the insurgents walked their fire into the road. Kent's driver and radio operator, Specialist Jason Winslow, moved the vehicle slowly toward Spike, Michael, and Shad. Kent kept pace on the right fender, still firing over the hood until they stopped a few meters away.

Damn that looks impressive, thought Shane as he saw his Joes fighting back with everything they had.

Winslow called in an evac chopper and the QRF team. Back at Camp Cooke, some four or five miles distant, a Blackhawk dusted off even as Vinni led his 3d Platoon section out beyond the wire. Behind him, Captain San Miguel followed with the HQ section.

Gradually, the firing died away. The Humvee still burned. Ammunition still cooked off, but the engagement was over. As Spike ceased firing, a 2-7 patrol rumbled up the road from the south. It was a platoon from Apache Company, to which 2nd Platoon had recently been attached.

Colonel Rainey was with them in his beat-up 1025. He dismounted and went forward. He'd done everything he could to minimize the chances of this day happening, but now as he stared at the smoke boiling from Davis' Humvee, he knew there was no safe place to put the 998s. The scene reminded him of some of the photos he'd seen from the Pacific War when he was a kid fascinated by military history. Now, he experienced it firsthand and saw the gruesome details the photos could never convey. This would not happen again. Not on his watch. The 998s would stay inside the wire and somehow he'd get all his boys 1114s.

Vinni's platoon arrived. They swung to the right across the field in front of the cement factory, ready for anything. Vinni led two Humvees north to set up security. His other two covered the eastern and southern flanks.

Captain San Miguel showed up and used his HQ section to sweep around the cement factory. Demian dismounted his men and searched the nearby buildings. They found some of the workers huddled in a room, but no sign of any insurgents.

A civilian truck showed up. Coming down a dirt side road that ran along the north side of the cement factory, it made straight for Vinni's Humvee. It looked hostile, and his men wanted blood after what happened to their buddies.

But Vinni told his men to hold their fire. The truck stopped. Inside, the thirty-year-old sergeant found a small boy and his father. They had nothing to do with the ambush and were terrified by the heavily armed Oregonians. Jacques' men searched their truck, then let them go. He had just saved two civilians who happened to be in the wrong place at the wrong time.

Down the road, Lieutenant Kent's RTO got into an argument with the helicopter pilot. The Blackhawk driver, convinced the area was still under fire, announced he wasn't going to land on the road. He wanted to land several hundred meters away in the field to the left. They argued back and forth even as Eldred, Caulkins, and Z worked on both Shane and Sean Davis.

Shane had started to bleed. He mentioned it to Z, who cut off his IBA and blouse. His back exposed now, Z could see the source of the bleeding: Shane had been nearly filleted by shrapnel. A chunk of metal had cut through his IBA's armhole to cleave an eight-inch by five-inch chunk of flesh and muscle off his shoulder blade. The flesh on either side of the wound had curled back. Matt found the shrapnel embedded in the back of Shane's IBA. Eldred and Z worked to staunch the wound as best they could. Shane began to cough up blood. The shrapnel had bruised one of his lungs.

Meanwhile, Specialist Winslow lost patience with the Blackhawk crew. Shane heard him shout, "Land that fucking chopper on the road now!"

The Blackhawk crew split the difference. The bird settled to the ground next to the road about fifty meters from the ambush point. Four men carried Shane in a stretcher to the helo and got him aboard with Sean. In seconds they were airborne, bound for the Green Zone hospital.

Matt watched the Blackhawk disappear over the horizon. The adrenaline drained away. To the north, his Humvee still burned. McKinley was still in the back. The emotions he had earlier suppressed welled up again. He could hardly bear the thought of Eric still inside that rig. None of them could.

Lieutenant Kent walked up to him and asked, "Zedwick, you doing okay, man?"

"Yeah, sir, I'm fine. I'm just shaken up. Feels like my arm's dead, though."

"Shit. Let me check you out."

Kent examined Z's arm and exclaimed, "Zedwick! Why didn't you tell me you were injured?"

That came as a surprise to Z. "I didn't know I was, sir."

His arm had been peppered by shrapnel from the second IED. An ambulance arrived. Spike and Z climbed aboard. As the doors closed, the last thing they saw was the smoke coiling up over the 998. It sent a stab of grief through both of them.

"Matt," Spike managed as they embraced, helmets touching, "Z. Eric, man. Eric."

"I know. I know."

THIRTY-ONE

AFTERMATH

Following the June 13, 2004, ambush, Bravo Company never left Camp Cooke in anything less than an M1114. Colonel Rainey made sure of that. Through the grapevine, the company heard their new battalion commander had taken a stand on their behalf. To the 39th Brigade, he flat-out told the Arkansans he would not send a single patrol outside the wire until he had all the 1114s currently being used as base hacks. In the meantime, he refused to let another 998 outside the wire.

The Bulldogs loved him for it. Rainey fought for them. He understood the significance of McKinley's death—and did something about it. In the process, his actions cemented his relationship with Bravo's Oregonians. He had their best interests at heart, and they would follow him anywhere.

The truth, versus the rumors Bravo had heard, was a little less dramatic. Colonel Rainey had his staff study the allocation of the 1114s. They found that by asking some officers to share rigs and doing a bit of juggling, enough armored Humvees could be shaken loose to equip every patrol. However it all came down, the results were the same: Colonel Rainey got the Oregonians the 1114s they so desperately needed.

As for the insurgents who launched the attack that day, most would not live out the week. The Bulldogs learned that two wounded insurgents escaped the firefight. They were found a day later, dead in their car. Word was they were Saudis, and none of the locals would help them.

The 2-7 S-2 shop also discovered the insurgent cell that had placed the IEDs the night before the attack. A witness came forward and described two cars that had parked in the area.

A few nights later, the same cars returned to almost the exact same spot. Three men jumped out and began digging. About a thousand meters up the road, Captain Glass and his men opened fire and killed two of them. A third was badly wounded. Part of 1st Platoon, Bravo, showed up and Lieutenant Wood brought the insurgent back to the battalion aid station.

The incident highlighted a favorite insurgent TTP. The men laying the IEDs were frequently a different group from the ones who executed the ambushes. First, a team would go dig a hole. Then another group would show up to place the IED. Sometimes, yet another group armed it. Finally, another element would wire it and execute the ambush. It was an extremely compartmentalized operation, centrally controlled but with sections that knew nothing about each other. Far from a bunch of ignorant goat herders, the insurgents around Taji possessed cunning and skill.

Within Bravo Company, the fate of the missing Blue Force Tracker and the MP Humvees remained unknown. Rumors abounded about the 1114s. Some of the men heard the MP rigs had been taken out into the desert and used for target practice by the insurgents, who learned from the exercise where the weak points were in the armor. Others heard the BFT was later discovered in a van down in Baghdad. The insurgents had been using it to track high-value targets and rain indirect fire on them. Both stories were likely myths and untrue. The fate of the vehicles and the Blue Force Tracker became one of many little mysteries to emerge from the deployment.

Back in Oregon, Eric's death delivered a devastating blow to the families of 2-162. Coming on the heels of McCrae, Linden, and Eyerly's deaths, Eric's passing left the Guard in shock.

The contact team paid its terrible visit to Eric McKinley's family, and funeral arrangements were made. Darcy Woodke, Laura Boggs, and Kay Fristad from the public affairs office worked hard to help the family where they could.

Later that week, the Bravo Company family support group met at the Corvallis armory. Mandy Ferguson, Spike's fiancée, attended that night to be with people who shared her pain. Her circle of civilian friends did not understand what she was going through. They couldn't comprehend the daily angst, the spear of dread that hit her every time she heard a radio report about soldiers dying in Iraq. She had tried to avoid the news, but at times that proved impossible. Some of her closest friends regarded her as mopey. One long-time college friend could not figure out why she hadn't gotten over Spike's absence, after all it had been three months.

The strain of it all had started to redefine Mandy's relationships. As a gulf grew between her and some of her longstanding friends, she and Spike's sister came together, bonding through the mutual experience of Spike's service in combat. In this, Mandy's experience differed little from everyone else in 2-162.

The family support meetings helped her, but they did not provide the answer. To be surrounded by people enduring the same things she was made a huge difference. It was a relief to have that, but at the same time most of the families who showed up were older than she was. Most were married, some had children. They had known each other for years. She knew no one. Even in this place, she could not find true solace. She remained an outsider.

The meeting began. The families went around the room and talked about June 13, each one relating what their soldier had told them. The pieces started to fall into place; the information sharing became one of the most vital elements of the meeting. The fear of the unknown was frequently worse than the actual reality.

Sean Davis' wife stood up. Through her tears she told of how Matt Zedwick had saved her husband's life. "If it wasn't for Matt, my husband wouldn't be here."

Ron Clement's dad stood up next. "We've known Matt Zedwick since he was a kid in high school. We think of him as a son. And right now, we could not be prouder of him."

And so it went around the room. When the families finished sharing, the real hard part of the meeting began. A Guardsman spoke for nearly an hour on how the families would be told if their soldier was killed or wounded. He detailed how the contact teams functioned, who would come to their house and who would be assigned to the families. Rhonda Jacques sat with Julie Howell and Kelly Clement. This last discussion pushed her to the edge of emotional overload.

This isn't happening. This isn't my life right now. I'm not supposed to be sitting in a meeting being told how someone will tell me that my husband has died.

She left the armory at the end of the night feeling like a five-hundred-pound weight had been dumped on her shoulders. Julie had first broken the news to her of Eric's death a few days before. Rhonda flashed to a memory of Eric she and Vinni had experienced at a park in Corvallis when Eric came walking up to them with his dogs. As they chatted, Rhonda couldn't get a handle on McKinley. He didn't seem the soldier type. He looked like a punk-rocker, skateboarder. After he left, Vinni said, "That's a really good kid there, Rhonda. A really good kid."

She knew of the Ward brothers, and knew Matt Zedwick. The TV news, the radio, and the newspapers had repeated their names so often by now that Rhonda had felt trapped in a vortex of unreality. These were people she knew. Her life was suddenly front page news. It was painful, disorienting, and almost, but not quite, unbearable.

THIRTY-TWO

SHEIK MAJEID

Major Mike Warrington was an idealist. He saw the world through two sets of lenses: those of a realist and those of a blue sky dreamer. If those seemed mutually incompatible ways of viewing the world, in Mike Warrington they were not. He used both to his advantage to develop a vision of what could be, while understanding how to see that vision realized. It gave him a blend of pragmatism and idealism that was well suited for the three-block war in Baghdad. At times, though, it left him terribly vulnerable.

In Sheik Majeid, Warrington saw much hope. To this native Montanan, Majeid had come to symbolize the relationship the coalition needed to cultivate with the civic leaders in Iraq. If those connections could be forged, Iraq could someday re-take its place on the world stage as a regional leader. It had so much potential in agriculture, oil, and tourism. It could be a great country someday—if the Sheik Majeids out there could be given the reins of power. For now, they needed to protect him and give him the tools to make his community a better place.

This was why Major Warrington was resistant to the 39th Brigade's order to provide a sheik for the upcoming media blitz and mosque opening fest scheduled for June 17 at Taji. For weeks, the brigade's IO (information officer) had pressured Warrington to supply a sheik. He told Warrington that the reconstruction of the Taji mosque had become the 1st Cav's main effort on the civil affairs front. The media was finally on board: Fox News, CNN, the *Washington Post,* and the *New York Times* all had agreed to cover the event. It would be big, and the opening would become a signal moment in OIF II: a gesture of goodwill that would demonstrate that America respected Islam. The 39th needed some sheiks to show the world they were on board with the American effort. And if they were not there? Warrington heard all manner of gloom and doom what-if scenarios come out of that discussion. Privately, he began to call the affair the *Sky Is Falling Mosque Opening.*

An order was an order. He asked Sheik Majeid if he'd be willing to attend the event. Majeid considered it an honor and happily accepted. Warrington had half-hoped he would refuse, as he considered the event a security risk. The 39th Brigade's IO ignored his security concerns.

As it happened, Eric McKinley's memorial took place the morning of the mosque opening. At 0900, Lieutenant Colonel Hendrickson and Warrington met with Majeid and the Rusapha DAC chairman, Doctor Khadam. Together, they drove to Camp Cooke.

Eric McKinley's funeral profoundly affected Sheik Majeid. Afterward, he spoke to Major Warrington about what it meant to be there.

"The sacrifice that Eric McKinley made to set my country free means a great deal to me," he told Mike through their interpreter. "I would like to match that sacrifice, honor it. Anything you want me to do, I will do it."

Majeid's sincerity profoundly moved Major Warrington. In that moment, they shared a bond: the idealist who came to help Iraq and the Iraqi who so wanted that help to become a reality. Despite their differences of religion, language, and culture, they had found common ground. They understood the cost.

That afternoon, they went to the mosque opening. Sheiks from Baghdad sat as guests of honor on the platform through the keynote speeches. Geraldo bounced around for Fox News. Media types swarmed. Afterward, they drove back to Patrol Base Volunteer right as the first mortar attack since November 2003 hit the base. It added something to the poignancy of the day.

Sheik Majeid and Doctor Khadam said farewell to Major Warrington. Mike watched them go and felt an upsurge of hope. The battalion needed to forge more relationships like this one. But Majeid's was unique; it was the test case that proved such connections were possible.

Three days later, Sheik Majeid and Doctor Khadam stopped for breakfast at a local deli. Two assassins came through the front door and in broad daylight murdered Majeid and shot Khadam in the head. The scouts showed up not long after the attack. Lieutenant Boyce went into the deli to investigate. Andy Hellman and a few others pulled security. Andy looked down and saw a bloody tangle of cloth lying in the gutter. It was Sheik Majeid's headdress. Sergeant McDowell recovered it and later brought it back to the battalion TOC.

Mike Warrington walked into the TOC that morning and knew right away something was wrong. When he asked what had happened, somebody told him that Majeid had been murdered. The news hit him like a physical blow. All that hope vested in that one relationship, to have it destroyed by an assassin's bullet sent Mike reeling with grief and guilt. Instinctively, he knew a tipping point had arrived. And when he'd look back, he'd look back on so many lost opportunities.

I shouldn't have done it. I shouldn't have let them put Majeid on stage.

Was Majeid killed because he attended the mosque opening? Probably not. Since 2003, he had been the target of repeated death threats. Late night phone calls, a chilling voice, whispers of murder and violence: these things were part of his life. They were part of the risk he took for his people. In the end, he matched Eric McKinley's sacrifice measure for measure. Majeid saw it as the only honorable path.

And who profited from his death? Nobody. Ultimately, those who lost were his people of Sheik Umar. The assassination of their leader left them paralyzed with grief. His loss left a leadership vacuum that the community never filled. While many good things still came from that initial relationship, and Sheik Umar benefited from the projects 2-162 helped undertake, the lost potential, the element of *what could have been,* haunted Mike Warrington long after Majeid had been put to rest.

It haunted the HUMINT team leader as well. Sergeant Hess sat down shortly after Majeid's death and wrote:

He was the best I had met and he will be missed. The Volunteers of Oregon, those who knew him, were fond of him. But it was his people, the people of Sheik Umar, who dared to hope again who are feeling this the most. And I, who aided in making him important enough to kill, will have to bear this burden until we can engage in our game of chess again. There is a chance that I will have the satisfaction of bringing his assailants to justice. But this will not bring him back.

What Sheik Majeid did for his neighborhood was what every leader hopes to do. In the wake of his death, the work will continue. The progress in Sheik Umar is undeniable, but it came at a horrible cost. That cost is the worst part of a good thing.

In summer 2005, the Volunteers learned the two assassins had finally been brought to justice. It was a victory, but a hollow one. Majeid died. Iraq lost. Nothing could even that score.

There was one glimmer of hope in the tragedy. Somehow, Doctor Khadam survived a 9mm gunshot wound to the back of his head. The locals rushed him to a nearby hospital, where doctors judged him beyond saving. They parked Khadam's bloody body on a gurney and left him to die.

Another Rusapha DAC member happened to find Doctor Khadam lying comatose in a corridor. He pleaded with the hospital staff to help him, but they refused. Desperate, the DAC member called Major Williams and explained the situation. Williams reported it to Lieutenant Colonel Hendrickson, who thought the matter over. When he had first met with the Rusapha DAC, he had said, "We are here to help you, and I will do everything I can to help you and keep you safe."

Now, the time had come to prove he meant those words. He spun up a D Company platoon and sent it out to get Doctor Khadam. Hildebrandt's men took the dying Iraqi to the Green Zone CSH, where neurosurgeons saved his life.

The BC visited Doctor Khadam while he still lingered in a coma. He talked with the neurosurgeons and learned he had suffered brain damage and would need a long convalescence. He wouldn't get that at the CSH, which was designed to stabilize tramautic injuries before sending the patients back to Germany. Doctor Khadam would need a safe place to recover.

The local Iraqi hospitals were out. The assassins would surely find him there and finish the job. Same with his home; besides, his wife and son did not have the skills needed to take care of him.

That left the battalion aid station at Patrol Base Volunteer. It was an unusual option, as the BAS was even less prepared to handle convalescing patients than the CSH. The BC made his decision; Doctor Khadam would recover under the protection of the Volunteers.

At first, the medics protested, but Hendrickson's order stood and a patrol brought Doctor Khadam onto the base. When he first emerged from the coma, Doctor Khadam could not walk and could speak only a few words. His wife and son joined him and lived on the base, nursing him along as best they could. The medics were touched by this, and soon their attitude changed. Here, in the midst of so much violence, they found an opportunity to do a good thing. They cared for Doctor Khadam as if he were one of their own.

He made remarkable progress. He began to walk again with the aid of a cane. His speech returned, and soon he could converse in both Arabic and English. His recovery amazed everyone. Who survives a 9mm shot to the head at point-blank range and can live to hold a conversation again? Not many people; Doctor Khadam became a living miracle.

Late in 2004, he and his family departed Iraq for a hospital in Jordan, where he would undergo long weeks of physical therapy and rehabilitation.

When he left, he personally thanked Lieutenant Colonel Hendrickson for everything he had done for him. The BC could have left him to die, but Hendrickson was a loyal officer who kept his promises. He bent the rules and, in doing so, had saved the life of a good man. *Do the right thing* was not something Lieutenant Colonel Hendrickson urged his men to do without taking it to heart himself.

THIRTY-THREE

TROLLING FOR TERRORISTS

The day after McKinley died, Vinni and the Hell Hounds got hit. They'd been out clearing Route Ram when they discovered an IED under some trash. Vinni called it up and wanted to shoot it with his .50-cal, but the 2-7 TOC told him to sit tight and wait for EOD to come out. There were civilians downrange near another road, and the 2-7 battle captain decided the risk was too great.

Third Platoon sat on that IED for hours. Word came back to them that the EOD team had rolled a Humvee and would be delayed. Six hours later, they showed up with a section of 39th Brigade Engineers providing security for them. They blew up the IED.

By now, every insurgent in the area knew Vinni's platoon had been sitting on Route Ram all afternoon. He knew it and called his NCOs together. They had a dilemma on their hands, and Vinni wanted to be totally straight with his leaders. He told them, "Either way we come out of here, we're probably going to get hit."

They remounted and drove for the MSR. En route, Vinni heard a rumble, and his new 1114 shook violently. Ben Ring, his home-schooled, devout Christian gunner, shouted, "IED! IED!"

Vinni turned to his driver and RTO, Kenny Leisten, and said, "Call it up, Kenny." Then he dismounted and called to his gunner, "Hey Ring, start shooting!"

Ring swung his machine gun out and opened up. Vinni watched him and couldn't stifle a grin. Ring, all of nineteen years old, never swore and never looked at porn even when the men stuck it under his nose. But now Vinni knew the kid had no problems pulling the trigger.

Nearby, John Rosander and Jeffrey Vondross did the same thing, unleashing the "Breathing Dragon" to drive the insurgents away. Meanwhile, Vinni looked back down the column. The IED had hit the EOD team. Their Humvees didn't even have doors. Third Platoon had no commo with them. They were stuck on this narrow stretch of road and couldn't turn around. They could back up, but Vinni decided to go back for them himself. He ran into the kill zone. Behind him, the Hell Hounds dismounted, and Bill Stout, Jeremy Turner, and Staff Sergeant Kevin Devlaeminck covered Vinni with a barrage from their M4s.

Vinni reached the EOD guys, who were shaken but unhurt.

To the driver he shouted, "Can you drive this thing?"

"Yeah, I think so. But we've got two flat tires and I won't be able to go very fast."

"Good, we're gonna get you out of here."

The EOD Humvee limped forward, its antennae shot away, shrapnel scars on its fenders. Vinni ran back to his rig. The column moved forward and reached Route Senators just as some Bradleys showed up, Kiowas overhead in support. Kenny had calmly called everything up to the 2-7 TOC. The cav had reacted with remarkable speed once again.

Minutes later, Captain San Miguel rolled up with a section that included Brian Ward, Matt Zedwick, and Pete Salerno. They'd been down in Baghdad checking on Shane at the CSH. Shane would live, but he had many surgeries and a lot of rough times ahead.

Matt Zedwick dismounted and found Vinni. When Z asked what had happened, Vinni replied, "Holy fucking shit, Z, we just got nailed!"

In the heart of the Sunni Triangle, a lot of American patrols were getting nailed that June, including Lieutenant Dewayne Jones' platoon from Alpha Company, 2-162. Jones had been sent to Taji to work with Commanche 2-7 in the western sector of Jim Rainey's AO. They covered down on the central communication avenues between Taji and Fallujah, the very nexus of the Sunni Triangle.

Compton and Sergeant Phil Disney had linked up with Sergeant Jacques shortly before they started patrolling the countryside. Vinni had passed along some tactical advice and cautioned them. Patrols were finding IEDs every day. He told them to expect to get hit.

First Platoon, Alpha, had been used to the streets of Baghdad. They felt comfortable out there among the people and buildings. Now, they found themselves in a totally different environment among a hostile population. It required different tactics and it would take time to learn the rules of this new game. In the meantime, the insurgents did their best to educate them.

Shortly before midnight on June 23, 2004, Disney led a section home after evening patrol west of Taji. As in Baghdad, they had their headlights on. They didn't know that was a bad idea in the Sunni Triangle.

They turned onto Route Raiders and started to cross a small canal where the dirt road narrowed and went over a culvert. Inside the culvert, an insurgent cell had placed an IED built around three 155mm artillery shells.

It detonated right under the lead Humvee, sending Staff Sergeant Travis Sigfridson's eleven-thousand-pound 1114 spinning skyward. Max Corrigan, Staff Sergeant Bruns' gunner during the Serial Five ambush, had been in the turret manning a .50-cal when the explosion catapulted him into the machine gun face first. The impact broke his jaw, knocked out his front teeth, and fractured his cheek and ocular cavity. Then, as the Humvee hurtled upward, the centrifugal force flung him out of the turret. He plummeted into the crater left by the IED.

In the trail vehicle, Phil Disney saw a white flash that grew so intense it blotted his vision for a moment. Then his Humvee shook as the concussion wave passed through it. A second later, he heard a metallic crash, like somebody had just dumped a car in a junkyard scrap heap.

He turned to his driver, "What the hell was that?"

In front of them, Sergeant Don Neilsen's Humvee suddenly sped up. First platoon had been trained at Hood to blow through the kill zone. That's exactly what Don's driver tried to do. The rig barreled into the smoke cloud and fell right into the IED crater. It ran over Max Corrigan.

Disney called out to Sigfridson's rig, "Commanche 32, this is 33." No answer. He tried again. Still no response. He sent his combat lifesavers forward. Private Caleb Torgerson and Specialist Ken Flick dismounted and ran forward to help. Disney called 2-7 Cav and reported the situation just as his men opened fire in the "Mad Minute."

Disney thought they were taking incoming. He requested the QRF and medevac, then threw his door open and went forward himself.

He ran through the night unsure of what lay ahead. All he knew was his Joes needed help. And then a shape formed in the darkness. He veered toward it and realized with a shock it was Travis Sigfridson, lying face down on the roadside. He wasn't moving.

"Sig! Sig!"

Disney felt like he was running in peanut butter. Time slowed. It took forever to reach his friend. Just as he reached him, Sigfridson moved his arm. A wave of relief washed over Phil as he knelt down and turned Sig over.

"Dis, you gotta get me outta here."

"I'm working on it, Sig. I'm working on it."

"My back. It's screwed up."

Disney checked him over and found no wounds. For the moment, Sig would be okay, though he remained in considerable pain. Phil went to check on Flick and Torgerson. They were nearby, working frantically on Bill Congleton, Sig's driver. Congleton's right ankle was twisted at an impossible angle. A bone stuck out above his boot.

"Sergeant Disney, give me something for the pain," Congleton asked.

"Don't have anything, man, but we're going to get you out of here."

Flick and Torgerson went back to work. Congleton was in good hands.

Disney asked, "Hey, where's Corrigan?"

"Don't know," Flick answered.

Then somebody said, "He's underneath the truck."

Oh my God. He's been crushed.

Disney took a deep breath, taking a moment to compose himself. Phil switched on his Surefire light and swept the beam under the wreckage of Sig's vehicle. No sign of Corrigan.

"Where is Corrigan?" Disney demanded.

Somebody called back, "He's under the truck in the IED hole."

Phil checked under it. No sign of the steady .50-cal gunner. Now he was starting to get really worried. Disney yelled out again, and this time Max's voice replied, "I'm right here, Dis."

Disney looked up and saw Corrigan in the turret of Neilsen's Humvee. The vehicle was tail-up, half-in and half-out of the crater. Corrigan's face was covered in blood. Phil couldn't understand what he was doing in Neilsen's rig.

"What are you thinking? What are you doing up there?"

"Well," Max replied through his broken jaw and ruined teeth, "It was the only thing I could think of to do."

Max Corrigan, a resident of tiny Canyonville Oregon, had been blown up and run over in a matter of seconds. His face smashed, his back broken when the Humvee struck him, he nevertheless crawled out from under it and saw Neilsen's turret was empty. The gunner, Sergeant Mike Blanchard, had suffered whiplash when the 1114 fell into the crater. It knocked him out of the turret so he dismounted and opened up with his M4.

At that point, Max climbed into the rig and laid down suppressive fire. It was the bravest, most selfless thing Disney had ever seen a man do. Dis coaxed him out of the turret and brought him over to Sigfridson. The other men eased Congleton onto a stretcher, which caused him intense pain. Moments later, the QRF arrived just as Disney was moving Congleton to the casualty collection point (CCP).

A lieutenant from the 39th Brigade's QRF showed up and demanded, "Do you have accountability on your sensitive items?"

Disney gaped at the young lieutenant. "What? I'm dealing with my wounded men right now."

"Listen," the lieutenant scolded, "you need to get accountability on your sensitive items."

Disney lost it. "I've got four injured soldiers and three men on the perimeter. What I need from you is to set up a perimeter around us. Then I'm going to get my men medevaced, and then I'll worry about sensitive items."

Disney turned back for his Humvee and the one working radio left in his platoon. He called up the 2-7 TOC and asked where the medevac chopper was. The TOC replied it was twenty minutes out. Not acceptable. Disney grew angry and frustrated, "I need that medevac chopper right now. I've got a litter surgical priority and a possible airway obstruction. They need to be picked up now."

The TOC told Phil they'd send out an M113 ambulance.

"I need air, not an ambulance."

Just then, a Blackhawk arrived. It touched down, and the men took Congleton to the chopper first. The other two wounded men followed. In seconds, the bird dusted off bound for the Green Zone CSH.

Colonel Rainey later visited them at the CSH. Though little was ever said about it, these three Oregonians owed their lives to Colonel Rainey and his stand to get them all 1114s. Had they been in a 998, not a man would have survived such a blast.

Sigfridson suffered four compressed vertebrae in the attack and was sent home. Congleton fought for more than a year to keep his lower leg, but in November 2005 it had to be amputated. Corrigan, face broken and back fractured, was also evacuated home, where he faced a long and difficult recovery. Disney put Corrigan in for a Bronze Star. It was denied.

Later that night, Disney rolled into Taji with the remains of his patrol. The

rest of his platoon greeted him at their pod. When he saw these men he had grown to love, the emotions held in check broke loose. Soldiers are tactile human beings. They touch, they embrace. They do not fear man-to-man contact as homophobic male civilians frequently do. It is not a threat to their manliness. For the soldiers it is a question of comradeship. Disney started to fall, but his men caught him. Hugs, pats on the backs, a few words telling him he did a good job: this was the solace he needed after losing three fine young men. As he looked around at the faces of his fellow Oregonians, he understood what it meant to be part of the blood brotherhood of combat veterans.

Three weeks later, Disney's section got hit again. The IED blast nearly severed Specialist Nicholas Bright's arm. Disney and Specialist Jason Rich managed to stanch the bleeding and stabilize Bright while Lieutenant Jones called in the medevac chopper. When they returned to Taji that night, both Phil and Rich were covered in Bright's blood. As they got out of their Humvee, Bright's brother, Rich Lamphere, stood waiting for them. He took one look at Rich and Disney's uniforms and began to lose control. Disney moved for him. Now it was his turn to be the support. That's how the brotherhood worked.

THIRTY-FOUR

THE KNEE-HIGH SNIPER

One look at Staff Sergeant Kevin Maries and anyone would peg him for a jovial, spectacled accountant. Easy with a grin, cordial to strangers, Kevin Maries looked like everyman's next-door neighbor. He was also a crack shot and cool hand in a crisis.

Before leaving Oregon, the BC had handpicked Maries to lead the battalion sniper section. Kevin had joined the Guard in '85 and had been a sniper since '93. The BC selected the right man; Maries possessed experience, skill, and leadership. At five foot five and a half, he was also one of the shortest men in 2-162. Sergeant Fields, one of the scouts, nicknamed him "Knee-high Sniper." The name stuck.

The battalion sniper section consisted of five two-man teams, which Maries commanded. The section fell under the scout platoon.

During the early weeks of the deployment, things had been pretty quiet for the snipers. About the only excitement they'd seen took place while a team was up on one of the hotels housing the Western press corps. Kevin had authorized the team to test their zeroes by firing their weapons into an abandoned barge in the Tigris River. When the Oregonians opened fire, a passing MP patrol thought they were under attack. The MPs machine-gunned the hotel. A French reporter in one of the rooms overlooking the road nearly got shot before somebody stopped the MPs.

Kevin had just arrived at Volunteer after coming off a shift when the event took place, and the BC really chewed him out over the incident.

Shortly after that, the snipers settled into an overwatch position atop the Ministry of Interior, not far from Patrol Base Volunteer. From this vantage point, they could see much of Rusapha and 2-162's AO.

The MOI building turned out to be a perfect sniper hide. They had an excellent view of all the major routes in the area, including Pluto and Highway Six.

Toward the end of June, two of Maries' snipers noticed a commotion around a building within the Iraqi police academy complex. They heard two gunshots and then, as they watched through their scopes, saw several IPs drag two limp bodies across a courtyard into another building. Neither sniper could tell if the men were dead or just unconscious, but it looked suspiciously like the aftermath of an execution.

The snipers reported the incident. The next day, some American MPs showed up at the compound. Later, Maries learned that there had been a riot at a prisoner holding area, but that nobody was killed. Whatever happened there,

154

the incident served to heighten the sniper section's interest in the IP academy and the nearby MOI complex. Something wasn't right.

Later that week, the IPs raided a Baghdad neighborhood and rounded up scores of people. The police brought them to a walled compound attached to the rest of the MOI complex by a common section of wall. A single story, rectangular-shaped building took up one corner of the compound. The IPs housed their prisoners inside.

Maries and the other snipers took an interest in this development. Over the next few days, they spied on the compound from their perch about three hundred meters away. Every now and then, the guards pulled a prisoner outside. They looked like Africans, not Iraqis or Arabs. Though Oregonians tried, they could not get a good count on the number of prisoners inside the building. Maries figured it must have been a lot because they counted eighteen guards.

A pattern developed. The guards would congregate on a concrete pad in front of the building, protected from the sun by a small overhang. Then, in pairs they would enter the building, covering their noses with a hankerchief. Usually, they carried a rubber hose or an aluminum bar from a U.S. Army cot. They'd disappear inside then emerge a few minutes later to rejoin the other guards. The snipers observed that once out of the building, the guards would laugh and mimic the torture they'd just inflicted on their captives. Iraqis are very hand-gesture-oriented, and these guards were particularly enthusiastic raconteurs. They'd pantomime beatings, then cringe and cower as if they were the victims. The guards always laughed at that.

Maries reported it to battalion and told his men to keep an eye on the compound. Since April, the snipers had watched other IPs inflict violent beatings elsewhere in the city, especially while at the hotels. This was part of how they did business. Here, while the evidence pointed to prisoner abuse, the snipers hadn't seen anything yet to confirm it. Concerned, the Oregonians monitored the situation.

Specialist Keith Engle, Kevin Maries' partner, happened to be on watch during the late afternoon of June 28, when the door to the building flew open and several guards dragged a prisoner out into the courtyard. The IPs had bound and blindfolded him. Once outside, they kicked him repeatedly, punched him, and threw him against a car. He struck the vehicle and fell in the dirt, unconscious.

Engle notified Maries, who reported the incident to the 2-162 TOC. Now they had proof something very wrong was going on down there.

The next morning, Maries watched as several of the guards grabbed their blunt objects, including a 2x4, and went inside the building. The rest of the guards stood outside watching through windows.

A half hour later, a group of Iraqis dressed in civilian clothes entered the compound from a driveway that led to the main gate of the MOI complex. Kevin concluded one balding man with glasses and a yellow shirt was a person of authority. The others seemed to defer to him. In his hands he carried a stack of paperwork.

Moments later, the IPs started taking prisoners out of the building. The snipers watched in shock as thirty to forty men and boys emerged, their hands bound by yellow cord. They had no idea so many people had been crammed inside such a small building. In all the time they'd watched the place, neither sniper had seen the IPs bring them food or water.

The guards kicked, punched, and bullied their captives into the courtyard and made them kneel in the dirt. A few collapsed. The random beatings continued as a couple of other guards brought out a pair of tables and some chairs, which they set up in the shade of a tree. The yellow-shirted leader placed his paperwork on the tables and sat down.

Snipers are trained observers. They notice the little things most people never see. One minute behind a scope, and a good sniper can learn a lot about anyone by his manners, movements, and attire. Kevin and Keith had a natural gift, which years of training had refined to a veritable art form.

Given the paperwork he carried, the way the IPs deferred to him, and the fact that he'd come in through the MOI complex, Kevin surmised he must have been a member of Iraqi intelligence. What happened next reinforced this assessment.

The IPs dragged a prisoner over to Yellow Shirt, who talked to him and motioned to the paperwork on the table. The prisoner said something back, which apparently Yellow Shirt did not like. The guards forced him to the ground, pulled his shirt up over his shoulders, and whaled on his back with rubber hoses.

The Oregonians watched this in horror. Here was Abu Ghraib, only worse. And Abu Ghraib was still a major issue in the news, having been broken only a few weeks before. The level of violence the two Oregonians just witnessed would be raw meat to the media.

The guards slapped and punched the prisoner a few more times before dumping him back with the main group of captives. Then they selected another one and brought him before Yellow Shirt, who said a few words. More beatings followed. A few captives signed Yellow Shirt's paperwork and were not harmed. Maries concluded they were signing confessions. Those who did not sign had a rough time. The guards were not very inventive, but they were experts at thuggery.

After a half hour, Kevin radioed battalion and let the TOC know the situation.

About that time, the IPs brought forth another prisoner. Yellow Shirt talked to him, but this man refused to even answer. Yellow Shirt motioned to the guards, who hammered into him with a vengeance. They whipped him with the rubber hoses; they slammed a spreader bar down on his head. Another guard kicked him in the head. The level of violence escalated. Keith watched in utter frustration as the captive endured the spreader bar again.

At some point, the Iraqis slid the bar under the prisoner's legs. One guard stood on either side and used it to elevate his feet. Another guard lashed the soles of his feet with a rubber hose. Kevin had just about had enough. This needed to stop, and stop now.

Then Yellow Shirt reached for a pistol. Maries called the battalion TOC and said, "All right, you've been taking our reports. Nothing's been done. If they continue to escalate, I'm going to shoot somebody."

A sergeant at the TOC replied, "Well, that's not within the rules of engagement."

Kevin's temper flared. "I know what the ROE is. And if they escalate, I will engage with deadly force."

Lieutenant Colonel Hendrickson came over the radio and told him to sit tight. He was coming to personally investigate the situation. The news brought relief to both snipers. Something would be done after all. In the meantime, Yellow Shirt decided not to shoot the prisoner. Instead, the guards worked him over and dragged him back to the group.

Maries and Engle snapped pictures of the abuse through their scopes. Yellow Shirt and his IP thugs went through two more captives before things got really ugly. The guards yanked a teenage boy over to the table.

Kevin saw that and exclaimed, "Oh Jesus Christ. What are they going to do to that kid?" The boy was presented to Yellow Shirt, who spoke a few words. Maries grew tense and anxious. Would they start beating him too?

The boy refused to sign the paperwork. Fortunately, Yellow Shirt had him returned to the group. The boy collapsed next to an older man, probably his father.

At that moment, Lieutenant Colonel Hendrickson and the scout platoon stormed into the compound. The proverbial cavalry had arrived. Eleven stories up, the two snipers breathed a big sigh of relief.

THIRTY-FIVE

COMMAND DECISION

Do the right thing.

That was Lieutenant Colonel Hendrickson's mantra for himself and his battalion. Now, as he walked into a courtyard full of bruised, bloody, bound, and blindfolded human beings, the BC grew livid. He'd lived his life with honor. He'd served in law enforcement or the military his entire professional career. Rarely did he see the gray area between right and wrong. Not that it mattered here. This was no gray area. This was torture, abuse, and a human rights violation. Well, he would put a stop to this right now.

Hendrickson entered the compound with Lieutenant Boyce's scout platoon, Sergeant Major Brunk Conley, Lieutenant Gilman, and Captain Jarrell Southall. Southall, his 9mm drawn, looked around at the scene with utter horror. He was a teacher, highly intelligent, empathetic, and a Sunni Muslim. He went with Hendrickson to talk with the blue-clad IPs.

"Who's in charge here?" Hendrickson demanded. In the courtyard, the prisoners moaned. Some were screaming. They'd been in the blazing Iraqi sun without water all morning. The IPs reacted with smug surprise at the BC's arrival.

"What's the matter? Why are you here?"

Tyson Bumgardner stood near the BC and heard this exchange. As he looked around at the cruelty inflicted on the people in the courtyard, his anger swelled.

What are you doing here? Are you not catching on to what we're trying to fix in your country?

The BC turned to Saad, his interpreter, and told him to repeat the question. The IPs did not want to answer it.

While this two-language argument waged back and forth through Saad, Southall, Boyce, Bumgardner, and Master Sergeant Jeff McDowell went around to the back side of the building and found a door. When they entered it, the acidy stench of stale urine assaulted them. No wonder the IPs had covered their noses every time they went inside.

They moved down a hallway and found two more doors. Tyson threw the first one open and discovered three IPs in the middle of torturing a bound and blindfolded prisoner. One was about to kick the helpless man.

Bumgardner rushed forward, pushed the prisoner out of the way, and slammed the IP up against a wall. Pinned to the wall by Tyson's hand on his throat, fear bloomed in the IP's eyes.

Tyson roared, "What are you doing?"

The IP shrieked back, "No! No! No! Not what you think! This is Okay!"

The *hell it is.*

Behind him, McDowell said, "Tyson, why don't you come out now?"

Tyson returned to the hallway as the other Volunteers cut the prisoner loose and gave him water.

Moments later, Boyce, Southall, and Bumgardner opened the second door to discover another scene of horror. What they saw looked like images of a German concentration camp. More than a hundred people had been crammed into a single room. They sat Indian-style, hands bound. Some had passed out in their own excrement. Others were covered with gashes, bruises, and welts. They had no food, no water. The room was well over a hundred degrees. Boyce went inside, and the stench hit him. It reeked of filth, feces, urine, sweat. Mingled into it was the pregnant sickliness of rotting flesh.

Southall went to a group of six or seven men and began a conversation in Arabic. "What is going on? I am a Sunni Muslim."

One of the prisoners began to talk, "I was in the market working when they picked me up." He was a Sudanese, and the IPs demanded a bribe from him. The man paid it, but the police took his passport and arrested him for having no identification. Another man told a similar story. He'd been caught up in the sweep, but didn't have enough money to bribe his way out of the situation.

Well over half the men in the room were Sudanese. They'd simply been caught in the wrong place at the wrong time. Tyson studied the prisoners and concluded only two or three, both Arabs, looked like hardened criminals. Their expressions showed no fear, only hate. The rest looked terrified and broken. Every man in the room suffered from untreated wounds delivered by the IPs and their blunt objects.

Lieutenant Boyce went back to get the BC, who was still arguing with the IPs. "Sir, I think you need to see this."

Boyce led the BC inside the building. The BC saw the people, the conditions, and his rage boiled over. Then the scouts showed him the interrogation room. A lamp had been found with its bulb broken so that it could be used to electrocute prisoners. Chemicals had also been found; the Sudanese said the IPs poured them in their eyes. The spreader bar added to the pile of torture implements.

The BC went back outside. He demanded to talk with whomever was in charge. Finally, Yellow Shirt admitted he was the leader. Apparently, he was a major, either in the Iraqi police or in the intelligence service.

Lieutenant Colonel Hendrickson engaged in a heated discussion with Yellow Shirt, who denied any wrongdoing. Defiantly, he told the BC that his men had not harmed anyone. There was no abuse, no torture. In fact, he was conducting an investigation on a bunch of hardened criminals and drug dealers.

Bullshit.

Long ago, the Volunteers learned never to lie to the BC. He hated that form of dishonor. Yellow Shirt's obvious lies infuriated the BC even further. The conversation devolved. Boyce half-expected it to turn into a fist fight.

As they argued, Sergeant Major Conley moved the prisoners inside the building out into the courtyard. The scouts were already taking care of them. Mike Giordano, the platoon medic, was busy giving IVs to the most dehydrated captives. Kyle Trimble, a combat lifesaver, assisted Mike. Others passed out water and shot photographs of the injuries the prisoners had sustained. They found the teenage boy and learned he was just fourteen. He'd been badly beaten, and later the scouts found a camera with photos the IPs had taken during a torture session with the boy. His father sat nearby, his wrist broken and his hand hanging at an odd angle.

The BC radioed the TOC at Volunteer. He explained the situation to Major Tanguy and told him he needed guidance from brigade. The Oregonians had stumbled into a potential international incident, one that was far worse than Abu Ghraib.

Major Tanguy served as the unofficial "big picture" guy in the battalion. His hard-core realism balanced the BC's idealistic, law-and-order streak, and on this morning Ed's alarm bells went off. Paul Bremer had just turned over power to the provisional Iraqi government. The United States no longer controlled Iraq, its police or intelligence branches. The transfer of authority had seen to that. But what exactly did that mean? Nobody knew.

Two hours into the transfer, even as Paul Bremer was airborne on his way back to the United States, the nature of the new relationship between the provisional government and the U.S. Army was put to the test by Lieutenant Colonel Hendrickson's request for guidance.

Major Tanguy talked to the XO at the 39th Brigade. He told Ed to stand by while he talked with General Chastain. Tanguy figured they would tell the BC to leave. Yes, the torture was brutal and grim, but this was the Middle East. This was Iraq. Such behavior is commonplace and has been since the days of the Hammarabi Code. The confrontation at the compound was more than humans trying to help other humans: it was a clash of values as well. The fact was, Western values and Iraqi ones were sometimes very different.

Meanwhile, the scouts continued to give aid to the prisoners. Some of them began to cry. Others kissed the Americans' hands. The Volunteers saw all manner of wounds, including one man who had a gunshot to his knee. The scene sickened the Oregonians, and they worked hard to get as much water, food, and medical attention to them as possible. The BC had sent a request for more medics and supplies, but for the time being, the scouts had to make do with what they had brought in their rigs.

Not long after noon, some MPs showed up as the scouts disarmed the Iraqi guards. Tyson had just taken an AK from one when he saw the 89th Brigade MPs come into the compound. They began to help, and they soon had a stack of guns and torture implements laid out in the main courtyard.

Then Major Tanguy called back. "The 39th Brigade says to stand down."

The BC, standing at his Humvee with Lieutenant Boyce, went rigid.

Shocked, Ross wasn't sure he heard correctly. "What? What?"

The BC picked up his mic. "You need to tell brigade this is not something we can walk away from."

Major Tanguy relayed it. The order stood. The BC resisted. "We can't just turn this over to the Iraqi police."

"You need to leave. There is no discussion about this," came the XO's reply.

"Have you talked to 1st Cav? Do they know about this?"

Tanguy repeated the 39th's order to leave.

Lieutenant Boyce came up with an idea. The 1st Cav's assistant division commander for support, Brigadier General Jones, had his office not three hundred meters away at the MOI main building.

"Hey, sir, we can walk over there and grab somebody from his office. Or, if he's there, we can get him to come see what's happening."

The BC agreed. They started walking that way.

The TOC came over the radio again. "We need confirmation that you are leaving."

The BC replied, "I'm having trouble reading you."

"We need confirmation you're leaving."

"You're breaking up."

The BC was out of options. Boyce sensed that if he pushed it any further, the 39th would relieve him on the spot. The tension over the radio had grown markedly in the past few minutes.

They had to leave. The BC turned and called, "Okay, 2-162, we're leaving. Now."

The order stunned the men. Captain Jarrell didn't want to leave at all, and one of the scouts had to pull him to the Humvees. Everyone felt like they'd just been gut-kicked for doing something noble.

They packed up and headed out. As they left, Brunk Conley saw fear swell in the prisoners' eyes. Jarrell turned around and got once last glimpse. He saw the IPs going straight for their guns.

THIRTY-SIX

THE GRAY-HAIRED MYSTERY MAN

The Volunteers never learned who gave the order to pull out. It took twenty minutes for the brigade to send the order to the BC, which in Ed Tanguy's estimation was plenty of time for the question to be kicked up to Central Command or even higher. The fact was, with the transfer of authority, 2-162 did not have any legal basis to be in the compound.

It was still the right thing to do. Iraq sometimes tested the boundaries of what was legal and from a bureaucrat's point of view—as well as what was moral and humane. This was one of those times.

As the BC returned to Volunteer with his dispirited men, Kevin Maries watched as the IPs went right back to beating the hell out of the captives once the MPs left. Keith Engle, a focused, dedicated soldier with loads of talent and heart, went from zero to pissed in seconds. Both men were heartsick, furious, and confused.

But they didn't stop watching. And at 1600, a motorcade of armored SUVs drove into the compound. A dapper, well-dressed gray-haired man emerged from one. Maries studied him. He was a Westerner, not an Iraqi. He didn't move with the usual fluidity of an American, in fact his movements were stiff. He did not use many hand gestures. Maries examined his bodyguards. They were all Caucasians, equipped with armor and AK-47s. This was unusual. American security companies used M4s and .45-automatics. The only PSD team Kevin had seen with AKs was a British company called Parson's Limited. Based on that, he guessed that Gray Hair was British, and somebody of importance.

Gray Hair gathered the IPs and spoke to them. A half hour later, he walked into the MOI main building. Maries told Keith to sit tight. He wanted to go find this guy. He left the hide and went downstairs. He searched for Gray Hair but came up empty.

An hour later, an Iraqi official showed up at the compound. He addressed the IPs, who then brought out ninety-three prisoners, thirty-five of them Sudanese. They lined them up in the courtyard, where the Iraqi official held what looked like a question and answer session with them. The snipers studied the captives, and they noticed one effeminate-appearing Caucasian male in the group. That puzzled them.

The meeting went on for thirty minutes. Afterward, the IPs brought the prisoners food, water, and cigarettes. Late that afternoon, the IPs released twelve prisoners. The next day, the teenage boy and his father walked out of the compound.

Altogether, the snipers saw the IPs release about sixty prisoners. Those who left received food and water, and the guards let them bathe in the courtyard during the course of the next week.

Exactly what happened to the remaining prisoners remained a mystery, but the vast majority returned to their lives. Maries and Engle took great pride in this. They had walked the walk. They had done the right thing, and their actions had saved lives. Kevin considered it the most important thing he did in Iraq.

For Hendrickson and the battalion staff, the June 29 incident was something the American public needed to know about. Here was a great example of something noble: U.S. soldiers putting a stop to abuse and torture. It could serve as a counterbalance to the legions of stories about the American guards at Abu Ghraib. It could show the world that this was how the army responded to such events. It looked like a golden opportunity to showcase something good.

It didn't happen. The brigade ordered everyone to remain silent. The incident never happened. Boyce tried to put Maries and Engle in for Bronze Stars, but for what? The event never officially took place.

The story did get out. A well-respected reporter from the *Oregonian* named Mike Francis picked up on it while embedded with 2-162 that summer. Several Volunteers shared information with him. Later, when it was evident the story would not come out through military channels, several key officers talked to Francis. Mike had earned the battalion's respect with his professionalism and discretion. Of all the media-types the Volunteers encountered in Iraq, Mike was the one man they trusted. They shared the story with him and even provided photos.

Francis broke the story later that summer. It created a flurry of international attention. The torture and abuse was decried and the fact that 2-162 had been pulled out of the compound made the U.S. Army look bad. In fact, 2-162's arrival clearly triggered a high-level investigation that led to the end of the abuse and the release of most of the prisoners. Gray Hair's subsequent arrival demonstrated that.

Had the military controlled the release of the story, this element could have been the central theme presented, not the fact that the BC was ordered out.

Mike Warrington chalked it up as another lost opportunity. The army's own paranoia for bad press in this instance destroyed any chance that it would get any good coverage from the events of June 29, 2004.

THIRTY-SEVEN

THE HELL HOUNDS' LAST RIDE

"My boys. How are my boys?"

"They're fine Sergeant Jacques. They're fine."

"Make sure my boys go before me. Get them on the bird first."

"Okay, Sergeant Jacques."

"Get them on the bird first."

"Okay, Sergeant Jacques."

"Marty."

"Yeah, Vinni."

"Tell Rhonda and Gabe I love them. Okay?"

"I won't have to. Tell them yourself."

"No. Tell my wife and boy I love them."

"Vinni, you're going to do it yourself."

"TELL THEM I LOVE THEM."

"Okay, Vinni. I'll tell 'em."

"And make sure my boys get on the bird first."

"Everyone's on. They're waiting for you."

Sergeant Ezelle looked up from some inventory paperwork and saw his longtime friend Sergeant First Class Tim Bloom standing in the door to his platoon's CP.

"Hey E. Z., you got a minute?"

Ezelle regarded Bloom's narrow face and his soft-spoken words. The news was bad, really bad. He put down his paperwork and grunted, "Yeah, I got a minute."

"Wanna sit down?"

Oh shit. Somebody's dead.

"Sure."

Ezelle found a seat. Bloom sat down next to him, took a breath, and said, "Vinni got hit today. We don't know a lot about it, but there's a good chance he's not gonna make it."

Silence.

And there's that.

Bloom left E. Z. alone as he struggled to get a handle on the moment.

Ezelle felt numb. Memory flashes of Vinni flipped through his mind. The bond they shared defined the best part of soldiering. That bond was the reason why Ezelle had made the Guard his life.

Rhonda and Gabe.

The scenes of backyard barbecues and barroom brawls played out in his mind. Vinni's wedding and his bachelor party rolled by next. These memories filled Ezelle with sadness that quickly morphed into cold fury. He surrendered to it.

Goddamned motherfuckers.

He stood, grabbed a SAW, and banged through the CP's door. He headed for the battalion aid station, where he found the medic platoon Sergeant First Class Bruce Cutshall. Cutshall and Ezelle went way back, having been buddies and sparring partners for years. When Ezelle and his wife split up years before, Bruce was there to help him through it. Their friendship ran deep.

Ezelle broke the news about Vinni. They talked about how hard the battalion would take his loss. He was one of the invincible types, the sort of NCO that cannot be killed by the human flotsam they battled in Iraq. It would make everyone feel vulnerable now. Ezelle said good-bye to Cutshall and left. Unsure of what he was going to do, he knew clearly what he *wanted* to do. He wanted revenge.

These motherfuckers . . . I hate these fucking people. I hate them. They're fucked up. They don't have a fucking clue how much we're trying to help them.

He wanted to stand in the street and drop every last Iraqi he could find. A soldier all his life, Sergeant First Class Ezelle was one of the toughest and most respected NCOs in the battalion. He was the rock of Charlie Company, the soldier everyone knew could handle anything thrown his way.

At that moment, none of that mattered. Neither did consequences. Death or Leavenworth and a life without his son, Chuck, awaited him on the other side of the gate. With each step, that meant less and less to him. The bond with Vinni, that mattered now. That was everything. They'd taken out his best friend, a man closer than any brother. *Uneducated cock suckers. There isn't one of them that's half the man Vinni is. A million of you fucks aren't worth him.*

Discipline had always been the cornerstone of Ezelle's life, but here in the middle of Baghdad on this terrible day, his self-control vanished in a firestorm of murderous hate. SAW in hand, he turned for the gate.

"E. Z., where are you going?"

Ezelle looked over his shoulder. Bruce Cutshall had followed him through the doorway and intuited where he was heading. He realized this could only end in a nightmare. Ezelle took another step. Cutshall caught up to him.

"E. Z., What are you doing?"

He looked into Ezelle's eyes and knew. "Man, if you're doing what I think you're doing, you need to stop. You need to stop *now.*"

Ezelle let out a long breath. His feet paused, his momentum faltered, he sucked air and seethed with pain. It stabbed him like an ice pick, but it shocked him back into control. He would not go out the gate on this day.

Not today, not like this. We'll get the right ones, and we'll do it the right way.

Head down, he walked back to the CP and returned the SAW. His rage drained away. In its place came the one emotion every soldier, no matter how tough, no matter how brave, dreads: despair.

It started as a routine patrol. There had been a lot of routine patrols that July. Vinni's section had been out on the roads day and night. They'd found dozens of IEDs and had done a lot of good, but Vinni could see his men were smoked. He asked for a day off. Captain San Miguel couldn't give it to him. The Op Tempo was too demanding.

Something told Vinni it was time to get his affairs in order. He grew ultra-serious, almost morose, which was very unlike him. Everyone, including Tommy Houston, noticed it. Vinni couldn't help it: he knew his time was up as surely as Eric McKinley had.

He wrote a last letter to Rhonda and Gabe. He squared a few other things away and made his peace. Then he went to take care of his platoon.

They left Camp Cooke in the early afternoon of July 28, three Humvees strong. About fifteen kilometers west of the gate, they drove into a small village near Route Mallet. Nobody came out to greet them. The day before, Vinni had stopped his section nearby to eat lunch in the shade of a house under construction. The owner appeared and had asked them to leave because the people in the village didn't like Americans and he was afraid they would retaliate against him. Vinni had decided to visit the village on their next patrol.

Vinni dismounted with his interpreter. Kenny Leisten climbed out of the driver's side to join him. So did Doc Rhodes, an African-American medic from 2-7 who'd been temporarily assigned to the platoon while Doc Smith was on leave.

At first, nobody came out to greet them. The village sat practically dead center in the Sunni Triangle—the people did not like Americans.

An Iraqi male sidled past. Vinni tried to talk with him, but he was very reluctant. After awhile, some kids appeared and walked over to a sewage culvert. They started drinking from it. One washed his face.

"Not, just no. *Fuck no!*" Vinni exclaimed as he saw this. He turned to the Iraqi and through the interpreter said, "Come on, you need some water. We'll give you some water."

Before he could even tell Kenny what to do, he'd gone back to the truck. Along with several of the other Joes, they handed the water out to the kids. Now adults cautiously approached the patrol. Leisten handed out water to them as well.

They had about ten hours left on a twelve-hour patrol in 130-degree heat. It didn't matter, the Joes turned over their water supply to the villagers. The sight of kids drinking filth had been too much.

The village sheik introduced himself to Vinni. He detailed all the things his people needed, including the completion of the village school. The school sat unfinished, mainly because the Iraqi contractor hired to complete the job had been assassinated. Vinni wanted to tell the sheik that if he wanted things built, his people needed to stop blowing up the help. The sheik talked about the lack of electricity, running water, and medical attention. The Oregonians wrote everything down and Vinni promised to report it after he returned to Taji.

Then he noticed the little girl. She was heartbreakingly cute with huge dark eyes and a playful grin. She hid behind her father, who was about Vinni's age, and would pop out every few seconds to giggle and wave at the Oregonians. Vinni waved back. He asked the girl's father, "Would it be okay if I gave this to her?" The Iraqi nodded. Vinni presented her with his flashlight.

"I hope I have a daughter as cute as yours someday."

The Iraqi father laughed. That broke the ice. He asked Vinni if he had any kids.

"Yes, I have a son."

"A son? What's his name?"

"Gabriel."

The Iraqi lit up, "Oh, like the angel Gabriel!"

Vinni smiled back and said, "Oh yes, like the angel. But he's not always an angel!"

The two men chuckled over that, finding a common bond in fatherhood.

The Iraqi wished him well. Vinni was about to load his men up when a man with a bandaged foot asked for help. Vinni called to Marty Theurer and Doc Rhodes, who came over with their medical gear. Marty thought this was pretty strange; he'd seen Bandaged Foot hovering on the outskirts of the crowd. He looked standoffish. Now, as they got ready to leave he wanted some attention? It didn't feel right.

They tended his minor wound, and soon others came to them for help as well. They examined and treated a sick baby, somebody with a tooth abscess, and three or four more people until Vinni told them it was time to go.

The Oregonians mounted up. Vinni climbed into his Humvee with Doc Rhodes and the interpreter in back. Kenny Leisten took the wheel as Ben Ring manned the gun. They drove back onto Route Mallet, heading south for the intersection with Route Raiders. They were in the same area where Phil Disney's patrol had been hit in June.

Vinni looked over at Leisten and asked, "Whaddya guys think? Did you see anything weird?"

"It seemed a little weird," said Doc Rhodes.

Kenny, sporting a mischievous grin joked, "Yeah, but there were some hot chicks checking me out over there!"

Vinni roared with laughter. "I imagine they were, you little fricking stud!"

Everyone cracked up.

Vinni continued, "I'm married now. I can't be doing that stuff. But there was a cute little girl back there. I gave her my flashlight."

Vinni turned to see Kenny laughing. It was a good moment. The banter had broken the tension they'd felt in the village. Then Kenny vanished.

Marty Theurer drove the lead 1114 that day. They passed by the unfinished house, and the road narrowed as it crossed an irrigation canal. He rolled over it. The second Humvee followed, doing about 40 mph. Suddenly, a deafening roar engulfed Theurer's Humvee, and his TC, Sergeant Duffer, started yelling "Turn around, turn around!"

Marty flung the wheel over and started a Y-turn. Halfway through, chunks of metal rained out of the sky all around them. He looked right. Part of a transmission and an engine block plummeted into the road.

He got the truck turned around. The second vehicle, TC'd by Sergeant Lucas Smith, had also pulled a one-eighty. Now Marty could see why. An IED in the irrigation culvert had blown Vinni's rig at least twenty feet in the air. Spinning right to left, it flipped over and crashed back down on the driver's side facing north. All Marty could see was the mangled back end. And now, AK fire cracked overhead. Bullets whined off the gravel road.

At least sixty feet from the wreck, Doc Rhodes was in the road, slumped forward on his head and shoulders. His lower legs had been snapped below the knee. He was standing on his ruined leg bones, the rest of his legs and feet bent impossibly backward under his body.

Marty stopped about fifteen meters from the wreck. Bill Stout leapt out, M4 raised. Back up the way they'd come, a car suddenly shot out of a concealed position and turned onto the road. In the turret, John Rosander opened up on it. Bill didn't hesitate either. His M4 barked until both men inside the car stopped moving. Rosander shifted his fire. Bill did as well, suppressing the area along with Sean Jenkins, Lucas Smith's M240 gunner.

Marty grabbed his medical bag and charged forward. For him, everything happened in silent slow motion. He didn't hear his guys pouring rounds downrange. He didn't hear the incoming fire. He remained uniquely focused: get to Doc.

Bill Stout saw Marty take off, then his attention turned to Vinni's Humvee. The entire front end was nothing but twisted metal. Without a thought of his own safety, he sprinted to the rig and climbed up onto the passenger-side fender. Completely exposed to the incoming fire, he braced himself in the wheel well and shouted, "Sergeant Jacques, Sergeant Jacques, are you okay?"

The passenger door had been blown off. Through the opening, he could see Vinni dangling upside down with his legs trapped under the ruined dashboard. A chunk of shrapnel jutted out of his leg. He could see another poking through the back of his IBA.

"What the hell's going on?" Vinni mumbled.

"You got hit by an IED."

Bill leaned forward. All of five foot six, maybe a hundred and forty pounds, Stout surely didn't have the strength to get Vinni out. Jacques outweighed Bill two to one. Bill grabbed Vinni's vest and pulled. Vinni was conscious, but couldn't move. His life was in this man's hands.

"I'm not in control here," he mumbled.

Bill tugged hard, bringing Vinni up an inch at a time, but he couldn't get his legs freed. Bullets snapped overhead. Rosander continued laying down fire. So did Jenkins. Bill ignored the firefight and focused on saving Vinni.

He tugged again, pulling with every bit of strength he possessed. With a sudden bloom of pain, something gave way in his back. Though he didn't know it,

Bill had just cracked his pelvis bone in two places and slipped several disks in his vertebrae. He ignored the pain and pulled again. Vinni was stuck fast.

"Hey, Clark, I need help."

Stout's call sent burly Christopher Clark running for the Humvee. He squeezed into the remains of the driver's side and lifted Vinni upward. That took the pressure off his legs, and Bill was able to free them. Jacques sagged into Clark. They pulled him through the engine compartment, put him on a stretcher, and carried him to Marty's truck. Seconds later, Marty, Duffer, and specialist Jame Walker laid Doc Rhodes down next to Vinni.

Bill went back to the Humvee, Marty and Clark right behind him. They reached the turret and could see the interpreter lying on top of Ben Ring. Stout reached in and yanked the interpreter clear. His leg was torn up, so Marty put him in Lucas Smith's Humvee.

Bill and Marty took hold of Ring and pulled hard. Ben flew through the turret and collided with Stout. They fell backward into a heap. Blood saturated Ben's uniform. The Joes got him on a stretcher. As they carried him to Marty's Humvee, Theurer tripped on something in the road. Looking down, he realized he'd just stumbled on an unexploded 155mm artillery shell. They kept going and put Ring on the hood of the Humvee. Even as Rosander kept triggering off short bursts with the M240, Theurer climbed onto the hood and went to work on Ben. Initially he thought Ring had a chest wound. He opened his vest and found nothing. *Where's all this blood coming from?*

He cut off Ring's IBA and tore open his right sleeve. He found the wound. Ring had taken a piece of shrapnel right under his armpit. It left an inch-wide gash through which dark-colored blood was seeping out. The shrapnel had hit a vein, and Marty knew he needed to staunch the bleeding fast. Ben, who'd always been a bit socially awkward, looked at Marty and quietly said, "I'm not going to die today."

I'm glad you think so, Ben, 'cause I'm not so sure.

"You're not going to die on me, Ben."

Beside the Humvee, Doc Rhodes was being treated by several of the Joes. Rhodes tried to help the other guys working on Vinni. From his litter, he offered advice and suggestions despite his own intense pain. He had compound bilateral fractures of both legs. The bones were sticking out of his flesh.

Vinni asked about his boys. He mumbled a few words, then drifted into incoherence. He'd suffered a severe concussion and wasn't making much sense. But his heart was intact, and it wanted to know if his men were okay.

On the hood, Marty wrapped an Israeli pressure dressing around Ben's wounded arm. He secured it as Walker got an IV started.

At that moment, Rosander eased off the trigger and asked, "Hey, where's Leisten?"

Theurer stood up on the hood and shouted, "Where's Kenny?"

He saw something in a drainage ditch alongside the road. He jumped off the Humvee and sprinted for it. Bill appeared by his side. Kenny was his boy. Kenny was his responsibility. Back at Polk, he had promised him he'd get them through this alive. They found Kenny's remains alongside the ditch. The IED explosion traveled at about twenty thousand feet a second. It struck Kenny with unbelievable force, tearing him apart as it vaporized his side of the Humvee.

Bill reached for his boy, "We've got to turn him over."

Theurer had seen many terrible sights throughout his career as a paramedic. Car crashes, brutal injuries, dying people, those were his days back in Oregon. He'd seen everything imaginable, but he did not want to see Kenny this way.

He touched Bill's shoulder. "No! There's nothing we can do for him."

Anguish raked Bill's face. Kenny was the son he'd never had. He loved the kid. He'd sworn to bring him home alive. Now, he'd welched on that promise. All this was his fault. Guilt and rage welled in him and mingled with despair. It became fertile ground for revenge. Bill wanted revenge. He lusted to kill those who'd taken his boy. It burned in him.

A pair of Blackhawks appeared on the eastern horizon. Through all the chaos, Lucas Smith had calmly reported the situation and called in a pair of medevac birds.

They moved like automatons now, simply reacting to the training Vinni had drilled into them in countless exercises. Bill and Marty both popped smoke for the choppers. Walker put 800 CCs of fluid into Ring. Stout and Lucas Smith worked together to secure the area and hold a perimeter. The birds landed. A crew chief ran to Marty.

"What do you have?"

"I've got two critcals and two others."

"Okay, put the criticals on the last bird."

Marty headed back for his Humvee. He'd been running in full battle rattle without water in 130-degree heat. Now it caught up with him. He staggered and vomited. The horror, the tension, the despair struck him a double blow. He dry heaved in his grief and dehydration.

Vinni refused to be carried to the helicopters until all his men, including the interpreter, were loaded aboard. With that done, the men carried Vinni toward the Blackhawks. As he moved passed Marty, he grabbed him by the vest and pulled him down until their eyes were only inches apart.

"Tell my wife and boy I love them."

The Hell Hounds were no more.

Part IV

THE AL SADR
SMACKDOWN

THIRTY-EIGHT

MOQTADA REPRISE

The Shiite fascist reemerged on July 23, 2004. After laying low for two months, Moqtada Al Sadr gave his first public sermon since the end of May. In it, he spat venom at both the United States and Prime Minister Iyad Allawi. This was not the conciliatory speech of a repentant. It was the opening blast of a new campaign.

In the spring, Al Sadr could count on less than 5 percent of his countrymen for support. Ironically, his military defeat in June became a strategic victory. He had stood up to the Americans and survived. That earned him political clout with his fellow Shiites. His base of support grew. A poll at the end of July showed 80 percent of Iraqis had a more positive view of him than they did in April.

He spent his political capital rebuilding his Mahdi militia and consolidating his hold on the 2.5 million people in Sadr City. After attacking the IP stations in June, he switched tactics and started working with the local cops to catch thieves, drug dealers, and kidnappers. Most of the time, Mahdi execution squads would kill these people.

For their part, the Iraqi police seemed either cowed or content to turn over the streets to the militia. Now in charge, they organized the community much the same way the National Socialists did in the 1920s in their pockets of support.

Mahdi militiamen gave religious instruction to youth groups at the local mosques. They taught ten-year-olds the history of the Mahdi militia and the beginnings of the struggle against the American juggernaut. A *Christian Science Monitor* reporter named Dan Murphy visited Sadr City, and in an August 4, 2004, article noted the kids re-created the Mahdi's first battle against U.S. forces in August 2003 with real AK-47s and RPGs as props.

In Najaf, his militia took control of the holy sites revered by the Islamic world. It was a rerun of the spring, and once again the reign of terror began. More liquor stores were firebombed, more video stores ransacked. People vanished. Death squads kept order. The people lived in fear. The IPs refused to interfere.

The Americans and Allawi's government decided to act. Instead of fighting the Mahdi in the open again, this time they planned a series of joint raids designed to take down the Mahdi's senior leadership.

On July 31, a team of Iraqi National Guardsmen supported by American troops captured Al Sadr's top leader in Karbala, Sheik Mithal Al Hasnawi. Moqtada denounced the move and demanded his release. The coalition ignored him.

On August 3, U.S. troops surrounded Al Sadr's house and tried to either kill or capture him. A firefight broke out. Al Sadr escaped again.

Moqtada called out his troops. Two days later, eastern Baghdad erupted.

THIRTY-NINE

THE CHARGE OF THE MODOC WARRIOR

Fate dealt 2-162 a rough hand. Earlier in the summer, the 39th Brigade had changed the boundaries of AO Volunteer to include Zone 22, otherwise known as North Sadr City. Hendrickson gave the new sector to Captain Granger's Alpha Company. Unknown to anyone, this area would soon become one of the key battlefields in the second Shia uprising.

It began on August 5 with massive Mahdi attacks all over Baghdad designed to cut the main supply routes into the capital. The Cav units assigned to Sadr City waged pitched battles in the streets again. Mahdi units descended into Zone 22 to strike at the IP stations and gather more weapons and ammunition.

That afternoon, Patrol Base Volunteer received a report that Mahdi militiamen had entered Zone 22. The battalion launched the QRF platoon to investigate. Doug Jackson, Alpha Company's Modoc warrior, led 2nd Platoon out the gate. Lieutenant Cory Jones was up at Taji that day and had left Jackson in charge. The platoon raced north with six rigs, five 1114s, and a turtleback. Between them, they carried a .50-cal, four M240 Bravos, and an MK19 grenade launcher. They crossed over Route Pluto on Route Grizzlies, which divided Sadr City from Zone 22. Doug ordered his lead rig to get off the main road, and the patrol slipped into a dense residential neighborhood. They zigzagged through it until the lead driver accidentally took a wrong turn and they returned to Route Grizzlies again. They popped out a few blocks from an intersection that connected Route Grizzlies and a northerly running road code-named Route Gold. Up ahead, Jackson could see a tire barricade blocking the road. The platoon's gunners called out targets and 2nd Platoon found itself in its first firefight since April.

The Oregonians were ready for a fight. They'd been looking for some payback for Luke Wilson for months. Now, as Mahdi militiamen boiled out of alleyways and materialized on rooftops, the men cut loose with everything they had. Jackson radioed his lead truck and told the crew to turn left and get off Route Grizzlies. They'd hit this nest from the flank, not head on. The column swung onto a side street parallel to Route Gold. Still under fire, they went up a few blocks then cut right on another side street. The fire died away.

Inspiration hit Jackson. He put his rigs three abreast with his in the middle of the front rank. With two M240s and an MK19 online, they hit the gas and roared onto Route Gold north of the Alpha Hotel intersection. They skidded right and charged headlong into a hornet's nest of Mahdi militiamen.

The gunners opened up. The MK19 thudded. Militiamen died. The charge caught the Mahdi in the open as they crossed Route Gold to reach the neighborhood Jackson's men had just vacated. The sudden appearance of a phalanx of thundering Humvees on their flank caused chaos and sent the militiamen scuttling for cover.

Twenty-five Oregonians strong, they drove straight into a force six times their size. Rockets raced by as the insurgents started to react. An insurgent loosed a volley from his AK. His bullets left five spiderwebs on the driver's side windshield of one Humvee. More RPGs. More AK fire. They had almost reached the Jamelia Power Station on the northeast corner of the Gold-Grizzlies intersection when Doug saw even more Mahdi flooding into the area. It was time to break off the attack. The platoon ducked left and plunged down a side street before turning back on Gold. Going north this time, they paused at IP Station Six about a mile up from the power station. They tried to enlist the help of the Iraqi police. Fat chance. The Oregonians suspected most of them were Mahdi sympathizers anyway. This was a fight 2nd Platoon would continue on its own.

Jackson checked on his guys. "We're going back there. Does anyone have a problem with that?"

"Fuck no. Let's do it."

"Yeah."

"Okay then," Jackson said, "get ready to shoot everybody."

They wheeled south and pushed down Gold again. Midway between Jamelia and the IP station, the platoon found a wide open spot that stretched across both sides of the road. The fields of fire here were awesome; nobody could sneak up on them. Jackson circled the wagons, dismounted, and set up a perimeter. It soon attracted all manner of attention.

Mahdi moved around the buildings on either side of the southern end of the fields. To the southeast, it looked like the militiamen were using a parking garage as a rally point. The platoon came under AK fire. Moments later, a blue pickup truck with an RPG gunner in the bed burst out into the field to the east and bounced straight for the patrol. Jackson's .50-cal gunner hosed the truck. The bullets sent up a rash of blue sparks as they impacted into the vehicle. It rolled to a stop, everyone on board torn apart by the fusillade.

A Jeep bored at them from the northeast, crossing into the field even as Jackson triggered his M4. In one of the Humvees, Specialist James Mercado trained his M240 on the rig and let fly with a long burst. He soon added his SAW to the barrage. Doug's RTO added his M4, and one of the grenadiers popped off an M203 round. That ended the one-way firefight. The grenade exploded right on the vehicle, killing the two insurgents instantly.

Carloads of AK-toting militiamen tested the perimeter next. The .50-cal barked. The cars exploded. Militiamen died. When the vehicular counterattack failed, the Mahdi tried to flank the Volunteers from the west, moving through buildings and laying down covering fire. AK bullets snapped and cracked around the Humvees. RPGs came next. The rockets sizzled by in reddish blurs.

Jackson's men held the enemy at bay. They met every probe with a wall of bullets, killing or driving the Mahdi away. Then they started to run low on ammo. Doug had the drivers dig into the loose 5.6mm rounds in boxes stored in the Humvees. As the firefight continued, the drivers carefully reloaded the empty M4 magazines.

Meanwhile, Specialist Patrick Silva, a six-foot-seven-inch jovial Irishman stayed on the .50 and inflicted much damage with his marksmanship. He towered out of the turret and made quite a target, but Doug never once saw his gunner duck. Silva personally took out more than a dozen Mahdi-driven vehicles that dared countercharge their perimeter.

Here in the middle of downtown Baghdad, it was the Wild West all over again, except this time the Modoc was in the middle with the circled wagons. They wrought utter havoc, these twenty-five men and their handful of heavy weapons.

Now the insurgents deployed more firepower. They struck at the Volunteers with more RPGs, then added mortars to the mix. Second Platoon had planted itself dead in the middle of a sea of insurgents who peppered them from every urban nook and cranny. In return, the Volunteers blazed back in all directions. The platoon knocked the Mahdi down, but more took their place. They were relentless and threw away dozens of lives in their effort to dislodge 2nd Platoon. It was Jackson's last stand, and his men stood fast.

Finally, they exhausted their ammunition. The platoon mounted up and exfiltrated north up Route Gold, enduring fire the entire way up to the IP station. This time, they found an MP platoon there who shared their ammunition with the Volunteers. As they reloaded and made ready to get back into the fight, the fight came to them. In minutes, they were besieged by Mahdi who fired from rooftops at them from every compass point. An RPG gunner leapt out into the street not fifty meters from the platoon. Before he could cook off his rocket, Silva saw him and blew him to pieces with his .50-cal. Only a red mist, his shoes, and the RPG remained. Three more insurgents went down as they tried to sneak up on the platoon.

Jackson's men remounted and pushed south to circle the wagons again, daring the insurgents to enter their kill zone. Meanwhile, the battalion TOC told them reinforcements were on the way, including a platoon of 2-7 Bradleys attached to Alpha. Jackson wanted to push the Mahdi back down toward Route Grizzlies and drive them into the inbound Bradleys. With their 25 mike-mikes, the Mahdi would be decimated.

This time down Route Gold, the fighting was not as fierce. A few Mahdi cars charged them across the open fields. The heavy weapons stopped them cold. When that failed, the insurgents resorted to harassing fire. Jackson moved around the perimeter, keeping his guys pumped as they fought back. By now, they'd been engaged for well over forty-five minutes. They were getting tired, but Doug could see they had plenty of fight yet in them.

Jackson started for Sergeant Tim Edwards' 1114 to check on his gunner, Specialist William "One Speed" Bahler. Right then, an RPG lanced into Edwards' truck. It detonated against the left rear tire, destroying it and throwing both Bahler and Edwards flying into the Humvee. A spray of shrapnel wounded Private First Class Rene Lizama and Specialist Jeremy Weir. Bahler climbed back into the turret and reengaged before anyone could even check on him.

Jackson did not have a medic with him that day, but his combat lifesaver, Tyson DeFrance, rushed over to give assistance. He found a five-inch chunk of shrapnel sticking out of Lizama's calf. Weir had been hit in the back of the head, but the wound was not serious.

Jackson decided it was time to pull back to the IP station again. The men remounted and escorted Edwards' crippled 1114. They reached the station and the platoon established a perimeter again. They pulled a pair of M240s off the trucks and put them on the station's roof. The gunners went to town engaging Mahdi targets all around them. It was now almost 1800 hours. Jackson's men had been fighting outnumbered and surrounded for almost two hours.

Now they needed help.

FORTY

THE BATTLE OF JAMELIA POWER STATION

Back at Volunteer, Sergeant First Class Phil Larson and his 3rd Platoon, Alpha Company, got the word to launch for IP Station Six. The news sounded bad. Second Platoon reported they were out of ammo and had two wounded. Larson's men were off duty at the time, but they threw on their IBAs and mounted up. In ten minutes, they rolled for the gate.

Everything happened so fast that several men from 3rd Platoon didn't make the movement. This included Sergeant Mike Brase. He linked up with Alpha's first sergeant, Randy Mefford, and learned what had happened. Together, they loaded a trailer with more than twenty-five thousand rounds of ammo and joined up with Captain Welch and Sergeant First Class Terrel's platoon as they left the gate to enter the fight.

Larson's platoon tore across Route Pluto on Route Grizzlies and entered Zone 22. The rigs veered left and took a side road onto Route Gold. Moments later, they reached the IP station and Jackson's men.

Their timing could not have been better. They arrived during a brief lull in the fighting to discover three of Jackson's M240s were empty. Silva was down to his last round for his Ma Deuce, and Doug's MK19 gunner didn't have a single grenade left. Larson cross loaded the ammo, giving Jackson half of what they were carrying.

As the men worked, Captain Granger radioed Lieutenant Rogers and told him to take 3rd Platoon down Route Gold and secure the Jamelia Power Station. Few facilities in AO Volunteer had more strategic significance than Jamelia. It had recently been rebuilt and served as the main electrical supply for much of eastern Baghdad. If the Mahdi destroyed it, the power issues in the capital would drastically worsen.

Third Platoon pushed south down Route Gold. Three hundred meters from Jamelia, they ran into Terrel's platoon as it pulled onto Route Gold from a side street. Mike Brase and First Sergeant Mefford dismounted and hooked up with Larson. As they discussed the situation, an RPG sailed into the traffic circle at the intersection of Route Grizzlies and Route Gold. The explosion three hundred meters away acted as a spur to the leaders. Mefford, Larson, Brase, and five other men instinctively bounded forward, covering one another while the vehicles trailed behind them.

Mahdi militiamen appeared on the rooftops on either side of Route Gold. Brase shot one insurgent as he popped up on a roof only a few meters away.

Another one slipped from an alley and leaned back to hurl a grenade. Larson saw him and was so startled by his appearance that when he brought his M4 to his shoulder, he forgot to flip the safety off. He pulled the trigger. Nothing. The insurgent finished his wind-up. Phil switched to semi-auto and drilled him.

The leaders pressed on, covering one another as they bounded toward the intersection. AK fire rained through the street. The Americans fired as they ran until they reached the northwest wall of the power station. Here, the station's security force had placed giant empty cable spools in a serpentine to prevent car bomb attacks. They came in handy now. The Americans ducked behind them and used them as cover as they moved the last few meters to Jamelia's southwest corner.

Mike Brase found cover behind a stack of tires next to the power station's cement wall. He popped up and scanned for targets. Next to him, Sergeant Nathan Lundquist did the same. They spotted some Mahdi moving around in an auto repair shop across the intersection. Several slid behind a blue Opal and opened fire on them. The Humvees arrived and took position behind the dismounts. The rigs took fire from the auto shop; an M240 and Larson's .50-cal strafed the Opal and killed the insurgents. But the militiamen came back, and a pitched fire combat erupted.

Another RPG zipped into the traffic circle and exploded. Then another. Larson had taken cover across the street from Brase. Nearby, Lieutenant Foley and Staff Sergeant Ellifret used a trash pile in the middle of Route Gold as cover. They engaged to the east of the traffic circle while Larson burned through his ammo, firing at targets down an alleyway on the other side of Route Grizzlies.

Mike Brase caught sight of an RPG gunner. He was hiding about three hundred meters down the alleyway behind a building with a vinyl blue awning. Every few minutes, he jumped into the street, let fly with a rocket, and scooted back into cover before anyone could get a bead on him. The RPGs always fell short, but he got off at least three before Mike spotted his launcher poking out from behind the building.

Brase shouted his location to Larson, who shouted back, "Well, shoot the motherfucker!"

Brase had a 4x32 scope on his M4. He settled down behind it and waited for a shot. As he did, he flicked his safety off and put the M4 on semi-auto. Then he thought about that.

Fuck that, this guy is pissing me off.

He flipped to three-round burst mode. The RPG gunner made his move. He jumped to the sidewalk, squared his shoulders, and brought the RPG up. Mike emptied almost a full mag into him. The stunned militiamen stumbled backward and triggered the RPG as he fell to the street. The rocket shot upward right through the awning, hit the building, and spiraled skyward like an out-of-control firehose. Two militiamen dragged the dead RPG gunner into a side alley.

A short lull followed that development. Larson went back to his rig to reload M4 magazines for his boys. He had personally gone through 240 rounds in thirty minutes. While he sat on the back of his 998, an insurgent popped up on Route

Grizzlies and triggered a couple of rounds his way. They cracked past Larson, who yelled, "Get that guy!"

Brase and Lundquist scanned for him. No luck. The insurgent fired again. Two rounds went over Larson's head. Annoyed, Phil shouted, "Somebody kill that motherfucker!"

Mike called out that he wanted a machine gun up at his position. A Joe hustled across the street and set up next to him in the tire barrier. Brase looked over to see the platoon medic, Specialist Chatlofsky, holding the SAW.

"Doc, what the fuck are you doing?"

"I've got the SAW, man! I'm gonna shoot these guys."

"Get the fuck back to the platoon, sergeant—you knucklehead!"

Disappointed, the medic returned to Larson's 998. The militiaman popped up again and put a few more rounds into the 998. Larson erupted, "Kill that motherfucker, *please!*"

Nobody could see him.

Phil slipped off the rig and dashed to the trash pile to give some magazines to Foley and Jimmy Ellifret. The militiaman seemed to take a personal interest in Phil. This time, he emerged and put three rounds right past his ear.

Brase saw Larson go rigid, but not with fear. Weapon up, he spun around until he faced Route Grizzlies. "Oh, you *motherfucker.*"

Brase shouted, "Get out of the road, Sergeant!"

Instead, Larson eased down into a sitting position, never taking his rifle from his shoulder. He kept it aimed at the insurgent's position and waited. When he didn't appear, Larson taunted him, "Go ahead, shoot again you motherfucker!"

Legs crossed, he waited. The insurgent never appeared. Everyone was disappointed; they really wanted to shoot that guy.

As part of the platoon battled the Mahdi at the end of Route Gold, John Neibert fought his own private battle with his squad on the other side of the power station.

When the platoon initially bounded down Route Gold, Neibert looked to the left and saw a series of tall apartment buildings overlooking the north and east side of the power station. He realized he would need to keep those clear, lest the insurgents get an overwatch position on the platoon's left flank.

His trucks turned off on a small road that ran along the north side of Jamelia. It narrowed to an alleyway, then opened up into a long cul-de-sac with a paved street that stretched back to Route Grizzlies. Neibert tried to reach Lieutenant Keelan Rogers, to report his movements, but he received no response. He told his men to sit tight and he went back to Route Gold and explained his intentions to Larson. Phil told him to do it, so John ran back to his men. Leaving the gun trucks lined up across the circular end of the cul-de-sac, their weapons trained down toward Route Grizzlies, Neibert took Sergeant Eric Cole and Private Second Class Joel Presler to recon the route. He hoped to get his whole squad up to Route Grizzlies. That way, they could catch the Mahdi in a crossfire.

The Oregonians ran alongside the power station's east wall and encountered no resistance. They reached Jamelia's southeast corner and could see an open field ahead dotted with construction vehicles and equipment. On the other side of it stretched Route Grizzlies. To the left, an apartment complex dominated the area.

A hail of gunfire greeted their arrival at the southeast corner. Without any cover, the three men hit the asphalt. At least twenty militiamen were shooting at them from a dirt berm on the other side of Route Grizzlies. Others used the berm to fire to the northwest at Larson and his crew.

More Mahdi slipped out of some houses behind the berm to join the fight. Just then, AK fire sang past from the left. That was coming from a warehouse to Neibert's ten o'clock. The Americans fought back with their M4s. Presler, Neibert's grenadier, launched several M203 rounds onto the berm.

Suddenly, Neibert heard a wooosh right over his head and thought an A-10 Warthog had just arrived. He looked up, very happy to have air support, only to realize the sound wasn't a friendly aircraft at all, but an RPG. More followed that first one. They exploded on the other side of the cul-de-sac and in the street nearby. They came in quick succession, but Neibert counted at least a dozen. They couldn't move. The Mahdi had them pinned.

Then a machine-gun team opened fire from their left flank. Neibert swung that direction and saw three Mahdi operating the gun from a window in the apartment building. Moments later, an RPG nearly hit them coming left to right from around the apartment. Another one followed. They exploded on the power station's concrete wall just above the Oregonians.

Caught in this crossfire, Cole went to work on the two Mahdi at the warehouse. He dropped them both while Presler rained grenades on the berm. Every time he killed somebody, another insurgent would scramble out of a house and take his place. Neibert focused on the machine-gunner in the apartment. They were able to cut the volume of incoming fire. This was their chance to get back to the rest of the squad. Neibert called for help. Dale Beshara brought his Humvee to them as his gunner laid down suppressive fire. The three Americans scrambled behind the truck and retreated back to the rest of the squad. It had been a very close call.

Neibert maneuvered his squad to the alley on the north side of the power station. He called for help. He needed more gun trucks and more ammo to hold this sector. Larson told him to push up again and hold the northeast corner.

Neibert tried it. He led his guys back to the cul-de-sac. Just as they reached it, AK fire laced across their vehicles. John set his rigs up in an inverted "L." The squad took incoming from the north, south, and east. They held their own for several minutes, dishing out everything they had against the Mahdi. Then several RPG teams arrived. Using the apartments as cover, they cooked off rockets at Neibert's Humvees.

They couldn't hold without taking casualties, so the squad retreated to the alleyway again. The fight had outgrown their available firepower. Worse, one of his M240s had run out of ammo, and the other two were just about done.

Neibert left his squad and went to find help. On Route Gold, he found Sergeant First Class Terrel from Charlie Company, and he agreed to slice out a pair of trucks and give Neibert some ammo. John led the two Humvees back to the alley, where his men reloaded their weapons. Ready once again, the hybrid Charlie-Alpha force drove back into the cul-de-sac.

The Mahdi gave them a hot reception. Most of the incoming still came from the dirt berm, about two hundred meters to the south. Neibert called up to Lieutenant Rogers and said, "Lieutenant, I can take out that dirt mound with 203s."

Rogers came back, "Smoke 'em."

John got both of his grenadiers together and told them, "Pour everything you've got into that dirt mound. I want it gone."

They took aim and sent their grenades down range. The barrage killed six insurgents and the incoming ebbed away. Then the squad ran out of grenades. The militiamen backfilled the berm from the houses behind it. An RPG gunner stood up, made ready to fire, but was cut down by a volley of M240 bullets spewed from Specialist Jesse Ginestar's gun.

About then, Sergeant First Class Larson appeared with Doc Chatlofsky, who checked out both Neibert and Presler. Joel Presler had suffered a broken hand at some point in the skirmish, but had remained in the fight. Neibert discovered he had RPG shrapnel in one hand, but it was nothing serious. The medic squared them away.

Seconds later, a rocket arrowed out of the apartments to the north, just missing Larson and exploding nearby.

"Jesus, they're all around you!" he exclaimed.

Neibert nodded, "I need more gun trucks."

"Well, I'll go back and talk to the lieutenant and see what we can do."

A few minutes later, Larson told Neibert that Captain Granger would be up soon with Alpha's attached Bradleys. Everyone was to hold their positions until they arrived. The men stayed in the fight and waited for the armor to deliver the knock-out blow.

While Neibert fought his pitched battle on the flank, Nate Lundquist and Larson took note of an alley between the south side of the power station and a small covey of buildings on the corner of Routes Gold and Grizzlies. Worried that this might provide an avenue for the insurgents to hit them from the east, Larson and Lundquist moved down the alley and came to the field littered with construction equipment across from the dirt berm.

Larson realized they needed more people. He radioed Lieutenant Rogers, "Mustang, we've got to have more men."

"I've got nothing to give you." The platoon was spread over three positions on Route Gold, the southeast and northeast corners of the power station.

"I don't give a shit. Just get me somebody."

Moments later, Staff Sergeant Ellifret, the FSO (fire support officer), walked up the alley.

Larson saw him and was puzzled. "Sergeant Ellifret, are you alone?"

"Yeah."

"Oh crap."

"What are we doing?"

"We've got to hold this corner."

Ellifret, thoroughly unconcerned, asked, "Okay. Where do you want me?"

Larson told him to head over to a series of concrete blocks near the power station's wall. Ellifret sauntered over there, only to draw a burst of AK fire from the apartments to the east.

The bullets scarred the wall behind Ellifret, who hit the dirt and shouted, "Goddamned, I can't believe they're shooting at me!"

Larson called Rogers, "Okay, we're being shot at. We need more people here right goddamned now!"

Mike Brase and Specialist Dustin "Swamp Donkey" Pennington showed up a minute later.

Brase piped out, "Hey, are you guys getting shot at over here?"

"Yeah, get over to Sergeant Ellifret."

Brase walked over to Ellifret. Right then, a Mahdi rifleman in the apartment building touched off a burst from his AK. The bullets spattered the ground all around Brase. He fell face-first into the dirt.

"They're shooting at me!" Brase yelled.

"I know, now get your ass up to the concrete blocks!"

Brase scurried like a turtle on his stomach to reach the cover.

"I can't believe they fucking shot at me. Those goddamned assholes!"

Ellifret looked at Brase and said, "Well, you better get used to it. They've been doing it the whole time I've been here."

In the heat of the moment, their adrenaline racing from the close calls, both men burst out laughing.

"So Sergeant Ellifret, what do we have going on here?"

"Well, there's three guys in that apartment over there."

Several more rounds snapped overhead. These had come from the warehouse Neibert had earlier suppressed. Brase molded himself to the concrete block, and seconds later, two bullets smacked into the dirt where he'd just been lying.

Ellifret half-rose and shouted, "Come on, let's go fucking get them! Let's attack them!"

"Dude, Jimmy, have you lost your mind? There's two of us and a great big fucking apartment complex! We've got these nice concrete blocks here!"

Disappointed, Ellifret settled back down and started shooting.

Larson wanted to call in artillery fire to wax the warehouse, but the rules of engagement prohibited this. Then, from an alleyway near the warehouse a group of militiamen carrying a belt-fed PKM (Soviet 7.62mm) machine gun let rip with a long burst at Larson and his four men.

Phil told Pennington to take his M203 and drop a grenade on the PKM team.

Pennington moved forward, peeked around some of the construction equipment, and saw the position. The militiamen saw him and sent a burst his way.

"Okay, I think I've got it."

Pennington loaded a grenade, flipped up the leaf site, and popped off a round. The grenade sailed down the alley and landed hundreds of meters long somewhere in Sadr City.

"Goddamn it, Swamp Donkey! I want the position right there!" Larson yelled, pointing at the PKM team.

"Okay, Sergeant." Pennington reloaded and fired again. The grenade vanished into Sadr City.

Suddenly, an RPG sizzled into the top of the power station's wall directly behind Brase and Ellifret. Larson turned, the PKM forgotten for the moment. He saw the rocket's vapor trail and knew right away it had been fired from the roof of the apartment building. The top of the power plant wall had saved Brase and Ellifret. If it had been a foot shorter, the RPG would have landed right between them.

A volley of fire kept the Oregonians down. They fought back, shooting into the apartment complex in a frantic effort to suppress the Mahdi on the high ground. Ellifret and Mike banged away with their M4s, which sparked a fire amid some trash in front of the concrete blocks. Both men gagged as they inhaled the acrid smoke.

"Gah, garbage dust." Mike pulled out a canteen and tried to stifle his stomach with a fresh drink of water. It went through him at record speed.

Oh fuck, now I have to piss.

Brase turned to Ellifret, "Hey Jimmy, are you gonna make fun of me if I piss my pants?"

"What, are you scared?"

"No, dude, I'm pretty hydrated. I really gotta go pee!" Brase shouted over to Larson, who was hunkered down behind a back hoe, "I gotta pee!"

Normally, Phil would have sent somebody to take his place, but there was no one. He yelled back, "Roll over and whip it out!"

Brase assessed the situation. If he moved to the right, the Mahdi in the apartment would kill him. If he rolled left, he'd urinate on Ellifret's leg. It was a conundrum not covered in basic training.

Mike stayed in place, dug a small hole out of the trash around him, and let fly. Then he rolled over on to it. Better that than pissing on a buddy.

The sun went down and darkness engulfed the battlefield. The five Oregonians remained in place, popping off shots whenever the insurgents exposed themselves. Conversely, they drew fire every time they moved. Finally, they drove the insurgents out of the apartment complex, but the Mahdi still held the south side of Route Grizzlies. The five Oregonians could not dislodge them.

That was the situation until the Bradleys showed up; two thundered down Route Gold and parked at the intersection on the north side of the traffic circle. The insurgents there either fled or died. Moments later, a Brad reached Larson's five men. It fired a single shot from its 25mm and blew the PKM team to bits six hundred meters away.

The PKM lay in the road, and the insurgents wanted it back. Every few minutes, a daring soul would dash into the street, unarmed. The Bradley crew couldn't fire at him. According to the ROE, they had to be holding a weapon. But as soon as the militiaman touched the PKM, the Brad crew lit him up. They killed at least eight militiamen who tried to get that gun.

The Mahdi could not stand in the face of the deadly Bradleys, and they melted to the fringes of the fight to snipe at 3rd Platoon sporadically through the night.

FORTY-ONE

THE FIGHT ON
THE PERIMETER

While 3rd Platoon, Alpha, fought its battle around the power station, Captain Granger coordinated the engagement with Captain Welch from a position farther up Route Gold. Nearby, Sergeant Terrel's platoon set up a blocking position behind the apartment complex. As night fell, Captain Granger consolidated 3rd Platoon around the power station, pulling Neibert from his cul-de-sac back to Route Gold near the intersection with Route Grizzlies.

Terrel's platoon took intermittent contact throughout the night. At one point, a car came speeding toward them. The gunners shot it up, only to discover an Iraqi man and his son were inside. Fortunately, both survived and they were able to get them to a hospital in an ambulance. Not long after, an AK-wielding insurgent appeared on the roof of one of the apartment buildings. Specialist Trevor Hutchinson killed him with a burst from his M240.

At 2130 hours, Captain Welch ordered them back to Volunteer.

Wyatt had set up around the IP station with Jackson's platoon. He'd come out with 2nd Platoon, Charlie, and some of the Bradleys. Welch resupplied Jackson's men and provided security while a wrecker arrived to repair Edwards' rocket-damaged truck.

They fought a sporadic battle around the IP station for several hours before Welch moved the platoon north to the intersection of Routes Gold and Hamms, where they established an outer cordon for the rest of the Volunteers. Not long after, a car drove headlong into the concertina wire the platoon had placed across the road. Thinking it was a VBIED, the gunners opened fire and set the vehicle ablaze. The flames trapped a woman inside, and despite the Oregonian's best efforts to get her out, she perished in the blaze.

Not long afterward, insurgents opened fire on the platoon and launched an RPG at its Humvees. AK-47s barked, and Private First Class John Karrantza suffered a grazing wound to his face.

While Charlie covered the north side of the engagement area, the scout platoon set up another blocking position on the Route Grizzlies overpass across Route Pluto. Some of the Iraqi National Guardsmen the battalion had been training came out in support. They could hear the fighting rage up Route Grizzlies and in Sadr City. In fact, much of the eastern half of the city seethed with countless small-unit skirmishes.

An RPG shot out of Sadr City and passed over the scouts from the south-east. Randy Mitts tried to find the gunner, but he ducked back into an alleyway. A few minutes later, Sergeant Andy Hellman heard sledgehammer-on-metal crashing above him. He spun around just in time to see debris cascade down around him. Mike Giordano, the scout's medic, ran over to Andy and threw him on the ground. Giordi told him an RPG had struck a road sign right above Andy's head. The collision deflected the rocket downward, and it plopped onto the road about two feet from Andy. It did not detonate. It was the first of multiple close calls Andy Hellman received that August.

Alpha Company spent the night spread from Jamelia up north to the power station. Every time the Bradleys moved or returned to Volunteer to resupply, the fighting flared again, but never with the intensity of the earlier skirmishes. The Oregonians remained in place until mid-morning when the BC called them home. Third Platoon departed first. Granger and the Bradleys followed. When Jackson's men left the IP station, the Mahdi turned out to bid them adieu. The platoon took AK fire and more RPGs all the way into Rusapha.

The battle for the Jamelia Power Station lasted eighteen hours, the battalion's longest single engagement in Baghdad. The Volunteers suffered five casualties, all of whom either stayed in the fight or returned to duty shortly afterward. In return, the Mahdi sustained heavy casualties. Exactly how many went down will probably never be known, but it certainly numbered at least a hundred. Unlike in Vietnam, the army in Iraq was not obsessed with counting bodies. Moreover, the insurgents made that very difficult, as they went to great lengths to recover the corpses of their dead comrades.

August 5 signaled a new phase in the 2-162 deployment. Aside from the June 4 incident and a few scattered IED ambushes, the Volunteers had not engaged in a stand-up fight until Jamelia. It was the opening round of a series of battles and small-unit actions that would turn Zone 22 into a bullet-scarred madhouse for the next month and a half.

FORTY-TWO

KILOMETER-LONG KILL ZONE

Just after lunchtime the next day, the battalion TOC received a desperate phone call from the Iraqi police in Zone 22. Mahdi militiamen were everywhere, storming both Station Six on Route Gold and Station Two not far away. The IPs also reported the Mahdi were laying mines on the road. Lieutenant Colonel Hendrickson ordered the scout platoon to investigate.

Lieutenant Boyce rolled with five Humvees. Sergeant Paul's led out, followed by Boyce's vehicle and Andy Hellman's Rat Rig. Bumgardner and Mitts, both in 1114s, brought up the rear.

They sped to Zone 22 and found nothing. At Station Six, Boyce discovered only three IPs had shown up for work. No mines littered Route Gold. Nobody was getting overrun. A check at Al Quids, Station Two, revealed the same thing: the facility was minimally manned and no Mahdi lurked nearby.

Boyce decided to patrol the area. They drove down to Route Grizzlies and spotted tires burning and people moving on the rooftops. Boyce ordered a U-turn to get them back up to Route Hamms, which ran southwest to northeast through Zone 22.

Just as they reached Hamms, a four-Humvee column from Bravo 3-153 Infantry blitzed past them. Their MK19 gunner launched a few rounds down Hamms, then yelled to the Oregonians, "Don't go down there!"

The Arkansans bolted. As the Volunteers watched them disappear, Paul came over the radio, "What do you want us to do, sir?"

Boyce replied, "Let's go check it out." It was the scouts job to find the enemy. This looked like a good place to start. The Volunteers turned right onto Hamms and drove headlong into a fight. Boyce had fourteen men in the five rigs.

Up ahead, the Volunteers saw a gaggle of black-clad men standing in the street. None appeared to have any weapons, but the men wore the pseudo-uniform of the Mahdi militia: black with green arm- or headbands. The Mahdi scampered for the side streets and alleyways.

In Bumgardner's vehicle, his iPod cranked "Cowboys from Hell," an old '90s, death-metal tune by Pantera. It seemed particularly appropriate at the moment. As it blared, an explosion rocked the column. Tyson looked over at his driver, Trevor Ward, and the two broke into a grin. It was on now.

The Americans drove into the kill zone at 35 mph. Paul's vehicle had transmission trouble that day, and Specialist Trimble, his driver, had the gas pedal floored in hopes of coaxing extra speed out of the ailing Humvee. No luck.

From the rooftops, alleyways, shop fronts, and even the curb, Mahdi militia boiled out, weapons blazing. Bullets flew, and the RPGs soon followed. Boyce looked out on a sea of muzzle flashes and knew his men were in for the fight of their lives. Tyson opened his window and laid down fire with his M4. In the rig behind his, Randy Mitts did the same. Every bit of firepower would be needed to get through this.

An RPG skipped across Tyson's hood. Another one ricocheted off Andy Hellman's softtop. In fact, the Rat Rig attracted all sorts of attention because it looked so different from the other Humvees. The Mahdi took potshots at it with AK-47s, RPKs, and rockets. Somehow the vehicle emerged unscathed.

Not Mitts' 1114. An RPG gunner jumped out behind them and sent a rocket right into the back bumper. It blew the vehicle's rear end into the air.

Mitts keyed his mic, "We just took an RPG in the ass!"

Another RPG hit Paul's rig but failed to explode.

The Mahdi had set up a clever ambush. On one block, all the insurgents would be on the right side of the road. On the next, they'd be on the left. This forced the American gunners to constantly traverse their turrets.

Tyson emptied his magazine and grabbed another one. Just as he slammed it in place, a militiaman with an AK-47 stepped into the street not five meters away. Bumgardner put a three-round burst into his chest, and he spun out of sight. Behind Tyson, Randy spotted at least a dozen Mahdi in an alleyway, some with RPGs. Mitts emptied a full magazine into them.

An RPG-armed Mahdi ran from an alley to the left and aimed his weapon at Recon Six, Lieutenant Boyce's rig. Less than ten feet away, Ross' gunner, specialist Ash, saw the threat and engaged him with his .50-cal. The militiaman exploded. One dismembered arm spun crazily across Recon Six's hood. Ash laid on the trigger and hosed the alley and nearby building. The entire front of the structure collapsed.

In the lead rig, Sergeant Paul's gunner, Specialist Nathan Gushwa, suddenly whipsawed against the back of the turret and fell into the cab. The insurgents had strung a wire across the road, right at head level for the gunners. It had caught Gushwa and inflicted a severe neck injury that left him with lasting nerve damage. He went down so hard that Tyson thought he'd been killed. Then Gushwa climbed back into the turret to engage the enemy again. At some point, an IED detonated near Sergeant Paul's truck. A thick, jagged hunk of shrapnel struck the back of the turret and fell behind the rear shield. Gushwa stayed on his gun, and his fellow scouts estimated he killed at least thirty insurgents. As the rear of the column reached the alleyways he had sprayed, they saw Mahdi corpses sprawled in heaps.

The Volunteers drove through the kill zone and realized they had hit the militia before they'd been able to fully establish their ambush. Stacks of artillery shells stood by the road. Obviously, they planned to set up a host of IEDs but hadn't had the chance to do it yet. It was a good thing, too. If any one of the Humvees had been immobilized, the men inside probably would have died. And if the platoon had stopped to defend the stricken vehicle, Ross might have lost every man. Their Humvees' mobility, armor, and firepower kept them alive that day. So did the marksmanship of Gushwa and Ash. The scouts credited them with saving the entire platoon that day.

Boyce estimated eight to ten RPGs had been fired at them, but that was probably conservative. Tyson counted at least twenty crisscrossing over and between their Humvees.

They ran the Mahdi gauntlet for more than a kilometer before breaking into the clear. Even then, the militiamen shadowed and chased them in five bongo trucks before peeling off and leaving the scouts alone for good.

But the fight was far from over that day.

FORTY-THREE

THE FACE OF THE ENEMY

Lieutenant Colonel Hendrickson linked up with the scouts at an intersection on Route Wild. Captain Welch, who'd brought a platoon-plus out to support Ross, showed up a few minutes later. The three leaders conferred.

Wyatt had part of 2nd Platoon and all of Sergeant First Class Terrel's platoon with him. Ezelle and his platoon were down at the hotels.

Hendrickson turned to Welch. "How many vehicles you got?"

"Fourteen, sir."

"I have two. How many you got?"

Boyce replied, "Five, sir."

Twenty-one gun trucks was a lot of firepower. The BC formulated a plan.

Captain Welch and his 2nd Platoon would advance down Route Portland until it intersected with Routes Montana and Hamms, which was where the scouts first engaged the Mahdi. Sergeant Terrel's men from 3rd Platoon would advance along Route Dechutes and form the northern flank. Terrel would go all the way down Dechutes until it intersected with Route South Dakota, which would take the platoon to the far end of Hamms. Between Routes Portland and Dechutes, the BC and the scouts would push down Route Rogue. Route Montana intersected all three of these roads, and dead-ended to the south at Route Hamms. Once the three elements reached Route Montana, they'd hold and the BC would decide where to maneuver next. To reinforce the Humvees, the BC called up Alpha's attached 2-7 Bradleys. Brunk Conley jumped in the back of one track as they left the wire to join the Volunteers. When they arrived, Hendrickson ordered them to go with Sergeant First Class Terrel's platoon down Route Dechutes.

It would be the battalion's first combat advance to contact, and never had they had this much firepower available.

The miniature battle-groups dispersed to take their assigned roads. The BC climbed into his Humvee and joined the middle of the scout platoon's column. Together, his two rigs and Boyce's five turned onto Route Rogue looking for trouble.

Route Rogue looked like a ghost town right out of a spaghetti Western. Only the tumbleweeds were missing. Not a soul moved on the street and every shop was closed. Mitts, who had switched positions with Bumgardner and was now next-to-last in the formation, spotted perhaps the only noncombatant out on the street that day. It was a kid. He made a throat-slashing gesture, then mimicked a man firing an RPG. As they approached Route Montana, Gushwa sighted two RPG gunners in an alleyway to the left. His vehicle passed it before he could get his gun to bear, and when the next vehicle came to it, the two insurgents had vanished. Now they knew bad guys lurked on the fringes of Route Rogue. The BC halted the column, the vehicles spread out to cover down on the alleyways. The scouts dismounted, ready for a fight.

To the south, Captain Welch, 2nd Platoon, Charlie Company, advanced down Route Portland. To the north, Terrel and the Bradleys ran into trouble on Dechutes. They began taking fire and the Bradleys discovered a roadblock that prevented them from getting to Hamms. Inside one of the Bradleys, Sergeant Major Brunk Conley could hear the 25 mike-mike unloading on something. The noise inside the armored box was absolutely deafening, and he didn't hear the RPGs whizzing by. Only later did the Brad commander casually mention that. The Bradley gunners tried to destroy the roadblock, but their 25 mike-mikes did little damage to it.

The skirmish raged and the Brads came to a halt. They would be unable to get through to Route Hamms. Meanwhile, at the intersection of Deschutes and South Dakota, Terrel's platoon found itself in the middle of the fight again. Small arms fire laced their Humvees, and several insurgents dashed from cover, AKs blazing. A bullet struck Staff Sergeant Joseph Tumbaga in the right forearm. The platoon got him back to the battalion aid station, and he later became the first Charlie Company soldier to be evacuated from theater due to a combat wound.

While the Bradleys and 3rd Platoon, Charlie, fought their own skirmish on Dechutes, the enemy struck the scouts a few blocks to the south.

On Rogue, a small crowd of unarmed males gathered in an alley about a hundred meters from Tyson Bumgardner's trail rig. Tyson dismounted and eyeballed the Iraqis. On the other side of the street, Randy Mitts also dismounted while his gunner Chuck Mangus covered another alleyway.

Suddenly, an RPG zipped overhead and exploded into one of the southside buildings on Route Rogue. Mitts looked around. So did Lieutenant Colonel Hendrickson who was standing only a few meters away.

Behind Bumgardner's rig, an RPG gunner burst from the crowd in the alleyway. The onlookers scattered. The gunner's loader, a slim youth, followed him out into the street. The BC carried a snub-nosed Barretta submachine gun that day. He used it as his personal weapon when visiting the NACs and DACs in AO Volunteer. For close-range firefights, it would have been an excellent weapon. On the street was another matter. He pulled the trigger and the Barretta spewed rounds. He missed. After this mission, the Barretta went in the trash and he carried an M4 for the rest of the deployment.

Tyson saw the RPG team break through the crowd. Before he could react, the gunner cooked off his rocket. Time stopped for Bumgardner. The RPG flew in ultra-slow motion straight for his chest. He knew it would hit him. He dropped to one knee, shouldered his M4, and just before he pulled the trigger, the RPG deflected downward. It exploded in the street fifty feet from him, showering him with bits of roadway and dirt.

On the other side of the street, Mitts saw the loader slam another rocket onto the tube. Randy dashed behind a blue Chevy Suburban parked on the northside curb. He leveled his M4 and drew a bead on the gunner through the SUV's windows. He fired. His first two rounds shattered the windshield. The third one struck the gunner in the chest. Simultaneously, Tyson triggered his M4. He watched his tracers disappear into the center of the target. A split-second later, Bumgardner's gunner unleashed his M240.

The RPG gunner staggered, bent forward, and let his launcher droop down. In his dying agony, the insurgent triggered his freshly reloaded weapon. The rocket exploded between his legs. He disintegrated. Only his shoes, feet still in them, remained on the street. The blast also threw his loader under a nearby minibus.

The BC called Randy on his Motorola, "Sergeant Mitts, can you retrieve the RPG?"

"Roger, sir."

Mitts ran over to the back of Bumgardner's Humvee and saw Tyson still kneeling at the right rear fender. Even after the gunner blew himself up, Tyson had continued to fire. He'd emptied his magazine into the carnage. Now, Tyson reloaded and moved to help Trevor Ward, whose M4 had jammed.

Randy explained the BC's intent. Tyson finished reloading while he and Mitts made quick plans to recover the RPG. As they talked, a militiaman opened fire on them. An AK round went right through Tyson's grenade pouch. Later he found it had destroyed his compass.

They bounded down the street, using the parked cars for cover. As they advanced, Bumgardner's gunner fired short bursts into the minibus. Nobody knew if the RPG loader was dead or alive, but they weren't taking any chances. Mitts and Tyson also fired as they ran. Now they could see a bloody heap lying under the bus. The loader had met his end.

Rounds kept cracking around their heads. Neither American could see who was shooting at them. The street was alive with echoes of gunshots and 25mm fire from the Bradleys, still engaged a few blocks to the north.

A bongo truck pulled up a northside alley right in front of Mitts' rig. In the turret, Chuck Mangus saw a militiaman pop up from the back and fire a rocket at him from fifty meters away. The RPG sailed high. Mangus went cyclical with his M240. In seconds, three hundred rounds bored through the front of the bongo truck, killed the driver and the passenger, and knocked the RPG gunner off the back. He fell to the alley peppered with bullets. He died before he could escape.

Mitts reached the minibus and moved beyond it to a loading dock, where he took cover and scanned for the AK gunners shooting at them. Tyson reached the bus. Underneath it, the corpse stirred.

"Help, please." The plea came in English. Tyson swung around, M4 shouldered, ready to kill.

Cargo pants bathed in blood, hand shredded with more blood pulsing from its ruins, the RPG loader somehow found the strength to roll from under the bus. He reached out to Tyson, entreating mercy with the mangled hand.

He shouldn't have been alive. His body was nothing but organic wreckage. Bullet wounds riddled his arms, legs, torso, and head. Tyson had never seen so much blood pouring from so many places.

Mitts saw the insurgent move and thought only of Tyson's safety. The Mahdi had been known to beg for mercy, only to detonate a grenade as an American went to their assistance. Others carried explosives and blew themselves up as soldiers approached. Bloody, wounded, dying or not, he represented a clear military threat.

"Finish him, Bum," Randy said.

Tyson stared at him through the sights of his rifle. Not six feet away, the insurgent struggled in a widening pool of his own blood. With a start, Tyson realized that under the horrible damage their weapons had inflicted, this tormented creature had once been a teenage boy.

Randy was right. He should shoot him. This was the enemy that embraced suicide bombers, VBIEDs, and self-destruction as a form of warfare. He could still be lethal.

"Please, am student. Student."

"Where's the RPG?" demanded Randy.

"No! No RPG! Help. Mercy."

"Kill him."

Tyson fingered the trigger. A deep upwell of terror, raw and keen, rose in him. Involuntarily, he took a step back. He'd never felt fear in a firefight. In fact, he had considered them more a rough team sport than killing. Now that he could see in excruciating detail what pulling the trigger meant, he stood on the edge of an abyss that could transform him from warrior to executioner. Fall into that, and this image would linger for a lifetime—this misguided kid twisting in his death throes.

He made his decision.

Finger on the trigger, barrel of the M4 pointed right at the boy's head, Tyson said, "No, I won't do it. I won't kill him."

Randy held his fire as well. A bullet cracked overhead. Then another. They were still under attack by those unseen militiamen.

Tyson steeled himself. "Come here."

How much was mere instinct? How much was this kid's monumental will to live? Tyson would never know. But as he motioned to him, the teen warrior rose shakily to his feet. He looked like he'd been run across a cheese grater.

"Please, student." He burbled an Arabic prayer and begged for his life. He took a step. Tyson braced himself. He keyed his Motorola and called Lieutenant Boyce and asked for a medic. The student took another step, then fell across the curb, his flayed hand reaching for Tyson, falling across the soldier's pant leg. A smear of blood marked the effort. The student bled out, face down, inches from Tyson's boot. Even had a medic arrived, his wounds were far too numerous to treat. Lieutenant Boyce ordered them back. Randy and Tyson left the dead insurgent and returned to their vehicles.

The BC told them saddle up. He had tried to get air and armor support, but nothing was available. With the Brads unable to push forward, a wounded man in Terrel's platoon, and his Humvees vulnerable to RPG fire, Hendrickson decided to break contact. They'd have to hit this hornet's nest later with more force, more firepower, if they were to be decisive.

The Oregonians returned to Volunteer. Later that night, Randy found Tyson and thanked him for not shooting the student. Militarily, it would have been justifiable. They were still under fire, and he'd only moments before loaded the rocket that had nearly killed Tyson.

But doing what was militarily correct and defensible was not always the *right* thing. By holding their fire, Tyson and Randy—who could have just as easily killed the boy–had proved that they would not let the horrors of war strip them of their humanity.

FORTY-FOUR

THE PRIVATE WAR OF
SERGEANT HELLMAN

Sergeant Andy Hellman was not a man who would ever stand out in a crowd. In fact, he went to great lengths to avoid notice. At parties, he was always the silent guy in the back of the room. Andy relished anonymity and used it like a cloak.

Fate has a sense of irony. Somehow, the Gods of War selected this shy scout for extra-special attention during the August chaos in Baghdad. His buddies noticed it and nicknamed him the "RPG Magnet." It was an apt description. On August 5, an RPG hit a sign directly over his head. The next day, Andy and the Rat Rig endured a thorough rocketing on Route Hamms. As the second week in August began, the Mahdi militia put in overtime trying to kill Andy.

It started with a mortar barrage at lunchtime on August 9. The first blasts rocked Patrol Base Volunteer and sent the KBR (Kellogg, Brown and Root) employees scurrying for the bunkers. Andy and Sergeant George Gordon heard the first explosions and stepped outside onto a second floor veranda to watch the attack.

A mortar landed near the maintenance bay. Another one exploded halfway between the bay and the scout hooch. Gordon said, "Wow, that one was really close."

A third one detonated less than a football field away, prompting Andy to say, "That's too close! Let's get back inside."

As they turned to leave, a fourth 82mm mortar landed next to their front door. The blast sent Andy and Gordon diving for cover.

On the floor below them, the scout's irascible medic, Michael Giordano, lay in a pool of his own blood. He'd been standing in the doorway shouting at the KBR employees when mortar landed. It blew him back into the building as shrapnel peppered everything inside the room, including a mortarman named Ben Freilinger who had been manning the radio.

Lieutenant Boyce had been walking back from lunch with Lieutenant Boeholt when the attack began. When they heard over their Motorolas that two men were down, Boeholt looked at Boyce and said, "Come on, let's go."

They ran through the mortar barrage to reach their wounded men.

Andy and George stormed down the stairs and found Giordano sprawled in the smoke-filled room. Every window had been shattered, and the stench of cordite mingled with the coppery smell of blood. Gordon bent down and went to work on Giordano. This was no easy feat. Giordi was not an affable man under the best of circumstances. He used to tell the scouts, "I'll save your life if I have to, but I'm not your personal Jesus." Now, he was pissed off, scared, and in tremendous pain. He made a lousy patient. He kept telling Gordon what to do.

"Check my eye."

"Your eye is fine."

"Is my liver okay?"

"You've been hit in the neck, Giordi."

Boyce and Boeholt burst through the door. They could see that their men had things under control. Freilinger, whose wounds were not serious, was already bandaged and would soon return to duty. But Giordi's neck wound looked pretty bad. They called for an ambulance, and the men loaded their medic aboard.

Giordano recovered from his wound at Walter Reed Hospital in Washington, D.C. Somehow, he talked his way back to Baghdad and returned to the platoon. The scouts were overjoyed to have him back—but that was months away.

Losing Giordano outraged the scouts. The base had been mortared from Sadr City almost every day in August, and the Volunteers could do nothing about it because Sadr City was 2-5 Cav's battlespace. The BC had tried to get 2-5's help in dealing with the attacks, but they had their hands full.

Well, enough was enough. Randy Mitts approached Lieutenant Boyce soon after Giordano's evacuation and said, "Sir, we have to do something about this."

The two men came up with a plan. If they couldn't go into Sadr City, they could use their sniper assets to kill the mortar crews. Boyce told Randy to load a trailer full of ammo, food, and water while he cleared their idea with the BC.

That night, the scouts slipped out of Patrol Base Volunteer and made the short run to Martyr's Monument, carrying enough supplies to last them four days. They hid their Humvees in the underground parking garage, where Boyce set up a mini–command post. He divided the platoon into three sections. One would be back with the rigs while the other two patrolled and looked for a good overwatch position.

One of the patrols returned and told Lieutenant Boyce that they'd found a ten-story building with an underground garage with a perfect view of Sadr City. Boyce decided to move to it at about 0230 that morning. When they reached the building, they discovered the Humvees were too tall to fit inside the parking garage. Boyce elected to hide them near the rear entrance behind a concrete wall. The men threw debris on top of their rigs to camouflage them further.

The building had been badly damaged in the past. The upper floors were little more than steel beams and scaffolding where intermittent repairs were under way. Above the fourth floor, there weren't any exterior walls at all. The single stairway upward was missing many steps, and parts of it seemed ready to collapse. Nevertheless, the view from the building could not be matched. The scouts set up an overwatch on the seventh floor and settled into a rotation. One section would stay on duty while the other two rested or pulled security by the Humvees.

It was an eventful night in Baghdad. Off to the north, Mahdi militiamen launched salvos of rockets that lit up the dark sky with brilliant red glows. They'd streak for the Green Zone and impact behind the scouts. Periodically, an AC-130 gunship would open fire with a sudden "brrrrrrrr" as its guns chewed up some target in Sadr City. Tracers arced back and forth as skirmishes raged between the 2-5 Cav and Moqtada's street army.

Andy Hellman had been dozing down by the Humvees when the first faint fingers of dawn crawled over the horizon. A tremendous explosion jarred Andy out of his repose. Whatever it was, the scouts grew extra alert, and most of the men down at the vehicles headed upstairs filled with a sense that they'd soon be in a fight.

Up on the seventh floor, the scouts scanned Sadr City looking for anything suspicious. Andy took that opportunity to snap a few photos of the sunrise and the view of Baghdad from their position. From Sadr City, they could still hear bursts of small-arms fire, punctuated by an occasional RPG. But in their line of sight, the enemy eluded them.

The hours dragged on, and as lunchtime approached, Andy came off watch and returned to the Humvees to get something to eat. He sat down on a stack of tires and was just about to tackle an MRE when a mortar round exploded back by Patrol Base Volunteer.

On the seventh floor, the scouts heard the mortar launch, but they still could not see any Mahdi fighters. A half hour passed without further incident. Finally, some kids emerged from a few houses along Route Florida, a road inside Sadr City that ran parallel to Pluto. They dragged tires into the street and set them afire. Either it was a signal or the kids were trying to melt the asphalt so IEDs could be planted in the road. The scouts watched this intently.

A few mintues later, a white four-door sedan screeched to a stop next to the tire fire. Four men poured out of the car and sprinted behind a house and a checkerboard fence. Tyson watched them through his binoculars and grew suspicious. He was lying prone behind an M240 at the far right end of the building. The rest of the scouts were on line in what would have been a room to Tyson's left, only it didn't have any intact interior walls.

Tyson stood up and went to tell Sergeant Paul and Sergeant Buchholz what he'd just seen. Buchholz, behind the platoon's .50-caliber Barrett sniper rifle, quickly picked out the men with his scope. So did Sergeant Paul. Only seconds later, the two scouts heard the "thunk" of a mortar launch and spotted a puff of dirt right behind the house they were watching. Paul observed a second launch a short distance up the street. They'd found their Mahdi mortarmen.

Lieutenant Boyce asked, "What's going on? Where's the launch?"

Buchholz explained the situation. Boyce told him to take the first shot, then everyone would open up and finish off the mortar teams. Buchholz hunkered down behind his .50-cal's scope, picked out a target, and fired. As he chambered another round, everyone else opened up.

It was pure slaughter. The Mahdi had no idea where the scouts were hiding, and as the mortar teams went down, fighters boiled out of every house and ran into the street with AKs and RPGs. At first, they thought the Americans must have been firing at them from the north, so they ducked behind walls and houses and peered up Route Florida. Of course, this gave them no cover at all from the scouts, who were six hundred meters to the west and seven stories above them.

Bumgardner used his M240 with telling effect. As the snipers engaged, he spotted the four black-clad militiamen as they ran back to their white sedan. Several bursts and he'd dropped them all. Then he lit up the car for good measure. Buchholz's .50-cal roared, and every time he pulled the trigger, the entire floor vibrated. His accuracy was deadly and gruesome. At six hundred meters, the .50-caliber sniper rounds blew the militiamen apart like cherry-bombed watermelons. On the street, it caused total confusion. One moment a militiaman would be there, the next, he was nothing but pieces sprayed across his comrades. They had no idea what was causing the carnage.

Simultaneously, the platoon's two M240s raked the street. With Trimble spotting for him, Tyson hit or killed at least a dozen militiamen, but more poured into the neighborhood. They ran around, totally confused, unable to find who was shooting at them. Some of the Mahdi tried to take cover in a nearby tire yard, but Bumgardner and Buchholz took a terrible toll on them there. Others ducked behind a cement truck and a garbage truck for cover. The M240s cut them down.

For ten minutes, it was a one-sided shooting gallery. For once, the Americans had actually ambushed the enemy, and it left Al Sadr's minions paralyzed and vulnerable.

Tyson used up most of his ammunition. He changed barrels, swept the brass from under his gun, and called for resupply. Meanwhile, Lieutenant Boyce radioed for indirect fire. The scouts had thought they were going to get 155mm artillery support, which would have been perfect. One fire mission would have taken out all the militiamen below them. Of course, the neighborhood would have been little but smoking craters afterward, so the request was denied. They'd have to continue the fight with only their direct fire weapons.

Boyce got down behind an M24 sniper rifle and engaged targets. He could see the kids who had started the tire fire were now carrying mortar rounds for the adults.

The mortar teams saw no mercy. Their tubes had been dug in behind the houses on Route Florida. Once discovered, the crews had no place to hide. They died under a hail of sniper and M240 fire.

Slowly, as more militiamen showed up, the insurgents rallied. They located the scouts, and scattered fire soon came their way. At first, only a few bullets pinged off the steel beams. Gradually, the intensity of the incoming swelled. Two RPGs slammed into the building. Machine-gun fire swept across the seventh floor. The scouts stayed low and kept shooting, but there were more targets than they could handle. They started to lose fire superiority. Fewer than twenty Americans suddenly found themselves fighting scores, if not more than a hundred, militiamen.

The platoon's pair of M240s helped even things out, and the two gunners sustained an amazing rate of fire. Bumgardner was soon surrounded by ejected shell casings again, some of which slipped down his sleeves and burned his arms.

It didn't matter, he stayed on his targets and systematically eliminated them as Trimble called them out.

The M240s ran low on ammo again. Randy Mitts dashed down the stairs to get more ammunition from the trucks. As he reached the Humvees, he said, "Sergeant Hellman, help me! We need to get more ammo for the 240s."

Andy pulled eight boxes out of the rigs. As they worked, new Mahdi mortar positions opened up on the building. One exploded a hundred feet from Andy. It was his fourth close call in five days.

Carrying as much ammo as they could, Mitts and Hellman risked the mortar fire and ran back for the building. Just as they reached the exterior stairs, a mortar round struck a concrete column less than a dozen meters away. The shrapnel splash miraculously missed them both. Make that five close calls for Andy.

They charged up the stairs. By the fourth floor, Andy's legs started to cramp and he made a mental note to do more PT in the future. He was carrying all his own gear, plus at least thirty to forty pounds of 7.62mm ammunition in four metal cases.

They reached the seventh floor. Randy took his ammo to the other M240 gunner while Andy delivered eight hundred rounds to Tyson Bumgardner. Trimble left to check on Sergeant Paul, so Tyson asked Andy to spot for him. He grabbed the binos and talked Tyson onto a green trailer some insurgents were using as cover. Once on, Tyson started rocking and rolling. Andy picked up his M4 and engaged as well.

Just then, a bullet ricocheted off a nearby beam. It had come from the right. The Mahdi had flanked their building. Tyson tried to get eyes on the shooter, but there were a million positions he could have used in the urban jungle to the south. So he settled down behind the gun and went back to work, staying as low as possible.

Another round smacked close at hand. The guy on their flank was a sniper. He knew what he was doing, and his shots were accurate and calculating. This meant trouble. Andy had been standing up, shooting down into the city. Now, he dropped to one knee. As he did, another bullet bounced off the scaffolding not five feet in front of him. Sobered by the near miss, Andy shouted to Tyson, "Get down!"

Tyson, already prone, tried to mold himself into the floorboards. But he stayed on his gun and kept shooting to the platoon's front. Another round impacted in a piece of dry wall leftover from the building's better days.

Andy looked through his four-power scope and snapped out several shots at militiamen running in the open along a brick wall. Next to him, Tyson unleashed burst after burst, seemingly unconcerned at the incoming sniper fire. Andy finally decided he was too exposed. He looked around at the near-misses and realized he needed to lower his profile. But the Mahdi sharpshooter found his mark.

Probably using a Dragonof sniper rifle, he could see Andy on his knee. He squeezed off another round. The bullet skimmed Tyson's helmet, tearing off the mounting bracket for his night vision goggles. Another two inches to the left, it would have gone through his temple. The bullet continued on and struck Andy

Hellman a sledgehammer blow. His whole body went numb.

Lieutenant Boyce heard somebody shout, "Oh Fuck! I'm hit."

Ross moved toward the voice and shouted, "Who's hit?"

"Sergeant Hellman, sir."

"Where are you hit?"

"My right knee, sir."

The sniper had put his bullet into the side of Andy's knee. The entrance wound was so clean it was hard to see. But inside his body, the bullet tumbled, exiting sideways and left a perfect impression of the slug in his flesh. Tyson flung himself on top of Andy to protect him. Then he dragged him clear into one of the semifinished rooms in the back of the building.

"This is just like you, always trying to get out of work!"

"Shut up."

Tyson began to bandage the wound. He told Andy, "It's not bad. You just got nicked."

Andy was actually kind of disappointed. If he was going to go down, at least it could have been more serious. At the same time, he was scared and going into shock. The pain roared through him and made him cry out. Nevertheless, he thought this would be a good Kodak Moment.

"Grab my camera! Take a picture of this!" Andy said.

"No man, I can't do that."

After Giordi went down, Andy had told his roommate that if he ever got hit, he wanted to be photographed. "I wanna see that shit later."

Now, in the heat of battle Andy's Kodak Moment never came. Everyone was too busy either bandaging him or fighting the enemy.

As he slipped further into shock, he apologized to Lieutenant Boyce for getting hit. It almost embarrassed him. He was causing trouble; he'd become the center of attention. Andy's cloak of anonymity had been torn away by that sniper's bullet, and he felt uncomfortable without it.

Tyson finished up, turned Andy over to a couple of the other scouts, and returned to his gun. Without him suppressing the Mahdi below, the volume of incoming fire had grown considerably. Now they stood on the brink of losing control of the fight. Tyson hunkered down low and hoped the sniper had moved away. That was wishful thinking. As he fired off the last of the eight hundred rounds Andy had delivered, the sniper took shots at him again and again. He stayed there, exposed to that sniper until the last round went through his M240. With the gun empty, he pulled out and joined the rest of the platoon in the main room to the left.

Lieutenant Boyce assessed the situation. They needed to medevac Andy. Getting him down from the seventh floor would be a real challenge. He called back to Volunteer and asked for the QRF to come support them. Lieutenant Williams' 2nd Platoon, Delta Company, the New York boys, came up to assist. Williams had a hard time finding their building. The platoon drove by several times before Boyce finally said, "We're in the ten-story building that all the fire is coming out of."

Williams got the message and found the right spot. Boyce wanted to join up with Williams and attack into Sadr City to recover the mortar tubes, but Lieutenant Colonel Hendrickson nixed that. They couldn't cross Route Pluto and enter the 2-5 Cav's AO. Again, that unit boundary was inviolable.

It was time to leave. Andy insisted on walking down himself. Specialist Ward stayed with him, but Andy limped most of the way on his own. He had gone into shock, and he kept repeating, "We've gotta get outta here. We've gotta get outta here." It made Ward nervous, and he got jumpy listening to Andy's creepy, wound-induced mantra.

On the seventh floor, Buchholz continued to fire his .50-cal Barrett, unaware that the rest of the platoon had pulled out. He'd been firing his weapon without earplugs. Now he could hardly hear. Tyson and Randy stayed behind as well. They laid down cover fire and then, as they moved to the stairs, spotted Buchholz. They went and got him, and as they moved back toward the stairs, Randy observed an insurgent on Route Florida.

"Hold up. I got this shot."

Randy squeezed off a shot with his M4. Seven hundred meters away, an insurgent tumbled to the ground. It was the most remarkable shot Tyson had ever seen. Together, the three scouts left the seventh floor to join the rest of the platoon at the Humvees.

Part of Charlie came out to block off traffic around the base. That gave the scouts a straight shot from the skeletalized building all the way to the battalion aid station (BAS). Andy was in the BAS in less than ten minutes, still apologizing to everyone for spoiling the day.

A raft of visitors flooded into the BAS. Sergeant Major Conley, now totally over whatever it was that kept him from the BAS earlier in the deployment, came to check on him. So did Lieutenant Colonel Hendrickson. The entire scout platoon clustered around him. For all his shyness, Andy never had trouble making friends. He got along with everyone, and now as he suffered, they showed him that the anonymity he craved never hindered the bond that had long since melded the scout platoon as one.

At first, Andy figured he'd be off his feet for a week or two, but when the medics looked him over one said, "Well, looks like you're going to need a new hinge."

They called for a medevac chopper. Andy would be going to the Green Zone CSH. As the helicopter landed, the scouts ran back to their barracks and pulled a huge American flag out of Andy's room. The Volunteers were not allowed to fly Old Glory over their base, but for this one moment, that rule was forgotten. The platoon congregated on the roof, and as the Blackhawk lifted off with Andy inside, his fellow scouts waved that flag in broad strokes as their send-off for their brave, wounded brother. They kept waving it long after the Blackhawk had slipped from view. Hidden for all these months, the Stars and Stripes never looked better than they did that moment in the afternoon Iraqi sun.

FORTY-FIVE

ZONE 22 RODEOS

Later that day, the BC sent the entire scout platoon to talk with a combat stress team. They'd been in three significant fights in less than a week and had lost two men. Most of the men chafed at this. All they wanted was some sleep, then another shot at those mortar tubes. Instead, the men found themselves face-to-face with a Green Zone chaplain who asked them questions like, "Do you miss home? How do you feel about killing?"

The scouts weren't having any of it. They just wanted to fight. Later, the chaplain told Lieutenant Boyce that he'd never seen a more professional group of soldiers in his life.

Yet, for some of the scouts, the *could have beens* lingered in their minds. At the top of that list was the kilometer-long ambush on Route Hamms. If even one of their Humvees had been disabled, the entire platoon probably would have been wiped out.

That thought haunted Lieutenant Boyce, who had taken the loss of Andy and Giordi particularly hard. Though not an Oregonian, he had bonded with his men so tightly that their safety had begun to eat away at him. How could he keep them safe in such hostile conditions? As he worked through his feelings, he realized his own judgment had been compromised by his love for them. A good platoon leader cannot hesitate to send his soldiers into harm's way. Indecision in combat puts everyone at risk. Boyce understood that. More than anything, he wanted to lead his platoon and continue with the scouts, but he knew his best was behind him. And anything less than that was apt to get somebody hurt.

Lieutenant Boyce sat down with Lieutenant Colonel Hendrickson and explained how he felt. He thought he could give a month, maybe two, more to the scouts, but after that he'd be shot through. He wouldn't trust himself to make the life-or-death decisions every platoon leader had to make in combat. The BC understood. Ross Boyce was a fine leader who recognized his limits. Hendrickson pulled him into the battalion staff. Lieutenant Akers would take over the scouts.

It was one of the hardest decisions Ross ever made, but not a man in the platoon ever faulted him for it. In his time with the scouts, Boyce had acted with cool intelligence and tremendous courage. Everyone respected him for that.

The mortar attacks continued unabated. Later that day thirteen rounds fell on the base while rockets sizzled into the Green Zone. In one of those strange twists of urban guerilla warfare, the insurgents had access to indirect fire weapons while the Americans, who traditionally rely on such firepower, did not. In fact, the United States displayed more restraint and concern for collateral damage than the insurgents did.

As the August uprising continued, the Mahdi militia deliberately targeted the downtown hotels with rockets and mortars. Why they devoted so much effort to trying to blow up the Western press corps hunkered down at the Palestine, Sheraton, and Baghdad hotels didn't make much sense at first. But it became apparent that the Mahdi leadership had put together a concerted information warfare campaign. By terrorizing the Western journalists and inhibiting their movements, the militia could control who reported on the events in Baghdad. And those doing the reporting more often than not were the Iraqi and Arab stringers, such as Karim Kadim and Cerwaan Aziz.

When the barrages started hitting the hotels again, Sergeant Ezelle's platoon from Charlie Company had the security detail. Every day they endured rocket and mortar fire as they patrolled around the hotels and stood guard on the rooftops. It was harrowing work.

On August 7, Ezelle conducted a battle hand-off and turned the hotels over to another platoon. His men came down out of the Palestine and Sheraton and gathered at the Humvees while still under indirect fire. Then the call came that two of E. Z.'s men remained on the roof of the Baghdad Hotel. One of them had experienced a seizure and couldn't move.

Ezelle and his medic went to investigate. They found the soldier rigid and shaking violently. Rockets sizzled past; mortars exploded all around them. The soldier stared into space as if this latest barrage had hit his last nerve. Ezelle bent down and talked to his panicked soldier.

"We gotta go. We gotta get back to the vehicles. All you gotta do is get down the stairs. Are you gonna be able to do that?"

The soldier stared with vacant eyes and didn't move. E. Z. hoisted the kid over his shoulders and carried him, body armor and all, down five stories to the street. They took the soldier straight to the battalion aid station, where the medics could not find anything physically wrong with him.

The next day, E. Z. went to see him. The soldier broke down. His self-respect was shot. He loathed himself for what he'd done on the roof.

Ezelle, this bearish, fearless warrior, put a hand on his shoulder and said, "Nobody thinks you're a piece of shit, man. Everyone's got a cup. And when it's full, it's full. Maybe your cup is full."

The soldier gained control. He listened intently as E. Z. continued, "You need to figure out what you want to do. Only you know how far you can go, but I need you to keep this in mind: when you're an old man sitting on your porch looking back on your life, whatever you decide now will affect how you'll deal with that. If you can't go out anymore, it'll be a ghost in your closet and it will haunt you for the rest of your life."

The soldier nodded his head.

"Nobody's gonna bang on you for what you decide. What you've already done is more than most people will ever do. But understand this: there's a whole platoon of guys who need you out there. Without you that's one less man, one less gun that can take it to the bad guys. So think about what you've got inside you. If you've got more to give, give me all. Give me everything you've got."

E. Z. left the kid to his thoughts.

That day, E. Z.'s platoon rotated onto QRF duty. A call came to mount up and head for Zone 22. Ezelle grabbed his Kevlar, picked up his M4, and went to check in with his squad leaders. As he stepped outside, he could see his men sprinting to the Humvees. The young soldier from the Baghdad was with them in full battle rattle.

Ezelle allowed himself a moment of pride. Seeing that kid get into that Humvee represented one of the highest moments of leadership he'd experienced in his military career. Honor intact, the young soldier would ride into battle with them one more time.

And ride into battle they did. With Captain Welch in the middle of their column and Sergeant First Class Tim Bloom functioning as the platoon leader, Charlie's 1st Platoon rolled up into Zone 22 and made contact while driving westbound on Route Rogue. The drivers flexed from a column into a staggered box formation, and the six Humvees drove right into another Mahdi ambush. The gunners opened fire. Ezelle directed them onto targets on rooftops along both sides of the street. Suddenly, a white flash to the front caught his eye. Ezelle watched the rocket almost hit Captain Welch's rig. Then in a furious blur it whipped past E. Z.'s right door, missing his windshield by a matter of inches. It came so close that the rumble of the rocket motor stirred his guts.

It exploded in the street a few meters behind Ezelle's Humvee, throwing up a curtain of dirt that rained down on staff Sergeant DeGiusti's trail Humvee. The rocket's shank spun clear of the impact and bounced onto his hood.

DeGiusti jumped out of his vehicle to clean off the windshield. As he did, Ezelle dismounted to check on him. Bullets cracked overhead and richoted off the roadbed, but neither man was hit. With the windshield clear, they remounted and stepped on the gas.

Minutes later, they emerged on Route Wild. To Ezelle, it was like crossing a finish line. Except for the Mahdi militiamen shooting at them, Rogue had been deserted. Crossing onto Route Wild brought them into everyday Baghdad traffic with people and vehicles going in all directions.

And so it went in Zone 22 during August 2004. Just about every platoon in every company ended up in a running vehicular firefight while up in the North Sadr City area. Zone 50, to the north of 22, was no different. Charlie Company took fire again while going to the rescue of IP Station Two, which had reported its chief had been kidnapped and the building overrun by militiamen. When Captain Welch brought out two platoons to check on it, he found the place manned by almost forty Iraqi police and Iraqi national guardsmen (INGs). The call had been made to orchestrate another ambush, and the Mahdi hit Charlie with RPGs and small-arms fire again.

Staff Sergeant Aaron Cochran led the column that day, and as he turned onto Route Montana from Rogue, they took small-arms fire. Halfway down Route Montana, Cochran looked out the left side and saw a militiaman rise up from behind a rock pile only a few feet away from them.

"Three o'clock!" Cochran called out. Then he realized his mistake. "No, nine o'clock, nine o'clock."

Standing erect, the militiaman hoisted an RPG onto his shoulder. He had Cochran's rig dead to rights. Aaron's gunner saw it coming and ducked down out of the turret. He didn't have time to bring his weapon to bear.

A flash, and Cochran's 1114 reeled from a close-order explosion. Exactly what happened remains unclear, but the nearest vehicle later reported the rocket actually impacted on the cooler strapped to the back of the Humvee. It richocheted back into the rock pile and exploded, blowing the Mahdi RPG man to pieces. Talk about just deserts.

The Volunteers repeatedly went to the rescue of the IP stations up in Zone 22, only to find they'd cried wolf or actively helped set up the Americans to be ambushed. To counter this, the companies used the back alleys and narrow streets not normally traveled by the military. That helped, but the fact of the matter was the IP stations remained a millstone around the battalion's neck.

Captain Granger led one mission into Zone 22 on August 10 with 3rd Platoon and Commanche 2-7's element Humvees and Bradleys, which were on loan to the battalion. En route, 3rd Platoon suffered a vehicular breakdown and diverted to the Alpha Bunker near Route Pluto. That left Granger with the Brads. He pressed on, and they ran into a coordinated ambush. The insurgents demolished one of the Commanche Humvees in the attack, wounding several men. Captain Granger pulled out of the kill zone, but the BC ordered him to go back in and recover the Humvee. The 1st Cav Division had issued standing orders to recover all destroyed vehicles. This was a result of photos and film taken by the Iraqi stringers depicting insurgents celebrating around burning American vehicles. The propaganda value of such images was enormous, and the American high command wanted to avoid such incidents in the future.

That meant nothing to Granger and his men at that moment. The fight had been a furious one, and his outnumbered Joes were now supposed to risk their lives for a wrecked vehicle? He protested the order. Hendrickson angrily ordered him to execute. Granger did so, and his men dragged the Humvee clear with a Bradley, but the incident destroyed the tenuous working relationship between the two men.

A few weeks later, Granger elected to go home with the first of the COT-TADs (contingency operations temporary tour of duty) from Alpha Company. The COTTAD law had been passed after 9/11 and it restricted Guardsmen from being required to serve more than twenty-four months overseas. Much of Alpha had been in the Sinai, and their twenty-four months came up that September. Some chose to stay, but many went home with Captain Granger. The BC gave Alpha Company to Captain Eric Riley.

*   *   *

The Zone 22 rodeos continued with two more major engagements fought by Delta Company in mid-August. The first pitted the Old Man platoon, now under Lieutenant Brandon Ditto, against scores of Mahdi militia in a midnight ambush near IP Station Six. The second came during recon of a warehouse complex near the Jamelia Power Station that the battalion had slated for a raid. Sergeant Brian Zacher's 3rd Platoon stumbled across a two-mile-long ambush on Routes Rogue and Copper established by scores of militiamen. Fortunately, the battalion suffered no casualties in either engagement. The same could not be said for the enemy. Delta Company had more heavy weapons than any other unit in the battalion, and they used them to telling effect in both firefights.

Nevertheless, these battles frustrated the BC, who wanted to go in with a battalion plus and wipe the Mahdi out. He wanted tanks, Bradleys, and air support. This was the right way to deal with this hot spot. The assets weren't available. The uprising taxed every unit in the 1st Cav and the Americans were spread thin. It was the cost of trying to fight the insurgency without the troop levels needed to do the job.

FORTY-SIX

BUDWEISER BRIDGE

At lunchtime on August 15, the Volunteers received a routine call to check out a possible IED at a traffic circle near Budweiser Bridge. Third Platoon, Alpha Company, drove through the daytime Baghdad congestion and reached the traffic circle, where the platoon dismounted and cordoned off the area.

The platoon sat on the IED and waited for EOD to show up. A few minutes later, a convoy of Iraqi soldiers rushed through their traffic control point and disappeared across Budweiser Bridge. John Neibert saw them pass on by in a pair of Nissan pickups, a van, and a bongo truck, each one stuffed to the gunnels with Iraqi troops.

A half hour passed. Phil Larson heard gunfire coming from the bridge. At first, it sounded like a few scattered shots. Then it swelled into a full firefight. Larson asked Lieutenant Rogers if he could investigate. Keelan agreed, and Larson took Neibert, Mike Brase, and Eric Cole up to the north end of Budweiser Bridge.

They climbed up a stairwell that led up to the bridge, then moved onto a catwalk over it. Eight hundred meters across the Tigris River, a battle raged around the south end of the bridge. Larson spotted a whole group of Iraqi soldiers pinned down under the bridge's main ramp on the far bank. From positions on either side, dozens of insurgents were shooting into the broken Iraqi force with AKs, crew-served weapons, and RPGs. Small groups of insurgents moved down to the riverbank, where they got behind the ING troops. Terribly exposed, the INGs were taking heavy casualties.

The four Americans opened fire with their M4s, but the range was too great to inflict much harm. Larson reported the situation to Rogers and called for help. The fight was on.

Rogers came forward to check on Larson just as the insurgents discovered the Americans on the catwalk. They began to fire at Larson's group. Rogers asked for a target. Larson called out a position, and Rogers observed an insurgent shooting near a vehicle.

"Oh, yeah. You mean that guy?" he asked Larson.

"Yeah! Shoot him!"

Rogers triggered his M4. The rest of the Volunteers followed suit. A few minutes later, the lieutenant left to report back to battalion.

At the traffic circle, Rogers ran into a lieutenant from the 1-9 Infantry. The lieutenant told him he was providing security for a sniper section that was on the roof of a medical complex to the right of the bridge. He told Keelan to make sure his men didn't open up on the snipers.

Rogers ran into an Iraqi captain next. Obviously upset, the ING drew his pistol and waved it around as he shouted that his men were trapped on the other side of the river. They were a brand-new special forces unit with the new Iraqi army, and this was their inaugural mission. It wasn't going well.

While Rogers and his interpreter, a three-hundred-pound monster named Josef, tried to calm the captain down, an Iraqi general drove into the traffic circle with another SF platoon. He dismounted and was briefed as he was led up to the bridge. Once at the river, the general pulled out a cell phone and called one of his officers on the other side of the bridge. When he finished, he turned to Josef and said that his men had taken many wounded and several killed. He was going to send his other platoon to their rescue before the insurgents wiped them out.

Rogers said his men would lay down suppressing fire for the movement. The general returned to the traffic circle to organize his men. Right as the Iraqi general led his platoon to the base of the bridge, Sergeant First Class Alan Ezelle arrived with an EOD team in tow. He dropped off the EOD guys and took his section up the bridge. As they reached the ramp, two RPGs arched overhead.

He dismounted, linked up with Staff Sergeant Neibert, and quickly got a handle on the situation. With Larson and his men on the catwalk to the left, E. Z. moved his men to the right side of the bridge. As he did, an Iraqi security guard ran up to him. He told Ezelle he'd seen three insurgents down in the weeds along the river only a few meters off to the right of the bridge.

Ezelle peered over the bridge and saw the three men. The insurgents sent a few bullets his way. E. Z. had only Sergeant James DeGiusti's squad and a fire team led by Corporal Steven Warming. Altogether, he had eighteen soldiers. He ordered DeGiusti to dismount and assault the river bank. Meanwhile, E. Z., Warming, and Sergeant Richard Newton provided covering fire from the bridge.

DeGiusti, a friendly NCO who prided himself in his professionalism, dashed to the stairwell and charged down with his men. As soon as his boots hit the riverbank, his men took fire. At first, it came from the three men hiding in the weeds nearby. Later, as they maneuvered on the insurgent trio, two more insurgents targeted them from the opposite bank. Caught in crossfire, DeGiusti's men kept moving and shooting. They flushed out the three insurgents, who broke cover, scampered away from the Americans, and took cover near a light pole.

On the bridge, E. Z. told Warming to put some M203 grenades down on the trio. His first shot almost landed on DeGiusti, who keyed his Motorola and shouted, "Little short!"

Warming adjusted his aim even as the men on the opposite river bank took potshots at him. Warming ignored that and triggered another M203 round. It exploded well behind the three insurgents. His third shot killed them all.

DeGiusti led his squad to a low brick wall that ran parallel to the river. His men came on line and poured bullets into the two men across the river. Newton, E. Z., and Warming added their fire, as did one of the M240 gunners. Both insurgents died.

Meanwhile, the EOD team showed up on the catwalk and gave Larson's men a .50-caliber Barrett sniper rifle and a spotting scope. Neibert got down behind the scope, while Cole and Brase took turns on the .50-cal. Now they had a weapon that could reach out and touch the bad guys.

Through the spotting scope, Neibert could see two Iraqi SF vehicles to the left of the bridge. Both had been knocked out, but were full of ammunition that the insurgents wanted. Periodically, an insurgent would make a run for the ammo. Neibert called him out, and Brase or Cole would drive him back with a few shots from the .50-cal. Most gave up, but one insurgent refused to be dissuaded. This enemy fighter had somehow scored a pair of U.S. Army PT shorts, which he wore along with a bright pink shirt.

For fifteen minutes, they fought a strange battle with Pink Shirt. He'd jump over a wall and streak for the wrecked Iraqi SF rigs, only to be stopped cold as the .50-cal. barked. They sent close to thirty rounds downrange at Pink Shirt. Though they never killed him, Pink Shirt didn't reach the ammunition in the Nissans either. The duel ended in a standoff.

Meanwhile, the trapped Iraqi soldiers got desperate. Several broke cover and dived into the river. Swimming frantically, two made it across as bullet spouts erupted around them. Ezelle saw several more try, but the insurgents cut them down mid-river. Obviously, the Iraqis under the bridge could not hold out much longer.

Sergeant First Class Larson had seen enough. The men across the river may not have been Americans, but they were friendly forces. It was time to help them. The other Iraqi SF platoon wouldn't be much use. As soon as their general left, they milled around in confusion on the north end of the bridge.

Larson grabbed Neibert and said, "Let's go."

They ran to Ezelle and formulated a quick plan. They'd go forward across the bridge while Ezelle's Humvees covered them with their M240s. E. Z. got his rigs on line, two abreast. They moved up the bridge, which arched gracefully over the Tigris. At the apex of the arch, he stopped his men, and his gunners went to work.

To the right of the bridge on the opposite bank stretched a series of apartment buildings. The insurgents were all over those, firing from windows and rooftops. Ezelle called out target floors and his gunners unleashed hellacious carnage. They scissored their fire back and forth, chewing up the buildings and dropping bad guys. From the bank, DeGiusti could see bricks, masonry, and other debris spinning off the buildings after every fusillade. Ezelle's rigs took fire from the left. A squat, one-story warehouse-looking building seemed to be the source of the fire. His men returned it, raking the warehouse with M4s and M240s. A burst of return fire tore apart two tires on one of Ezelle's Humvees. Several of his men had to run back down the bridge ramp to pick up two spares. They returned, rolling the tires ahead of them. Under fire the entire time, they changed out the tires. Heroism isn't just about charging machine-gun nests.

The TOC radioed E. Z. and told him the 1-9 Infantry would soon join the fight. The unit was coming from the north across the Tigris River with Bradleys and tanks. They'd be on the scene any minute now, and that made Ezelle nervous. He was fighting a battle with friendlies to the front, bad guys to the left and right, and the cavalry coming to the rescue in the middle of it all. He did not want to draw 1-9's fire by accident and see his men go down in a fratricide incident. He held his men at the apex of the crest and waited for the situation to develop.

While Ezelle's platoon laid down fire in two directions, Larson and Neibert started across the bridge. Initially, most of the second Iraqi SF platoon followed them. They moved through Ezelle's Humvees and out over the crest of the bridge. As they did, the insurgents unleashed a hurricane of bullets at them. They pinged off the railings and snapped off the roadway in high-pitched ricochets. Larson and Neibert kept going; most of the Iraqis did not.

Instead of advancing, the Iraqi SF cut loose with their AKs in a 180 degree arc. Their shooting was wild and uncontrolled. Some shot right over Larson and Neibert. Just then, the first 1-9 Bradleys appeared to the right. Ezelle charged across the crest and screamed at the Iraqis to cease fire. Nobody heeded him. "Americans! Americans!" he called out. The Iraqis kept firing.

Well, fuck, maybe they want to kill Americans.

"Americans and ING! ING!" This got some of them to stop firing, but others kept at it. Ezelle rampaged from man to man, drop-kicking them in the head until they got the message. Sergeant DeGiusti, who was still at the river bank, watched Ezelle's mad-dash across the bullet-swept bridge. His heart leapt to his throat and later he admonished his platoon sergeant, "E. Z., don't ever fucking run out in the open like that again. You scared the shit out of me!"

If E. Z. was exposed, Neibert and Larson were sitting ducks, totally exposed in the forwardmost position on the bridge. The fire grew so intense that they finally had to flop prone. They were in quite a pickle. Larson asked, "What the fuck are we doing? We've got no protection."

They lay there on the bridge for several terrifying minutes until Larson realized they had to move. If they stayed in place, they'd die. Larson stood, motioned to Neibert, and the two lone Americans bolted for the far side of the bridge. Fewer than a half dozen Iraqi SF soldiers followed them.

They reached the south end of the bridge and moved down the ramp. To their front and left, insurgents in a series of buildings near Haifa Street opened up on them. So did the ones in the apartment buildings Ezelle's men had targeted. The two Americans found themselves in a triple crossfire. Larson leveled his M4 and started shooting into the apartments. Neibert worked over the buildings between the bridge and Haifa Street.

Then the 1-9 showed up. The Brads pushed through a clover leaf and set up an inner cordon around the shattered Iraqi SF platoon. Several M1 tanks drove into the neighborhood and attracted RPG fire. A few main gun rounds took care of those bad guys . . . and the buildings they used for cover.

The arrival of heavy armor drove most of the insurgents away. The firing ebbed. The few Iraqis on the bridge with Neibert and Larson found a stairwell down to the river bank. They used it to link up with their comrades under the bridge, and moments later almost thirty men boiled up the stairs to run back across the bridge.

At the crest, Ezelle and his men were still taking sporadic fire from the left side. E. Z. busily coordinated the fight. He called targets out for his gunners while giving the BC updates every few minutes.

While engaging the warehouse to the left, Ezelle's men watched the broken Iraqi SF platoon stagger up the bridge to their position. A colonel limped to Ezelle and screamed, "Please, you must help my men. We need weapons and ammunition! We are out of ammunition and seven of my men are dead!"

"You're gonna have to stand by," Ezelle said. The colonel disappeared to the rear with the rest of his men.

Moments later, an Iraqi SF soldier carried a bloody comrade up to Ezelle. He pleaded, "Help him! Help him. He's my friend." E. Z., who was still directing the fight, turned to see the desperate Iraqi. One look at his friend's glazed eyes and E. Z. knew there was nothing he could do.

"Stand by," he repeated as he went back to directing the fight.

"No, you *must* help him."

Ezelle grew angry. He was trying to kill bad guys. "Your friend's deader than fucking fried chicken. You need to move out."

The platoon medic, Specialist Miller, showed up to help before the Iraqi could respond. Miller, all of five foot three inches, already had his hands full that afternoon with walking wounded and Iraqi heat casualties. Not all of the Iraqi SF escaped from under the bridge. When the Iraqis made their break for Ezelle, they had abandoned fifteen seriously wounded men. They'd also left their dead.

From the south ramp, Neibert could see one Iraqi special forces soldier KIA lying in the street not far from the two Nissan pickup trucks. His head had been shattered. Now, as the Bradleys took control of the scene, Neibert and a fire team of Iraqi SF retrieved the dead Iraqi.

As the fighting died down, the Bradleys' dismounts cleared the buildings between the bridge and Haifa Street. Neibert and the Iraqi SF team entered the warehouse on the left side of the bridge. Inside, they found Pink Shirt hiding in a back room. They also found two terrified families who explained that Pink Shirt had threatened to kill them if they revealed his presence.

The Iraqi SF soldiers dragged Pink Shirt out of his hiding spot to beat him. Pink Shirt sobbed. He begged. He pleaded. In his hysteria he denied being a part of any insurgent group. Neibert entered the room and told the Iraqi SF to stop beating him. They did, at least for the moment. Pink Shirt remained on the floor mewling for mercy. Neibert was disgusted. With his buddies around, this insurgent had had plenty of courage. Alone, he acted like a "six-year-old who had lost his momma."

Neibert turned his back for a minute, and the Iraqi SF started kicking Pink Shirt again. Neibert stopped it one more time, then went and found an Iraqi SF captain who had stayed behind. He told the Iraqi officer that the prisoner was his responsibility. He needed to make sure he was not harmed. The captain agreed, went inside the warehouse, and put an end to the abuse.

Later, they brought Pink Shirt out and put him under the bridge with the wounded SF soldiers. Each time the captain or Neibert looked away, the Iraqis whaled on Pink Shirt again. Some things in a culture just can't be changed overnight.

One of the Iraqi SF bongo trucks rolled across the bridge to pick up the wounded men. The Americans and unhurt Iraqis loaded the dead and wounded aboard. They stuffed Pink Shirt in the back. When the truck went through the New York–Budweiser traffic circle, Lieutenant Rogers observed the Iraqis beating the hell out of their prisoner again.

Rogers had spent the fight coordinating all the different engaged units. Between the snipers on the roof, the Iraqi SF platoons, the 1-9 Cav on the far side, and Ezelle's men, it was a supreme challenge for this young, intellectual lieutenant. He handled it all with aplomb until one of his men at the traffic circle suffered a brain fart and unloaded a burst from his M240 at the sniper team on the medical complex. The SF guys were not happy about that. Fortunately, nobody got hurt. With all the coalition units involved in this engagement, it was miraculous that this was the only friendly-fire incident of the day.

Across the Tigris in 1-9's battlespace, the fighting flared anew off to the northwest. Haifa Street, which was one of the main roads into the Green Zone, had been the scene of bitter fighting for much of the summer. Despite every effort, the coalition could not keep it clear of insurgents. The new flurry of gunfire prompted the 1-9 element to pack up and drive north. Within minutes, the Brads and the tanks disappeared into the cityscape.

That left Neibert and Larson alone with an Iraqi SF captain and a handful of his men. The insurgents returned. They crept into the nearby buildings and took shots at the Oregonians under the bridge. This was exactly how the first Iraqi SF platoon was trapped in the first place.

Larson radioed Ezelle, "Hey man! We're all alone over here."

"Roger, I'm on my way."

Gathering his rigs, plus the EOD Humvee and one Alpha vehicle, Ezelle's men thundered across the bridge to the rescue. They reached the south ramp and swung around the cloverleaf that took them under the bridge. Ezelle established a perimeter near the two Iraqi SF Nissans.

The EOD team dismounted to destroy the ammunition in these two vehicles. Rockets, boxes of 7.62 ammo, and hand grenades lay scattered around the two pickups. The EOD team gathered all this up and piled it in a field near the warehouse. As they worked, DeGiusti's men came under fire from the buildings the 1-9 Cav dismounts had cleared only a half hour earlier. They shot back furiously, but several cagey insurgents maneuvered on them. DeGiusti, a short, spitfire of a man with relentless energy and a cheerful spirit, suddenly found himself in a point-blank firefight. With only a wall between them, the insurgents pitched hand grenades at the Oregonians, who dove for cover as the first one rolled into their position and blew up. Three more grenades soon followed. The Americans poured lead into the enemy and either killed them or drove them away. It had been a close call.

As the fight raged, the BC had come out with the battalion's QRF and had taken a position on a bridge just to the south. There he monitored the fight and waited to see if the QRF would be needed. When Ezelle radioed back and told him they were on the far side of the Tigris out of their AO, the BC ordered everyone out of 1-9's battlespace. The Americans saddled up under fire and drove back onto the bridge. The Iraqis climbed up the stairs and sprinted across on foot. Ezelle saw this and turned around to give them support. He and Corporal Warming's Humvee covered the Iraqis as they raced for safety. They took sporadic fire all the way, but nobody got hit.

Once clear of the crest, the entire force moved back to the north bank and reconsolidated at the New York–Budweiser intersection. The firefight had lasted four grueling hours in the stifling Iraqi heat.

By its very nature, combat is an extreme event. Those involved in it witness the extremes of human behavior from raw depravity to self-sacrifice. On August 15, Phil Larson, John Neibert, and Alan Ezelle embodied the best of human nature under fire. Larson and Neibert can be called reckless for their dash across the bridge. Some can argue that Larson had no business being there. As a platoon sergeant, his doctrinal position was back at the traffic circle handling the "beans and bullets" aspect of the fight. None of that mattered when he saw friendly soldiers dying across the river. Without Larson's decision to go to their rescue, many more Iraqi SF soldiers certainly would have been killed or wounded. Their actions that day represented one of the finest moments in the history of the Oregon Guard.

As did Ezelle's. Without a second thought, he crossed the bridge and came to the rescue of his fellow Oregonians. Ezelle, always the tough guy, reacted solely on instinct. His instincts obviously trended toward the best of human character.

Part V

THE BATTLE OF NAJAF

FORTY-SEVEN

THE COVER OF
STARS AND STRIPES

Back home, Mandy Ferguson's phone rang just before 7:00 a.m. It was Spike. He sounded morose, and right away Mandy knew something was wrong. He was supposed to come home on August 20, only twelve days away. She had expected him to be excited.

"I can't tell you where we're going, but you won't hear from us for a while."

A million questions tumbled around in Mandy's head, none of which Spike could answer. Instead, she listened and told him how much she loved him. As the conversation continued, Spike's fear of what they would soon face transmitted to Mandy. Already tense, the future looked positively terrifying now.

"Mandy, I know we're going to lose somebody."

They said their goodbyes and hung up, each turning to the morning to face what lay ahead without the other's support and comfort. Spike would have his buddies with him, though, and they would get through it together. Mandy would not. Her apartment became her own version of solitary confinement, her imagination a prison where hope and fear wrestled for her heart and spirit. It was a war every loved one back home was fighting.

"Pack your gear, we're going to Najaf."

That was Captain Toepfer's announcement to Lieutenant Dewayne Jones and Sergeant First Class Shannon Compton that night. Their Alpha Company platoon had spent the summer attached to Toepfer's Charlie 2-7 and had taken several casualties in the two IED incidents in June and July. Now they were headed to the biggest fight in Iraq.

They went to work gathering ammo and gear.

Two mornings later, the battalion was staged and ready to go. Colonel Rainey came by 2nd Platoon, Bravo, to check on his Oregonians. Pete Salerno greeted him with a big grin.

"How you guys doin'?"

"Great, sir!"

Rainey said, "Yeah, I looked at that task organization and I said, 'This ain't gonna work. I ain't goin' nowhere without 2nd Platoon.'"

Pete swelled with pride. Colonel Rainey was a fighting man's leader, and such a compliment meant more than all the Bronze Stars in the army.

"Right on, sir!"

Salerno and his student-warriors would soon be in the fight of their lives.

Later that morning, the 2-7 Cav, plus two platoons of Oregon infantry, set out for Najaf. Going through Baghdad turned out to be an all day affair, and they reached Scania late that evening. The next morning, they continued their journey into the vast desert expanse of southern Iraq. To some of the men, the colors seemed remarkable. The flat landscape contained every shade of brown imaginable from tan to burnt umber. It was the flip-side of Oregon and the cornucopia of lush greens every native grows to love. The barren desertscape stretched in every direction over the horizon, offering nothing but 140-degree heat and the occasional pack of camels. It made Death Valley look hospitable.

They sweated in the Humvees and swapped out of the turret every few hours. At least the 1114s had air-conditioning to temper the heat a little bit. The old cardboard coffins and turtlebacks had no climate control systems, and regulations prevented them from rolling the windows all the way down. Until McKinley's death, they patrolled in the hundred plus heat in what amounted to portable ovens. To stay cool, they brought ice and drank constantly, but long after patrols, their own body temperatures would hover around 103 degrees. They had called it "baking brain cells."

Now, only the gunners had their brains baked. They stood watch over this gypsy column of Hemmits and Humvees and tried not to think about the violence they would soon experience.

On the 10th, Rainey's men reached FOB Duke, a searing "shithole" in the middle of nowhere comprised of circus tents and foot-deep talcum-powder sand that clung to everything. Kris Peterson called the stuff "moondust," and for the vista in every direction, they might as well have been on the moon. They languished at Duke for two days as Colonel Rainey's staff developed a plan of attack.

The situation was a tricky one. Muqtada Al Sadr had holed up in a fortified area around the Imam Ali Shrine, the second holiest site in the Muslim world after Mecca. The marines of the 11th Marine Expeditionary Unit (MEU) and the mech infantry of the 1-5 Cav had tried to tackle the Mahdi by themselves. They found themselves locked in a macabre battle north of the shrine amid the crypts and tombs of one of the world's largest cemeteries. The Mahdi had interior lines and superior numbers. The marines needed help. They called in another marine unit and asked the army for a mech battalion. Colonel Rainey's men had come to fill that request.

Rainey and his S-3, Major Tim Karcher, drafted a daring, somewhat risky plan. While the marines continued the fight in the north end of the city, 2-7 Cav would assault Najaf from the south. The battalion's AO was a three-by-three-kilometer square in the southwest section of the city. In the northwest corner of the AO stood the Imam Ali Shrine. On the east side, the main road into Najaf, Route Miami, rolled up a steep hill into the city and stretched to an intersection with Route New York, the main road into the shrine complex.

The U.S. Army handled urban warfare as a distinctly different type of battle from fighting in rural terrain. During World War II, the army methodically cleared hundreds of towns and cities in western Europe with block-to-block, sometimes room-to-room advances.

Rainey didn't have the men for that sort of operation. Clearing Najaf room-by-room would take months—time they didn't have. Instead, he decided to handle the terrain as he would any other battlefield. He would seize the high ground and use it to inhibit the enemy's movements.

The 2-7 Cav's attack would launch a two-pronged attack designed to capture footholds at the edges of the city. Charlie 3-8's tanks would form the main effort and assault up an escarpment at the southwest corner of the city. First Platoon, Alpha, 2-162, would provide the tanks their infantry support.

As Charlie 3-8 fought its way uphill, Captain Twaddell's Apache 2-7 would strike from Route Miami and grab a foothold in the southeast corner of the AO. Once established inside Najaf, Colonel Rainey would send in Commanche 2-7's tanks and Brads to leapfrog past Apache and storm an IP station on the corner of Routes New York and Miami. If it worked, by nightfall the battalion would control three of the four corners of the AO. From there, they would advance on the shrine on two fronts. While Rainey's tankers fought in the streets, his infantry would seize high-rise buildings, where snipers, machine-gun teams, and forward observers would rain death down on the Mahdi and negate Al Sadr's advantage of interior lines.

Risky, but borderline brilliant, the plan would either pay big dividends or fail spectacularly. Rainey bet his career on it. Outstanding leaders know when to take calculated risks. This was one of those times, and Rainey was one of those leaders.

FORTY-EIGHT

CAPTAIN GLASS' FINEST HOUR

Charlie 3-8 moved out at 0400. The tanks—those lumbering, beautiful behemoths—led the way with their turrets forward, guns loaded. Behind them, an engineer platoon followed in M113 armored personnel carriers. Lieutenant Jones' Oregonians brought up the rear with Phil Disney in the front of the platoon column and Shannon Compton at tail-end Charlie.

At 0530, just as dawn broke, Captain Glass paused the column next to a tiny village on the outskirts of Najaf. The marines were supposed to prep the battlefield with an artillery mission. Binoculars up, the Cav troopers scanned the escarpment and waited for the 155s to open the door for them.

Silence. No shell landed. No gun barked. Colonel Rainey, who was with Commanche 2-7 to the east, had called off the fire mission after he learned civilians still remained in the area.

Captain Glass would have to go in without artillery support. Around them, curious Iraqi civilians lingered on the fringes of the column. Any chance of surprise was long gone now. The original plan of attack called for a night assault. But delays the night before scuttled that. Now they'd go in at daylight without the 155s to pave the way.

Captain Glass gave the order to move. The tanks crawled down the hardball road and broke out into the open at the base of the escarpment atop which Najaf is built. The road bent to the southeast, putting the high ground to the left of the column. Charlie 3-8's broadside now faced the enemy. Dug in along the crest, Mahdi militia mortar teams readied their weapons. Nearby, dozens of RPG teams stayed concealed in buildings and alleyways around the first intersection inside the city.

The tanks passed through a palm grove. The road began to bend gently eastward again for the final run up the escarpment and into the city. As the M1s approached the curve, the militamen detonated an IED planted by the side of the road. It struck Staff Sergeant Laverra's tank in the column's van. The blast was so loud that Vinni Jacques' brother, Ryan, heard it while rolling into the city several miles to the east.

A roiling mushroom cloud of smoke and flames boiled up over Laverra's Abrams. But the IED had been all bang and no buck. The M1 blew through it, little worse for wear. The IED detonation was the signal for the Mahdi defenders to engage the Americans. Small-arms fire rattled through the column. Mor-

220

tar fire soon followed. Captain Glass ordered the tanks forward. They rumbled up the escarpment and into an inferno.

RPG teams swarmed over the lead tanks. They came out of buildings, fired from alleyways, and shot from behind fences and walls and dug-in positions. Rockets whirred. The tanks took hits. Then they took more. The RPG teams worked with reckless abandon. They charged the tanks in waves, sprinting to point-blank range before sending their rockets downrange. As the coax machine guns cut them down, more poured in to take their place. The tanks took more hits. The rocket strikes rocked them on their treads. At one point, several RPG-armed militiamen ducked behind a wall. One of Captain Glass' tanks crashed through the wall and crushed the enemy beneath its treads. The fighting was close quarters: rocket-toting fanatics against the fearsome M1 Abrams.

The American attack stalled. The tanks could not move forward. Mahdi militiamen seemed to be everywhere, firing from the south, north, and east. The tanks battled back, main guns booming, machine guns ripping off long bursts. An RPG strike disabled Staff Sergeant Laverra's turret. Unable to traverse it, Laverra stayed in the fight and used his M1 like a WWII German assault gun. Pivoting on the treads, he brought his weapons to bear and hammered the RPG teams.

Major Karcher, the battalion ops officer, took a look at the volume of fire and the veritable human wave assault the tanks now faced. He radioed Colonel Rainey.

"It ain't lookin' real good, Colonel," he reported.

Fortunately, the plan had a built-in contingency for this development. If Charlie 3-8 got stuck on the escarpment, Commanche would move into the city after Apache secured a foothold and would turn left to attack westward. That way, Commanche could drive into the rear of the enemy fighting Captain Glass. They wouldn't get their northeast corner secured, but at least they'd capture two of the three objectives for the day. Rainey didn't want to do that. If the plan was to pay off big, he needed that leap into the northeast corner.

As he mulled over the situation, Captain Glass cut in over the radio, "Colonel, I got it, sir. I can do it. Just give me thirty minutes."

Rainey gave it to him.

The battle on the escarpment continued.

As the tanks fought on, the Southern Oregon boys drew heavy mortar fire while they waited to get up the escarpment. Compton could see some of the tubes on the crest to their left. He called out their locations and his gunners hosed the mortarmen with 7.62mm and .50-cal fire. Shannon's MK19 gunner took out two of the tubes with well-placed grenades.

The hillside came alive with winking AK-47s. Bullets snapped overhead or pinged off their Humvees. Mahdi militiamen, dug in at the base of the escarpment, laced the column with fire. First Platoon's Joes, especially the men in the trailing rigs, were getting hit hard.

A mortar exploded not far from Sergeant C's 1114. Another one soon followed. Some Mahdi mortarmen had him zeroed, and now they walked their fire straight for his vehicle. Shannon spared a passing thought to his five kids and his wife back in Oregon and grew "anticipatory" about the mortar fire.

"We need to move," he called to Lieutenant Jones.

At the head of Alpha's part of the column, Phil Disney listened to the tankers over the radio.

"RPG team left!"

"RPG team right!"

"RPG team destroyed."

Chaos reigned around that final bend. The engineer APCs (armored personnel carriers) wanted no part of it. They came back down the road, leaving Alpha as the next formation in line.

"Dis, we need to move forward. Move up to where the tanks are."

Lieutenant Jones' order surprised Disney. He answered, "Hey sir, I don't know if you can hear what they're going through up there, but I don't think we have any business going into it in Humvees."

"Listen, we need to move forward until we can see the tanks."

Another mortar round rattled Compton's rig. This one was less than a dozen meters away. Compton knew the next one would probably land on his gunner's head.

"We need to move *now!*" Shannon shouted over the radio.

Disney looked over at his driver, Specialist Benito Najera, and said, "Okay, here we go, man. Pull forward."

Phil's gunner, Arthur Duryea, groaned, "Oh shit."

The accelerator hit the floor. The Humvee bolted forward. Behind Disney, the rest of the platoon followed him up the escarpment. They moved just in time. Another few seconds and Compton surely would have been hit.

Disney's rig rounded the bend and reached the crest of the escarpment. They could see the tanks, still heavily engaged, a few hundred meters ahead. Every few minutes, one would disappear in a ball of smoke and flame as another RPG struck home. This was far enough.

Suddenly, a huge explosion hammered the Humvee. The concussion tossed his crew around and Disney exclaimed, ""Holy shit! IED!"

Sergeant Compton radioed back, "No! It was a Hellfire missile. An Apache just took out a house next to you."

Disney looked to the right. Two Apaches rose over the hillside, looking like giant, futuristic insects full of menace. They had launched a missle *over* Disney's rig.

At the intersection, a wedge of RPG teams assaulted the tanks from the northeast and northwest. The attack faltered in the face of the M1's incredible firepower. Their coax machine guns swept the streets and dropped dozens. The human wave attacks stopped. The tanks moved deeper into the city.

In response, Disney's Humvee pulled forward. At the first intersection, the platoon established a perimeter while the tanks continued to fight a block or so ahead of them. Lieutenant Jones ordered everyone to dismount and clear the nearby buildings. Seconds after Disney's boots hit pavement, a mortar round exploded in the traffic circle. Another soon followed.

"Come on!" Disney shouted. He led his squad into a stable next to a slaughterhouse. Mortars rained down, bursting all over the intersection. Part of the platoon, led by Staff Sergeant Harold Cunningham, broke into the slaughterhouse. Blood and organic debris littered the building. The men couldn't tell if what had died here was animal or human. The scene was ultra-macabre, like something straight from a Stephen King novel.

The mortar barrage intensified. Disney's men rode it out inside the stable. An 82mm landed right next to their building. The ground quaked; the building quivered. The men were unhurt. They hunkered down and waited for the barrage to abate.

In the traffic circle, Compton was forced to maneuver his Humvees to avoid the incoming. The Mahdi delivered amazingly accurate indirect fire, probably with the help of well-trained forward observers. Though not quite an army, the Mahdi did possess some advanced combat skills.

Finally, the incoming ceased. The men returned to their Humvees to mount up. Occasional small-arms fire stitched the traffic circle. An RPG sailed past. Jones ordered them two hundred meters east into the city. They stopped at a three-story schoolhouse. This looked like an excellent base of operations. The platoon dismounted. Disney led his squad inside to find stacks of ammunition, rockets, RPG launchers, and sniper rifle ammo. The latter worried Compton quite a bit when he examined the bullets. They were larger than the 7.62mm rounds the M240s used.

They set up positions on the third floor and the roof of the school. A sniper team joined them. From this piece of high ground, they could see all the way to the Ali Shrine three kilometers away. It gave them an excellent overwatch of the southwest section of Najaf. It did not take long for them to get engaged.

A crowd of adult civilians gathered in the streets a few blocks north of the school. Most were women who stood in the open and watched the tank battle only a few blocks up the street. The scene reminded Sergeant Compton of the Battle of Bull Run in 1861 when well-dressed civilians picnicked on the battlefield. Over 140 years and 5,500 miles later, the curious civilians in Najaf carried no picnic baskets, but were equally fascinated by battle. It was a surreal moment, the first of many that would demonstrate how combat kaleidoscoped reality into a bacchanal of the bizarre.

The Mahdi capitalized on the crowd. They sent fighters to infiltrate it. Periodically, the Oregonians would see one unveil an AK or RPG launcher. Before they could get a shot off, C's boys would kill them with well-placed shots. Seven died this way throughout the day, but the Volunteers remained selective with their violence. The women in the crowd remained unhurt. The Volunteers were warriors, not butchers.

By now, it was late afternoon and Captain Glass' tanks ran low on ammunition and fuel. In pairs, they pulled off to go refuel at Camp David, a special forces base on the southern outskirts of Najaf.

Those thirty minutes Glass had asked for had made all the difference in the day. His tankers had repelled the massed militia countercharges, and had set the table for Alpha 2-162 to establish the battalion's first foothold in Najaf. It was an outstanding accomplishment.

Colonel Rainey believed that every battle has a decisive moment. The best leaders recognize its arrival despite limited intelligence and limited vision on the battlefield. To do so requires knowledge, awareness, and intuition. To Colonel Rainey, Captain Glass displayed all that and more. This was his victory.

Late in the day, Tim Karcher radioed Colonel Rainey, "Sir, they fucking pulled it off!"

FORTY-NINE

KRIS HANEY'S
CHUNK OF HISTORY

As the battle on the escarpment raged to the west, Apache 2-7 and Bravo Company's 2nd Platoon plunged into the fight from the south.

Captain Twaddell's Bradleys led the way. Behind them came 2nd Platoon's five 1114 armored Humvees. They would seize the second foothold of the day.

The moment the Bradleys drove up the escarpment and reached the edge of the city, the Mahdi unleashed a storm of bullets, rockets, and IEDs on the Americans. The 25 mike-mikes barked out high-explosive rounds. Helicopters buzzed back and forth, working over the insurgents with Hellfires and 30mm chain guns. Coax M240s chattered. PPKs and AKs rattled. Grenade launchers boomed.

Second Platoon, this special group of students-turned-Guardsmen, watched the battle develop from their Humvees and steeled themselves for their entry into the fight.

Pete Salerno stared at the shrapnel-torn scene ahead and whispered, "Oh my fucking God." He had long since resolved to never show fear in front of his men. He would be their rock, no matter how scared he was inside. The toughest part of soldiering is controlling the natural fear a Joe feels when he is in harm's way. Everyone felt it that morning, but not a man succumbed.

In the middle of the column, Spike Olsen held on to his M240 Bravo and scanned for targets as the city loomed. Fleeting thoughts of Mandy flipped across his mind like a slide show. The day he proposed, all the talks about their wedding, that first night they met in Independence at Lenora's Ghost: these were the things that had sustained him thus far. Now he longed to linger on them, to turn each one over and capture even the tiniest details: Mandy's grin, her laugh, the way she brushed her hair behind her ears. But now was not the time; his head needed to be in the game. He stowed the memories. A wave of fear and anticipation gripped him, but like the others, he refused to give in to it. A college student, yes, but today he was all warrior.

Twaddell's Bradleys ground into the city. Bullets sprayed their armored hulls. Rockets flew. The 25 mike-mikes banged out their deadly response. The fight bloomed, intense and desperate across a nightmare cityscape where every window, doorway, and rooftop posed a deadly threat.

In the back of Captain Twaddell's track, Staff Sergeant Kris Haney watched the fight on the Bradley's three video monitors. Connected to cameras that showed what the driver, gunner, and track commander were seeing, these view screens gave him a good idea of what he would soon face once dismounted. It wasn't pretty. The driver's view showed IED explosions detonating in rapid-fire succession. Bullets pinged off their hull, and RPGs zipped here and there.

Haney was unused to this form of fighting. He was a Bravo Company NCO, long since at home in a Humvee. Crammed in the back of a metal can with treads, taking fire from three sides, was not his way of fighting, but the platoon had run out of room in their overloaded rigs. He and Private First Class Jaerod Case were orphaned, taken in temporarily by Apache 2-7 until they got into the city.

Haney was prior service navy, a devoted soldier who'd gone to SEAL school before a knee injury cut short his career. He'd been with Bravo Company for years before leaving for special forces training after 9/11. When he learned Bravo had been mobilized for Iraq, Kris returned to Oregon to go with his old friends, taking a demotion to do so. Instead of getting his own squad, he became a team leader under Vinni's brother, Ryan Howell.

Now, this moment in combat became his unique chunk of history. He was about to be the first Bravo Company soldier to plant his boots in Najaf.

Tough, experienced, and used to hardship—he was born in a log cabin in Missouri and lived part of his childhood in a teepee in the Teton Mountains— Haney knew this was the pivotal event in his life. Older and more experienced than many of the Bravo Joes, the company had high expectations of him. His actions today would be judged like no one else's. He must set the example. It was his moment. He seized it.

Twaddell's Brad crashed through a cement wall, and the soldiers in back were tossed around like bowling pins. Haney held on for dear life. The driver stopped and spun on the treads. The ramp dropped. Haney stared out at the burning city. The moment had come. He looked over at Private First Class Jaerod Case. Their eyes locked, and Haney knew the young soldier was looking to him for leadership.

He turned to the ramp. Bullets bounced off it and smacked the asphalt around the back of the Bradley. Haney's mind flashed to the scene in *Saving Private Ryan* when Tom Hanks' landing craft came ashore and dropped its ramp, only to face a hail of machine-gun bullets.

The volume of fire increased. More rounds smacked into the ramp. To step onto it seemed like a sure ticket to a combat support hospital.

"What the hell are we doing?" Case asked as another fusillade of bullets swept the ramp.

The look in Case's eyes broke the spell. Haney soldiered up. Time to be a leader. He stepped into the maelstrom. His boots slammed onto the ramp. A short jump and their tan soles hit pavement. Case followed his team leader. Together, they crouched down, using the Bradley for cover as a 2-7 sniper team dismounted behind them.

The sounds of the raging firefight enfolded Haney, disorienting him. Staccato bursts of machine-gun fire filled his ears, punctuated by thunderous explosions that made the ground tremble. Rifle reports mingled with the sound of

SAWs and RPKs (Soviet light machine guns). The 25 mike-mike barked. The *thup-thup-thup* of the Apaches overhead provided the bass line for this cacophony of battle.

It wasn't like any movie Kris had ever seen. In *Platoon* or *Apocalypse Now,* the men could always tell the direction of the incoming. Not here, not with the crazy acoustics the buildings created. The sounds bounced off their walls and created deceptive echoes.

He stayed calm and studied the scene. Twaddell's driver had dropped them at a gas station. They were next to a huge aboveground fuel tank, which one of the 2-7 snipers had just climbed atop to get a better view of the fight. Kris thought that was a ridiculously dangerous idea. One RPG and a ball of flaming gasoline would burn the sniper alive.

He peered up the street. He couldn't see much, just explosions and damaged buildings. Then an insurgent appeared in a window about seventy meters away. The militaman raised an AK and opened up on Twaddell's Bradley. The turret spun. The 25 mike-mike erupted. The insurgent disintegrated.

Figures moved and darted around on the fringes of his vision. It was eerie. They loped like the cretins in *Escape from New York,* using the shadows to mask their movements. Yet, they could not escape the Bradleys and their awesome firepower. The volume of fire diminished. The Americans were winning. Bullets ricocheted off the aboveground fuel tank. Haney called up to the sniper.

"What are you doing? Get the hell off the giant gas tank!"

The sniper saw the light. In his haste to dismount and find something less volatile to use, he slipped and fell. He clattered to the ground a few feet from Haney, luckily unhurt.

For Haney and Case, fighting in the van meant separation from the rest of 2nd Platoon, Bravo Company. Until he could find Lieutenant Kent and Ryan Howell, Kris decided to stay with the snipers.

Twaddell ordered the men to remount. They would continue the advance north.

The Bradleys cleared the way for the rest of 2nd Platoon. When the Humvees reached the city, they faced general fire. Stray rounds snapped overhead, and an occasional RPK flared to life to the northeast. But the rockets weren't flying anymore, and no IEDs struck the 1114s. The platoon moved a couple of blocks north and dismounted to clear their first objective, which was a series of houses.

The platoon went to work, kicking in doors and sweeping through the narrow confines of these dwellings. At one house, Staff Sergeant John Ashford prepared to lead an entry team through the front door. Somebody leaned against the side of the house, and the entire front of the building collapsed to the inside, leaving nothing but the door in its frame still standing. The men broke out laughing at this ridiculous Buster Keaton moment.

"Well, guess that house is clear!"

They moved on to the next house.

Within a few hours, 2nd Platoon and Apache had secured the southern foothold, though the initial objective turned out to be a poor position. As a result, 2nd Platoon advanced another few blocks and moved into a sports complex, which they dubbed the Rec Center.

With a thick, tall concrete wall surrounding the entire facility, it was a veritable urban fortress. The gymnasium's roof was at least fifty to sixty feet tall and gave the platoon an excellent view of the neighborhood.

As 2nd Platoon settled in, Rainey launched the final element of his plan. Commanche 2-7 leapfrogged through Apache and bored through the Madi defenses until they reached their IP station objective. There, surrounded by disorganized resistance, Captain Toepfer's men became a dagger in the rear of the outer Mahdi defenses. From the IP station, they could snipe, machine gun, and call fire down on any militiaman foolish enough to break cover.

Not long after Commanche captured the IP station, Colonel Rainey arrived and set up his forward command post there, despite the fact that the position remained under mortar, rocket, and small-arms fire. To him, there was nowhere better to lead than from the front.

The plan had paid off. The 2-7 Cav now had a solid grip on the three corners of their AO, and Commanche in the northeast had penetrated to the rear of Al Sadr's outer defenses. The maneuver left the militia with few options. They could either flee and die, or die in place as the Americans brought their tremendous firepower to bear. Though nothing ever goes exactly according to plan, this was about as good as it got. In the process, Rainey and his staff had validated a new method of urban warfare. The 2-7's plan and attack into Najaf would be studied by students of warfare for years to come.

Lt. Erik McCrae sits glued to his laptop while he writes another e-mail to his fiancée, Heather, back in Oregon. Lt. McCrae wrote her so often that the other officers in Delta Company good-naturedly teased him about it. Lt. Bailey, commander of 3rd Platoon Delta, is at left. *Courtesy of Brandon Ditto*

Delta Company's Old Man Platoon in September 2004. *Courtesy of Brandon Ditto*

Rebekah-mae Bruns at work at Fallujah, November 2004. Bruns had the grit of a foot slogger and the eye of an artist. As a result, her photographs from Fallujah rank among the best images captured by a U.S. Army photographer since World War II. *Courtesy of Spike Olsen*

The unbridled Hellhound. Nineteen-year-old Kenny Leisten had been a computer clerk for the Oregon Guard before volunteering to go with 2-162. Bill Stout and Vinni Jacques molded him into a fine infantryman, but could never curb his wild side. *Courtesy of Josh Smith*

Brandon Ditto with his veteran platoon sergeant, Sfc. Kerry Boggs. *Courtesy of Brandon Ditto*

In this scene, one of Rebekah-Mae Bruns' finest photos from Fallujah, a medic comforts a wounded 2-7 Cav trooper who has just learned of the loss of several brothers-in-arms. *Courtesy of Rebekah-mae Bruns*

Spike Olsen, college student-turned-infantryman, scans for targets atop the Rec Center during Bravo's first day in Najaf. *Courtesy of Spike Olsen*

Left: Charlie Company's legendary Sfc. Alan Ezelle on patrol in Baghdad. Ezelle was widely regarded as one of the best small unit tacticians in the entire Oregon Guard. *Courtesy of Rebekah-mae Bruns*

An Alpha Company Cardboard Coffin. This was Lt. DeWayne Jones' rig, which was hit during the Serial 5 ambush. *Courtesy of Phil Disney*

Sfc. Pete Salerno and Lt. Chris Kent in Baghdad in the spring of 2004. *Courtesy of Spike Olsen*

Vinni Jacques smokes a cigar next to John Rosander after a patrol in April 2004. *Courtesy of Ron Clement*

Eric McKinley atop one of Bravo Company's Cardboard Coffins shortly before the drive into Iraq in April 2004. *Courtesy of Spike Olsen*

Maj. Mike Warrington inside a Humvee on election day, 2005. *Courtesy of Mike Warrington*

Staff Sgt. Randy Mitts. Fearless in combat, he had the respect of every Scout. *Courtesy of Andy Hellman*

Justin Linden atop one of the battalion's TOW-armed anti-tank Humvees. *Courtesy of Brandon Ditto*

Sfc. Shannon Compton takes a break at the school house in Najaf, August 12, 2004.

Ryan Tuttle on a M240 machine gun inside the Apache Hilton, Najaf, August 2004. *Courtesy of Spike Olsen*

Brandon Hern and Ryan Tuttle with their M240 machine guns in Najaf. At the Apache Hilton, they wrought havoc on the Mahdi Militia. *Courtesy of Spike Olsen*

Phil Disney poses next to the remains of the IED crater that Max Corrigan fell into during the June 23 ambush. When the 155mm shells detonated under Staff Sgt. Travis Sigfridson's Humvee, the crater they made extended all the way across the road. In this photograph, the locals have filled most of it in so the road could be used again. *Courtesy of Phil Disney*

Andy Hellman sits astride the Sharif Brothers' getaway vehicle used during the June 4 attack on Route Pluto. *Courtesy of Andy Hellman*

Staff Sgt. Travis Sigfridson's 1114 after it was hit by an IED composed of three 155mm artillery shells. An unarmored Humvee would have been pulverized.

Lt. Col. Hendrickson and Maj. Tanguy in Baghdad on the morning of June 29, 2004. *Courtesy of Ed Tanguy*

From left to right: Sgt. Timothy Galloway, Staff Sgt. Jerry Kinman, Staff Sgt. Doug Jackson, Staff Sgt. Harold "The Big Mexican" Cunningham. *Courtesy of Doug Jackson*

Capt. Welch and Sheik Majeid together during the first patrol into the Sheik Omar district of Baghdad. Sewage puddles dot the street, trash lies strewn about, and the men of Charlie Company could hardly stand the wretched stench. This would be the place where 2-162 would devote its main civil affairs effort. *Courtesy of Mike Warrington*

Tyson Bumgardner (at left) with unidentified soldier between battles on August 6, 2004. *USAF photograph courtesy of Wyatt Welch*

Dr. Khadum, Lt. Col. Hendrickson, and Sheik Majeid at Eric McKinley's memorial service in June 2004. *Courtesy of Mike Warrington*

Battalion commander (BC) of 2-162 Lt. Col. Dan Hendrickson patrolling his area of operations with an M4 rifle. Later, when Hendrickson led the first patrol into the St. Bernard Housing Projects in New Orleans, several of his soldiers shouted, "BC on point . . . again!" *Courtesy of Dan Hendrickson*

Medevac, Fallujah. Second Platoon, Bravo, helps carry a wounded 2-7 Cav trooper to an awaiting helicopter. The Oregonians operated with the Cav. *Courtesy of Rebekah-mae Bruns*

Charlie Company on patrol in AO (area of operations) Volunteer. *Courtesy of Mike Warrington*

Kevin Maries snapped this photo through his scope on June 29, 2004. Here, one of the guards beats a prisoner with an aluminum bar as "Yellow Shirt" gazes on. *Courtesy of Kevin Maries*

In the waning days of the deployment, Alpha Company was detached from 2-162 to assist the marines in operations south of Baghdad. The Oregonians discovered an enormous stockpile of ammunition, rocket fuel, shells, and other ordnance buried in a cemetery. Shannon Compton's 1st Platoon stands in the enormous crater made after EOD blew up the stockpile. *Courtesy of Phil Disney*

Bravo Company's commander, Captain Demian San Miguel, on patrol west of Taji in 2004. San Miguel took Bravo to New Orleans, and in August 2006 commanded the company during a joint exercise with the Mongolian, Chinese, and Russian armies. Bravo Company represented the entire U.S. Army in Mongolia. *Courtesy of Demian San Miguel*

Bill Stout, a marine in the 1980s, joined 3rd Platoon Bravo Company, and formed the backbone of Vinni Jacques' Hellhounds. Courageous and utterly devoted to his fellow Joes, Bill helped save two lives on July 28. In the process, he suffered devastating injuries for which he never received a Purple Heart. *Courtesy of Bill Stout*

Matt Zedwick earned Oregon's first Silver Star since World War II when he rescued Sean Davis from their burning Humvee on June 13, 2004.

Spike and Mandy reunited at last, March 2005.

Vinni Jacques' brother, Ryan Howell, was on patrol in Najaf. Wounded twice, Ryan returned home to his young wife, Julie. They're seen here moments after reuniting at Fort Lewis the night Bravo's 2nd Platoon came home from Iraq in March 2005.

Vinni Jacques finally reunited with 3rd Platoon. Ken Kaiser barely got off the aircraft before he was engulfed in a giant Jacques bear hug at McChord AFB, March 2005.

Medevac, New Orleans. Will Coker (front on right), the gentle medic who bonded with Mimi Bartholomew, one of our hold-outs, helps carry an injured soldier to an awaiting helicopter.

Gretl Jugl, an ER nurse from Long Island, left her job and drove straight to New Orleans to save lives in the wake of Hurricane Katrina. For two weeks, she saw the worst of the human tragedy in the city as she worked in a hospital established in LSU's baskeball arena. Her selflessness restored my faith in people after seeing the aftermath of depravity, violence, and looting in our New Orleans area of operations.

John Bruning and Staff Sgt. Chris Johnson on the back of a 5-ton truck just prior to departing on Bravo Company's final search patrol in New Orleans, September 2005.

FIFTY

ZERO TO CRUSTY
IN NO TIME FLAT

Spike Olsen sat on the roof of the gymnasium and studied the Iraqi studying him. Both men had binoculars, but Spike could see no weapon on the Iraqi. He was up on a rooftop to the northeast, and it looked like he was directing the mortar fire now falling around the Rec Center.

Spike descended the stairs and reported the man to Pete Salerno, who said, "Well, go fucking shoot him!"

Spike climbed back onto the roof. Nearby, "Sweety Petey" Peterson watched his buddy kneel down and take aim. Peterson grabbed his digital camera and filmed the scene. Spike peered through his ACOG four-power sight. Patiently, he waited until the Iraqi popped his head up again. When he did, his M4 bucked twice.

"Nice shot Spike," Brian Ward called out.

"Hey Spike, whaddya doin'?" Petey asked.

Spike lowered his M4 and casually replied, "I'm tryin' to kill a guy."

A half day in battle, and already they'd become inoculated to the violence.

Pete Salerno saw that transformation in all his soldiers that day. He and Lieutenant Kent had deployed them around the Rec Center to guard every avenue of approach. Three Humvees took up positions along the westside wall. There, they covered down on the alleyways stretching off toward Charlie 3-8's base at the schoolhouse. Two more Humvees stayed on the south side of the gym, while a squad plus used the roof to eyeball the north and east.

Salerno stayed with his gun trucks along the west wall. The wall itself shielded the Humvees from enemy fire, but the gunners could see over it to shoot down the alleys. It was a good position.

Pete and Staff Sergeant Chris Bailey were talking next to Salerno's .50-caliber-equipped Humvee when suddenly the Ma Deuce boomed. The reports startled both men, and Pete looked up to see Shad Thomas in the turret. Shad, a southern Oregonian with black hair and a narrow face, sent another burst downrange. He paused, leaned back in the turret, and let fly again. Shad had rolled his sleeves up and undone his chin strap. His eyes were covered with a pair of Wiley-X sunglasses, and a cigarette dangled from his lips.

He looked down at Pete, plucked the smoke from his mouth, and nonchalantly remarked, "Yeah. Couple of guys in black tried to cross that alley over there."

He returned the cigarette, took a drag, then opened fire again.

Salerno howled with laughter. *Holy shit! This is cover of* Time *magazine back in the day!*

Later that day, Doc Bagnall, the platoon medic, spotted Shad on the .50-cal. Pete was dozing in the front right seat when Bagnall kicked him.

"What, Doc?"

"Sergeant Salerno! Three guys in black just ran south to north across the alley over there."

"You dumb sonofabitch, why are you *telling* me? Why aren't you shooting at them?"

Contrite, Doc apologized, "Oh, yeah. Sorry."

"Fuck man, it doesn't do any good now."

"Oh fuck. Okay. You're right."

Twenty minutes passed. Pete started to doze again. Suddenly, the .50-cal roared.

"What's going on, Doc?"

"Okay, Sergeant Salerno. This time there were three guys running from north to south."

Pete could only grin again. Even his medic had become a bad-ass, .50-cal-firing Muldoon. The whole platoon had gone from zero to crusty in less than a day. He couldn't have been more proud of his boys.

As the afternoon wore on, the situation on the roof grew dangerous. Periodic mortar fire rained down on the men. Bullets smacked into the low-lying wall that skirted the roof. A Mahdi sniper zeroed in on them. He peppered the roof with well-placed shots.

Not long before this, the prodigal team leader returned. Kris Haney and Private First Class Case finally found the platoon and rejoined Ryan Howell's squad. As Haney moved onto the roof, the sniper took a shot at him. The bullet embedded itself into a wall only a few inches from Haney's head.

Moments later, Brian Ward and Ryan Howell climbed onto the roof and ran to join the rest of the men there. The sniper fired again. The bullet went right over Ryan's head and struck a wall behind him.

Enough was enough. This insurgent needed to die. John Ashford had an idea. He built a dummy with his Kevlar helmet mounted on a pole. While he raised it over the roof's parapet, other members of the squad peered over to see if they could find the sniper's location. Sure enough, this classic trick worked. The dummy drew fire, and the men identified the sniper's building.

Another mortar attack began. On the south side of the gym, John Michael's Humvee took three near-misses in quick succession. Other rounds exploded on the basketball court and soccer field that stretched to the west wall and Pete Salerno's position.

In the middle of the barrage, Ashford radioed Salerno, "Sergeant Salerno, I want to . . ." The rest was lost to Pete in the din of the attack.

"You want to what?"

Ashford tried again, but again the mortars drowned out his voice.

Exasperated, Salerno shouted, "What the fuck ever, John. I gotta situation down here. Just fucking execute."

Ashford did just that. On the north side of the roof, he assembled a dozen men with M4s and two SAWs. On his command, the entire group stood up and volley-fired into the sniper's building. The din was overwhelming as the men drained their M4 magazines and the SAW gunners stitched the target. When everyone had expended a mag, they dropped back down and reloaded. One more time, they popped up and let the sniper have it again.

Down at the Humvees, the sudden din piqued Pete Salerno's interest. What were his knuckleheads doing now?

Pete keyed his microphone and called Ashford.

"John, what the fuck is that?"

"Hey, I told you what we're doing."

"Bullshit! What's going on?"

What was going on was the demise of the sniper.

They put at least eight hundred rounds in that Mahdi sharpshooter's hide. Later, one of Twaddell's patrols told Spike that they had found the insurgent riddled with dozens of bullet holes.

They didn't have time to savor their victory. The mortar barrage shifted from the soccer field to the gym. One shell landed right at the eastside entrance and blew part of the building's façade off. The men on the roof scrambled for the stairs and beat feet back down into the shower room. The chaos left Sweety Petey and Spike in stitches. That irritated somebody who barked, "It isn't fucking funny."

A goofy grin crossed Petey's face. "Come on guys, they haven't hit us yet!"

Pete Salerno entered the shower room and announced, "We need gunners out in the Humvees." The guys out there were getting smoked in the 140-degree heat and needed relief.

Peterson volunteered and headed out for Lee Davidson's Humvee, which was parked on the south side of the gym. Just as he reached it, a mortar exploded on the basketball court not forty feet away. The blast sent Petey flying for his turret. He plopped down into it as Davidson remarked, "Ah hell fellers, that one was really close."

At forty-nine, Davidson was a legend in Bravo Company. He'd been a grunt longer than some of the men had been alive. Just to be safe, he moved his rig to the northeast, using the side of the gym as a shield from most of the mortar fire.

During the barrage, Salerno and three relief gunners crossed the basketball court and the soccer field to reach the gun trucks. It was a three-hundred-meter open stretch without so much as a pebble for cover.

Brandon Hern, a 187-pound, lantern-jawed Oregon State wrestler, climbed into one of the turrets and began his watch. Salerno suddenly heard a rapid-fire *prrrrrrrr!* An RPG skimmed over his head and just missed Brandon Hern. Before anyone could even curse, the rocket skipped off the basketball court, bounced back into the air, and sailed mere feet past Sweety Petey in Davidson's turret. With its momentum spent, it impacted about fifteen feet from their Humvee. The blast showered them with dirt and shrapnel, which cracked their windshield but left Petey unscathed.

Toward evening, the fire slackened. Peterson swapped out of Davidson's rig and returned to the roof. While still blazing hot, the coming of nightfall had dragged the temperature down a few degrees. Birds chirped in the nearby trees. Even the occasional burst of machine-gun fire or mortar explosion failed to dissuade these lusty avian singers.

Night fell, and the men bunked down on wrestling mats inside the gym. The air grew stale and oppressive. The heat of the night was almost unbearable to the Oregonians raised in far more temperate climes. They spent their first night in the city in sweaty, sleepless misery.

FIFTY-ONE

FIVE THOUSAND
NEW MARTYRS

Dawn on August 13 brought calm to the schoolhouse and Rec Center. First Platoon, Alpha, had spent the night running patrols around their new home. The men moved stealthily through the city streets, but encountered no Mahdi. To the east, 2nd Platoon, Bravo, pushed out patrols as well, but the militiamen had abandoned the streets. Either by design or because of 2-7's commanding positions on the corners of the AO, Al Sadr's men had fallen back to the northwest. Now they formed a hard defense line around the Imam Ali Shrine.

Aside from distant gunfire and explosions, the day began in relative quiet. At the Rec Center, the men pulled security and waited for more attacks. Then they got word that a cease-fire had gone into effect. Negotiations between Al Sadr and the coalition resumed. The fighting was put on hold.

At 0900, the first protesters appeared. They marched up Route Miami right past Apache's foothold. At the Rec Center, Petey and Spike gazed down as a procession of chanting Iraqis streamed past. Hundreds, perhaps thousands, of them filled the street. Beat-up vans and bongo trucks intermingled with the foot-bound protesters.

Lieutenant Kent observed them and asked an interpretor what the protesters were saying.

"America is friends with Saddam and is only fight for Israel!"

Some carried signs. Some clung to the bongo trucks. None wore the black and green of the Mahdi militia, and none carried weapons.

At the IP station, this new development concerned Colonel Rainey. He now had an estimated five thousand angry Iraqis clogging up his MSR. Should they turn hostile, his battalion would be hard pressed to fight so many fanatics. At the same time, he couldn't order his men to kill them. The protesters were unarmed. Shooting them would have been a war crime. Rainey put his Bradleys on line and waited. The chanting Iraqis shouted insults at his soldiers and tried to provoke a confrontation. It didn't work.

Inside the column, Khalid Mohammad, an Iraqi stringer for the Associated Press, snapped photographs of the crowd. The men were fired up, angry, and loud. Mohammad had ridden down from Baghdad to cover the event. He stayed with the protesters as they made their way up Route Miami and turned left past Colonel Rainey's IP station forward command post. The rear of the column reached Bravo Company's position. Spike and Sweety Petey watched as the last of them walked on by, still chanting anti-American slogans.

"They're pretty pissed off," Petey said as he filmed the scene. He was one of the platoon's inveterate shutterbugs.

"God, I love my life. This is freakin' awesome."

Spike gave the crowd one more glance and spit.

The protesters marched right into the Imam Ali Shrine complex and picked up AK-47s and RPGs cached there in preparation for their arrival. The protest was nothing more than a cover to reinforce Al Sadr. They walked right through the American cordon. It was a brilliant move—and practically unique in military history.

The Americans took a philosophical view of this. The protesters had not been combatants when they first entered Najaf; they were merely exercising their new right to free speech. But if they wanted to fight, the Americans would oblige them. A brilliant move, yes, but for most it was also a death sentence. American firepower made sure of that.

FIFTY-TWO

THE DAY OF DONKEY DEATH

For two days after establishing the foothold at the schoolhouse, Captain Glass and his task force fought pitched battles with the insurgents in the southwest streets of Najaf. Sergeant Compton and the rest of 1st Platoon, Alpha, spent those days at the schoolhouse, engaging targets of opportunity. On August 15, their third day in the city, the platoon loaded up in their Humvees and drove north to test 2-7's new thesis on urban warfare: seize the high ground, control the battle.

First Platoon cleared and occupied a five-story hotel that dominated the south-central section of Najaf. Surrounded by two- and three-story buildings, this new base of operations provided the southern Oregonians a spectacular view of the battle. A 2-7 sniper team joined them, along with a Special Operations Command (SOCOM) marine sniper section. Both set up shop on this new chunk of high ground and went to work shooting insurgents to the north and northwest. They could clearly see militiamen moving around on the rooftops to the north. For those Mahdi, their once-secure positions became deathtraps; the American snipers saw to that.

Down at the vehicles, the gunners engaged a lot of targets. The .50-cal and the M240 became hot commodities, and Compton had to kick his NCOs out of the turrets at times to let his Joes get a turn behind these weapons. The rigs were deployed around the hotel to provide ground-level security. The men also strung concertina wire across a nearby four-way intersection to give them protection against VBIEDs and other suicide attacks.

Initially, the insurgents sprayed the building with occasional long-range rifle fire. A few mortars dropped on them, but nothing like the first day. The day after they moved into the hotel, several militia teams infiltrated some houses three to four hundred meters to the north. There, they laid down inaccurate but steady fire on the building. The snipers had plenty of targets.

That morning, the platoon received a very unusual order. The Mahdi had been observed moving weapons and supplies around the city on donkeys. They had also used RPG-armed donkey carts to attack Captain Glass' tanks. Now, to interdict their ability to resupply, these enemy donkeys needed to die. When the order reached Sergeant Compton, he mumbled, "Oh, shit."

Within easy rifle range of their hotel, the platoon had seen a donkey pen. Dozens of donkeys had been tied up there, and Shannon feared his men would wax the animals wholesale. He had nothing to worry about. His men established that these were not enemy combatant donkeys, but neutrals minding their own business. They lived. The ones carrying supplies did not.

Using M4s and M14s, the platoon spent the day scanning for donkeys as well as insurgents. They could see the Mahdi darting across alleys pulling the beasts along with short ropes. Atop their backs, these donkeys carried ammunition and rocket reloads for the RPG launchers.

The men obeyed orders and dropped those donkeys. Lieutenant Jones' driver shot one with his M14 at four hundred meters. It got up. He shot it again. It got up again. He finally killed it on the third shot. Disappointed in his marksmanship, he tried to look on the bright side.

"Hey Sergeant C," he said. "It's all good. Now I know that if I aim at somethin', I can pretty much hit it!"

As the day wore on and the donkeys died, some of the insurgents tried to recover the supplies still on the fallen animals' backs. They would dash into the street, start stripping the rockets and ammo off them, only to die at the hands of the snipers and 1st Platoon's dismounts high in the hotel. They killed close to a dozen that way, and each donkey became a baited trap that the men watched carefully.

Later that day, as the fight continued, a donkey galloped down the street in front of the hotel. In its terror, it didn't notice the concertina wire in the intersection, and it soon got hopelessly fouled in it. This was not an enemy donkey; it carried no supplies. The platoon held its fire. It brayed and keened, kicking all the while, but could not free itself. Nobody wanted to go out and free it; they'd be too exposed.

Combat turns reality on its ear. Life in battle becomes a journey through the bacchanal of the bizarre. This was one of those moments.

A second neutral donkey appeared down the bullet-swept street. It sauntered up to the concertina wire, sized up the trapped donkey, and mounted it. Here in this cauldron of battle, the men of 1st Platoon, Alpha, bore witness to all the raw horror of donkey lust gone wild. They were probably the only two creatures having a carnal encounter in the entire city that day.

Their unbridled passion complete, the trapped donkey tore free. It loped back up the street with its new friend in tow. The platoon held its fire and laughed like hell.

Some donkeys didn't just carry ammunition, they became weapons.

Late that afternoon, Pete Salerno went back to Camp David to get supplies. A dusty, dirt-splattered M1 rolled into the base. Pete watched as one of Captain Glass' officers, Lieutenant Wojcik, threw back the commander's hatch cover and pulled himself out of the tank. Drenched in sweat, wearing little more than his underwear and body armor, Wojcik was about as filthy as a man could get. The young lieutenant peeled off his IBA and T-shirt, and then jumped off the track.

"I'm fucking smoked," he said to Salerno.

The rest of the crew popped out as well. All of them sported a thick swath of stubble and grime so thick it could have been a second layer of skin. The exhausted crew moved like automatons as they refueled and re-armed their tank. While they worked, the lieutenant shared a story with Pete.

During the raging battle on the southwest escarpment, their tank had taken thirty-six rocket hits and kept going. The Mahdi tried a new trick. Wojcik's crew watched as a donkey appeared from an alleyway ahead of them, prodded by a stick held by a militiaman hiding behind a building. The donkey edged into the alley. Attached to it was a cart with an RPG launcher mounted on it. The insurgent had tied a string to the trigger.

Wojcik called out, "Gunner, coax, donkey cart."

The militiaman yanked the string. The rocket shot forward, but as it did, the back blast caught the donkey square on the hindquarters. It jerked out of the way and spoiled the shot. The rocket flew off into the city. Disappointed, the insurgent pulled it back into cover. A few minutes and modifications later, the donkey re-emerged. This time, the RPG had been buttressed by sandbags.

Wojcik saw it again and grew tired of this. "Gunner, main gun, uparmored donkey cart."

It was an order unique in the annals of American military history. Wojcik finished telling his tale and turned to help his exhausted men. A few minutes later, they climbed aboard their Abrams and drove back into the fight.

Donkeys aside, the killing of humans continued unabated.

Back at the hotel, daring Mahdi militiamen spent the afternoon harassing 1st Platoon's Humvees. The Mahdi had been told that American vehicles were made of plywood and could be destroyed by AK-47 fire. They spent the day trying to prove that correct. Every so often, an insurgent would pop out of an alleyway and snap off a shot. Others would swing around the corner of a building and spray the Humvees with their AKs on full auto.

The platoon killed several of these fighters with well-placed bursts from their crew-served weapons. That dissuaded others from trying the same thing. The insurgents changed tactics and came at the platoon with snipers.

Up at the top of the hotel, Phil Disney's squad spotted one of the sharp-shooters on a rooftop about two hundred meters away. He was crouched behind a wall that skirted the edge of the roof. They soon discovered he was a cagey fighter. He'd leap up, fire a single shot with remarkable accuracy, and dive out of sight before anyone could draw a bead on him.

The sniper's marksmanship impressed Disney. His bullets cracked and whirred right over his squad, forcing them to keep their heads down. To counter this, the Oregonians knocked a hole in the side of the hotel and laid down fire on the sniper's last position. It didn't work. He popped up elsewhere on the roof and sent another bullet so close it practically scraped scalps. Everyone ducked.

Frustrated with this cat-and-mouse game, Disney turned to Mike Blanchard and said, "Hey, Blanchard, lob a 203 at that sonofabitch."

Blanchard did one better. He sent a veritable mini-barrage down on the lone sniper. The 40mm grenades sprayed shrapnel all over the roof. The insurgent did not reappear. Twenty minutes passed without a return shot. Disney decided to take a team and check it out.

They went downstairs, dashed across the street, and broke into the building. A sweep revealed nothing. Disney led his men upstairs. They searched the roof but found neither a corpse nor any blood. Somehow, the sniper had escaped to fight another day. He'd been one of the best enemy fighters the platoon had seen in Najaf.

FIFTY-THREE

THE APACHE HILTON

With the three corners secured, Colonel Rainey's men squeezed the Mahdi militia back into the Medina Complex around the Imam Ali Shrine. Charlie 3-8 and its Oregon platoon advanced from south to north. Commanche, operating from the IP station, drove west down Route New York along the southern edge of the cemetery.

Several hundred meters west of the IP station stood a series of multistoried hotels that catered to the tourist industry centered on the shrine. The Najaf Hilton was the tallest one in the area. It became Rainey's next major objective.

Colonel Rainey borrowed a company of marines from the 1-4. At night, the marines swept forward and cleared every building between the IP station and the Hilton. By the time they reached the hotel, the strenuous work left them exhausted. When morning came, they occupied the high ground but could not exploit it. The insurgents laid down accurate sniper fire into the building. The marines moved away from the engaged side and hunkered down in the basement and back of the hotel.

That morning found 2nd Platoon, Bravo Company, moving up to the IP station from another hotel at the southwest. They'd moved there earlier in the week to act as a hinge between Charlie 3-8 and Commanche. They found little sign of the enemy. They'd simply been pinched out of the area by the other two companies.

Rainey ordered Apache to relieve the marines at the Apache Hilton. Upon reaching the IP station, 2nd Platoon learned it would have to leave its Humvees behind. The trip up Route New York was too dangerous for wheeled vehicles. Twaddell had just returned from a leader's recon, where his Brads had been thoroughly shot up. He climbed out of his track and shouted over to Salerno, "Man, it's pretty fucking hot up there."

Lieutenant Kent left ten of his men behind to stay with their Humvees. The other eighteen men of the platoon—Ryan Howell's guys plus a fire team from John Ashford's squad, Doc Bagnall, Salerno, and Kent—climbed into the back of Captain Twaddell's Bradleys and headed off to what would become the most important chunk of real estate in Najaf.

The ramps dropped, the Oregonians had reached the objective. Now known as the Apache Hilton, they could see it was a towering, six-story hotel whose front faced west. Pete Salerno and Chris Kent led the men inside.

They found the marines waiting for them. Spike looked around and saw many vacant stares. After days of continuous operations, the marines looked absolutely smoked. As Salerno got a handle on the situation, he was surprised to learn that the marines hadn't even set up security, let alone returned the fire coming into the building. Instead, they'd gotten out of the line of fire and let a SEAL team on the roof handle the bad guys for them. Second Platoon wondered what Colonel Rainey had gotten them into.

As the marines prepared to pull out, Twaddell's first sergeant told Salerno to take the platoon up to the top floor. Pete led the way up a spiral staircase carrying four boxes of 7.62mm ammo for the M240 Bravos as he went. When he got to the top floor, he found more marines sitting out the fight. "Don't go over there, man," said one of the marines as he pointed to the west side of the building, "There's really accurate sniper fire."

Pete ignored him. He took Chris Bailey, and together they scouted the rooms on the west side. They discovered that the last ones on either end of the corridor had unrivaled views of the shrine complex and everything around it. They could see for miles to the west. Second Platoon had been placed on the highest piece of ground in the most important sector of Najaf. Now, they just had to execute.

Salerno and Bailey deployed the M240s. Brandon Hern's gun, with Spike Olsen as his spotter, went into the room at the south end of the hallway. Shad Thomas' went into the north end. The rest of the men took up positions in between the two guns, and in the northside hallway to keep eyes on the cemetery. Within minutes, the platoon was ready to fight.

Four hundred meters to the west, the Oregonians could see a tangled mass of metal and debris in a blackened stretch of cityscape surrounded by hotels. The day before, it had been an open-air marketplace, which the 2-7 discovered was being used as a major base of operations by the Mahdi militia defending this area of Najaf. The night the marines reached the Hilton, an AC-130 turned the market into a smoking, rubble-cluttered pile of junk.

Spike stood alongside Hern and pulled out his Oregon-made binoculars he'd carried since leaving home. They came in handy now. As soon as he got eyes on the boneyard, three militiamen broke cover and sprinted south to north through it. They dodged around the debris, climbed over some of the mangled metal, and reached cover on the far side.

A few minutes later, another group tried to do the same thing. Spike saw them slipping around some shacks on the south side of the boneyard. He called them out to Hern. "Tin shacks. Two guys. Left of the yellow sign. They're gonna move left to right."

Hern sighted through the ACOG (advanced combat optical gunsight) four-power sight on his M240. Finger on the trigger, he waited. "Okay, the skinny guy will have the RPG. The fat one in back is carrying the reloads."

They broke cover. Hern's M240 blazed. Almost half a kilometer away, the 7.62mm bullets sprayed a pattern in the dirt and ashes of the boneyard and kicked up a cloud of dust that partially obscured the scene. Hern laid on the trigger. Spike gave him corrections. The skinny Mahdi with the RPG died halfway across the boneyard. The second one went down not long afterward.

Moments later, another group tried the same thing. They died in a hail of Hern's gunfire. Meanwhile, Shad Thomas was doing the same thing. The guns chattered mercilessly.

At first, the incoming fire seemed to confuse the Mahdi. Unsure of where it was coming from, they continued to try and run the gauntlet of the boneyard, ducking and weaving through cover as they went. Few made it across. When that kept failing, others tried another approach to get across. They would move off a street that bordered the boneyard and run east along a wall. When they reached the corner of the wall, they'd break north and try to cross that way. It didn't work. In fact they made excellent targets for Hern and Thomas. Whenever they followed the wall, they moved toward the Oregonians and gave them a zero-deflection shot.

Hern was a natural M240 gunner. Muscular, precise, and willing to listen to his spotters, he could get on a target faster than anyone else. Once on, he stayed on, using his strength to hold the M240 down as he snapped out bursts.

Spike alternated spotting for Hern and shooting his ACOG-equipped M4. He wanted to shoot; it made him feel like he was contributing. Plus, after months of chasing phantoms around Taji, the enemy had finally come into the open. It was like the Tet Offensive, and fate had given him a ringside seat to history. He took advantage of it.

His M4 barked frequently. At one point, he spotted a black-clad Mahdi fighter with a red sash around his waist. The man was pretty chubby, but Spike could clearly see the weapon he carried. He ran through a parking lot near the boneyard with four or five other insurgents. Spike got him in his crosshairs. His first shots missed, but he walked his bullets across the lot until they hit home. Red Sash staggered, fell, and twitched violently in his death throes. Seconds afterward, Shad and Hern brought their M240s to bear and lit up the entire parking lot. Few of that group survived.

Spike looked out at his kill.

I just shot a fat guy in a robe.

Resting the crosshairs on another human being had been an eerie experience. Now that the man had died in the street, Spike felt nothing for him. He had chosen to fight Americans. Yes, he probably had a family, a mother, kids. But so had Eric McKinley. Besides, it had been a good, two-hundred-meter shot. Spike's M4 barked again.

The morning wore on. The men continued to kill. It became a shooting gallery, one of the few times they were weapon-free and laying it to the enemy without any significant counterfire. It was so one-sided, these college-kids-turned-soldiers laughed and shouted and one-upped each other with the shots they made. They jostled for time behind the M240s. Ryan Howell and Salerno had to set time limits. Everyone wanted a piece of this moment.

The SEAL team on the roof was astonished at this development. They'd gone all the previous night and morning without any help against the Mahdi from the marines. Fifteen minutes after showing up, 2nd Platoon uncorked its machine guns. After the first burst, Salerno heard one of the SEALs shout, "What the fuck was that? Who's shooting?"

A moment later, a puzzled voice answered, "They say they're some sort of National Guard platoon."

"You're shitting me?"

Salerno grinned. The machine-gunning continued.

A few hours into the fight, Ryan discovered why the boneyard attracted so many insurgents. He observed several groups recover ammunition among the tangled metal. The militiamen were trying to salvage what they could from their AC-130-ravaged base.

Ryan had an idea.

"Hey, Sergeant Salerno, can I shoot this thing at some guys over in the boneyard?"

Ryan was hefting an AT-4 rocket launcher.

"Well, Ryan, we didn't bring them all the way up to the fucking sixth floor just to look at them."

Ryan grinned like a kid, and the two NCOs worked out a plan. Moments later, Ryan went up onto the roof. The SEALs had established their hide in a small shack up there, and they were busy spotting and shooting targets of their own.

Ryan and Kris Haney eased over to the wall that skirted the edge of the roof. Hunkered down on the west side, they waited for Pete Salerno to activate their plan. The M240s erupted. Tracers flew downrange, marking the target area for Ryan. He stood erect, his six-foot-four-inch frame exposed above the thighs. Carefully, he took aim. The AT-4's crosshairs settled onto a car near the back of the boneyard. Behind it, six ammo-hunting insurgents lurked.

The AT-4 spewed flames. With a tremendous *whoosh* the rocket sped downrange like a fiery meteorite. The launch shook the entire building. Ryan ducked down behind the wall. One story below, Spike and Pete Salerno watched as Ryan's rocket drilled the car center mass. The AT-4's HEAT warhead blew it apart, sending pieces careening in all directions even as a fireball engulfed the area. Not so much as a toe remained of the six men.

In their hide, the SEALs started to shout.

"Holy shit!"

"What the fuck was that?"

A pause, then another voice, full of awe replied, "I think those National Guard guys just shot at those fuckers with an AT-4."

"Right the fuck on!"

From that moment, the SEALs virtually adopted 2nd Platoon. After showing up the marines and letting fly with everything they had, these collegiate warriors had proven themselves one "bad-ass bunch of Muldoons." It was the start of a wonderful relationship that lasted almost until the end of the battle.

As the afternoon wore on, the shooting gallery continued. The men swapped out behind the guns. Blond-haired, blue-eyed Private First Class Ryan Tuttle's turn came. Tuttle was not a recruiting-poster type of Guardsman. With thick, industrial-strength "birth control" glasses and a helmet that seemed too large for his skinny head, he looked more like a geeky kid playing soldier than an actual one.

He got behind the M240, which the men had mounted atop a pair of sandbags. Behind him, Spike leaned into a metal railing, Kevlar long forgotten. Spike gave Tuttle a target. Eyes behind the ACOG, he scanned for it and opened up.

"Go! Go! Go!" shouted Spike.

The M240: *shattattattaatta.* Spike watched Tuttle hit the side of a building instead of a nearby alleyway. He corrected him.

"Lower right! Lower right!"

The towheaded, former chicken farmer and student snapped out a short burst.

"Lay on the trigger!" called Spike.

Tuttle held it down this time, spraying a four-second burst into the target area. Salerno loved this kid. Easily bored, Tuttle needed to be constantly challenged. Pete tried to keep him busy. Spike watched his latest burst stitch across the building to the left of the targeted alleyway.

"Lower right!"

Another fusillade.

Spike raised the binos and looked down at the back of Tuttle's flat-topped head.

"You're hitting the side of the building. Hit the alley!"

Tuttle tried again. This time, he took careful aim. The gun chattered. Ryan kept the M240's stock tight against his shoulder while his left hand atop the ACOG held the gun steady. He flayed the alleyway. Spike was pleased.

"There ya go!"

Later, Lieutenant Kent estimated that Tuttle, Hern, Shad Thomas, and Spike had killed at least twenty-four insurgents. The count was probably much higher.

For Pete Salerno, this first day at the Apache Hilton showed him what sort of moxy his men possessed. Before leaving the States, he'd read a book entitled *On Killing,* which described the psychological effects soldiers face when they enter combat.

Evan Johnson, one of Howell's NCOs, got behind one of the M240s. Pete watched him spray the boneyard and drop a militiaman. The Mahdi convulsed in the dirt, something the platoon called the "kicking chicken." A second burst killed him. Evan looked back at Salerno. Pete, his mind flashing to some of the passages of *On Killing,* went to reassure his young NCO.

"It's okay, son. You keep doing your job."

Evan gave Pete a quizzical look. "Are you kidding, Sergeant Salerno? That was for McKinley."

No anguish. No guilt. Pete decided right then and there that *On Killing* did not apply to 2nd Platoon.

They were all steel-eyed killers.

FIFTY-FOUR

ELDRED'S FIST OF GOD

The capture of the Apache Hilton was the turning point in 2-7's Battle of Najaf. With 2nd Platoon on this piece of high ground astride the Mahdi lines of communication, the insurgents lost their freedom of movement. Any attempt to reinforce or flee the fighting against Charlie 3-8 to the southwest was now met with the raw fury of American firepower. Soon after 2nd Platoon set up shop on the sixth floor, Captain Twaddell moved his command post into the basement and sent one of his platoons up to the fifth floor. With multiple M240s covering down on the north-south roads, any insurgent moving within sight was sure to draw fire.

With the Hilton serving as a base of fire, Twaddell's Bradleys probed west. At one point, Colonel Rainey joined one patrol in his command track. They drove straight into the teeth of a Mahdi defensive position and Rainey's Bradley took an RPG and three near misses. Luckily, everyone emerged unscathed, and Rainey's gunner killed at least one of the Mahdi rocket teams.

As the Brads trolled and probed, 2nd Platoon searched the nearby buildings. Salerno led the first of these patrols. As he and his men gathered in the basement, the SEAL team's officer in charge (OIC), Lieutenant "P," came downstairs to join them. He'd velcroed all sorts of gear to his helmet, and 2nd Platoon's Joes all stared enviously. Pete thought the young lieutenant looked like R2D2 with all the stuff hanging from his Kevlar. When he saw the look in his own boys' eyes, he laid down the law, "Don't even think about it. He gets to put shit all over his hat because he's a SEAL."

Salerno never was one for adhering to all the uniform chickenshit. That attitude drove Rainey and his sergeant major crazy. But even Pete had his limits. No cool-guy stuff on the Kevlar. That's where he drew the line.

They cleared a multi-use building across the street. It had a big drill-hall-like open room inside, plus a lot of offices and a prayer room. In the latter, the men found AK-47s under every pillow. Pete Salerno uncovered a stash of photos showing Iraqi soldiers during the war against Iran in the '80s. Later, some of the men uncovered Iranian currency.

A subsequent patrol advanced west down a road at the southwest end of the Apache Hilton. In broad daylight, the men moved through the street. Tall, eight-foot walls ran along both sides of the road, and the only cover in sight was a derelict dumpster squatting amid a pile of trash on the sidewalk. Spike felt the hairs on his neck stand up. They were terribly exposed.

The objective of the patrol was a schoolhouse about halfway down the street. Earlier, a few militiamen had crept into it and fired from its windows into the Apache Hilton. They came to the school's gate, a heavy ten-foot-wide by eight-foot-tall metal barrier the men could never force open with their bare hands. Salerno turned to Kris Haney, "Hey, Kris, have Case launch a 203 at the gate."

The SEAL OIC looked unsure. They were all pretty close to the target. Haney turned to his grenadier. Case took aim. Nearby, Sweety Petey Peterson grew alarmed. They were less than twenty-five meters from the gate.

"This is freaking crazy!"

Just as Case fired, Lieutenant "P" said to Salerno, "Isn't he a little close?"

Somehow, Case missed the gate entirely. His grenade exploded on the second floor of the schoolhouse.

Salerno erupted, "Case, how the fuck did you miss that huge fucking gate?"

Somebody else, mimicking the words of the Comic Book Guy in the *Simpsons* judged, "Worst shot . . . *ever!*"

"Sorry. Let me try again."

Petey covered him with his SAW as Spike snuggled with a SEAL against one wall. A few stray shots had passed overhead. If they got caught in this road, it would not be pretty. The SEAL with Spike muttered, "What's taking so long?"

Case popped another M203 round. This one hit the top of the gate on the right side. Petey felt a sudden sting in his knee. He looked down to see blood trickling through a hole in his pants.

"Case? You fucking shot me!"

Doc Bagnall came forward just as Salerno shouted, "Breach that fucking door!"

Petey looked down at his wound. A rush of happiness seized him. "Yes! I'm going home! See you fuckers later!"

Then he got up and started to move for the gate. His knee worked fine. It was just a scratch that didn't even need a Band-Aid. Petey cursed. "Guess I'm staying."

Thanks to the second M203 round, the men were able to get the door open. They cleared the school, found nothing, and returned to the Apache Hilton. All the way home, Case endured the merciless heckling of his fellow Joes, who called him a "Gate Blasting Buddy Fucker."

Corporal Patrick Eldred was the platoon anomaly. Attached to Bravo Company as one of Major Warrington's forward observers, he had endured six months of flak from the infantrymen he supported. Brian Ward especially liked to heckle him. "Patrick, what is it that you do here? You're not infantry."

Eldred inevitably replied, "I am your fire support." Around Taji, though, there was no need for fire support because most of the time indirect fire was forbidden. Eldred had spent almost half the deployment as the platoon's third wheel.

Because Eldred was not an 11 Bravo infantryman, he would never be able to wear the combat infantryman's badge. The CIB is the universal sign that a soldier has seen combat. It is worn with great pride, and is coveted. Second Platoon never let him forget that.

Just because he didn't have an 11 Bravo MOS did not make Eldred any less of a soldier. Far from it. One afternoon at the Apache Hilton, he stunned everyone by killing an RPG-toting militiaman with a single M203 round at more than four hundred meters, well beyond the effective max range of the weapon.

The SEAL team also had a forward observer, known as a Joint Tactical Air Controller (JTAC) in navy parlance. Lieutenant "P's" JTAC possessed an outstanding radio system, but he was a little green. Eldred hooked up with him. Together, they turned western Najaf into their personal playground.

On the second night at the Hilton, Eldred and the JTAC called in an AC-130. Eldred talked directly with a female AC-130 gunner, whose sultry voice and incredible marksmanship earned her the nickname "The Angel of Death." Whether she was the same Angel of Death of Afghanistan fame is unclear, but she and Eldred formed a working relationship that cost the Mahdi a lot of its people. Eldred picked out individual buildings, then individual floors and windows. The Angel of Death demolished everything targeted.

The next morning, Eldred found his stride. Marine Harriers, F-16s, Apaches, Cobra gunships, and Hornets circled overhead just waiting for targets. Eldred put them to work.

By the end of the second day at the Hilton, the enemy figured out that the Americans were up on the top floor in strength. They laid down small-arms fire on the building from a series of other hotels to the west. At first, 2nd Platoon traded shots with these thorns in their side. Spike played cat-and-mouse with a couple of sniping insurgents around a fire station. He shot up the entire area with an M240, peppering the fire engines with 7.62mm-sized holes. It was frustrating work trying to keep those insurgents suppressed.

Eldred had a better idea. He wielded the aircraft overhead like a fist of God, calling them down to smash Mahdi-held buildings. He had a ball doing it; this was his chance to shine and he seized the moment. He started to strut.

After leveling a building, a feat that earned him numerous cheers, he exclaimed, "You guys can keep your fucking CIBs. Look at what I'm doing!"

Somehow, he'd lost his protractor, a vital tool for any FO. He sat down and carved a new one out of an MRE box. Later, somebody snapped a photo of him working with his cardboard protractor alongside Colonel Rainey and Captain Twaddell as they reviewed the battalion's fire support plan. Eldred's work in Najaf became so well known that his MRE protractor later ended up on display at the fire support school back in the States.

The boneyard was a prime target for Eldred's fist. He called in a JDAM (Joint Direct-Attack Munitions) strike, and a five-hundred-pound bomb fell from two miles above the city and obliterated the boneyard. Later, he went with a patrol that skirted the edge of the boneyard. The men looked out in awe at the huge crater left by the JDAM. Eldred pointed at it and proudly reminded them, "I did that. See that! All of that was me!"

Early on August 20, the fourth day in the Apache Hilton, the dynamics of 2nd Platoon's battle changed. While the M240s engaged targets, Lee Davidson and Pete Salerno scanned for targets from inside a room between the two machine guns. They had created an excellent position behind two walls. They could see outside without obstruction, but anyone wanting to hit them would have to put a bullet through a narrow opening in the exterior wall. No militiaman with an AK-47 could do that.

A bullet cracked past them at eyeball level. It exploded a brick in the corridor wall and embedded itself in another one directly above Sweety Petey, who had been sitting on the floor behind Salerno and Davidson. Pete and Lee froze. They burst out in gales of hysterical laughter.

"That was pretty fucking close!"

"Holy shit, man!"

In the next room over, Evan Johnson called out, "What's going on over there?"

Spike Olsen was on the M240 in that room. He had Evan behind one shoulder and a 2-7 trunk monkey on the other. Both were spotting targets for him. Before Salerno could answer Johnson, the sniper fired again. This time his bullet blew apart a brick right above and behind Spike's head. Everyone hit the floor, eyes as big as silver dollars. It had been so hot that nobody was wearing their body armor or helmets. Salerno dug the first bullet out of the wall in his room. It was a football-shaped boat-tail round.

"We've got a sniper!" he announced.

Second platoon pulled into the east side of the building, safe from the sniper's reach. This guy was so good, they decided to let the SEALs take him. A cat-and-mouse game began. The SEALs in their hide searched for the sniper and waited for him to make a mistake. He was good; he made none.

For the next day and a half, the cat-and-mouse game continued. The sniper would lie silent for hours before snapping off one or two expertly placed shots that drove the platoon back into the east part of the Apache Hilton. They'd return, only to be driven out again. At one point, Tuttle and John Michael felt the sniper's wrath when he put a bullet right over their head as they remanned one of the M240s. The round splintered the door to the room they were in, causing the two men to duck into a stairwell. Tuttle, who'd been keeping a video journal of Najaf with his digital camera, explained the situation for posterity and ended the entry with, "I think he's got us pinned. Zoinks!"

The next morning, August 21, the SEALs thought they saw him in a hotel near the boneyard. Eldred called in an air strike. The building was flattened. That sniper bothered them no more.

Other snipers moved into the area. Eldred called down his fist of God again. He used everything he could get his hands on. If it flew and dropped bombs, Eldred found it a target. The cat-and-mouse game became less a contest between the SEALs and Mahdi snipers, and more a gigantic display of aerial firepower.

Jim MacMillan, a daring AP photographer, had joined 2nd Platoon just in time for the Apache Hilton. He photographed much of the platoon's experiences in Najaf, and one of his 2nd Platoon photos earned him a Pulitzer Prize. Another one, showing Chris Bailey using Ashford's Kevlar-helmet dummy technique, made the front page of the *New York Times*.

Thanks to Eldred, he got the photo of a lifetime as Patrick called in an F-16 on the sniper's suspected building. With his Canon 10D, he captured the bomb in midflight just before it impacted and exploded.

Second Platoon cheered like kids at a football game as that building came down. For the moment, it looked like the end of the sniper plague.

FIFTY-FIVE

THE TUTTLE CHAPTER

Mixed in with the sniper attacks, the Mahdi around the shrine launched mortar barrages against the Apache Hilton. Several times, they managed to hit the roof of the building, and one attack slightly wounded the SEAL who'd been with Kris Haney at the gas station on the first day of the battle. That same attack also destroyed a $1,500 scope, which thoroughly bummed the SEALs.

As one barrage fell around them, part of 2nd Platoon took a break in one of the eastside rooms. The men ate MREs and tried to ignore the explosions, the dust showers, and the shake of the building after every direct hit.

A lull descended, broken a minute later by a loud, hollow *pop!*

"What was that?" somebody asked.

Lieutenant Kent answered, "That was a mortar hit, but it didn't explode."

Tuttle burst out laughing. The men turned to look at him. Tuttle had a mischievous streak in him a mile wide, mixed with a healthy serving of smart-ass. Once, when Salerno had heard Tuttle claim he was a chicken farmer, he howled with laughter. He'd known where Tuttle had worked. He cleaned eggs for his pay.

When Pete confronted him, Tuttle shrugged, "I prefer the term 'chicken farmer' to 'egg washer', thank you very much." Now, he stared back at the rest of the platoon with a huge grin striping his face.

"No, that wasn't a mortar," he confessed. "That was an MRE bomb."

Tuttle had stuck an MRE pouch in a water bottle. He'd activated it to chemically heat, and the bag swelled until it blew the water bottle apart. Salerno looked at Tuttle as if he were a Martian.

"Are you fucking high?" he demanded.

"Well, no. I'm bored."

"Bored? Oh you're bored are you?" Salerno bellowed. "Fucking Private Tuttle is bored. Oh, okay. Well, I've got work for you!"

Pete made Tuttle clean out 2nd Platoon's bathroom on the sixth floor. With no running water, they used cans and bags for their business. There, in the middle of the Battle of Najaf, as bullets rattled off the building and more mortars fell around them, Tuttle carried bags of shit from one room to the next.

He never set off another MRE bomb.

FIFTY-SIX

18TH AND CHRISTIES

While the fighting flowed around the Apache Hilton, Lieutenant Dewayne Jones and his men prepared to bound a full kilometer and a half north toward the shrine. Jones formulated a plan to put all six Humvees on line on six different north-south roads. They'd sweep forward to Routes 18th and Christies, where Charlie 3-8 had ordered them to secure a three-story building.

In the dead of night, 1st Platoon, Alpha, rolled into the gutted heart of old Najaf. Fires burned in the distance. Tracers lit the sky. The platoon made it to Christies without contact. They formed back up on 18th and dismounted. There, the platoon discovered the only easy access to their objective was from Christies itself. The Mahdi militia had Christies zeroed with mortars, RPGs, and machine-gun fire. Any movement on that road sent a cascade of fire pouring into the Americans.

Disney and Cunningham led their men down an alley behind the target building. There, they scaled a wall, entered a house next door, and accessed the objective from the roof. It was not an easy thing to do, and after clearing it, the men had to open a hole in the wall along the alley to allow easier access to the rigs. Compton deployed his six Humvees behind the house. Tucked in tight, they could be seen only from directly east or west.

Dawn broke to reveal most of the platoon on the roof, ready to support the marine SOCOM sniper team. Down at the alley, Lieutenant Jones grew concerned that militiamen might try to flank the building and take side shots from the west and east. He told Compton to push his rigs out of the alley on both ends so they could fire northward into the city.

Compton didn't like the idea. He and Jones shared words. In the end, C inched his trucks out of the alley. A furious volley of small-arms fire lashed the vehicles. The enemy had not known that 1st Platoon had advanced so far until that moment when the Humvees broke cover. Now, the insurgents poured everything they had into displacing the Americans.

It was the start of a rambling, desperate six-hour firefight in which some of the Mahdi actually tried to close with the Americans and assault their positions. They came out of buildings less than twenty-five meters away, AKs blazing. The platoon cut them down. The Humvee gunners had their hands full suppressing these insurgents. They moved with expertise and military knowledge, and they shot better than the other Mahdi they'd encountered earlier in the battle. Al Sadr was saving his best for last.

Phil Disney was up on the roof with his squad. Soon, the men attracted a storm of fire. It seemed to be coming from a ten-story building across Christies, but nobody could get eyes on the shooters. Every time they popped their heads over the roof's parapet, well-aimed bullets drove them back down. Lieutenant Jones called for armor, and a Bradley came waddling up 18th. When it reached the intersection with Christies, it hammered the ten-story building with coax and 25mm fire. Disney peered over the parapet. No sniper fire greeted him.

The SOCOM team licked its chops as they studied that ten-story high-rise. From there, they could do all sorts of bad things to the insurgents. They asked for an escort to go with them and clear the building.

Crossing Christies in the middle of a sprawling firefight didn't appeal to 1st Platoon, but Lieutenant Jones ordered Sergeants Cunningham, Blanchard, Parks, and Neilson to give the marines some support. The Oregonians soldiered up and charged across the street.

The advance triggered an unbelievably accurate mortar barrage. This mini task force of special forces searched the building and found nobody left alive inside. Just as the marines began to get to work again, a mortar round fell right down the main elevator shaft. It exploded next to a room a marine was using as his hide. He emerged covered head to toe with dust and dirt. Amazingly, he was unhurt.

After that, the marines decided it would be best to stay on the south side of Christies until this rodeo subsided.

Later that day, an Arab press crew emerged from a side street and started down Christies for the platoon's position. Jones took three soldiers and went to detain them. Recently, the Americans began to suspect these journalists were not really reporters at all, but Mahdi conducting reconnaissance on their positions. Jones and the three men dashed out into the street, only to be driven back by a hail of fire. More Arabs with cameras appeared, PRESS written on their body armor in two languages. Disney and his Joes drove them off with warning shots.

Two tanks came up to support the platoon that afternoon. They shot up the local hot spots, finding the enemy much more skilled than normal. Several times, they crossed Christies and pushed a block or so north. Each time, they ran into RPG teams and mortar fire. The tanks would back down and return to the intersection with 18th. At least with the tanks present, the Mahdi stopped maneuvering on the platoon's three-story house. Both sides settled down into another fire combat and blasted away at one another with every weapon at their disposal.

The militiamen had set up mortar tubes all around the Iman Ali Shrine. Somehow, they'd learned that the American high command had declared a hundred-meter radius around the shrine to be a no-fire zone. From the house, Alpha's Joes could see mortars firing from that exclusion zone. They couldn't shoot those, but the mortar tubes outside the exclusion zone were fair game. The platoon's grenadiers lobbed M203 rounds at them, destroying several mortars and their crews.

Throughout the day Marine JTAC with the SOCOM team called down helicopters and AC-130s on RPG teams and mortar pits. As night fell, the AC-130s kept up the pressure, devastating insurgent positions at the direction of the marine observer.

The crisis passed. The platoon would not be pushed off Christies.

The next morning, Compton was inside his Humvee riding out the most intense mortar barrage of his career. Using heavy 120mm mortars, they pummeled the house and all the surrounding buildings. He ordered his men to button up. The gunners descended into their rigs and slammed their hatches closed. They rode out the barrage cramped like sardines.

Eventually, the attack ran out of steam. The din ebbed away, and Compton was about to tell his men to unbutton.

Wham! A huge explosion rattled through the area. Phil Disney, atop the platoon's house, felt the shock wave roll through it. He turned to Private First Class Ivan Ventrella, the platoon's RTO, and said, "Call the rigs. Make sure they're okay."

Ventrella keyed his mic. A moment later he reported, "A mortar round hit in the middle of the Humvees. Sergeant Compton's rig is on fire."

"Oh my God." Disney replied. He organized a rescue team and sent it downstairs with the medic. The rest of the platoon remained in the building, dreading what the team would find. Sergeant C was the heart and soul of 1st Platoon.

Inside Compton's rig, Shannon and the rest of the crew were unhurt. Whatever had hit them had thrown everyone around and blew the Humvee six or seven feet into the air, back end up. Their ears buzzed, and now Compton's gunner said, "It's getting hot in here, Sergeant C. It's possible we're on fire."

Compton didn't want to dismount in the middle of the barrage. He told his men to sit tight. Over the radio, the platoon's chatter was tinged with near panic as the men called out to their platoon sergeant. Shannon couldn't respond. The blast had knocked out his transmitter.

They sat in the burning Humvee for about thirty seconds. It seemed like ten years. Finally, Compton ordered them out. The doors opened and the men hit the pavement with their weapons ready.

There was no enemy in sight. Compton examined his burning vehicle even as Caleb Torgerson and Benito Najera ran to them wielding fire extinguishers. They smothered the flames, and the men discovered they'd been hit by an RPG. Some ultradaring Mahdi fighter had crept into a position just west of the alleyway to torch off an RPG at point-blank range.

The rocket struck Compton's Humvee right between the tailgate and the bumper. It penetrated easily, smashed through two crossmembers under the rig, and exploded in the driveline. Shrapnel shredded the brakes and all four tires. The hit had deadlined the rig, and with the level of combat they faced on Christies, Compton doubted anyone would come and recover it for them. He decided to drive it back to Duke.

He told Staff Sergeant Manual Annear he was in charge of the alleyway now. Compton took two rigs to provide an escort for him, then he told his driver, Specialist Flick, to head south for Camp David.

There in the blackened, bullet-scarred city, Compton and his crew got the ride of their lives. The remains of the tires spun away. Flick drove on the rims or run-flats without brakes. When they reached Route Miami, Flick failed to slow down, and they skidded sideways as if on a sheet of ice.

"Flick," Shannon said, "you'd better slow down. I didn't come through all this only to die now."

Chastised, Flick agreed, "You're right. You're right."

Somehow, they made it to Camp David. As they prepared to make the turn, Compton said, "Okay, Flick, you'd better slow down here. I'll be really mad if you roll us now!"

They herked and jerked their way inside the compound. A crowd gathered and marveled at the damage and their fifteen-kilometer journey. Commanche's XO, Captain Morris, appeared and took Shannon aside.

"Are you guys okay? How're you doing?"

"We're okay, sir."

Morris started to smile. "You know, when you came in a minute ago, all I could think of was Fred Sanford!" Morris started humming the *Sanford and Son* tune. Compton burst out laughing.

It was funny now that they were safe at Camp David. But as Shannon thought about it, he realized just how narrow their escape had been. Four inches higher and that rocket would have gone right through the tailgate into a box of claymore mines and hand grenades.

FIFTY-SEVEN

OF BRAS AND
WEDDING GOWNS

Second Platoon was getting pungent. The men had been on line for almost a week now. They cleansed themselves with baby wipes and tried to scrub their uniforms with bottled water and laundry detergent. Everyone was covered with concentric layers of filth. Heat rashes, fungus, and other skin problems started to appear on the men. Brian Ward suffered particularly hard from one rash that confounded the medics. They gave him different creams and took bets on which would work. None of them did any good.

At least they had hot chow. After surviving on MREs for several days, Major Scott Jackson and Sergeant Major Tim Mace made sure the soldiers at the Apache Hilton received freshly cooked steaks. The men were extremely grateful for the good chow.

The killing continued. The Apache Hilton was prime real estate, and the American occupation of it denied the Mahdi the full use of their only advantage: their interior lines. Anything that moved got shot up by the M240s or got flattened by Eldred's fist of God.

On the night of the 23rd, Twaddell sent all of 2nd Platoon out to the schoolhouse whose gate Case had mangled with his grenade launcher earlier in the week. He wanted his Oregonians out there for the night, then they were supposed to return to the Hilton. Reinforced now by Staff Sergeant Dave Williams' men and the rest of Ashford's squad from the IP station, the platoon was again at full strength. The men left their personal gear behind, taking only their assault packs stuffed with ammo, MREs, and water.

They reached the school without incident and spent the night inside waiting for something to happen. The next morning, the rest of Apache attacked forward, and the momentum it created changed everything for 2nd Platoon. Instead of going back to the Hilton, Twaddell ordered the Oregonians into the attack. The men never returned to the Hilton and lost much of their personal gear to ransacking Joes.

Apache's Bradleys rumbled forward, supported by tanks from Commanche 2-7. They spread out on either side of the new objective, which was a hotel near the boneyard. From these new positions, they unleashed a storm of prep fire on the building and its environs, paving the way for the light infantry.

Meanwhile, 2nd Platoon waited for orders to advance. Inside the school, Pete and Doc Bagnall discovered some personal belongings left by a family who had been squatting in a room near the platoon CP. Pete rifled through and found a pair of bras, one red and one black.

Hoisting them up, he asked, "Hey, Doc? Which one do you think?"

"Oh, the black one for sure. It's your color."

Pete admired the bra, then peeled off his IBA and shirt and put it on as Bagnall belly-laughed. Salerno knew that the platoon was very tense about this new offensive. He figured the boys would need a good laugh at some point during the day.

The first lift of Bradleys arrived for them. Lieutenant Kent took the majority of the platoon and climbed into the tracks. Rather than wait for the second lift, which would be only one Bradley, Salerno wanted to hoof it over to the objective on foot. He told Ryan Howell his idea, then asked, "Sergeant Howell, are you afraid?"

"Sergeant Salerno, I am not afraid."

"Let's go."

They ran west along an open stretch of road, totally exposed should any Mahdi sniper linger in the area.

Fortunately, 2-7's armor had thoroughly suppressed the nearby buildings. A Bradley showed up as they reached the halfway point. The two NCOs climbed aboard.

They reached the objective, and the platoon cleared the hotel. It was a huge place with more than two hundred rooms. The Oregonians divided into two-man teams and spent hours in the stifling heat checking every nook and cranny. When they finished, they discovered the field of fire to the west was blocked by another one sitting directly across an alleyway.

They crossed into it and started the whole search-and-clear process anew. Another two hundred rooms later, the platoon was totally spent. So were the SEALs, who sent a few men up onto the roof while the rest of the team crashed on a set of stairs near the elevator.

Second Platoon set up the M240s and the gunners found they had an incredible view to the west. They'd soon find plenty of targets. Meanwhile, the bulk of the men congregated on the top floor with the SEALs to catch their breath. They sat around the elevator as Pete Salerno lounged on a couch. The moment had come.

"That's a goddamned smoker, man. I'll tell you, I am done." Pete said as he peeled off his IBA and shirt. Specialist Keith Dow noticed the bra first. His jaw hit the floor and he burst out, "Oh my God!" Heads turned.

Pete played dumb. "What? What?" he asked. Then he fingered the bra and said defensively, "I like nice things! It feels soft on my skin!"

The SEALs about split their sides. The platoon howled. Morale was restored. Their exhaustion forgotten, they went back to killing the enemy. They sure had the position for it. The M240s could range all the way to the Medina Complex surrounding the shrine. The JDAM-blasted, M240-raked, and AC-130-pummeled boneyard sat directly to their right.

Insurgents darted through the alleyways. The gunners opened up. Spike and Shad Thomas joined in with their M4s. The incoming fire surprised the militiamen. They fell like flies again. From the roof, the SEAL team later reported to

Lieutenant Kent that they killed eight insurgents in a matter of minutes. Second Platoon accounted for another twenty-two. Thomas scored the biggest moment of the day. He leveled his M4 and killed an insurgent five hundred meters away with a head shot. It was a remarkable feat of marksmanship, though Petey and the other Joes chalked it up to luck.

It did not take long for return fire to hit the hotel. Bullets smacked the outside of the building all day long. Some of it came from point-blank range from a junkyard across the street. The gunners tried to get eyes on the militiamen down there, but the angles were poor. The enemy was close: at one point Shad heard an insurgent working his AK's action.

Somebody suggested they use hand grenades to clear the junkyard. Brian Ward's eyes lit up. He'd loved grenade training back in Basic, and now his chance had arrived to actually do it in battle. He asked Lieutenant Kent for the job. He and Evan Johnson got it.

Together, they went up to the roof and took turns running from the stairwell to the edge of the roof and chucking the grenades across the street into the junkyard. One of Evan's didn't explode, but both of Ward's did. The blasts drove the enemy back.

As Brian returned, Spike and Hern were busy at work. They'd flipped a bed over, laid a pack of cigarettes on it, and were snapping out bursts whenever a militiaman appeared. After the initial carnage, the insurgents had grown cautious. They'd peer around a corner and dash through the shadows. It was a bit creepy, sort of like a bad drive-in vampire movie. Every time the men looked away it seemed another insurgent would zip across their peripheral vision.

"Come on, Brian. You need to shoot some rounds," said Spike.

"Hell yeah."

Brian got behind the M240 and thoroughly avenged his brother's wounds. He'd come to Najaf wearing the same IBA Shane had on when he got hit in June. As Brian sweated in the brutal heat, blood leached out of the IBA and trickled down his legs. The first time he saw it, he thought he'd been hit. After realizing what it was, he found no greater motivation than the sight of his brother's blood.

Shtatatatatatatatatat. "Shit. Missed." Brian corrected. The M240 bucked. Target down.

The fighting continued. Once again, the high ground gave the platoon an excellent overwatch position. They could rain down long-range fire on the Mahdi with impunity. Their weapons were better, their optics superb, and their marksmanship light years ahead of Al Sadr's fanatics. Like the Apache Hilton, it became a shooting gallery again.

Eldred got into the act. With the SEAL JTAC, he called down his fist of God again, blowing things up with alacrity. Any building the Mahdi chose to fire from felt Eldred's wrath. At one point, he approached Pete Salerno, "Hey, Sergeant?"

"Yeah, Pat? What's going on?"

"We, uh, got some CAS [close air support] coming in. You might want to have the men put their stuff on."

"Okay, lay it on me. What are you doing?"

Eldred sheepishly explained, "Well, this might, uh, be a little close. Yeah."

"*How* close, Pat?"

"Five hundred meters. We need to get everyone away from the windows."

Around them, the eavesdropping Joes scrambled to get their cameras. Soon, most were glued to the windows. Salerno rolled his eyes.

Brian Ward asked, "What's going on here, Eldred?"

Pointing to a structure they'd been taking fire from, he said, "See that building over there? I'm going to drop a JDAM on it."

"We're going to be okay, right?"

"We'll be fine."

Danger close for a five-hundred-pound JDAM is five hundred meters.

Spike overheard this and added, "You make sure they hit the right goddamned building!"

Moments later, an F-16 pickled off the bomb. As it flew to its target, somebody over the radio announced the drop had not been cleared. Too late now.

The JDAM hit its target dead center. The blast was so close it knocked bricks out of the wall in 2nd Platoon's hotel. Debris rained down on them. The men loved it and cheered as if they were at the Super Bowl.

Of the fifty-three air strikes he called in during the battle, this was the ballsiest thing Eldred did in Najaf.

The following night, the platoon advanced northwest to a market and office complex on Route New York only a short jump away from the shrine. The endgame had arrived.

The building was a horror to clear. Broken glass, debris, and dozens of rooms, nooks, and crannies made searching it an ordeal in the heat. Already exhausted, the work made them bone weary. Nevertheless, they still found time for moments of humor.

It took an hour to clear the building. When that was done, the platoon set up an overwatch on the top floor in what had been an insurance office. Some of the men covered the north side across Route New York with Staff Sergeant Dave Williams, while the rest covered down on the final approaches to the Medina Complex.

Ryan Tuttle encountered a wedding gown as he cleared the market. Now, he put it on and modeled it for his fellow Joes, who snapped photos and belly-laughed at the sight. He looked like a blonde bridezilla gone postal. When Salerno saw him, he blurted out, "Woah, simmer down there, Commando!" The wedding dress came off. Pete later noted that the gown actually fit Tuttle quite well.

Meanwhile, John Willingham found a mannequin. He picked it up and started carrying it upstairs when Salerno caught him. Shaking his head, Pete shouted up, "I don't know what you're doing, but the answer is *no*." Reluctantly, Willingham replaced the mannequin.

The platoon spent the next day in the mall, but daylight revealed its field of fire was restricted by taller buildings to the north and west. The SEALs moved across the street and got into another building to the northwest that afforded them a better sniper hide.

Second Platoon settled in, taking occasional small-arms fire and mortars. Further explorations of the mall revealed unexploded mortar rounds. It made the place a real hazard.

About 0100 on the second night in the building, an RPG ripped through the north wall and exploded near Staff Sergeant Dave Williams and Keith Dow. Williams, a taciturn, soft-spoken rock of an NCO suffered shrapnel wounds from the blast. Fortunately, it was not serious and he stayed with the platoon. Doc Bagnall fixed him up.

On the 26th, the time had come to establish a foothold in the Medina Complex. Apache's 1st Platoon leapfrogged past the Oregonians and assaulted the southeastern tip. Unfortunately, that platoon had lost a key leader earlier in the fight. They assaulted the wrong building. Once they moved in, their breaking point had been reached. Exhausted, worn down by the fighting, they needed a break.

Kent suggested to Captain Twaddell and Colonel Rainey that 2nd Platoon execute a relief in place. Rainey liked the idea and ordered him to do it. On the 26th, 2nd Platoon bounded forward right into the hornet's nest. They would have a ringside seat to Moqtada Al Sadr's Gotterdammerung.

FIFTY-EIGHT

THE PIRANHA KITTENS

The day after their epic drive through the city, Sergeant Compton and his three Humvees rejoined the rest of 1st Platoon, Alpha, back at the original foothold in the southwestern section of Najaf. Captain Glass had pulled them back from Christies to reconsolidate before they leapfrogged north and east. They'd been fighting for more than a week through the southern heart of the 2-7 AO. Now, the platoon was to be pushed up to support the westward drive into the Medina Complex.

In the meantime, the platoon patrolled back up toward Christies to keep the pressure on the enemy. This irritated Phil Disney, who thought giving up so much ground, then fighting for it all over again, was a foolish move.

The patrol was almost Disney's last. Jones arrayed the Humvees on a broad east-west front, each advancing on its own northern axis. It spread the platoon out, and when they paused just south of Christies, Jones stationed a Humvee at each intersection for several blocks. There, they waited to draw fire.

This made Disney very unhappy. His crew echoed his sentiments. As they dismounted, Sergeant Matt Roberts grumbled in anger and Art Duryea spat, "This is bullshit! Why are we doing this?"

He'd barely got his gripe out when a bullet hit the road only a few feet from them. Duryea dove behind a wall for cover. Disney and Roberts ducked behind the Humvee. In the turret, Specialist Aaron Links cursed and fired a long burst up the street.

All the noise attracted Lieutenant Jones' attention. He was on the next intersection over to the east, well within shouting range. He yelled over to Disney, "Whaddya got?"

"Sniper fire down the street."

Jones yelled back, "Get on the radio and tell me."

"Jesus Christ."

Dis went around to the driver's side, flung open the door, and grabbed the mic. By now, he was so disgruntled with the situation all pretenses of civility vanished.

"We're taking sniper fire, asshole!"

Links was equally pissed off. He took it out on the Mahdi sharpshooter.

"You want some more of that, asshole? Come on you motherfucker!"

The Mahdi gunman let fly another round. It whizzed past. Enraged, Links tore up the neighborhood again. "How's that now, fucker!"

A single bullet cracked overhead. Links and this militiaman played this game until a Charlie 3-8 tank thundered into the intersection. The militiaman stopped shooting at that point.

The tank commander appeared in his hatch. "What do you have?"

Disney filled him in. The tanker dropped back down into his track. The turret scanned left and right. Using their thermal sight, the crew locked onto the militiaman. The coax ripped off a long burst. A moment later, the tank commander reappeared, grabbed the .50-cal atop the turret, and hosed down the target.

The turret scanned one more time. The tanker turned to Disney and shouted, "One guy with an AK. He's done."

While at the schoolhouse, one of the 2-7 NCOs came face-to-face with an insurgent in a basement. The militiaman threw a grenade, which bounced off the American and exploded just as both men fled from it. Though bleeding from shrapnel wounds to the head, legs, arms, and stomach, the American chased the militiaman down, beat him into submission, and dragged him back to the school. First Platoon babysat the prisoner for several hours until some IPs showed up and took custody of him. They were not disposed to be merciful; the next day Compton saw the prisoner lying dead in the street.

The southern Oregon boys joined the last push to the Medina Complex on the night of August 25. They moved up to the IP station, then bounded toward the shrine complex with a Polish SF team and the SOCOM marines. They moved through a section of the city that had not been cleared, and heavy gunfire forced them to stay off the streets and advance from building to building, Stalingrad-style.

They reached their objective, but discovered they could not get into it without maneuvering onto the street. Jones led the platoon around back, and as the incoming buzzed around them, they hunkered down against a wall. They couldn't find a way inside from the back, so Lieutenant Jones ordered Disney to check the front. He sent Cunningham's team to reconnoiter. They took fire again, but found a way into the building's bottom floor.

The rest of the platoon found an entrance from the third floor and joined them. Once inside, they could see the building was a multi-story apartment complex that had street-level shops and an open courtyard in the middle. In one barred office, they found a sizable missile, still in its loader all primed and ready to be launched. It looked big enough to take out a tank.

The men stongpointed the upper floor and settled down into a new firefight. Dawn on the 26th found them taking plenty of small-arms fire. The windows became kill zones, and the men could not risk more than fleeting looks out to search for the source of the bullets.

The platoon lacked armor support. In fact, at the time they were told they were the forwardmost position for the 2-7 in Najaf. The insurgents wanted it back and spent the morning trying to drive them out. At one point, they cooked off an RPG, which sailed right through a window and exploded against an interior wall. It was a remarkable shot.

The SOCOM marines called in a Cobra gunship, whose crew misunderstood where the target was and ended up strafing 1st Platoon's building instead. Bullets ricocheted around the rooms, sending the Oregonians diving for cover. That didn't work, but at least they got the friendly fire to cease with a few choice words over the radio.

Later, a Bradley moved up in support. The bulk of the incoming fire originated from a building across the street that had a big Samsung billboard on it. The Oregonians directed the Bradley onto it. The track commander told them to stand by while he fired a few shots to make sure he was on the right target.

His 25 mike-mike belted out a couple of rounds. On the building next to the one the platoon wanted suppressed, a generator exploded in a ball of flames. Wrong building. First platoon told the track commander to hit the one next to it. An instant later, several 25mm shells tore up their own building. In a room overlooking the street, Roberts came staggering out with a wounded 2-7 Cav sniper. The sniper waddled along, his buttocks torn by shrapnel.

"Goddamnit, I'm hit," he barked.

Sergeant Robert Dalke, the platoon's medic, went to work on the 2-7 trooper, who had a chunk of flesh from his hindquarters hanging over his belt. He had also suffered shrapnel wounds to his legs and arms. As Dalke patched him up, the wounded trunk monkey shouted, "Hey, guys," he asked, "Get a camera! Take a picture of this shit!"

Fortunately, none of his wounds were serious, and he returned to duty.

After the second friendly fire incident of the day, the Bradley finally got on the right target and tore it up. The incoming ceased, and things quieted down. The Bradley lumbered away.

The men kept watch through the rest of the morning. A lull had developed around them. Suddenly, an M4 banged out, shattering the silence and sending the men for their weapons. Robert Dalke, the medic, had fired the shots.

"Whaddya got, Doc?" asked Disney.

"I got two down. There's a third one. He ran off."

From a position overlooking the interior courtyard, Dalke had seen the three militiamen creep into the building. He waited until they got close and opened up on them.

Disney looked into the courtyard. One militiaman lay dead, an RPG launcher close at hand. Dalke had shot the other once in the head and twice in the neck. Covered in blood, the insurgent had slumped onto his haunches. At first, they thought he was dead as well. Then he moved. Disney wanted to kill him, but Lieutenant Jones told him to hold fire.

"Lieutenant, he has a weapon," Disney reported. He still had a hand on his AK.

"Don't shoot!" Jones reiterated.

The insurgent's head jerked. Disney watched in horrified fascination as the blood-soaked man turned his head upward to stare at the Americans with flat, hollow eyes. The dying insurgent gazed at Dalke and Disney. Before either could react, one of the attached snipers shot the man in the head. He fell over backward and bled out into the courtyard.

The third militiaman was still in the building. Disney ordered Sergeant Cunningham to take his team and go find him. Cunningham descended the spiral staircase to the courtyard with Private Second Class Jesse Parks and Mike Blanchard in tow.

They reached the base of the stairs. Cunningham passed a door. Parks did as well. As Blanchard reached it, an AK-47 barked. Three rounds exploded through the door. One hit Blanchard's weapon. Another nearly tore his index finger off. All those Ft. Hood ready-up drills kicked in, and Blanchard swung his M4 up and pulled the trigger. It jammed.

"I'm hit!" Blanchard called out as he pointed at the door, "He's right in there!"

Parks grabbed a grenade and said, "I'm fragging the fucker." Blanchard headed upstairs to have Dalke treat his hand.

Parks edged along the wall to the door, Cunningham covering him. He tried to ease the door open, but the insurgent saw the movement and unloaded a few rounds. Parks tossed the grenade in reply. It bounced off the door and rolled into the courtyard.

"Oh shit! Grenade. Run!" Parks shouted. The team dove for cover. An instant later, a deafening boom echoed through the building. The door had been blasted away.

Cunningham tossed another grenade to Parks, who pulled the pin and popped the spoon as he ran. He threw it straight through the doorway. The grenade exploded and wounded the militiaman. Parks stepped into the doorway and finished him off with his M4.

A cry resounded through the courtyard. The Joes turned and listened. It was another insurgent.

"Akmed?" the voice asked.

"Akmed?"

An Oregonian answered, "Your buddies are dead. If you don't want the same, come out!"

Silence. Disney sent a few more men downstairs to help out while he and Dalke took care of Blanchard. Sergeant Neilson crept up to a barred office door. It was the same place that they had found the missile. He prepared to throw a grenade.

Somebody asked, "Should we be throwing a grenade in there with the missile?"

"Dude, that missile's long gone," replied Neilson.

He pulled the pin, flipped the spoon off, and lobbed the grenade through the bars. Another defeaning explosion shook the building. The Oregonians charged into the room. The insurgent was nowhere to be seen. He'd escaped out a nearby exit. The missile sat somehow unscathed in the middle of the room.

Corporal Baldwin, who'd been in Luke Wilson's Humvee during the Serial Five ambush, remarked, "Dude, you just threw a grenade into a room with a missile!"

Upstairs, Blanchard's index finger dangled against his palm, held to the rest of his hand by a single strand of skin. As Dalke clipped the finger off with a pair of scissors, Blanchard shook his head and said, "Sonofabitch shot my frickin' clutch finger off." Mike loved motorcycles. He'd have to figure out a new way to change gears now.

Dalke finished bandaging him up and Mike Blanchard was medevaced out of Najaf and sent back to Oregon to recover. As of 2006, he remained in the Guard, serving with 1-186 Infantry in southern Oregon.

The Mahdi seemed anxious to get their missile back. The platoon also noticed that the militiamen would risk their own lives to recover their dead so that they might keep with Muslim tradition and be buried within twenty-four hours. The Oregonians had three corpses and a missile to use as bait. They brought the corpses together in the courtyard, along with the missile. Then they settled down to wait.

Hardly had the last man returned upstairs when movement stirred in the courtyard. A black-and-white kitten emerged from its nest. Somehow, it had survived all the fighting, but it looked malnourished. Another kitten appeared. It was orange and white. Together, the two felines crept over to the insurgent bodies.

Disney heard one of his men exclaim, "Hey, check this out! There are cats down here eating the bodies!"

He ran to the railing, along with just about everyone else in the platoon. Sure enough, the black-and-white kitten had straddled one corpse's face. With its milk teeth, it tugged furiously at a loose strip of scalp. The orange one was feasting on an eyeball.

When something as innocuous as a fluffy little kitten turned into a man-eater, the men could either ride the wave or vomit and come apart at the seams. Psychologically, there was no middle ground.

They rode this wave and egged the kitties on. Black humor ruled the day. When trapped in the bacchanal of the bizarre, laughter was the only defense against the macabre and the insanity it offered.

FIFTY-NINE

THE DEAL

All through Najaf, the Americans prepared for the endgame against Al Sadr. After poking his fingers in the coalition's eyes for more than a year, Moqtada was toast. By the end of the 27th, he'd either be dead or captured. This last fight would see the end of the Mahdi militia, who had vowed to fight to the last man around the shrine. Finally, the Americans would win a decisive, strategic victory in Iraq.

It didn't happen.

Even as tanks and Bradleys moved into their final jump-off positions, even as the marines to the north checked their gear and sweated out the order to go, Al Sadr's own sworn enemy saved him. Al Sistani, the revered Shia leader whom Al Sadr had tried to assassinate twice, brokered a deal with Allawi's provisional government.

If Al Sadr and his militia gave up their weapons and left the shrine, their lives would be spared. Once again, Moqtada took the Americans to the brink, only to slip away at the final moment.

A cease-fire went into effect at 0600 that morning. From their toehold in the Medina Complex, 2nd Platoon soon saw the militia stacking their weapons at a nearby storefront. They held their fire and watched. The numbers grew. More militia appeared in the street.

Sistani and his supporters drove into town, passed through American lines, and reached the shrine. Lieutenant Jones' men peered out of their apartment building to see more than fifty men carrying RPGs, milling around in a traffic circle only a stone's throw from the shrine. They were mixed in with men carrying AK-47s. The shrine had been saved from a final assault, and a precious holy relic was spared for future generations. But the cost was high. Al Sadr and his brownshirts escaped final justice.

With Sistani's supporters that day was the Associated Press stringer present at the June 4 ambush. Karim Kadim snapped pictures of cheering Iraqis as Sistani's caravan linked up with the Mahdi militia.

The Battle of Najaf in August 2004 killed at least 1,600 Mahdi militiamen. The 2-7 Cav accounted for more than 350 of those in its AO alone. The exact numbers will never be known to the Americans, as the Mahdi fighters evacuated and buried their dead, as was Muslim custom.

Colonel Rainey's battalion did not lose a single man, and of the thirty or so wounded, more than half returned to duty. The 2-7 had shined in Najaf. Far from the 70 percent losses the training manuals taught the soldiers to expect in city-fighting, 2-7 emerged without a single man killed in action. Najaf represented perhaps the most one-sided tactical victory in 1st Cav history.

Najaf and the fighting in Sadr City broke the back of the second Shia uprising. Though heavy resistance continued through September in Sadr City, by early October Moqtada's brownshirts had taken so many losses that he was forced to throw in the towel. Overnight, on Al Sadr's orders, the Mahdi militia ceased resistance against the coalition. They became model citizens, assisting the police in northeast Baghdad and supporting the 1st Cav's reconstruction efforts in their neighborhoods.

Al Sadr himself took another path. Fighting the Americans twice and surviving earned him a broader base of support. He used that base as his entrance into mainstream Iraqi politics. At the same time, he rebuilt his Mahdi militia, recruiting again among the poorest Shiites.

In short, Al Sadr went legit, at least on the surface. He proclaimed his support for the upcoming January elections. And as he wormed his way into the heart of the forming Shia power structure, he would ultimately become the unseen presence that guided it from behind the throne.

Defeated in Najaf? Yes. Crushed in Sadr City? Yes. In neither case were those defeats decisive. Instead, they granted Al Sadr a reprieve, and he used it to wage his fight on another front. For him, politics became warfare by other means.

At midmorning on August 27, the day the cease-fire took effect, Salerno and the rest of 2nd Platoon watched as an IP patrol moved into the area. The insurgents who had been stacking their weapons moment before, suddenly turned and opened fire on the IPs. The police shot back into the crowd. From the ruined hotel they'd strongpointed, Lieutenant Kent ordered his men to only engage the insurgents actively shooting. The men killed two that way before the IPs pulled back and the fighting ceased.

When the firefight erupted, Ryan Howell had been catnapping on the floor. The gunfire woke him up, and he poked his head up into a window to see what was happening. He had not put on his helmet, a decision that almost killed him. An AK round struck him in the head and snapped him back onto the floor.

At first, the platoon thought he'd been killed. He stirred, sat up, and looked around. His head felt like it had been split. The wound bled copiously, as all head injuries do. Fortunately, as Doc Bagnall squared him away, they found that the bullet had only grazed him. A half-inch lower it would have embedded in his brain.

Not long after, the platoon was pulled out of the area and Ryan got a chance to call home. After talking with Julie for several minutes, he ended the conversation with, "Oh, and if you hear anything about me, don't worry. I'm fine."

After everything the family had been through—his first wound, Vinni, and now this—Ryan was not about to tell them just how close he'd come to death *after* the battle had ended.

Part VI

THE LAST HEROES

SIXTY

WHERE DO THE WOUNDED GO?

August. Vinni Jacques lay in a bed at Fort Lewis' Madigan Hospital. He'd lost a lot of weight. His burned back ached. His head still rang from the effects of the severe concussion. His knee was so jacked up, he couldn't stand. His shoulder and knee were so swollen the doctors would not be able to do an MRI on him for another month. Yet, he was alive, and for that he resolved never to complain about his own life again. God had given him a second chance; he would not squander it.

Vinni waited nervously for Gabe and Rhonda. After the flight to the Baghdad CSH, Vinni had been flown to Germany in a huge air force transport full of desperately wounded men. At Landstuhl, he received further treatment. But anyone who could not return to action in two weeks was automatically sent home. Vinni reached Fort Lewis the previous night.

From down the hallway, he heard his little boy coming. He soldiered up and waited to see if his son would recognize him.

"Are you ready to see Daddy?" Rhonda prompted Gabe as they headed for Vinni's room at Madigan. Gabe shouted an enthusiastic "Yeah!" and tore down the corridor. Rhonda trailed behind. The past two weeks had taken a huge toll on her, but she knew the hard part was just starting.

She had learned of the July 28 attack early the next morning. Rhonda was in her pajamas, and Vinni's stepmom and brother were visiting. The phone rang. Rhonda could tell from the caller ID that it was a call from Iraq. Something twisted in the pit of her stomach.

This is not good news.

"Hello?"

Silence.

"Vince?"

"I'm just gonna shoot it to you straight, Rhonda. I got blown up. I'm in the hospital."

"Okay," Rhonda said, her voice shaky. "I'm going to go sit down."

She found a seat. "Tell me what happened."

"Leisten's dead."

Silence. Vinni continued but he was so emotional and so pumped with painkillers it was hard for Rhonda to make heads or tails of what he said. She got that Ben Ring and Doc Rhodes had been wounded, but nothing about his own injuries. He rambled, talking about his men. The pain in his voice was palpable. It wasn't from his own wounds.

Rhonda cut in, "Vinni, what about your own injuries?"

"I can't move my left side."

"Why?"

"I don't know."

An officer with a thick accent took the phone. He told Rhonda not to release any information. The call ended, and the ordeal began. She spent most of the day on the telephone with the rest of her family as she waited for the contact team to arrive on her doorstep.

Vinni called back twice, but he made less and less sense. The morphine and his concussion made sure of that. Finally, an American doctor spoke to Rhonda and explained Vinni's injuries. The most serious were the third-degree burns on his back. He would have to undergo skin grafts for those, so he would be sent home.

A day or so later, the Oregon Guard released the news to the press. Within forty-five minutes, Rhonda had reporters and cameramen at her door. At first, she wouldn't talk to the media. Then she changed her mind. She gave two interviews to the local TV news stations. In both, she controlled the flow of the interview and focused on the soldiers. She told the media that Oregonians should be proud of their warriors. They were doing amazing things in Iraq, despite the hardships on themselves and their families. The press was looking for another "poor me" interview, but Rhonda didn't give it to them. She made it all about the Joes and never broke down.

In fact, for two days her family waited for her to crack. She didn't. She refused to give in to the tsunami raging inside her. She had Gabe, and she would not break down in front of him.

On the second day, Ryan called. As soon as she heard the pain in his voice, all her resistance crumbled. Tears streaked her cheeks as Ryan told her about the attack. "I saw the Humvee, Rhonda," his voice choked up. "I don't know how anyone lived."

The two weeks following that conversation left Rhonda in limbo. Vinni was moved from hospital to hospital, and it was tough trying to keep track of where he was. Finally, he reached Madigan, and the day arrived for their reunion.

Gabe scooted into the hospital room at a full two-year-old sprint. From the bed, Vinni laid eyes on his little boy and felt a surge of emotion. Gabe looked up and screeched to a halt. Father and son stared at each other. Not a word was spoken. Fear swelled in Vinni. Did he not remember him?

He broke the silence, "How ya doin', big boy?"

"Dada! Dada!" Gabe launched himself into Vinni's arms, and the big knuckledragger hung on to his son, suffused with love. He never thought he'd hold his boy again. But even before this first embrace ended, a finger of guilt stabbed Vinni dead center in the heart.

Why am I getting this moment when my Joes can't have it? I should be the last one to hold his family, not the first.

That finger of guilt was just the beginning. It would almost overcome Vinni in the months ahead.

Shane Ward understood the guilt all too well. He'd returned home in June, the wound on his back still raw and painful. He'd attended McKinley's funeral, then returned home to Alsea, where the entire town turned out to welcome him.

The luster of the homecoming faded. In its place, the wounds dominated Shane's life. The physical pain was bearable. The hole McKinley's death left in him was not. Neither was the overwhelming sense of guilt at being home. He felt helpless and raged at it. The guilt would not abate. He drowned it in alcohol and false cheeriness. To the world, Shane was his laughing, easy-going normal self. At night, alone, he was plagued by his innate sense of duty. All he wanted to do was get back to Spike and Pete Salerno and all his other brothers.

It would not happen. His wounds were too severe, and to a young man who prided himself on getting things done and controlling his own destiny, his own body's healing process became a trap from which there was no escape.

Guilt and Andy Hellman got acquainted at the Baghdad CSH. After his short helicopter trip from FOB Volunteer, the hospital staff wheeled the wounded scout off to get an MRI. Andy tried to be the model patient and did his best to joke and laugh with the nurses. He'd seen other guys yelling at the staff and did-n't want to do that. He was polite and friendly even as they wheeled him into surgery.

He woke up with a nurse yelling at him. She yelled again. Andy struggled to regain his faculties and understand what she was saying.

"Breathe!" she shouted. Andy breathed, and that appeased her. After the surgery, Andy had stopped breathing twice. The doctors had almost lost him.

They pushed him into a room with three other severely wounded soldiers. He tried to find the humor in the moment again, but the sight of his new room-mates silenced him. One, a large African-American sergeant named Applewhite, had been IED'd. His left side was paralyzed. Another young soldier had been hit in the genitals and leg. One kid had part of his face and arm blown off by an RPG. Andy looked around the room at these pain-wracked men and his mood inverted.

I have no right to be here. None.

The nurses got him to his bed. His knee started to ache. During the surgery, the doctors found that the bullet had fractured all three of Andy's legbones. The next morning, he was so stiff and sore he could not walk unassisted. He needed to urinate. He called a nurse. No one showed up for a half hour. When one did, he asked for crutches so he could go use the bathroom. A half hour passed. No crutches. Another nurse came by and Andy told him he *really* had to urinate, and would go on the floor if he had to. The nurse hustled off to get him crutches. An hour later, he hadn't returned. Bladder ready to burst, Andy started to get irritated. His irritation grew into anger. He had to pee.

Through his doorway, he saw several new casualties arrive on the floor. The sight of these men, some unconscious, some missing limbs, melted his anger. Guilt and self-loathing replaced it.

These people are trying to save lives. How selfish am I to ask for crutches?

Two hours later, the crutches arrived and Andy relieved himself. He didn't complain again.

That night, a nurse brought Sergeant Applewhite his dinner. He propped the sergeant's bed up, then put the food on his left side. Without a word, the nurse walked out of the room.

Applewhite studied his dinner. With his left side paralyzed, he couldn't reach it. He didn't complain. The sight stabbed Andy right in the gut, and it was made worse when the prop holding Applewhite's bed broke loose. The bed flopped back flat. The sudden collapse caused Applewhite tremendous pain. His face went ashen; his eyes rolled into their sockets. He never so much as moaned.

Andy found the strength to help him. The Oregonian propped his bed back up and moved his food tray to his right side so he could eat.

The next day, the 39th Brigade's commander, General Chastain, entered the ward with a pack of politicians in tow. He went from bed to bed handing out Purple Hearts.

He reached the soldier who had been hit in the crotch. As he pinned the award to his pillow, the kid's expression went absolutely blank.

The general turned to Andy. "Where would you like it, son? Should I pin it on your chest or your pillow?"

"I don't want the damn thing. Just keep it."

Andy looked away.

General Chastain persisted, "I've got to give this to you."

Andy looked at the open box in Chastain's hand. The Purple Heart, the award nobody ever wants. How could he take it? Andy considered his injury little more than a flesh wound. He didn't deserve it, not compared to the other men in the ward. Besides, accepting it would be an admission that he was going home. That was the absolute last thing he wanted. He had conned himself into believing he could return to Volunteer. Maybe he wouldn't be able to patrol, but he could work in the TOC or in Maintenance. Having that medal pinned on him would mean he would not return to his brothers. He couldn't face that, not now.

"I don't want it," Andy said again. "You can do whatever you want with it, just don't put it on me."

Chastain bent down and left the Purple Heart on his pillow. When the general left, the politicians tailing behind him, Andy plucked the medal up and tossed it on his nightstand.

He never wore it.

Once back stateside, the wounded Volunteers found their battles just beginning. Some, such as Sean Davis, got stuck in the nightmare of Fort Hood. Davis was billeted next to the mortar range, where day and night the explosions would startle him, inflicting bolts of pain on him every time. Others spent their purgatory at Hood dealing with REMFs and 39th Brigade malingerers who nursed phantom injuries that kept them out of the deployment. The chickenshit and sharpshooting drove them to distraction. They just wanted to get home.

When they finally did get home, the Oregon Military Department largely ignored them. To a man, they felt abandoned.

Luke Wilson, the hard-charging NCO who had lost his leg during the Serial Five ambush, probably had the worst time. The army sent him to Walter Reed Hospital in Washington, D.C., to recover from his amputation and learn to use his new prosthetic limb. His family and fiancée stayed with him until the fall of 2004. After that, he was on his own, living in an on-base hotel room. The physical therapy was exhausting and demanded a high pain threshold. If he didn't show up for it, though, the therapists hunted him down and made him work.

As his time at Walter Reed wore on, he sank into depression. Homesick, he missed his family. Each day became harder to get out of bed. Two emotional blows nearly sent him into a fatal tailspin.

During physical therapy, Luke had met another wounded soldier whose attitude had inspired him. They became friends, and their relationship was one of the bright spots at Walter Reed. In early '05, the soldier committed suicide. His death came as a terrible shock to Luke.

Close on the heels of that blow came another one. After the Serial Five ambush in April '04, Luke's chain of command recommended him for a Silver Star. Everyone thought it was a slam-dunk. He'd been selflessly aggressive that night, and had very nearly died from blood loss because he wanted his men fighting, not bandaging him. At Reed the following year, he learned that his Silver Star had been downgraded to an Army Commendation Medal with a V device for valor, the lowest award for bravery a soldier can receive.

After everything he'd gone through, to have the 39th Brigade tell him his life and his moment in combat were worth little more than an "atta boy" was too much. The award did not match his sacrifice. It belittled it.

He spent days in bed, searching for a reason to get up. He didn't shower. He didn't talk to anyone. Finally, one morning he realized he either had to get up or die. He got up, put on his prosthetic leg, and went down to Virginia and bought a dog.

Dogs were not allowed in this on-base hotel. Luke didn't care. He smuggled his pup into the hotel in a backpack. The animal became his lifeline. He named him Buddy, and the miniature dachshund became his reason for being while he searched for the will to live again.

After a year at Walter Reed, Luke Wilson was ready to go home to Oregon. Four days before he was discharged, a maid discovered his pup while he was taking a shower. She raced out of the room and told the staff what she'd found.

A few minutes later, somebody pounded on his door. Still in the shower, he told them to wait. The pounding continued. "Open up, *now!*" said a voice.

Fuck it. Luke hopped out of the shower and threw the door open. He stood on one leg, soaking wet and naked before two cleaning women. They fled down the hallway, any thought of removing Luke's pup forgotten.

Every wounded Joe hit rock bottom at some point. Some never pulled out. That fall, Vinni hovered on the brink. It started with Kenny's funeral. Vinni insisted on attending. The car ride there took a physical toll on him. As he arrived, he was offered a wheelchair. There was no way he would say good-bye to Kenny from one of those. He pulled himself from the car and hobbled into the service. On raw guts alone, he made it to a seat, only to suffer the far worse pain of loss. He sat, lost in it, as Leisten's dad, Kenny Sr., said good-bye to his son.

The nights went by with interminable slowness after that. The buzzing in his head was so bad that he couldn't sleep. During the days, he couldn't help Rhonda with Gabe, his wounds were still too severe. He couldn't even put on his clothes without Rhonda's help.

Life had thrown them a curveball. When they had first met, it was Vinni who took care of Rhonda after her accident. Now, this proud man was forced to let her care for him. It left him angry and frustrated. Vinni took it out on his wife and son with outbursts totally unlike him.

He seethed with pain. Guilt assailed him. Being home was wonderful at first, but it felt like a stolen pleasure. It was a luxury his own soldiers were denied. He didn't deserve to be home. They did. His wounds had inversed his world and left him at war with his sense of duty and values. His self-respect was on the line.

The nights were the worst. Rhonda would go to sleep. Vinni would stay in the living room, staring at the TV, his thoughts enveloping him. He replayed July 28 over in his mind so many times that it became a millstone. He second-guessed his every move. He blamed himself for everything.

Come dawn, Rhonda would find him sitting on the couch, the TV's glare lighting the room.

This went on for weeks. Even when he wanted to, he couldn't sleep. The buzzing in his ears was as loud as a fire alarm, which got worse if he drank.

He sweated out every day, worried sick about Ryan. His brother's second wound came as another severe blow to Vinni. He feared for his own platoon. Every dawn brought another waiting game: waiting to hear from his men, waiting for the dreaded word that his Joes had been in it again. Every evening brought a sleepless night of self-doubt and tormented thoughts of July 28. A month home, and Vinni continued to slide deeper and deeper into the prison of his own mind.

One Bravo Joe on leave came to see Vinni. Although he put up a good face, the Joe came away fearing Sergeant Jacques was heading for a full crash.

Three things saved him. The first was his refusal to use the pain meds the VA had given him. At first, he had taken a few, but they had made him feel too good. The pain pills scrubbed all the humanity out of him. He stopped feeling, stopped caring. It scared him, and he sensed that if he kept taking them, it would destroy his life. Instead, he lived in constant pain and never once complained. Vinni avoided a trap with that decision.

Unfortunately, some of the other wounded from 2-162 fell into it. For a time, Vicodin and OxyContin took over their lives, and getting clean after their recovery proved a brutal ordeal.

And then there was Rhonda. She endured his mood swings, his unfocused anger and sleepless nights. She offered nothing but support. She took care of him, helping him to dress, giving him encouragement. And when needed, she comforted him in the dead of night.

As Vinni slipped closer to the abyss, Rhonda stepped in with a good, swift kick in the butt. It was much needed, and she pulled no punches.

"We love you, Vinni. You don't need to be angry with us," she began.

Vinni blurted, "I love you, Rhonda. You're wonderful."

"Those are just words, Vince. If we mean so much to you, then get up and show it."

"How?"

"Have more patience with us. Get out there and do something. I need you to step up and help me."

Over the next few days, the talk sank in. One morning, about ninety days after he'd come home, Vinni lay in bed. His wounds had healed enough that he could move around now. He didn't need to keep his swollen knee elevated all the time. He could walk again, though any movement still caused him pain.

Under the covers, he stared at the ceiling. In his mind, he came to a cross-roads. Fight or give in. It would be so easy to give in and become another casualty of the war as sure as Kenny Leisten.

If I lie here any longer, I won't get up.

With stiff determination, Vinni climbed out of the bed. He put on his clothes and went to find Shane Ward and Andy Hellman. He wasn't done yet.

They were his third lifeline. The three wounded vets came together and discovered they all were experiencing the same pain. All three were tough as nails. They had no problem handling the physical pain. But all three ached inside. They began to meet regularly, turning within their small circle for comfort and understanding. They leaned on one another, inspired one another.

But it wasn't enough. The only way they were going to heal from this was to get back in the game. Returning to Iraq for the three of them was not an option; their wounds were still debilitating and would be for months to come. There was, however, another path. Shortly after Rhonda's talk, Vinni met with Shane and Andy.

"No matter how bad we're hurting," he told them. "We've got to get things ready for the guys when they come home. We need to be part of the team."

They formed the Blasted Bastards, three wounded vets who decided their salvation lay not from within but from without. They reached out to other wounded vets.

Bill Stout, his back so wrecked by July 28 that his career as a crew chief at the 1049th Medical was over, had the worst of it. He came home with vengeance for Kenny unrealized. In his mind, he owned Kenny's death. It was his fault because he'd let Kenny go to Vinni's rig to be his driver a month before the attack. He'd also made a promise to bring him home. Now that it was broken, he could hardly face himself.

Bill was a music lover, the harder metal the better. He took hundreds of CDs over to Iraq with him, and his favorite songs became the soundtrack to his experience in the Sandbox. Now home, those much-loved songs were nothing but torment. He'd hear one on the radio, and it would trigger a memory of Kenny or the Hell Hounds. The memories would lash his emotions, tearing apart his center, ripping at what kept him whole.

At times, he found himself in the bathroom, crying unashamed as the radio played in the background. He stopped listening to music. It was easier that way, but it came at a cost. He'd lost another thing he cherished about life.

Bill struggled every day. Vinni reached out to him, not as his platoon sergeant, but as his brother. In helping Bill, Vinni found his own way. He and Andy and Shane would not allow what happened to them to happen to anyone else. Not another man would come home from Iraq and be thrown to the wolves. They would have help. They would have support from Joes who had been there and understood what it took to return to the land of peace and freedom.

Unofficially, Vinni, Shane, and Andy formed what they called their "reintegration team." They helped out other wounded vets in the battalion by getting them counseling, or cutting through the massive red tape they faced with the VA and their health care provider. They also paved the way for the unit when it came home. They lined up job fairs, housing, and worked with Darcy Woodke and Laura Boggs to garner support around the state.

What they found was that the war did not end on the Kuwaiti border, it just changed form. The war at home was more insidious, more psychological, and in many ways more frustrating. But it was just as difficult, and could be equally deadly.

The Blasted Bastards waded in to that new fight, their passion unbridled and their will to succeed totally dominating. They got things done. They saved lives.

In the end, they saved themselves.

SIXTY-ONE

THROUGH HARDSHIPS –
TO THINGS OF HONOR

Mandy Ferguson sat in her little silver sedan on the side of the road and sobbed. She gasped with pain and struggled to breathe. She was caught in the agony of the unknown. Not knowing. That was the worst of everything related to this deployment. It left every family member in a state of perpetual anxiety. The unknown became the playground of the imagination, and left unchecked it could be a stiletto to self-control.

On this September morning, the local radio news had demolished her composure. She wondered how she'd survive the day. All across the Emerald Valley, Volunteer families felt the exact same anguish.

At the top of the hour, a Portland station had reported that two men from Bravo Company, 2-162 Infantry, had been killed in action. Their names had yet to be released pending notification of the families. Who were they? Was Spike among the dead? It was like a dreadful lottery, one in which she had a one in fifty chance of finding the contact team at her doorstep.

"Why do they do this? Don't these people know what they're inflicting on us?" she cried aloud to herself. If she hadn't already hated the media, she detested them now.

Mandy was no shrinking violet. She'd been tough all year, finding reservoirs of strength she never knew she possessed. Under her pretty face and engaging smile was a woman built of solid steel. Just to keep busy that summer, she had volunteered to be a juvenile rape counselor in Portland.

But even steel can be broken.

How long did she sit by the side of the road? Not long enough. She had just started a new job not a week before, working as a first grade teacher at Independence Elementary School. She had to get to work. She continued on her way to school. As the fresh face in the staff room, she had no shoulder for times like these. She was on her own. All day long, she fought the tears. She kept the kids on task, even though Spike's parents barraged her with phone calls asking if she'd heard anything.

Her kids saved her. One particular stinker picked that day to be extra naughty. He fell out of his seat. He chewed up a pen. He drooled and spit on his desk. He colored his hand black with a marker, and when Mandy told him to stop, he began spitting on it to wipe the ink away. At the end of the day, he balled up a worksheet and refused to give it to Mandy. She had to pry his fingers loose and take it from him. In the process, a corner tore off. Quick as a cat, he stuffed it in his mouth.

It was that kind of a day. Yet, it distracted her from the awful news. For that she was grateful.

As class ended, she learned who had been killed. First platoon had been hit. Spike was unhurt. A wave of pure relief flooded her. But guilt rode on the crest of that wave. Somebody else would see the contact team. She had no right to feel relieved.

At Camp Cooke a few days later, Bravo Company held its Memorial for Staff Sergeant David Weisenberg and Specialist Ben Isenberg. They had been killed as 2-7 returned from Najaf on September 13, 2004. Under command of the 206th Field Artillery Battalion, 39th Brigade, at the time, 1st Platoon, Bravo Company, was sent north of Camp Cooke to patrol a "red zone."

Earlier in the summer, the 2-7 intel staff officers had done their homework. They studyied the IED attacks in the area and found useful patterns. They were able to identify the roads most frequently targeted by the local insurgents. They discovered that the enemy most usually attacked during a two-hour period in the morning and a two-hour period in the late afternoon, the coolest points of the day. Based on this information, the 2-7 Cav structured its patrols to avoid those high-risk times. The various roads were also divided up between armor-only, mech-only (meaning Bradleys), and wheeled. By July, the battalion was finding more than 70 percent of the IEDs in its AO using these tactics.

The 206th did not function in the same way. In the absence of the 2-7 and the bulk of its armor, Bravo Company was forced to spend time on roads that were too dangerous for armored Humvees. When the attack came on September 13, Lieutenant Wood's 1st Platoon section was out in an area whose roads 2-7 had designated as mech-only.

Lieutenant Wood's rig was IED'd. Staff Sergeant David Weisenberg and Ben Isenberg died instantly in the blast. Wood's gunner, Private First Class Michael Johnson, was blown from the turret and fell into a canal. Wood, suffering a concussion and shrapnel wounds to his hand, continued to lead his platoon after crawling from the wreckage until Specialist Chad Erb sat him down and treated his wounds. Gabe Sapp took over at that point and called in the medevac.

Ron Clement saw Wood and noted his only concern was for his men. Though concussed and in intense pain, he tried to call in the nine-line himself until he was told Sapp had that covered. He also tried to help carry his wounded men. Pete Wood had his heart in the right place, and when the worst happened, he tried to do the right thing. Everyone had to respect that.

Wood also lost a friend in David Weisenberg, who had come to the platoon from the 218th Field Artillery as part of Major Warrington's fire support group. Wood and Weisenberg's sister had gone to high school together up in Portland back in the '90s.

After the attack, Ken Jackola took the rest of the platoon out of the wire to assist. Shortly after arriving, a second, cell phone–detonated IED went off. Ken and his men laid down suppressive fire, but the insurgents were long gone. Fortunately, the second IED caused no harm.

As the rest of the men went back to Taji, Ken shouldered one last and terrible job that day. He helped load the remains of Ben and David into a Bradley. He rode in back with them all the way to Taji, a solemn escort as the Bradley delivered them to the morgue. It was among the most difficult things Ken had ever done in his storied military career.

Major Warrington spoke first at the memorial service. Among his many assets, Mike possessed the rare ability to speak from the heart.

"I have feelings," he began, "but I don't have the words. The experiences we share with those we love are so unique and personal, that for me to convey my own to you would only do injustice to yours."

His head bent forward. He rocked behind the podium as he struggled with his emotions. "There were moments David Weisenberg inspired me, and I *miss* him." Mike's composure cracked. Unabashedly crying now, he pressed on. "Yet my grief pales in comparison to the pain a mother must feel for the irreplaceable loss of her child. I mourn for his family as well."

He searched for meaning in his soldier's death. "It is my observation that God takes the best first. I don't know why that is, unless it is to teach us something we don't want to learn."

Mike gathered himself and finished this touching and poignant eulogy.

"As fellow warriors, I am certain we will rise to the occasion with confidence and faith. Armed with the memories of our comrades-in-arms, we will not abandon the path we've chosen. Through hardship, to things of honor. Volunteers."

Moments later, Ben Isenberg's squad leader took the podium. In an emotionless voice, he praised David Weisenberg as one of the best NCOs he'd ever met.

He turned to Ben Isenberg. Reading his speech, he began, "One thing I've come to understand about the National Guard is that every company has at least a couple of soldiers who may not look like the personification of soldierly values, or be the most physically fit soldier in the world, but who have other traits just as important, if not more important to the unit. Traits such as commitment and a heart that doesn't know when to stop. Ben Isenberg was one of these soldiers."

The NCO's delivery was grating. The backhanded compliment about Ben enraged some of his friends.

"Over the years, I learned a couple of things about Ben Isenberg. One, no matter how many push-ups or hand claps I made him do, he was never, ever going to pass a PT test, or even do fifteen tolerable push-ups. Two, no matter how much crap we gave him, he was always there, maybe a little late, a little slow, but he'd be there, his annoying voice and whiney independent streak and all."

Jaws dropped. Even though the speech concluded with kind words about Ben, nobody heard them. To the Bulldogs, the NCO had crossed a line at a sacred moment. Already detested by much of the company, the antipathy his speech generated permanently destroyed the NCO's relationship with most of his peers and soldiers.

Unfortunately, a video of the speech reached Ben Isenberg's family and it inflicted utter anguish. It was traumatic enough to lose Ben. But to see him remembered this way was too much. The damage the NCO's words did will linger for years to come.

The Volunteers learned a huge lesson as a result of that speech. In such traumatic moments, when emotions are heated and grief wracks those at home as well as in the front lines, it is vital that words are chosen very carefully. It would not be an error that was repeated.

Was Ben Isenberg a bad soldier? No. He was a man of morals, devoted to his wife and two sons. He had spent six years as a specialist; he was overweight. That was the crux of the NCO's issue with him. He hung in there and did his job. He patrolled with courage. He was there for his fellow Joes.

A bad soldier? There were plenty of examples of that at Taji, where one 39th Brigade soldier died of an illegal drug overdose and the brigade's operation's officer was court-martialed for having multiple affairs with female NCOs while his wife was pregnant back in the States. Others stole equipment, including sensitive items. Some men found excuses to never leave the wire.

Ben Isenberg did none of those things. He stood fast, did his job, and he did it to the best of his ability. He died in battle, willingly sought. To paint him as anything other than an honorable soldier because he was not as physically fit as other Joes disgraced his memory.

On September 25, 2004, the Volunteers lost their cook, a man who had the heart of a warrior. Specialist David Johnson, who had volunteered for the deployment out of the 218th Field Artillery Battalion, was killed in a one-in-a-million IED incident. Johnson had been the thirtysomething cook whom Rebekah-mae Bruns had interviewed before the unit left Oregon. He'd been eager to support the men in any way he could. When he got to Baghdad, that chance came and he grabbed it. With KBR providing the food, the cooks were organized into another HHC maneuver platoon. Johnson volunteered to be a gunner. He knew how to handle an M240; he'd had 11 Bravo infantry training before leaving Oregon so he could deploy with 2-162.

During a supply run up Route Senators to Taji, a roadside IED exploded alongside his uparmored 1025 Humvee. The blast caused little damage beyond blowing out three tires. But a piece of shrapnel struck Johnson right under his helmet, killing him instantly. Had he been an inch lower in his turret, or had his head cocked another way, the shrapnel would have struck his Kevlar helmet and he would have survived.

Back home, Johnson's grieving mother joined the antiwar movement and later traveled to Crawford, Texas, in '05 to be with Cindy Sheehan during her vigil outside President Bush's ranch.

SIXTY-TWO

MUSHADA MARKET

The fall brought many changes to Lieutenant Colonel Hendrickson's companies. First, the COTTADs went home. Alpha and Charlie companies were hit the hardest by their departure. Captain Welch lost most of Sergeant First Class Terrel's 1-162 platoon. Alpha lost its company commander, Captain Granger, and about one-third of its total strength.

To fill these gaps, the Oregon Guard called for volunteers to serve as replacements. They arrived that fall to fill holes in every company.

The day the first replacements showed up at Taji, 3rd Platoon, Bravo Company, got IED'd twice. Tommy Houston was showing the replacements around FOB Volunteer when the platoon drove back in after the first IED. Sergeant Kevin Devlaeminck's rig had been hit. Skinny Joel Stinemann, the battalion's "token Jew," had been in the turret. As they gathered themselves inside the wire, Marty Theurer popped out of the turret of his Humvee and gave Stiney a huge hug. The IED had been detonated early, otherwise Stiney probably would have died.

An hour later, they went back out on patrol, this time heading north to the Mushada Market. Mushada had been a hot spot of insurgent activity. Earlier in the month, Captain San Miguel had been IED'd in that area. Using his law enforcement skills, he matched some of the metal in the IED to pieces found in a shop in Mushada Market. Thanks to the sleuthing, they had taken down one cell. Others remained in the area.

Third Platoon passed through the market and took another IED. This time, Marty Theurer's truck got hit. Marty had swapped out of the turret with Specialist John "Rosie" Rosander. The blast burst his eardrums and lacerated his face with shrapnel. They drove through the kill zone on four flat tires, only to take fire from a two-story house.

Despite his wounds, Rosie raked that house with his M240. He shouted out, "I'm hit!" and Marty looked over to see blood dripping out of the turret into the Humvee. Marty dismounted from the engaged side of the rig, climbed onto the hood, and jumped into the turret as Doc Smith rushed over to treat Rosander.

The platoon lit up the house until Staff Sergeant Chris Johnson, a wild, towheaded Ranger, ordered his men to stop shooting. A lull developed, and it looked like the insurgents had been driven off by the section's firepower. Then a shot rang out. A bullet skipped off the asphalt and struck Specialist Ivan Duble in the hand. Everyone ducked behind their Humvees and the fight was on again.

In the middle of this, Jeremy Turner noticed a soldier casually walk down the road from the north. He seemed oblivious to the gunfire. "Hey!" Turner shouted at him, "Get the fuck down! We're taking incoming!"

The soldier was Colonel Rainey. He had heard the firefight and had told his driver to move to the sounds of battle. When his own patrol arrived, he found 3rd Platoon pretty rattled and focused on CASEVAC. About a half dozen insurgents were shooting at them, so Rainey moved his four rigs into firing position and joined the skirmish. He dismounted and decided 3rd Platoon needed some bucking up.

He walked through the firefight and reached the Oregonians, eschewing cover the entire time. He didn't consider it reckless; he was setting an example.

His presence calmed the platoon. Soon the insurgents either died or ran away. Chris Johnson got his men down to FOB Animal, where the wounded returned to Cooke in field ambulances. Rosander had taken a chunk of shrapnel right between his eyebrows. Jeremy Turner fought through the entire engagement with a severe concussion. Marty Theurer had burns on his wrists from hot M240 casings. The IED also injured his right arm, and he couldn't bend it after the fight. Ken Kaiser had suffered burns on his back and buttocks.

Though everyone would return to duty, each man suffered. Turner spent several days in his hooch vomiting as a result of his concussion. Rosie was out of action for weeks with his ruptured eardrum. Marty took two days off to let the swelling go down in his elbow. Then he rolled outside the gate again.

When Johnson and the rest of the section returned to Cooke, Tommy Houston and the new replacements were there to greet them. It was Tommy's birthday, and it was his first day off in weeks. He was sorry he missed the fight, but the wide-eyed, *Oh my God what did I get myself into?* expressions on the new guys' faces almost made up for it.

A little more than a month later, on Veteran's Day 2004, 3rd Platoon fought the largest engagement around Taji during OIF II.

At 1800 hours that evening, Lieutenant Paul Metzdorff led four Humvees from 3rd Platoon north of Camp Cooke. In the rear of the column, Specialist Jason Becker, a medical supply clerk who had volunteered to come to Iraq as a replacement, served as the gunner for Staff Sergeant Bailey's Humvee. Bailey had shifted over to 3rd Platoon after Najaf. Marty Theurer drove Bailey's rig that night. Tommy Houston, the battalion's legendary scrounger, sat in back along with Sergeant James Mann.

The patrol moved through Mushada, which was nothing more than a scraggly collection of huts and rundown buildings with a mosque in the middle of town across from the marketplace. The place seemed quiet enough, though all the lights were out. The Oregonians figured there'd been another rolling blackout.

North of the market, the patrol spotted a joint ING-U.S. traffic control point (TCP) stretched across the southbound lanes of Route Senators. It looked like they had a handle on things, so the patrol continued north to a point about five kilometers north of Castle Gate.

Metzdorff turned around. By now it was dark, and the Humvees were driving in full blackout conditions. The drivers used their night vision goggles (NVGs) to find their way. As the four rigs came up to the TCP, Metzdorff decided to go around it. He crossed over to the northbound lanes with the other three vehicles in tow.

The INGs didn't like that. As the Oregonians went past, they unloaded a burst of automatic weapons fire past Metzdorff's Humvee, prompting one of the Bulldogs to scream, "Hey you motherfuckers! Can't you see we're a bunch of Humvees?"

Furious at the incident, the men swung back into the southbound lane and headed back toward Mushada. Inside the last Humvee, Chris Bailey yelled to his young replacement clerk now occupying the turret.

"Becker, when I tell you to, I want you to rotate right and fire a hundred rounds in ten-round bursts."

Marty looked out to the right just as they passed a gas station and could see nothing but reeds. If anyone was lying in wait for them, this would be a good spot. Becker charged his M240 Bravo and pulled the trigger. A single round fired, then the gun jammed. He charged the gun and fired again. Only one shot went downrange before the gun jammed with a stomach-churning *chunk*.

Becker's two single-shot bursts set off the mother of all sound and lights shows. Bailey had wanted Becker to recon the area by fire. It worked. The reeds came alive with muzzle flashes. Tracers zipped through the column. The American gunners engaged while Becker frantically tried to clear his weapon. He realized he'd loaded the ammunition in upside down. As the column blew through this prematurely executed ambush, Jason fumbled with the ammo and loaded it properly this time.

Metzdorff led them through Mushada. They sped through the market without taking any more fire. But as they passed outside of town, they drove straight into a second ambush. Tracers streaked over the Humvees from both sides of the road. An RPG speared the night and passed between the rigs before exploding to Marty's left.

The Americans raced through the second ambush, cleared it, and turned into another gas station. Bailey clambered onto his Humvee's hood and got right in Becker's face. When he found out why the gun had jammed, he gave Jason a hall-of-fame ass-chewing. When he finished, Bailey went off to find out from Metzdorff what they'd be doing next. His confidence blown, Becker slumped back in the turret.

Marty saw this and called Tommy over to him. Houston had a gift for gab so slick and reassuring that Pete Salerno once quipped, "Tommy could sell sand to Arabs."

"Hey, Tommy," Marty said, "You need to talk to Becker. He's fucking freaked."

Houston climbed up on the hood and used his golden tongue and friendly nature to buck the kid up. He checked the M240 and gave Jason some pointers. When he finished, Becker looked much better. Houston's veteran-to-replacement chat had done some good.

They were going to go back north. Lieutenant Perrin, the company's fire support officer, had called back to Camp Cooke and requested an illumination round be fired by the 206th Field Artillery right over Mushada. The timing was delicate, but the Oregonians wanted to have the round light the way just as they came into town again.

The men saddled up. Becker straightened in the turret. He'd come to Iraq in part to test himself. Tonight was the ultimate test.

They drove up to Mushada. No illum round burst over the town. They took fire again as they reached the southern tip of the town. The drivers stepped on the gas, and the rigs lurched up over 40 mph to get through the kill zone. Once clear on the north side, Metzdorff told the men they'd go back into the fight. Hopefully the illum round would be fired this time.

Well short of the ING-U.S. TCP, the platoon pulled a U-turn. Usually, patrols tried to avoid crossing through the same stretch of road even twice during a normal patrol. Now, they were heading through Mushada for the fourth time in less than two hours.

The insurgents were waiting for them. The two groups that they had encountered earlier now converged on the Mushada market. Toting RPGs, AKs, and RPK machine guns, they hunkered down in buildings, on roofs, and even on the mosque.

The column drove into range. Mushada exploded with gunfire and rockets. Jason Becker opened fire with his M240, but just as the engagement started, the illum round burst overhead. The entire market was bathed in artifical light, which blinded Becker because he still had his night vision goggles on.

He flipped them up and kept firing. From both sides of the road, he could see scores of muzzle flashes. A web of tracers interlaced through the column. Somebody rolled a pair of tires into the street; they rolled straight toward Metzdorff's vehicle.

In the trail rig, Marty could hear Becker banging away with the M240. He could see the fireworks engulfing the column. The insurgents cooked off RPGs. They flashed across the road in sudden red-orange streaks. Marty's whole world telescoped to one task: stay with the rest of the rigs. If he fell behind, they'd be singled out and killed.

Meanwhile Tommy Houston had cracked his window and was shooting fiercely out to the right with his M14. Every little bit helped. On the gun, Becker saw the enormous amount of incoming and his mouth went cotton-dry. Stabs of stark terror threatened to paralyze him in the middle of the chaos. He fought two battles that night: one against the enemy, one against himself. At that moment, he discovered self-control yet untapped. He plumbed its depth. His M240 ripped through his ready ammo as he sprayed the muzzle flashes and RPG launches.

Marty's Humvee reached the main intersection in Mushada. The amount of incoming swelled. A rocket arrowed through the night, fired from point-blank range. It center-punched the passenger door's window on the right side of Marty's 1114.

"Oh my God!" yelled Mann. The RPG had spiderwebbed the ballistic glass only inches from his head.

The Humvee convulsed. Another rocket blasted into the Humvee, this time from the left side. It struck the front fender well right at Marty's legs. The armor held, but the stench of cordite filled the rig.

Jason hammered back at the enemy, but the sheer number of AKs and RPGs was overwhelming. Every gunner in the column flayed both sides of the marketplace, but the Americans had no chance of gaining fire superiority. Still they emptied their M240s, reloaded, and kept shooting.

An RPG whipped past Becker. It came from behind. He traversed left and raked the area. The Humvee rocked again; he swung right and hammered muzzle flashes coming from a strip mall.

An RPG struck the gypsy armor next to Becker's gun. The armor deflected the rocket, but shrapnel dismounted the M240 and struck Jason in the hand. An eyeblink later, a bullet hit the AT-4 rocket launcher strapped to the back of his turret. The impact activated the rocket, which shot off into the night.

Becker was still shooting when a blistering wave of heat engulfed his back. The Humvee shuddered. Jason fell out of the turret and landed between Mann and Houston. His back felt like somebody had just kicked him, then set him afire with a blowtorch.

"Becker's hit!"

Marty had no time to look. Bedlam had broken out in the front of the column with more RPGs crisscrossing from every direction. Some came straight down the road, skipping along the shoulder. Others whirred by from behind. The other Humvees started taking hits.

Lieutenant Metzdorff's rig drove up alongside one of the rolling tires the insurgents had sent into the road. It was an IED. Marty saw one explode only a few feet from the lieutenant's left rear fender.

More RPGs swept through the column. The Humvees up front were hurting now. Another RPG slammed into Marty's rig. In a freakish example of marksmanship, the insurgent who had cooked it off managed to hit Tommy Houston's window almost in the same spot as where Sergeant Mann's had been hit.

Tommy turned from the window to check on Jason. "Becker, are you wounded?"

His back burned. His hand ached. "I don't know."

The defining moment of Jason's young life had arrived. All of nineteen years old, he'd set out to Iraq to see what kind of man he was. Now, the test had come. He could lie there in a heap between two veteran NCOs and let them check him for wounds, or he could find the strength to get back in that turret.

It's time to decide.

He struggled upright. A calm voice inside him said, *My responsibility is to protect this truck and everyone in it. That's more important than my safety.*

He pulled himself back into the turret, his DCUs covered with blood. He reached for the M240 . . . it wasn't there. He looked around. It had spun out of the turret and was about to slip off the Humvee's roof. Now, only the barrel was in grabbing range. Becker lunged for it with his unwounded hand. He had no gloves on, and as he grasped it, the muzzle's searing heat burned his palm and fingers. But he held on to it and dragged it back into the turret. He laid it down on the gypsy armor and engaged the enemy again. Bullets still buzzed like angry hornets overhead. Rockets lit the night's sky. The ambush stretched from north of town all the way through it.

Becker fired the last belt of M240 ammo. With the weapon empty, he grabbed his M4 and used the M203 to pump grenades into the insurgents. Then his turret jammed. He expended his last grenade, sending it into a building alive with muzzle flashes.

Tommy handed him another can of M240 ammo. He loaded the weapon, but the turret still wouldn't traverse.

Even as they reached the town's southern outskirts, new insurgent positions opened up on the column. Becker needed a weapon he could use. He reached for a SAW, swung it out, and pulled the trigger.

That night, Becker found out what sort of man lurked beneath his quiet demeanor. He was all sinew and steel. He earned everyone's respect that night.

A kilometer south of Mushada the incoming drained away. They'd reached the edge of the ambush. It was a good thing, too. Just as they cleared the kill zone, Lieutenant Metzdorff's Humvee broke down. Jeremy Turner's rig came up and pushed Metzdorff's Humvee down Route Senators for another half kilometer or so. Once they were sure they'd cleared the ambush, Turner swung in front of the platoon leader's vehicle and towed it back into Camp Cooke.

Inside the gate, the column limped into the 2-7 maintenance area. The platoon deadlined three of their Humvees right there. Marty's had taken four RPG hits. The other three had taken five more among them, including one that had hit Metzdorff's window. All the trucks were stippled with bullet holes and silvery nicks from ricochets.

During the fight, the platoon had received virtually no support. The reason? Colonel Rainey and his battalion had left for Fallujah a week earlier. There was little help to send. The 39th Brigade was stretched thin. It didn't help that the Bulldogs were left under the control of the 206th Field Artillery again. Bravo's men had little respect for that unit and its ability to conduct operations.

While the men gathered around the vehicles, Doc Smith tended to Becker's wounds. Doc found shrapnel in Jason's finger and around his kidneys. The AT-4 launch had also burned his back and neck. Becker later received a Purple Heart for these wounds, which he did not feel he deserved. He returned to duty a few days later, no worse for the wear, though to this day he still has a chunk of shrapnel in his finger.

Lieutenant Metzdorff walked over to the 39th Brigade TOC to report, where he was ordered to take his men back out on Route Senators and patrol north to Mushada. They wanted him to go right back into the lion's den. Twenty-nine RPG launches apparently weren't enough. Like August in Baghdad, the American forces in Iraq were stretched to the limit during Fallujah. On the grass-roots, tactical level, the Joes paid the price.

Metzdorff argued he didn't have any rigs left. The 39th arranged to get him three temporaries.

By now, the rest of the platoon had returned to the company area. Becker had been taken to the aid station, and John Rosander, shattered eardrums be damned, came out to take his place.

The temporary Humvees arrived. General Chastain's personal security detail contributed one. Another showed up from a military intelligence team.

Metzdorff returned. He huddled with the men. "Listen up, guys, we're going back out."

"What?"

"You've gotta be fucking kidding me!"

"This is bullshit!"

The platoon stared at Metzdorff in shock. The force they had faced totaled between sixty and a hundred and fifty insurgents. It was the largest single ambush in AO Ghost during OIF II. The insurgents were well equipped with antiarmor weapons and belt-fed machine guns. To go back without air or Bradley support seemed akin to a death sentence. Hell, they'd just lost three-quarters of their vehicles. Had even one been immobilized in the kill zone, the entire column could have been wiped out.

Three hours after they limped back in through the North Gate, 3rd Platoon rolled north again.

Fortunately, the 39th Brigade had scrounged around for armor. Several green-camouflaged Bradleys from another brigade showed up later that night and pushed into Mushada. But by then the insurgents had long since melted away.

SIXTY-THREE

FALLUJAH

Second Platoon had become FOB bitches, and they hated it. In early November, Colonel Rainey and the 2-7 Cav headed for Fallujah and the largest battle of the Iraq war.

He took his misfit Oregon platoon with him to guard his base of operations. Lieutenant Kent saddled up his men, many of whom now grumbled that they were getting more than their fair share of the fighting. The platoon had become vagabonds, moving from one major battle to another. They dubbed their Humvees the "gypsy wagons" and lived alongside them out in the field.

Instead of forming the tip of the spear as they had in Najaf, 2nd Platoon escorted convoys between Taji and Fallujah and pulled security outside the city while the tanks and mech infantry did the fighting.

When the attack began, the combined army-marine force assaulted Fallujah from the north. Ryan Howell, Spike Olsen, and Chris Johnson (who had swapped into 2nd Platoon when Chris Bailey joined 3rd), watched the initial marine assault from Rainey's FOB near the railroad station. A whistle blew; the marines poured over a berm and into the city, spawning a battle that would rage for weeks. The initial attack reminded Ryan of the movie *Gallipoli*. He wondered why the marines didn't use armor.

Rainey's battalion drove into the city and faced an entrenched and tactically savvy foe. Without the combat power to clear every house, 2-7's soldiers seized key points in their battlespace. The fighting was intense. If Najaf was a shooting gallery, Fallujah was a toe-to-toe slugfest. The enemy had acquired better RPGs, and they used them with telling effect. Captain Twaddell's command Bradley suffered a direct hit from one of these new RPGs. The rocket pierced the track's armor, killed his interpreter, and grievously wounded one other man. Nevertheless, Twaddell stayed in the fight.

Captain Glass and his tanks encountered similar resistence. They found the roads littered with Brazilian-made antitank mines. After clearing those, the RPG attacks began. One of Charlie 3-8's Abrams took a direct hit from one of the new RPGs. It penetrated the front armor and killed the driver, disabling the tank.

The battalion encountered booby-trapped buildings, multilayered ambushes, and even 23mm antiaircraft guns. The insurgents in Fallujah had months to prepare for the American attack, and they had barricaded buildings, thrown up roadblocks, and dug battle positions with interlocking fields of fire.

In such a fight, the light infantry would have been chewed up. Rainey left his Oregonians to cover his rear where they'd be relatively safe.

Relatively safe can mean a lot of things. In this case, it meant all the fireworks without the glory. The 2-7 FOB became a mortar and rocket magnet. Day in and day out, the Oregonians guarded the base. It was boring work, punctuated by moments of sheer terror as indirect fire rained down on them. At one point, a mortar shell exploded between two of the Humvees. Another one landed right on top of some nearby marines. Members of the platoon rushed to assist, but there was nothing they could do. One marine died instantly, but somehow the others were unscathed.

The platoon grew edgy. Morale dropped. Part of the problem was that Pete Salerno was no longer the platoon sergeant. He'd been transferred to Baghdad where he took over as the senior NCO in 2-162's intel shop. His iron hand and fatherly love had ruled the platoon for years. Now his alpha-dog leadership was sorely missed. Tempers boiled, and resentment burned. Lieutenant Kent grew so frustrated with Brian Ward's smart-ass remarks he physically assaulted him.

Rebekah-mae Bruns came out to Fallujah to report on the 39th Brigade's part in the battle. She was shocked at the transformation of 2nd Platoon. They seemed like a different outfit without Salerno.

She stayed with them through the mortar attacks. As casualties came back from the city and 2nd Platoon helped move and treat them, she photographed the scenes. It was poignant combat photography, and her natural eye for the work captured the emotions of the moment with heartbreaking clarity.

One night, a nearby Abrams fired a main gun at a group of insurgents moving near a collection of buildings to the east of the FOB. Spike, Petey Peterson, Chris Johnson, and Ryan Howell went off to investigate. Rebekah-mae went with them.

They moved into the area and found a decapitated body, blood spilling out its stump to form a puddle around its shoulders. By now, they were so desensitized to such scenes that they became curious by it, not horrified. They wondered whether the corpse was a male or female. They couldn't decide. As they were walking away, Petey looked over his shoulder and suddenly blurted, "That is the most fucked up thing I've ever seen."

The patrol turned around. A little white kitten was lapping up the blood. After seeing that, they swore they'd never own a cat.

On November 13, Apache 2-7 suffered the loss of almost a full squad of men during a street fight next to a house. One of Twaddell's soldiers fought to the last breath protecting his wounded comrades and was awarded a posthumous Silver Star for his sacrifice.

Spike, Ryan, Petey, and twenty-year-old Thomas "Dirty" Herb were sent forward into the city as replacements for Captain Twaddell.

The rest of the platoon remained at the FOB, though Lieutenant Kent tried everything he could think of to get them into the city. Colonel Rainey would have none of it. This was not a Humvee battle, not when the enemy had antiarmor weapons that could pierce his Abrams. Second Platoon remained in the rear enduring more rocket and mortar attacks.

Rebekah-mae wanted to get into the city as well. At one point, she climbed onto a track and was heading into the fight. Colonel Rainey got wind of this and ordered the vehicle back to the FOB. She was left behind; Rainey would not let her inside the city. The decision crushed and outraged her. He stood firm, though. He was not going to risk another soldier's life if he didn't have to do it.

Staff Sergeant Bruns stayed with 2nd Platoon and wrote a vivid piece about the men entitled *Recollections of Najaf, Vignettes of Fallujah.*

Meanwhile, inside the city the four Oregonians assigned to Twaddell's company saw limited action. By the time they arrived, most of the fighting in the 2-7 AO had ended. They took occasional mortar fire. A few times they were shot at, and they searched an awful lot of houses. Those searches paid off: many times they found caches of grenades, RPGs, and AK-47s.

One morning, Spike caught sight of several white-robed Iraqis as they emerged from a building. They carried AK-47s, and he was about to kill them when at the last moment, they were identified as ING. He breathed a sigh of relief that he did not commit an act of fratricide.

A week later, the four Oregonians rejoined 2nd Platoon. The men stayed in the area, pulling security and escorting convoys until early December. Upon returning to Taji, Captain San Miguel tried to give the platoon a break by putting the men on QRF. It didn't happen. Lieutenant Kent's father-in-law arrived to film a documentary at Taji. Though both San Miguel and Kent tried to stop it, 2nd Platoon was ordered out on a meaningless patrol so that Kent's father-in-law could film them in action. Kent was particularly furious with this unwelcome intrusion. His men had been going full tilt since August. They needed a rest. It would not happen.

Exhausted, the men climbed into their Humvees and rolled for the gate. Kent's father-in-law failed to show up. Apparently, he found other things to film that day. The whole affair ruptured Lieutenant Kent's relationship with his father-in-law and embittered many of 2nd Platoon's weary men. After that patrol, the student-warriors were all ready to just go home.

SIXTY-FOUR

THE WOMAN
ON THE ROOF

Major Mike Warrington stood in the battalion TOC at FOB Volunteer and dialed a number on his cell phone. Nearby, Major Tanguy and Lieutenant Colonel Hendrickson were talking with Captain Hildebrandt, who was on the phone in his CP. The Old Man platoon, now under Lieutenant Brandon Ditto, was in a major fight again. Adhamiya, Saddam Hussein's Sunni stronghold of power, had turned into a zoo. If the radio was any indication, every American unit in that district was under attack on that morning of November 20.

With the Battle of Fallujah raging, the Volunteers could not get any air support or armor. Delta was on its own. Warrington finished banging out the number and waited for the other party to pick up.

"Doctor Aladhadh," Warrington began as the vice chairman of the Adhamiya DAC answered his call.

"I am upset with the violence this morning!" the Iraqi answered as soon as Mike identified himself. The BC had long suspected Doctor Riyadh Aladhadh and the chairman, Hashim Ibraheem Hassan, of being dirty. If they were not outright insurgents or sympathizers, they certainly played both sides of the fence. Self-aggrandizement seemed to be their motive.

"I am upset with the violence!" Aladhadh said again. "This is no need! The soldiers come into our streets and the violence is not good!"

"I am upset as well. I need for you as a leader of the people to get the innocent civilians off the streets so that they can be safe while we deal with the fighters."

There were no innocent people on the streets of Adhamiya that day. The entire district had been warned in advance that the insurgents would fight the Americans on this morning. The shops were all closed. Every building was barred, windows taped.

Aladhadh skirted the issue. Instead, he played the blame game, "You know that the violence in Fallujah precipitated all this. . . ."

Warrington suppressed his growing anger, "Doctor Aladhadh, that is crap and you know it. We work in good faith with you and make frequent gestures of goodwill."

Mike didn't bother to remind him of the millions of dollars poured into civil affairs projects in Adhamiya to improve the power grid, water system, and schools.

The DAC vice chair conceded the point, "Yes, yes. We work together. It is the ING attack on the Abu Hanifa Mosque yesterday that causes this violence today."

Aladhadh spoke the truth this time. The raid on this sacred holy site, the most important mosque in Baghdad, had stirred a hornet's nest. Aladhadh's family had been inside when the raid began. Yet the Volunteers had had nothing to do with that raid. Warrington wasn't about to let Aladhadh use the mosque raid to justify the IEDs, rockets, and small-arms fire that had torn up elements of two American battalions.

"These are two different things. They are separate issues. We were attacked this morning without provocation, and you had better get your people under control, or we will come down there and do it for you!"

Fear tinged the Iraqi's response. "No! No!" he yelled into his phone, "*Don't!* I will do it. We just want peace, but the soldiers—"

Warrington's anger boiled to fury. He cut Aladhadh off with, "We want peace as well. Go now and take care of—"

"It was the mosque!" Aladhadh screamed. "The honor of the people is impugned, and this how they make things right, to get back their honor."

"The mosque is a different issue. You get your people under control and get a grip on them right now or we will!"

"No! No!" The Iraqi pleaded, "Please! I will have everyone in their homes immediately. I have connections. We have a system to communicate. I will do it now!"

Warrington yelled, "Good!" and hung up. Around him, the soldiers in the TOC gaped in astonishment. Warrington was usually the picture of self-control.

With Doctor Aladhadh that day was an American named Laura Poitras. She stood next to him on a roof with her video camera trained on the battle up the road.

The events of November 20 had really begun at the November 10 Adhamiya DAC meeting. Mike Warrington had shown up that morning to discuss issues the community had and to give a progress report on the civil affairs projects under way. The main effort in Adhamiya was the renovation of the school system.

A slim, dark-haired American woman, a civilian, arrived with Doctor Aladhadh. Her presence piqued Warrington's curiousity. Who was she? After the meeting, he introduced himself and discovered Laura Poitras was a documentary film producer from New York. She'd won the 2003 Center for Documentary Studies Filmaker Award for *Flag Wars,* a four-year study of a Columbus, Ohio, neighborhood riven with conflict between the African-American long-term residents and a wave of gay home-buyers who had begun to move into the area.

In his conversation with her, Warrington learned that she had been credentialed by the 1st Cav Division public affairs office. Once in Iraq, she left the 1st Cav and struck out on her own. At the time the two met, Poitras was living at Doctor Aladhadh's house. Major Warrington gave her his card and offered her any help or support she needed.

Back at Volunteer, Mike followed up on the encounter. He e-mailed the 1st Cav's senior PAO, Lieutenant Colonel James Hutton, and confirmed that Poitras had been credentialed by the division. Still, something seemed not right here. Warrington resolved to keep an eye on things.

Nine days later, on November 19, a platoon from 3-153 escorted an Iraqi special forces unit to the Abu Hanifa Mosque during a Friday prayer sermon. As the Iraqi SF entered the mosque, Sheik Mauayad Adhami was caught cold in the middle of an anti-American rant that included urging his followers to turn Baghdad and Mosul into another Fallujah.

Violence broke out inside the mosque. The 3-153 platoon had remained outside to pull security and had nothing to do with what followed. The Iraqi SF began beating the people inside the mosque. Shots rang out. Four people were killed. Dozens more were injured in the chaos. The raid nabbed nine men on the 1st Cav Division's most wanted list, including Sheik Adhami, but the timing and violence created a backlash that cost the coalition dearly.

As bleeding mosque-goers staggered outside, a stringer for the Associated Press named Khalid Mohammad—the same man who had entered Najaf with Al Sadr's reinforcements back in August—reached the area, and photographed the scene. Several of his photos depicted bloody civilians leaving the mosque as American soldiers stood nearby. From the photographs, it looked like the Americans had perpetrated the incident.

The people of Adhamiya reacted with outrage. They vowed revenge, and all over the district insurgents prepared ambushes with IEDs and RPG teams. Later, some intelligence reports suggested Al-Qaeda cells spearheaded this effort. By the next morning, November 20, they had transformed Adhamiya into a series of kill zones. The locals knew what was coming. Those not willing to fight stayed off the streets and barred their shops and houses.

Shortly before 0730 that morning, the battalion TOC received a report that shots were being fired in the northeastern section of AO Volunteer. The battalion launched the QRF platoon, which happened to be the Old Men from Delta Company.

Brandon Ditto had taken over the platoon after McCrae's death. Ditto was a tall, dark-haired graduate of Oregon State University. The events of 9/11 drove him into the guard, where his patriotism was matched by a keen intelligence and an ability to think on his feet. Initially, he served as a Joe in Shane Ward's squad in Bravo Company. He learned the ropes with the Bulldogs, and once commissioned in the summer of '03, he joined Delta Company after IOBC in January '04. Following Delta's reorganization at Hood, Ditto became one of the battle captains in the TOC.

After Erik McCrae died, Ditto inherited his platoon in early July. Kerry Boggs sat him down and made it clear whose platoon it would be, at least until the young lieutenant proved himself.

"I will be watching you," Boggs told Ditto. "This is *my* platoon. When I am confident you can handle it, I'll hand you the reigns completely."

Boggs didn't have anything to worry about with Ditto. The first week in the platoon, Ditto and the men ended up in a midnight firefight near a bridge over the Tigris. Ditto remained calm and focused. His decision making under fire impressed Boggs. After that night, Boggs concluded, "That kid's pretty good."

The firefight in Zone 22 a month later confirmed Boggs' assessment. Ditto had a knack for staying collected in the heat of battle. He was aggressive, but not stupid. He did not take unwarranted risks. The men of the platoon grew to respect him for that. By the fall of '04, Boggs had concluded that Ditto was one of the best young lieutenants he'd ever seen.

On the 20th, Ditto led the Old Man platoon out into Rusapha. They had four rigs that day, heavily armed with a pair of M240s, two .50-cals, and an MK19 grenade launcher. Many of the men were still half asleep. They'd been sent out dozens of times over the months to respond to reports of gunfire. Usually, such missions came up empty, and the men did not expect this Saturday morning to be any different.

The platoon had not been briefed about the Abu Hanifa Mosque incident. The column reached the northern edge of AO Volunteer where they heard gunfire to the northwest near an American base called Fort Apache. Ditto ordered the platoon to investigate.

As they made their approach, the Oregonians encountered an ING platoon blazing away at several cars and trucks to the north. The vehicles took off into Adhamiya. Ditto stopped long enough to learn from the INGs that they'd taken small-arms fire and rockets from these vehicles. The platoon gave chase, but the enemy eluded them.

Ditto decided to explore the neighborhood. The four Humvees, two 1114s and two up-armored 1025s, wound their way through alleys and side streets looking for trouble. It did not take long to find it.

In ones and twos, AK-wielding Sunnis popped up on rooftops and in alleyways to take shots at the Oregonians. The men returned fire but didn't chase any of the insurgents. The hit-and-run attacks continued. Ditto wondered why they were being so bold this early in the morning. It gave him a bad feeling.

Only a few kilometers away, Charlie Company, 3-153, launched its QRF platoon to investigate a report that the local IP station in Adhamiya was under attack. First Lieutenant Michael McCarty led his men out in a four-Humvee column. As they approached the IP station, well-placed insurgents opened fire on them. Two IEDs exploded nearby. McCarty maneuvered his Arkansans toward the IP station, but the volume of incoming grew. The insurgents started cooking off RPGs. The American gunners suppressed the rooftops and alleyways with their M240 Bravos.

They fought their way to the IP station. While paused in the road in front of the station, a car approached the rear of the column. The Arkansans laced it with gunfire, and the vehicle swerved into a wall between the station and a school about thirty meters from the trailing 1114.

The car was a VBIED. It blew up with such massive force that it left a six-foot crater in the road and demolished thirty feet of the wall. Two Arkansans were hit by shrapnel, and one of the 1114s suffered serious damage.

With two men down, McCarty needed to disengage. As he moved the platoon to a rally point a few blocks away, insurgents detonated two IEDs on their vehicles. Fortunately, these did no damage and the platoon reached Fort Apache without further casualties.

Devil 4, the Old Men, reached Fort Apache. Just as they did, a rocket whirred through the column and into the front gate of the American base. The Oregonians returned fire but couldn't find the RPG teams. The enemy proved particularly elusive that morning. Ditto and Boggs thought they were being baited, as if the insurgents were daring the Americans to pursue them so they could spring a trap.

The amount of fire swelled. The platoon's MK19 gunner, Specialist Daren Pfaender, matched the insurgents with a steady stream of grenades. Within minutes, he'd triggered off his entire load of forty. The platoon halted in a deserted stretch of road. In a box formation now, the gunners covered on the nearby houses and shops while Sergeant Brian Mumey leapt out of Pfaender's vehicle and ran to the trunk. Three shots rang out. Mumey didn't even flinch. He threw open the trunk, and with one hand pulled out a can of MK19 ammo. He lugged it over to the right side of the Humvee and pushed it up to Pfaender, who coolly reloaded even as more incoming pinged around the platoon. Mumey ran back to the left-side passenger door and remounted.

Mumey's act of bravery confounded Boggs, and he burst out laughing. Here was a soldier who had never figured out how to stay out of trouble. He'd lost several stripes through his career, and while Mumey had reached Baghdad as an E-6, he would leave as a specialist. Yet, in the heat of battle, he exposed himself without hesitation.

The platoon rumbled forward, and the fight continued. At 0720, Ditto requested permission to cross into 3-153's battlespace. The 2-162 TOC informed the Arkansans. The Old Men ducked into the labyrinth of streets in the heart of Adhamiya.

A running fight developed. The platoon kept moving and shooting. The insurgents bobbed and weaved around them. When the Humvees reached the Huskies–New York traffic circle, the insurgents tried to detonate an IED. It partially exploded just as Boggs' driver, Specialist Louis Bernhardt, shouted, "IED left!"

Another RPG shot out of an alley. It skipped into a curb, spun around wildly, and failed to explode. Suddenly, Boggs' rig disappeared in a cloud of smoke and dust.

"The PSG's [platoon sergeant] been hit!" someone shouted over the radio.

"No, I'm not," said Boggs. His rig had been lifted up on two wheels by an explosion.

Curious, Boggs asked his gunner, Specialist Andy Ashpole, "Andrew, what was that?"

"That was an RPG, Sergeant."

"Where did it hit?"

"You don't want to know. But it is time to leave."

The rocket had missed Ashpole by less than two feet before impacting on a wall. It had been an exceptionally close call.

One of the .50-cals opened up on that RPG gunner. The bullets sawed a palm tree in half. It crashed down as another burst finished off the insurgent. The gunners fired whenever a target presented itself. The insurgents masterfully used cover and concealment. The Oregonians couldn't find them.

Another RPG arched into the traffic circle. This one passed overhead and hit a statue. The insurgent disappeared before the Oregonians could get their weapons to bear. About this time, Captain Hildebrandt came over the company net.

"Sergeant Boggs, whatcha doing?" he asked.

"Well, driving around and killing people," the platoon sergeant replied.

"Where ya at?"

Boggs gave him the grid coordinates.

"You're out of your area. Get yer ass back in zone!" said Hildebrandt lightly.

Boggs relayed this to Ditto, who ordered the platoon south. As they consolidated back at the intersection of New York and Huskies, Ditto called for air support and armor. The battalion TOC replied they were working on it, but no armor was available. Much of the 1st Cav's armor was in Fallujah.

Ditto decided to move north again. They drove up parallel to Route New York, taking sporadic fire all the way again. A cat-and-mouse game developed as the Humvees snaked around the back alleys and side streets at the edge of AO Volunteer. The men could see insurgents darting between buildings, shooting and moving from rooftops, and firing from sidestreets.

They turned left onto Route New York. Ditto kept calling for air support. Nothing was available.

The Humvees roared south on Route New York right past Doctor Riyadh Aladhadh's house. On the rooftop, the men saw a man and a Western-looking Caucasian woman. She was filming them with a professional video camera. At 0745, the platoon reported that development to the battalion TOC.

Continuing south, the platoon broke contact and moved down past Route Huskies. Ditto needed reinforcements. The closest available unit was Devil 2, Hildebrandt's New York platoon, which had been at one of the ING bunkers. The two Delta Company elements linked up between Routes Grizzlies and Huskies. They'd soon have a new mission.

While Ditto and Boggs chased insurgents through the streets of Adhamiya, Lieutenant McCarty's Arkansans waded back into the fight. Driving through the empty streets, his platoon took sporadic fire until they reached the IP station. It was relatively quiet there, and the lieutenant learned that the insurgents had withdrawn westward to regroup.

McCarty decided to attack and decisively engage this group of insurgents. Using the alleys, he maneuvered toward them. Just after turning to the west to run down another alley, his platoon stumbled into a prepared ambush. A PKC machine-gun team opened up on McCarty's vehicle from a position to the right. Simultaneously, another group of insurgents on the left fired an RPG-7, the deadly new version that had been causing terrible damage in Fallujah.

The rocket penetrated McCarty's left rear door. It exploded, severely wounding the platoon radioman and McCarty's gunner. The lieutenant took shrapnel to the ear, and his driver was knocked unconscious.

All up and down the platoon column, the gunners blazed away as insurgents swarmed around them. McCarty saw the PKC team and realized his men would get machine-gunned if they dismounted to help the wounded. He jumped out of the Humvee. Standing in the middle of the street, he fired at the Sunni machine-gunners. They stood up and started running for a nearby building. McCarty gave chase and killed two and wounded the last one. He destroyed the PKC while under fire from other AK-toting fighters.

With the platoon stopped, the insurgents surrounded it and poured fire into the Arkansans. They fought back, using their grenade launchers and M240s with telling effect. McCarty sent three-man teams to clear the nearby houses and buildings, but that failed to drive the enemy away. There were just too many. Between twenty and thirty RPGs exploded around the platoon. Four of the six Humvees McCarty had taken out on this second sortie took damage. Twenty minutes later, with the fight still raging, another platoon of Arkansans arrived to resupply McCarty's men with ammunition and to get the wounded out.

With a fresh load of ammunition, McCarty's men worked to clear the alleys and rooftops seventy-five meters in all directions. The insurgents began to break contact. The Arkansans were winning.

Ditto and Lieutenant Williams, the platoon leader for the New York platoon, hooked up south of the engagement area and received new orders. The IP station in Adhamiya was under attack again. The 2-162 TOC reported the VBIED and that the Arkansans were stretched and needed help.

They'd have to drive back up into Zone 18 to get there. They'd be out of sector again, moving through an unfamiliar labyrinth of alleyways and streets. Worse, Ditto's Blue Force Tracker went down. Williams' rig had the only working BFT now. Ditto told him to lead out, but to use the side streets and to stay off Route New York.

Williams and 2nd Platoon roared off north, leaving 4th Platoon behind. Surprised, Ditto's drivers tried to catch up, but the spacing between the two elements grew to more than two hundred meters. When they reached Route Huskies, Williams didn't turn off New York. His 1114 in the lead, Williams drove his platoon right into the middle of the insurgents Ditto's men had just been fighting.

Bernhardt watched as the first seven Humvees went through the traffic circle and stayed on Route New York. His heart sank.

"Isn't this the bad road?" he asked.

"Yes," replied Kerry Boggs.

"Why are we on it?"

The platoon sergeant shook his head. "I don't know."

Moments later, the platoons came under scattered small-arms fire. The gunners shot back when they had targets, but the column did not slow down. They raced past Doctor Aladhadh's house. The Old Man platoon spotted the woman on the roof again. Her camera was angled down at them. Anger flared in both Boggs and Ditto. What was a Western reporter doing in the middle of a Sunni ambush?

They drove another few blocks. Second Platoon slowed down. The Old Men started to catch up to them. An explosion echoed through the neighborhood. Sergeant Carle shouted, "IED!" It turned out to be a rocket-propelled grenade.

At the head of the New York platoon, an insurgent jumped out in front of Williams' rig. His gunner tried to kill him with his MK19, but it jammed. Williams' Humvee screeched to a stop. The rest of 2nd Platoon stacked up behind it. In the second rig, the M240 gunner tried to kill the insurgent. His weapon jammed as well. The TC dismounted and started shooting with his M4. Just then, Williams' driver hit the gas, and the platoon leader's rig disappeared up the road and around a corner to the right. He was now alone, unsupported in the middle of a district-wide firefight with a jammed weapon.

The rest of the New York platoon lay exposed in the street. Mobility had kept the Volunteers alive. Now, that advantage was lost. The insurgents seized the moment. Rockets speared the platoon from the front, sides, and rear. At least nine exploded in or around the Americans. One hit the lead remaining Humvee, whose truck commander, Sergeant Hegedus, was furiously shooting at the insurgents to the platoon's front. The rocket impacted right on the front grill, drove into the engine compartment, but did not explode.

Another rocket ripped into the second rig in line. Commanded by Sergeant Postle, it was an uparmored 1025 driven by a Syrian-American named Dave Roustom. The RPG hit Roustom's door. The explosion blew it inward and turned the ballistic window into a projectile. The glass decapitated Dave and killed him instantly. Postle was splashed with his driver's blood, and when he dismounted, some of the Volunteers thought he'd been wounded himself.

Then the Humvee began to burn.

The last New York rig, an M1114, swung around to the right and edged past Roustom's. As it moved forward, an RPG exploded nearby and blew several of its tires out. The men dismounted and fought for their lives.

It was Lieutenant Boyce's worst August nightmare come true. How many times had Ross looked back on his kilometer-long dash through Zone 22 and thanked God the insurgents hadn't scored a mobility kill? He knew that if that had happened, the entire platoon would have been wiped out.

The New Yorkers now faced that end. The insurgents knew it and assaulted the platoon. From alleyways in front and to the rear, RPG teams poured into the street, ready to deliver the coup de grace. Devil 2 was surrounded.

One hundred and fifty meters behind the carnage, the Old Man platoon heard the RPG strikes and sped to the rescue. They closed the gap in seconds and arrived just as the final insurgent assault began.

In the lead rig, Sergeant Louis Esquivel saw the Sunni fighters flood toward New York from the nearby alleys. He told his driver to stop. Ahead and to the right, an RPG gunner turned around and stared in abject surprise. Obviously, they hadn't seen Ditto's vehicles. Esquivel dismounted and killed the RPG man. Daren Pfaender cut another one down his M240 Bravo. Pfaender kept firing, slaying insurgents all around the rear of Devil 2.

Ditto dismounted and ran forward. Ahead of him, Sergeant Mumey had already reached Roustom's vehicle and Ditto could see him tugging at Dave's seatbelt. To the right, Esquivel and Pfaender killed two insurgents in an alleyway. Boggs watched from the rear as an RPG exploded near Roustom's rig again. Everyone who had dismounted dashed for cover. To Kerry, they looked like of a flock of seagulls flying pell-mell in all directions.

Kerry keyed his mic and called Hildebrandt. "Contact report: two trucks down. Multiple wounded. I need air support. Get me some help."

Hildebrandt said something, but Boggs didn't hear him.

Ditto reached Roustom's rig. "Mumey, you getting him?"

"Yeah, I got him."

Ditto opened the right-side passenger door and discovered Specialist Bona, the gunner. Covered with blood, he stared at Ditto with saucer eyes and moaned, "Dave's dead." Ditto pulled him out and discovered Bona had shrapnel wounds to his face and legs. He dragged him back to his own Humvee and got him inside. Specialist Polly, who had also been in Roustom's truck, had suffered shrapnel wounds to his face and eye. He was taken to another of Ditto's rigs.

Meanwhile, Esquivel pulled forward so Sergeant Postle and Lonnie Harrison could hook a tow chain to the other immobilized Humvee. Ditto returned to Roustom's burning rig. Oily black smoke now filled the interior. He searched for sensitive items and found a set of night vision goggles as he waved away the smoke. He looked up into the turret and saw the M240. It had been mangled by the RPG. Ditto didn't worry about it.

Mumey still hadn't pulled Roustom out. Brandon called across the Humvee, "What's taking so long?"

"He's not going," Mumey replied.

Ditto ran to the driver's side to see Mumey pulling at Roustom. He could see right away that it wouldn't do any good. Roustom's body was pinned inside by the twisted remains of the door. A burst of fire raked the area. It had come from the left side. Ditto dashed back to the right and called for Mumey. He kept working to free his comrade and ignored the incoming.

"Get over here, Mumey!"

Reluctantly, Mumey gave up.

There was nothing they could do. Two of the three New York rigs had been immobilized or destroyed. For blocks around, scores of insurgents were moving to the sound of the gunfire. If Ditto stayed with Roustom's rig, his men would be overwhelmed just as surely as 2nd Platoon had been. What was already a tragedy would become a massacre. He made the decision. They'd break contact and come back for Roustom later.

Ditto told his men to mount up and make sure that all the New Yorkers had seats. Mumey ran back with Ditto to the platoon leader's rig. There was not a free seat. Undeterred, he jumped onto the back deck, wedged himself in place, and raised his M4. He was still firing as the battered column limped north. A later patrol estimated Delta's two platoons had killed at least thirty insurgents during the fight.

They dragged the one broken Humvee north to a traffic circle deep in AO Gunslinger. Just as they got there, Hegedus' Humvee gave up the ghost. The RPG in the engine finally took its toll. Ditto's crew hooked it to a tow chain. Now they had two rigs under tow.

At the traffic circle, they found Lieutenant Williams and his crew unscathed. Ditto dismounted and told him what had happened. The news hit Williams like a thunderclap.

"Dave's dead?" he asked.

Ditto nodded. Williams teared up.

Ditto set up a defensive position at the traffic circle while the men worked on their three wounded brothers. He got on the battalion net and gave a contact report. He requested ambulances and permission to go to the nearest American base, which was 3-153's FOB Gunslinger.

When the BC heard Roustom had been left behind, he erupted in anger and pain. He launched the back-up QRF, which was Tim Bloom's platoon from Charlie Company. Captain Welch went with them. He'd long since earned the respect of his men for his willingness to share their risks. He was the only company commander in the battalion to get in a fight with every platoon.

As they drove north, Welch tried to get a fix on Roustom's location. Williams and Ditto weren't able to do it. The death of one of his soldiers had profoundly affected Williams; he gave Welch the wrong coordinates.

Meanwhile, Ditto was in the middle of a shouting match with the BC, who had ordered him to continue to the IP station. Ditto refused. He had two rigs available to maneuver. His other two were towing 2nd Platoon's Humvees and would be of minimal value in a fight.

As the debate continued, Boggs tried to go back for Roustom. Louis Bernhardt threw the Humvee in reverse and crept down Route New York. After about a block, an RPG sailed down the street and exploded right behind them. That ended the experiment. They weren't going to be able to get Roustom.

The BC hated the idea of leaving a man behind. It was bad enough to give up a vehicle to the enemy, who would surely climb on it and celebrate as news photographers snapped pictures. It had happened too many times in Baghdad already. Now it looked like it would happen to 2-162.

The BC ordered Ditto to the IP station again. Ditto refused, "You've got to understand, I don't have any combat power left." They could not afford to get into another fight, not with two dead trucks and three wounded men. Ditto said he'd go to FOB Gunslinger or the Green Zone CSH.

Hildebrandt called the TOC and said to the BC that the men had to get out of there. The decision was made. Major Tanguy went over the radio and told Brandon to go to Gunslinger.

The two platoons limped to the 3-153 FOB without further contact. After Blackhawks medevaced the wounded, Boggs learned that 2nd Platoon had stopped in the kill zone because two of their weapons had jammed. He told Lonnie Harrison and Daren Pfaender to check the weapons out.

They returned a few minutes later, extremely upset. Pfaender, who was easily the best gunner in the battalion and had won numerous marksmanship awards back in Oregon, told Boggs, "The fucking Mark 19's down because it doesn't have any grease on it."

The MK19 is a finicky weapon. It takes significant training and expertise to fire it effectively. Most army weapons use a type of lubricant called CLP. The MK19 uses a different type of grease that has a butter consistency like vanishing cream. Only certain parts of the MK19 are supposed to be treated with it, but if it is overlooked the grenade launcher simply won't fire.

Boggs reeled at the news. A few minutes later, Lonnie returned. "The 240's not oiled." The machine gun was bone-dry.

Welch and his men reached the IP station and drove into the middle of a firefight. Tim Bloom saw the IPs fighting back with vigor. This was a good development and far different from August in Zone 22. The platoon engaged as well, and in the ensuing fight took rockets and mortars. Welch took charge of the fight. The arrival of so many crew-served weapons on Charlie's Humvees tipped the balance. Within minutes, the volume of incoming decreased, and Welch told Sergeant First Class Tim Bloom to take a section out and find Roustom.

Bloom's Humvees had just departed when Lieutenant McCarty's platoon showed up at the IP station. He conferrered with Welch, then went off in search of Roustom as well. When he couldn't find him, he took his platoon to Fort Apache to repair and refit. Three of his six rigs were damaged. At least one had a leaking fuel tank.

Tim Bloom took his section out south of the IP station and drove to the nearest column of smoke. On the way, they made contact with more Sunni insurgents, and another running gunfight followed. Undeterred by the enemy, Bloom's men reached the source of the smoke and discovered it was a burning house. It had been a wild goose chase. He swung his rigs around and linked back up with Captain Welch.

While Bloom was gone, several 1st Cav Apaches arrived on station. They found Roustom's rig and reported the grid coordinates. When Tim returned, Welch passed the coordinates along to him.

He drove off in search of Roustom again. This time, he hooked up with a platoon of Bradleys from a unit across the river (probably the 1-9 Infantry). Together, they found Roustom. No insurgents remained in the area. They'd pulled out a few minutes after Ditto had broken contact, taking their dead with them.

Bloom dismounted with his medic. Together, they extinguished the fire inside the Humvee and bore the terrible task of getting Roustom out. It took about five minutes to do it. Later, when Roustom's body was returned to the States, his brother insisted on viewing it. The awful horror of that moment is simply unimaginable.

Two days later, Lieutenant Colonel Hendrickson, Major Warrington, and Lieutenant Gilman (the intel officer) met with the Adhamiya DAC chairman, vice chairman, and Laura Poitras. The BC wanted answers. The party was brought into a conference room and seated at an L-shaped table. The BC questioned the two Adhamiya leaders, whose answers proved elusive and unhelpful. The meeting continued for almost two hours and grew heated at times. The BC wanted to know who killed his men. Hashim Ibraheem Hassan said that he thought the perpetrators were locals from Adhamiya, but he made it clear he would not help the Americans track them down. Doctor Aladhadh echoed this at first, but later said the perpetrators came from outside his district. When the BC asked Aladhadh if he witnessed the attacks on Delta Company, he hesitated, looked up and to the left, then very tentatively said that he had not seen the attacks. Hendrickson asked him again. Again, Aladhadh hesitated before answering. Every officer in the room concluded Aladhadh was lying. He then stated that he had seen an attack two-and-a-half months earlier.

The BC turned to Laura Poitras and asked her if she had seen and filmed the attack on his men. Ditto's platoon had reported seeing windows taped around Adhamiya, a sure sign that the local civilians knew of the ambushes in advance. The fact that the shops were all secured, gates were locked, and nobody was out on the streets that morning also strongly indicated the locals had foreknowledge of the engagements. The BC and Major Warrington wanted to know if Poitras had advance knowledge of the attacks. It stood to reason that she did, because she was living with Doctor Aladhadh's family in the middle of one of the kill zones on Route New York.

If she had advance knowledge, she did not call and warn the battalion. Major Warrington had given her his contact information. She had the ability to report the pending attacks to her fellow countrymen. She did not do this. How much did she know in advance? The BC wanted to find out.

All through the meeting, she had looked extremely uncomfortable. Now, Warrington and the BC thought she looked terrified. Lieutenant Gilman saw her lips begin to quiver. She struggled to respond. When she did answer, her lower lip seized up and what was probably intended to be a "no" came out more like a nervous, slurring grunt. The Volunteers took that as a denial. But before the BC could press the issue, Hassan interrupted him and demanded reimbursement for his car, which he said had been destroyed in the fighting.

Poitras forgotten, the BC slammed his hand on the table and shouted, "You have a fucking lot of nerve coming in here and saying that. We already paid that price, and it was in blood."

Dead silence. The BC was so angry he left the room. The meeting ended. Poitras and the two DAC leaders were escorted out of the building and past two soldiers from Ditto's platoon. They identified her as the woman on the roof.

They had also initially misidentified her in a photograph found on the Internet that showed her with an African-American woman. They picked the African-American woman first. Both then changed their minds. Based on that uncertainty, Lieutenant Colonel Hendrickson gave Poitras the benefit of the doubt. If the ID had been 100 percent positive, Laura Poitras' fate would have been sealed. The BC would have detained her on the spot, and she would have faced a raft of charges.

She left Patrol Base Volunteer that afternoon as a free woman. She never returned to the base, and none of the Volunteers ever saw her again. In 2006, she released a documentary called *My Country, My Country,* which was based on her experiences inside Iraq and Adhamiya. Doctor Aladhadh and his family featured prominently in it.

In January 2006, Laura Poitras admitted in an e-mail to the author of this book that she had been filming on the roof that morning.

Summing up his feelings one Volunteer later said, "I hope she's dead in some hole right now."

SIXTY-FIVE

THE INK-STAINED FINGER

The deployment drew to a close. In those final months, Baghdad had become much quieter. Al Sadr and the Mahdi licked their wounds. The Sunni insurgents had been thrashed in the Anbar Province and were trying to regroup. Between the Battles of Najaf and Fallujah, plus the suppression of the two uprisings, any hope the enemy had at creating a national, unified resistance had been lost. It was the most significant accomplishment of OIF II, and the Volunteers could justly take pride in their role in it.

From this point on, the Sunni insurgency and the Shia militias would find themselves at odds. Yet, the failure to unify the resistance created new problems that the Americans would have to deal with in OIF III, IV, and V. As of mid-2006, Al Sadr's militia had become one of the key players in the sectarian violence that gripped Baghdad earlier in the year.

That couldn't be foreseen in January '04. Real progress was being made, even in places like Sadr City. Alpha Company and Captain Eric Riley took advantage of the relative tranquility to reach out to one of the communities in Zone 22. Riley became personal friends with the leadership there, and just before they left, the Volunteers helped initiate several civil affairs projects in this neighborhood that only a few months ago had been shooting at them.

Though Sheik Majeid's vision of a complete Iraqi-American partnership was never realized in Sheik Umar, some progress had been made in the wake of his death. The streets looked better. Much of the garbage had been cleared out. Water and sewer projects had been initiated. Thanks to the Majeid's memory, his people benefited from 2-162's presence.

Trouble still lingered. Down toward the river, a hostile cell moved into AO Volunteer in early '05. These insurgents launched grenade attacks on Bradleys and laid IEDs again. Sergeant Michael Creech, a bespectacled Eugene resident, was wounded in one such IED attack and was among the last of the Oregonians to be medically evacuated from Iraq. Ezelle later ran into these insurgents, who sprayed one of his patrols with AK fire before darting away.

In late January, a sniper killed an engineer from the 39th Brigade. Rebekah-mae Bruns had been friends with him and had just spent a week with his unit. She was part of the group of Volunteers who responded to the incident in northeast Baghdad. Arriving just after he'd been removed, she went with a group of soldiers to clear a nearby building. She slipped on the stairwell and fell to the first floor. The mishap compressed or cracked several of her vertebrae.

She hid the injury from the Joes. In utter agony, she soldiered up and continued to search for stories out beyond the wire. Not long after, she went out with a 39th Brigade unit and got into another firefight. A bullet pinged off her Humvee only inches from her head.

Election time came. In the intel shop, Pete Salerno kept receiving warnings that the insurgents were planning an apocalyptic campaign of destruction across Iraq. The battalion's force swelled as units surged into Baghdad to control the streets so the people could vote for the first time in their lives in a free election. The Volunteers guarded ballots, covered down on the polling sites, and prepared for the worst.

Election Day came without a wave of terror. The people of Rusapha flowed into the streets wearing their finest clothes. They voted en masse as families and neighborhoods. As they left the polls, they proudly held up their ink-stained fingers. Something good started here. It gave the country momentum. And it gave the Joes a reason for everything they had endured. Election Day became redemption to them, proof that their time in Iraq had not been in vain. The pain, the losses, the lost brothers: this moment validated everything as Iraqis took control of their own fate. It was a glorious capstone to the deployment.

And yet, the battalion made history one more time. Captain Riley and Alpha Company spent February working with the marines south of Baghdad. Their patrols in the countryside resulted in numerous IED attacks; the disenfranchised Sunnis had refused to give up after the election. Between the IED incidents, an Alpha patrol discovered an enormous weapons cache hidden in a cemetery. At least 140 tons of explosives, rocket fuel, mortar rounds, RPGs, artillery shells, and mines were hidden in this location, buried layer upon layer so deep the men quit digging. When EOD blew it up, the company watched from more than a kilometer away. That wasn't far enough. The blast wave struck Alpha's veteran Joes with such intensity that it knocked some of them off their Humvees. It was one of the largest caches found during OIF II, and its destruction saved countless lives.

In early March, the battalion left Iraq and returned to Kuwait. After several weeks crammed together in a warehouse exchanging colds, the battalion flew home in three chalks.

Ezelle and 1st Platoon, Charlie, flew home on St. Patrick's Day. On the way, E. Z. began to feel nauseous. He ignored it and sucked it up. He'd see his son soon; that was what mattered. But the pain wouldn't go away. When the plane stopped in Ireland, he climbed off to go drink a green beer with his men. The BC was buying. Instead, he collapsed in the bathroom. Some of the other men found him curled up on the floor, his face wrenched with pain. But he refused to be left behind. He returned to the plane and lay down for the rest of the flight.

That night, the plane reached McChord Air Force Base in Washington. A thick crowd of press, onlookers, and family members awaited them at a Fort Lewis gymnasium. Behind the gym, the Oregonians had filled the parking lot with colorfully adorned cars and SUVs. On one window, a sign read, "Bill's

Booty Call Baby! Fort Lewis or Bust!"

Sergeant Vince Jacques waited in the crowd that night. Though still in pain—his injuries kept him on medical hold until Labor Day '05—he would not have missed this moment for anything. He stood with Julie Howell, his mom, and the rest of the Jacques clan. Nearby, Shane Ward and his parents awaited Brian's arrival. Mandy Ferguson sat in the bleachers and counted down the last seconds of her year-long ordeal. Spike had lived. They would have a life together after all.

Exhausted by their journey, the men arrived to stand in one last formation. General Pritt addressed them, as did the BC. When dismissed, chaos broke out. Wives flung themselves into their soldier's arms. Kids ran helter-skelter under-foot. Grins striped every face, but a few tears appeared on cheeks as well. Spike and Mandy found each other. It was the embrace of a lifetime, and they held each other and cried as all around them the 2-162 families celebrated this moment. It was a shared catharsis. All of the angst and tension flowed away. Relief and euphoria dominated the night.

Vinni gave Ryan a moment with Julie, but couldn't contain himself any longer. The two brothers soon were locked together in a huge bear hug. They looked like wrestling Sasquatches.

Ezelle did not make it to the gym. As he got off the plane, his pain proved so intense the battalion rushed him to Madigan Hospital, where he underwent an emergency appendectomy. Somewhere between Kuwait and Washington, E. Z.'s appendix had burst. It would have killed a lesser man, but men like Ezelle don't go out that way.

The next morning, he woke up to find Vinni standing over his bed. It was quite a switch from the last time they'd seen each other. Vinni had been barely coherent, lying in the Green Zone CSH. Now, their roles reversed, Vinni looked at his comrade-in-arms and said, "Welcome home, brother."

EPILOGUE

The summer sun seemed hot to most Oregonians that July day in 2005, but the men of 3rd Platoon, Bravo Company, barely felt it. They stood in the parking lot at Willamette National Cemetery in Portland and exchanged hugs and happy grins. They laughed, welcomed the late arrivals, and compared notes over the medications they were taking. All had scars that only time and patience can hope to heal. Today, they would confront the worst: Kenny's death.

Ken Leisten Sr. hiked up the hill. Carrying his son's assault pack, he moved into the circle of soldiers. He was one of their own, as much a member of 3rd Platoon as anyone else.

Fourteen men showed up that day. When all were present and accounted for, they caravanned to Kenny's grave site.

The procession wound through the emerald hills past row after row of veterans of the Bulge, the Death March, the Iron Triangle, and the Ie Drang Valley. Name an American battle of the twentieth century, and in this cemetery there will be a participant.

This hilly cemetery gives mute testimony to the tradition of service that stretches across the generations here in Oregon. It is a tradition few know about, but for those who understand its quiet power, it symbolizes strength and continuity. It is a reminder that this state gives more than its fair share every time Americans are flung to foreign shores.

They gathered around Kenny's grave in awkward silence and formed a circle around their fallen brother. The stillness of the moment contrasted with the beauty of the day. The high sun had chased away the shadows, giving the men a spectacular azure sky.

Ken Sr. bent over his son's grave. His gravely voice broke the silence, "I need to see my boy. I've gotta see my boy."

From his assault pack, he withdrew two photos of his son. Both showed him in his National Guard uniform. In one, he wore his full battle rattle. A broad grin stretched across his youthful face. In the other, Ken stood at attention and tried his best to look serious in his Class A's. He almost pulled it off. But a close look at his eyes showed the reckless passion that inhabited him. It was that reckless passion that drove him to Iraq, and ultimately to this early grave. A year before, he was twenty-four days past his twentieth birthday.

In Iraq, he became a man. He served with the spirit of a mule, infused with a stubborn refusal to let the army completely erase his individuality. He stood beside his brothers and fought for them with devotion that earned lasting respect.

Though he died a man, he never had the chance to be an *adult*. He was denied those things that define the average American adulthood: a family, house, job, and someone to love.

It is true that he had many women in his short life. It is also true that abiding love eluded him. He died without a mate, without the chance to know the peace of hearing her soft breathing at night on the pillow next to his.

The men moved to Kenny's headstone to leave offerings for their brother. Two tins of Copenhagen chewing tobacco were laid atop the marker. A big wad of Redman soon followed. Vinni stepped forward and dropped two rounds, a 7.62 and a 223, next to the Redman.

They passed around a bottle of Wild Turkey Rare Breed. Each man took a swig and handed it along while others took dips from the Redman. Pretty soon, everyone was either drinking or spitting, toasting Kenny with irreverent reverence as only soldiers can do.

And then the stories came. Kenny Sr. broke the ice and told how it had just been he and his son for so many years. They were a team, a package deal. Take them or leave them, they were not separable. He laughed as he remembered Kenny catching a fly ball in Little League when he was nine years old. Sports were not for him. Kenny was the anti-jock, so this momentary fame on the baseball field caught him by surprise. For a while, the memory of that catch propelled him to pursue the game, but the luster soon faded and he went in other directions.

The 3rd Platoon stories flowed next. One by one, the men told their favorite stories about Kenny. The men bellowed with laughter as they remembered their young stud. Nobody had ever seen a guy take such huge chews as Kenny could. Half his mouth would be full of tobacco, and at Hood he and his roomie had tried to fill a two-liter bottle with chaw. They recalled how he'd play spades for hours on end, spitting into that bottle, then passing it around. That cut everyone up.

Here and there, a serious story was told. Vinni talked about how Kenny worked his magic on the fussy radios in their Humvees. He was a natural with electronic gadgets. That story prompted several more that highlighted Kenny's intelligence. John Martin noted that despite his youth, Kenny could learn things so quickly he made the others look bad. His natural intelligence caused them all to work harder to keep up with him. And they were a better platoon for it.

Ken Sr. listened intently, full of pride for his boy. He spoke only of his son in the present tense, as if by doing so fate would somehow be cheated. Kenny was not gone forever, his spirit walked with his father. They were still the inseparable pair. Then, Ken Sr. went silent for a moment. His chin fell on his chest, and in a chilling monotone he spoke of how the army had just sent him more cremated remains. "They sent me his foot and some teeth in a box."

The men looked stricken and stared hard at Kenny's grave, lost in grief.

Finally, Vinni stepped forward to pour some Wild Turkey into the grass at the base of his marker.

"God took Kenny for a reason," one of Vinni's men said in a hollow voice. "What that reason was, we'll never know."

"He probably needed some angels corrupted."

Lurid descriptions of Kenny befouling the purity of heaven's residents returned levity to the scene. That led to further stories of Hood and how Kenny had spent his last leave in Las Vegas, where he blazed through six grand in one grand salute to excess. He came back ready for war, his hell-raising sated at least for the time being.

Grief masked by humor and light memories cloaked the deeper emotions of the moment. Beneath the surface, the men ached with loss and guilt. From time to time, it boiled to the surface and opened a window to what really was going on that day within each man's heart. Then somebody would lighten the mood again with another funny anecdote. The wound left by Kenny's death was still raw. Getting toward the center of that pain made every one uncomfortable. Soldiers—men—fear that center most of all.

And then John Martin mentioned how nice it would have been to be able to read the 91st Psalm for Kenny. Vinni brightened and left the circle to return to the government van he and Tommy Houston had driven up from the Corvallis armory that morning.

Vinni never leaves the house without his laminated copy of the 91st Psalm. He loped after it, his men noticing his gait remained tainted with a limp. Though he'd never complain, though he'd never think to tell anyone of his pain, the fact was Vinni still suffered. He took elevators now instead of the stairs to spare his knee. He jogged every damn day so that he could pass the physical and get off Med Hold, but a lesser man would never have withstood the agony each run inflicted. Once, he dislocated his hip on a run and had to walk several miles back to the armory. "At best," he once remarked of the pain, "it's tolerable." He'd tolerate it, too. No way was the army going to kick him out.

He returned to the group and in a husky voice peppered with emotion, he carefully read the words that had bonded his men forever during those months in Iraq.

> A thousand shall fall at thy side, and ten thousand at thy right hand;
>   but it shall not come nigh thee.
> Only with thine eyes shalt thou behold and see the reward of the
>   wicked.
> Because thou hast made the Lord, which is my refuge, even the most
>   High, thy habitation;
> There shall no evil befall thee, neither shall any plague come nigh thy
>   dwelling.

The last words carried over the men, who stood with bowed heads and folded hands. Reverence and irreverence dwell deep within these soldiers. It defines them, this curious oxymoron. They are hard-drinking, hard-living hooligans. They are steadfast, loyal soldiers. Their humor is never muddied with good taste or the boundaries of propriety. They are devout in their personal relationship with God. They take nothing seriously. Deep within, in their most honest moments, they all know how easily hurt they all can be. Men who are idealists at their core will always try to hide that vulnerability with shields of laughter and bawdiness. They are contrasts of defenses and defenselessness. They are men with wounds yet unhealed.

Vinni tried to be tough for his Joes. Everyone was hurting as those final words of the 91st Psalm were spoken, but Vinni was their leader. He could not break. He wavered, turned away, and walked from the circle. A few feet away he stopped, struggling to contain himself, though the seas that raged within him mirrored the experience of every man there. His eyes squeezed shut, his head down, he forced control.

He returned, face red, eyes hardened. "We'll meet here again, noon next year." Around the circle, heads nodded. This was their sacred bond. Kenny would not be forgotten.

A day later, twenty miles west of the martyrs in the Willamette National Cemetery, a different ceremony took place. Spike Olsen and Mandy Ferguson finally tied the knot.

They could not have picked a more tranquil spot. Bridal Veil, Oregon, is legendary among those in the Northwest predisposed to matrimony. Set high above the Columbia Gorge, hidden among the tall firs, the wedding took place at the edge of a small mountain lake. Shane Ward, now recovered from his wounds and busy training Rangers at Benning, had flown in to stand up for Spike. On Mandy's side, her seven attendants could have stepped straight from the finals of a beauty pageant. As they arrived, the young single men in the audience ogled and dreamed while the married old ones lamented the passage of years and cursed their fate. In fact, the entire wedding party seemed taken from the pages of *Cosmopolitan* and *GQ*.

The ceremony was short and full of spirit and smiles. Mandy, deeply tanned, smiled with teeth as white as her dress. As she walked down the aisle, she fairly fluttered with excitement and joy. All those months of uncertainty, all those sleepless nights and the tears by the side of the road—this moment drove those demons out once and for all. Their time to be together had finally come.

Spike looked at his bride and his heart practically exploded. Later, some of the guests talked about that look, and how it seemed like all the pressure, the angst, and the near-misses with death were laid to rest right there. He had Mandy now, and that set his world in balance. Harmony, passion, and a life with this extraordinary woman would at last be his.

They kissed; the ceremony ended. The guests adjourned to the buffet on the other side of the lake. Somebody dropped baby booties next to Spike's dinner plate, the suggestion lewd and obvious. Laughter echoed through the trees as the sky turned crimson with the most beautiful of nature's gifts to Oregon: a sunset over the Gorge.

The drinks flowed, the party grew raucous. It was time to dance. Spike and Mandy went first, of course, and they held each other and swayed on the dance floor as a hundred friends and family looked on. Nearby, Shane stood with Ron and Kelly Clement.

Mandy danced with her dad next. The old principal who wrought terror on generations of high-school students held nothing back. As he held his little girl, all grown up to everyone but him now, the familiar strains of "Stand by Me" filled the evening. "Come on everyone!" he bellowed. "Sing!"

And a hundred voices rose as one.

"No I won't . . . be afraid . . . "

Not a guest remained silent. They all knew the words. Loyalty defines the core of who these people are.

Things just plain got silly from there on out. The country boys went crazy as the DJ spun "Save a Horse, Ride a Cowboy." The dance floor was filled with Bravo Company soldiers, hip-bumping and foot-pounding their way through the song.

A good time was had by all. This included Sweety Petey Peterson, who stumbled from group to group in his usher's outfit, looking terribly incongruous in a gray suit, vest, and tie, topped off with a massive black cowboy hat. He'd finally gotten himself a girlfriend, and he wanted everyone to know that Spike's teachings had served him well.

"I was Spike's Padawan!" he proclaimed. "But now I am mightier than Darth Vader!"

Ron Clement stole his cowboy hat, and the young Padawan-turned-master-of-the-force scampered off to retrieve it.

Long into the night, the wedding party rocked. The sky turned dark, and then black. Near the dance floor, some couples strolled up a low ridge and discovered they could see the lights of Troutdale, the easternmost Portland suburb, off in the distance. Some settled into chairs to drink and talk. Others slipped into the darkness for more attentive things.

Ron and Kelly Clement blew everyone off the dance floor with their sultry moves. Kelly would sway her hips, flip her dress, and swing around her husband, whose lusty grin threatened to split his face in half horizontally. At one point, Kelly slid around and pressed her back into Ron's chest, and they held each other in a semi-cuddled embrace as they moved in time with the music.

In the center of it all, Mandy and Spike had a ball. They danced and hammed things up with the bouquet toss and the slinging of the garter. They covered each other with frosting as they cut the cake. Shane stepped forward at one point and kissed Spike on both cheeks, which prompted another guest to grab Shane's butt and announce he was ready for some action as well.

The forest rocked until midnight. Then, couple by couple, the guests departed. As the last ones left, Spike and Mandy walked through the remains of the party. They snuggled by the lake, the stars their only audience now. It was time to start a new life, as far removed from the horrors of June 13, Najaf, and Fallujah as possible. Though those memories will always linger in Spike, he was one of the lucky ones. He cheated death. He never lost faith. When it all ended, he came home to love.

Together, they turned from the lake's empty shore and headed into the night. Perhaps, someday those baby booties will be needed.

POSTSCRIPT

THE REFLECTION
IN THE MIRROR

On the Friday before Labor Day '05, the Oregon National Guard was mobilized for service in the wake of Hurricane Katrina. I found out when I sat down to interview Command Sergeant Major Conley in Salem. As soon as he told me where the brigade was heading, I asked to go along. He made that happen, and my life changed forever.

Bravo Company, 2-162, adopted me. Captain San Miguel and First Sergeant Jackola spearheaded getting my paperwork signed so I could officially go as an embedded historian. Tommy Houston, ever the scrounger, scored me a pair of boots, some wool socks, a canteen, and other gear. Sergeant Young, Bravo's supply guru, gave me Lieutenant Metzdorff's IBA. Anything else I needed, he made sure ended up in my ruck.

Vinni, who had come off medical hold the day of the alert order, made sure my skull was protected. He gave me one of his helmets and an extra poncho liner (one of the greatest inventions ever). I left my writing desk behind and climbed into a bus that took 365 combat veterans into the heart of a national tragedy.

We arrived at night, a week after the levees broke. Northeast New Orleans and the 9th Ward became the brigade's AO. Though the 2-162 vets had been home only six months, they left their families behind yet again to answer the call to duty. As Spike Olsen, married all of three weeks, put it, "I am so fucking sick of goodbyes."

For Lieutenant Colonel Hendrickson, this would be his last hurrah as the BC. He'd been scheduled to turn over command to Major Tanguy in mid-September, but the new deployment had put that on hold.

We drove through New Orleans in the dead of night in commandeered city buses. Had the authorities only gathered up the municipal buses that had been abandoned all over town with the keys still in them and tanks full of fuel, thousands of people could have been evacuated from the Convention Center and the Superdome. Instead, they were left for us to find and use. The battalion owed its mobility to these castaway rigs.

Loaded with gear, stuffed with troops, we convoyed through the city. It was an eerie journey no one present will ever forget. Broken windows, trash, looted buildings, overturned cars, and windblown debris littered the landscape. We passed a Tower Records, whose purplish neon sign still glowed in the darkness. A block up from it, we saw our first corpse lying on a street corner in a body bag, suffused with purple shadows cast by the neon sign. A few blocks farther, Joel

Stinemann and I peered out the rear doors of our bus to see a man casually smoking a cigarette. He was standing on the sidewalk as if he had not a care in the world. Never mind the fact that he was the only living human we saw through this entire drive. Never mind that in a doorway not ten feet away lay two corpses clutched in a macabre embrace. Apparently, the smoker had grown used to the smell of rotting human flesh, something I can't say happened to me. It was the first of many bizarre moments in New Orleans.

In the middle of the city, our convoy stopped. The drivers had learned other vehicles had been shot at in this neighborhood, and they were loath to continue. We sat for nearly an hour before they reluctantly agreed to move.

Stiney and I engaged in a philosophical discussion about religion even as we studied the destruction and despair within our limited range of view. It seemed as if we'd driven straight on to the set of some creepy, post-apocalyptic drive-in flick, only there would be no escape after ninety minutes of good, clean terror. We were stuck in a nightmare.

Late that night, we moved into the New Orleans Baptist Seminary. Bravo Company set up camp along the covered walkways of the school's music building. Tommy Houston took 3rd Platoon and established it on the steps of the school chapel. Charlie Company and Captain Welch took the walkways around the school cafeteria. The battalion staff moved into the student union.

The next morning, with the temperature hovering near a hundred degrees with about as much humidity as anyone had ever experienced, the men pulled on their gear and patrolled the Orleans Parish. What we found that first day was more than a ruined city. It was more than receding floodwaters and dead fish on the freeways. We found a city that had torn itself apart. Each step became a journey of reflection on the nature of humanity, on the character of our fellow Americans. It was a raw, unflinching study, and the answers we gleaned shook many of us to the core. Americans take pride in being different from the rest of the world. We think we're better human beings with a better system of government and judicious laws that protect the weak. When we see scenes of panic during overseas calamities, Americans smugly think, *Well, those poor people. Thank God that can't happen here.*

The first patrol in New Orleans knocked the smugness out of us. We learned not only can it happen here, but it did. When the levees broke, the neighborhoods in north central and northeast New Orleans came unglued. We waded into the aftermath of an orgy of violence and looting. Two blocks from the seminary, we found a gas station and meat market that could have been a set from *Night of the Living Dead*. A van sat derelict at the pumps, its doors opened and its contents strewn all over the ground. Two or three other cars also sat abandoned, their trunks and hoods open, batteries looted. Lying in a pool of gelatinized blood by the pump island was a man with dreadlocks and no face. It had been blown off, probably by a shotgun.

I stood twenty feet or so from this corpse, which somebody had tried to cover with a piece of canvas. It was bloated and maggot-infested, and the stench wafting from it will never leave my memory. Ken Jackola tapped my shoulder and warned me, "If you get too close, you'll step in all that blood, and it's congealed like Jell-O. You'll slip in it and fall. Then you'll puke, and you'll stink of rotting flesh and vomit. Then nobody'll want to be around you."

It was a handy tidbit of advice; though not one I had ever imagined I'd need. Moments later, Ken entered the meat market and the reek of rotting flesh nearly overcame this two-war veteran. He gagged just as I took a photo of him. Later, the battalion discovered two more corpses in the back room of the meat market. Only Ken Jackola could have gone in there without losing the MREs we'd eaten for breakfast.

Across the street sat a devastated Winn-Dixie. It seemed all the anger and frustration and selfishness resident in the community exploded in one burst of violence and looting inside this supermarket.

The interior doors had been smashed to splinters. Broken eggs, wrecked displays, boxes, and even a shattered scooter for disabled shoppers cluttered the front entryway.

Inside, it looked like a herd of elephants had run amok. The store's generator was still running when we first stepped inside, but the looting had destroyed the refrigeration units. The stench of rotting meat and fish was almost unbearable. Amid the few remaining working lights, we could see bottled water, baby food, diapers, batteries, and other survival supplies still stocked in abundance on the store shelves. What had been stolen during all this destruction? Liquor, cigarettes, and prescription drugs. We later found dozens of drug vials in bags abandoned outside behind a dumpster sitting in the middle of Gentilly Boulevard.

The realization of what had been looted turned everyone's stomachs. This wasn't looting for survival, it was looting for self-gratification. They'd picked through the corpse of their own city like the crows we later saw pulling strips of flesh off the bodies in the streets.

I followed the BC into a shattered minimall that had endured some flooding. Lieutenant Colonel Hendrickson led the way past a toy kiosk stripped of every item. We peered inside a clothing store that had not a rack left intact. I stepped over a wedding veil somebody had dropped in the hallway in a hasty exit from that store. A sign saying "We Carry Gold Jewelry" in one store was its death sentence as the chaos unfolded. Nothing remained in it. At the end of the mall, another grocery store stood looted and demolished.

Later explorations uncovered a furniture store totally destroyed. What could not be stolen was simply smashed. In another surreal incident, the men found a ruined bank full of parakeets, happily chirping away.

Nearby, the Footlocker had been totally pillaged. We found new shoes dropped hither and thither all over the neighborhood. A wig store in the same complex had also been picked clean. On a later patrol, I saw a lump next to a curb and thought it was a human head. It turned out to be one of the wigs, dropped by a fleeing looter.

The Volunteers wanted blood for this. That some people capitalized on the tragedy made them angry. They wanted to find those responsible and, quite frankly, beat the ever-loving shit out of them. I would have been right there with them. We were ashamed at what we saw, and it made us take a hard look at our fellow Americans and who we really are. Nobody liked the answers our eyes provided.

We came across a pillaged postal truck. It had been used to haul all sorts of random loot until it broke down on the freeway. The occupants abandoned it, but not until spray-painting, "Fuck the City White Bitches—Black Power" on the side.

As the brigade came in contact with the New Orleans police, the Oregonians got a firsthand look at the level of racism resident in the community. Lieutenant Brandon Ditto listened as white cops casually used the word *nigger* in their conversations. The word grated on Ditto like nails on a chalkboard.

Other stories of the police flowed in. Major Warrington, who went out with 1-162, sat in a meeting with one of the few precinct captains in the city. A twenty-year veteran of the force, he was in no mood to sugarcoat the situation. "Five years ago, we could have survived this. Not now. Our average officer has four years' worth of experience." He continued on, telling the Oregonians not to trust his officers. The local gangs had penetrated his department. They were dangerous men with their own agendas, not true peace officers. When patrolling with the NOPD officers still remaining on the job, the soldiers of 1-162 found only a handful to be reliable and earnest in their desire to help their city. It was disgraceful, but at least their commander was honest enough to give an accurate picture for the 1-162's staff.

To the north, across a wide swath of flooded cityscape, 2-162 received little to no support from the local police. In fact, the NOPD became the most dangerous factor the men faced on patrol. On September 12, Tommy Houston led a patrol into a poverty-stricken neighborhood called the "Indian Village." While talking with one of the few holdouts in the area, six shots rang out. Two passed fairly close overhead. The men instantly ran to the sound of the gunfire. Running in full gear in the dreadful heat, they came to a railroad embankment near Gentilly Road. There, they found a group of police officers standing near a fire. Houston sent men to investigate, and the police told them they'd started the fire to burn cans of sausages, which exploded. The story seemed far fetched, and later, Vinni's platoon discovered a revolver in the ashes of the fire. The police had thrown a loaded handgun into a bonfire. The rounds cooked off into a residential neighborhood. What sort of professional law enforcement officers do this sort of thing? Not good ones.

Not long afterward, the BC confronted a group of Louisiana Guardsmen and NOPD who were trying to arrest the owner of a pawn shop who had returned to examine the condition of his business. Hendrickson would not allow them to detain the man, who had done absolutely nothing wrong. The situation grew intense, and disrespect for the Oregon colonel mushroomed into outright defiance. Bill Woodke, who had served as Captain San Miguel's gunner in Iraq and was now part of the BC's personal security detail, grew concerned that the scene might grow violent. The BC kept his cool and handled the situation with professionalism. Woodke watched as one of the NOPD officers reached for his holster. Without hesitating, Bill stuck the barrel of his M4 into the man's ribcage and said, "You really don't want to do that."

After these and other encounters, the Oregonians had little respect for what was left of local law enforcement. Many of the men concluded that much of the disaster could be attributed to the failure of the police department to hold things together. It seemed to the Volunteers that instead of fighting for the community, many of the police they encountered had been feasting off the corpse of it, just like the other looters.

At night, the men returned to the seminary to sleep on the ground or in cots. Mosquitoes plagued them. Chiggers left angry red welts on their bodies. They lived among toads and cockroaches and had little more than MREs to eat. It was rugged and depressing. The men missed home and some knew that this deployment had finished off their marriages. Some would come home to empty houses and eviction notices. Yet, every morning they rose, strapped on their gear, and went out to try and help this dying city.

And that is where I learned what *honor* really means. These men had so much to lose by being there away from home, new jobs, their children. Yet they never shirked their duty. They went out and patrolled, searched neighborhoods for survivors, and worked twenty-hour days without letting up.

Good came of that work ethic. Early in the deployment, Specialist Jim Schmorde, one of the scout platoon's snipers, pulled off an amazing rescue. He struck up a conversation with four Portland, Oregon, firefighters who had used their vacation time to go down to New Orleans and save lives. Hendrickson adopted them, and they lived in the battalion TOC. The firefighters worried that the exterior-only house-to-house searches the battalion was authorized to conduct would miss those survivors unable to shout for help. That gave Schmorde an idea. He went out to some high ground with his thermal optics and scanned our AO for heat signatures. He found one not two blocks away. Later that night Tyson Bumgardner led a patrol up a set of railroad tracks to get a better look. Sure enough, somebody was alive in an otherwise dead neighborhood.

The next morning, the firefighters set out in a boat and found an eighty-seven-year-old woman. She'd been trapped in her house for ten days by the floodwaters, which had swollen her doors and windows so badly she could not open them to call for help.

Without Jim, she would have died.

Later that day, Sean Davis led a patrol that encountered one of the few hold-outs in the area. Her name was Mimi Bartholomew. She'd spent her entire life in the Indian Village and lived in the house she was born in some forty-four years before we met her. Sean tried to get her to leave, but she refused. When the patrol learned she was diabetic, they became adamant. She dug her heels in and would not even let anyone examine her.

Mimi had survived the levee breaks by standing on a crate on her toilet. When we found her, she was running out of food, water, and insulin. At the time, the battalion had orders not to assist holdouts by giving them basic supplies. The men ignored this and brought Mimi MREs, cat food for her animals, and water. Will Coker, one of the brigade's medics, was the first to make a breakthrough with her. Though she was a poor, white Southern woman and Will was an educated Northern African American, the two bonded within minutes of meeting. She let him check her blood sugar, and after that he made a point of visiting her every day. I went with him several times and always marveled at his gentle manner.

Later that day, I met Gretel Jugl. One of Gretel's fellow volunteers had been bitten by a dog, and she asked Will for help in treating the wound. It was a chance encounter that profoundly affected us both.

Gretel was a New Yorker, an ER nurse who had just started the physician's assistant program at Adelphi University when Hurricane Katrina struck New Orleans. She worked a fourteen-hour shift at her hospital, then packed up and drove for Louisiana. As she left New York, her employer told her she'd lose her job if she went to New Orleans. Adelphi University refused to hold her slot open. She didn't care. She left her daughter with her family and drove straight through to go help.

She ended up at a makeshift hospital set up in the LSU basketball arena. Hundreds of patients poured through the doors. Sick and dying people were her stock and trade, and she worked tirelessly for two weeks taking care of them.

Once, while taking a rare break, a sick man showed up on the street in front of the arena. Before she could go help him, the media showed up. A cameraman filmed the man as he staggered forward, and then fell to the pavement. Gretel ran to his assistance. The cameraman complained that she had ruined his shot.

"Why don't you help?" she asked the cameraman.

"It's not my job," he replied.

"You're human. Of course, it's your job."

One day, a wave of nursing home survivors came through the doors. They had been left to die in their beds by their care providers. They came in with no names, no personal information. Instead, their care providers had printed their medical conditions on their shirts. In some cases, all Gretel saw was DNR, which means do not resuscitate.

Later, she volunteered to help evacuate people. In doing so, she saw hundreds of starving pets being left behind. She got on the Internet and called for volunteers. She organized them and saved countless animals after the last humans had been evacuated.

I stood next to her as she broke down and told me her story. Her courage and convictions left me in awe. How many people give up their career and their education to go save human lives? After patrolling through the darkest side of human nature, Gretel Jugl's story was nothing short of redemption to me. When she finished, I gave her a long embrace, the black, reeking floodwaters lapping nearby.

She was the most noble human being I've ever met.

The next day, Staff Sergeant Jason Obersinner rescued a dying orange kitten from a flooded motel. He handed the critter to me and I started to carry it back to the patrol bus. When I reached the parking lot, I ran into Mark Martin. Mark and his wife, Shannon, own Pet Supplies Plus in Athens, Georgia. On their own, they had driven to New Orleans to save animals. The BC, who is a dog-lover, recognized Mark was a sincere citizen with the power to do some good. He protected Mark and gave him supplies. We developed a great working relationship with him, and the battalion tipped him off to trapped animals whenever possible. I asked Mark if he could get the orange kitten to me when I got home. He promised to make it happen.

Later that day, Jason Obersinner was injured by glass. Doc Smith expertly bandaged him, then got him into a field ambulance for the ride to Belle Chase Hospital. Jason had surgery later that night; he had a torn tendon in his arm. He was subsequently returned to Oregon to recover.

A few days later, on September 13, I rode with Vinni, Spike, and Michael Johnson on a night patrol in one of the city buses. Come dawn, we dismounted behind a pawn shop. Somebody realized it was the anniversary of Weisenberg's and Isenberg's deaths. There, as the sun rose over this desolate city, Spike shared his memories of June 13. Vinni went next. Michael Johnson, who rarely says more than a few words at a time, talked about being blown out of the turret exactly a year ago that day. He was so sore he could hardly walk, but he was back patrolling with his platoon within days.

Meeting men like Johnson made New Orleans the epochal moment of my life. I lived on the ground with them, learned their stories, and learned to love them. And, of course, I learned to retaliate after they unleashed their devilish imaginations on me. Day one in the city and Matt Zedwick brought me a lovely bouquet of dead insects. They ended up in Vinni's BDUs. A toad made the rounds in several cots. Vinni nailed me good by pouring warm water on my crotch while I catnapped at the end of a patrol. I didn't even notice until we got off the patrol bus.

Later, Congresswoman Darlene Hooley arrived with other state officials for a tour of our base. Major General Raymond F. Rees, the new Oregon adjutant general, served as their escort. I'd been out with Bravo all day and returned to my patch of walkway for a quick nap before writing up the day's events. To be honest, I was trying to avoid the VIPs, who were over at the battalion TOC. I figured if anyone in authority knew an almost middle-aged, overweight, desk-bound historian was out patrolling with an infantry company, they'd want to get rid of me.

I awoke to Vinni's drill-sergeant voice, "On your feet, the general's here!"

Not sure of what to do, but positive lying on my butt in front of all these distinguished guests was not the way to go, I got up. The rest of the men stood rigidly at attention, waiting for the VIPs. I bent down to grab my glasses, only to discover I was surrounded by the most vile porno magazines I'd ever seen. Spread-eagled women abounded. I thought I saw a goat in one scene. I was horrified. Darlene Hooley knows me. I couldn't be seen like this. Frantically, I started to gather them up. The entire company howled. Vinni had set me up.

I still owe him for that one.

The days wore on. We patrolled down to Dillard University and then into the St. Bernard Housing Projects where a sniper was still shooting at firefighters. We found nothing but the ruins of so many lives. The scale of the devastation came to numb us. For me, the numbness was pierced only once when we came across an NOPD officer and his wife inspecting the wreckage of their house. Both were sobbing as they looked upon their shattered home. All of us were touched and saddened to see that they had lost everything.

Three weeks later, I was home. A small kernel of the battalion stayed in Louisiana for Hurricane Rita. They drove from Alexandria south to Lake Charles in open-backed five-ton trucks and doorless Humvees through the hurricane on Saturday the 24th. Then they assisted in rescue and security operations in various communities around Lake Charles. By the end of the month, the entire battalion returned to Oregon.

I returned with the bulk of Bravo and Charlie companies. When we reached Portland, the men assembled in formation and were formally greeted by Colonel Caldwell. He went to each man and gave him a campaign ribbon for his service.

I was very emotional at that moment. I was fighting tears through the entire formation. I didn't want to leave Louisiana. Now I didn't want to leave the company. These men had become friends; some had become brothers.

Right then, Vinni turned to me and said, "Here, John, you earned this."

In his hand he held a campaign ribbon.

Composure gone, I took this unique and priceless gift. Sure, it was a ten-cent chunk of fabric. But I wouldn't trade it for a mint, for the meaning was clear. It was a gift of respect.

The bodies, the sordid end of New Orleans, and all the lessons I learned rolled around in my mind and dreams for weeks after we returned home. At night, I'd sleep talk and tell my wife I needed to know when the next patrol was leaving. I didn't want to miss it. My subconscious still wanted to be where the story was: out there exploring the city with the men.

One day I was with 127 best friends. The next, I was in my office, alone. I couldn't work. I couldn't focus. Every time I returned to the armories to continue interviewing the men, I'd feel reborn. When I left at the end of the day, the loneliness returned.

I went to see a counselor, who assured me this was all a natural result of the experience of New Orleans. That was comforting, but it didn't ease the sense of isolation I felt. I was shut off, closeted away in my office, while my friends got ready for other adventures. It was almost unbearable.

And then, Mark Martin came through with his promise. He and his wife saved the little orange kitten. In mid-October, he arrived at Portland airport with a German shepherd pup Vinni had saved on another patrol. Vinni gave the pup to Andy Hellman, and for the next six months the dog was a fixture at the Corvallis armory.

I named the cat Volunteers, and he became my shadow. The local restaurants feed him; the kids at Independence Elementary School adore him. He's sat perched on laps as I've interviewed the Joes. He is lying beside me as I type these final words. Volunteers eased the loneliness for me and pulled me out of my own spiral.

Jason Obsersinner volunteered for an Iraq deployment a month after returning home with his injured arm. He went over as a replacement to Charlie 1-184, California National Guard. He got back just in time for the birth of his son in early '06.

And that is the story of my friends, my neighbors, and my brothers. As I write this, the battalion has experienced a bit of a baby boom. Vinni and Rhonda had twins in January. A month later, Ryan and Julie welcomed their first, a boy, into the world. Marty Theurer is a father now, too. So is Doug Jackson. And Captain Jack's blood line will now endure for another generation. Captain Welch and Gina are pregnant and due any day. There are many others, each one a celebration of life.

The men returned from the two deployments and picked up their lives as best they could. Some have had a rough time. There were lots of divorces. Some of the men have spiraled into drug or alcohol abuse. Some struggle with post-traumatic stress disorder every day. A few Volunteers have attempted suicide, but their brothers have moved swiftly to take care of them. They've learned that the war didn't end at the Iraqi border; it just changed form. They're still fighting, still taking care of one another.

Tyson Bumgardner is in flight school to become a commercial pilot. Brandon Ditto is now a member of the Salem police force. Kris Haney went back to school. Scott Hildebrandt works ful-time for the guard (AGR) in Salem. Ezelle returned to Eugene and is still an AGR. Tim Bloom is now Charlie Company's first sergeant. Eugene can be a tough town for Iraq vets. Some have been heckled and ridiculed. A Charlie Company vet was called a "baby killer," a taunt that caused a bar fight and resulted in the soldier being slashed with a knife.

Rebekah-mae Bruns spent eight months living in a motel outside of Ft. Lewis while in the limbo of medical hold for her back. She went through surgery and is okay now. She's working on her master's degree and wants to teach special-needs children. She made it a personal mission to get one of the battalion's Iraqi interpreters to Oregon. Against the odds, she succeeded, and the interpreter will be going to school at Portland State in the fall of '06.

Doug Jackson is back in southern Oregon working as an AGR in 1-186. Phil Disney is a recruiter in Coos Bay. Shannon Compton runs the show at the Roseburg armory.

In eastern Oregon, Luke Wilson has made quite a splash. He graced the cover of *Field & Stream* and hunts regularly. He works with Vinni and Pete Wood on the reintegration team, which is now a state-funded program; Colonel Scott McCrae, Erik's dad, runs it in honor of his son. Erik would have wanted to see the men well taken care of, and that's exactly what Colonel McCrae's team has done.

Matt Zedwick received the Silver Star for pulling Sean Davis out of the burning Humvee on June 13. He is the first and so far only Oregon Guardsman to receive the award since World War II. He's been highlighted in a National Guard ad campaign and has his own collectible action figure. He's back in college studying graphic design. His best friend, Ron Clement, left the Guard to finish up at Oregon State. He's in the ROTC program and will make a fine officer.

The BC came home to the Corvallis police department. He's in charge of the Oregon Military Academy in Monmouth. He's more emotional now, and I think he misses his Volunteers.

Mike Warrington commands his own battalion, the 1-41 Support. He'll be wearing a star someday for sure. Captain San Miguel is on the SWAT team in Eugene and took Bravo Company to Mongolia in August 2006, where the Bulldogs were the U.S. Army' representative in a multinational, antiterror exercise.

Lieutenant Colonel Tanguy is now Volunteer Six. He took over 2-162 after New Orleans. He's working hard to network with local authorities so his battalion can better function in the event of a natural disaster.

Ross Boyce is in medical school at the University of North Carolina, Chapel Hill. Daren Buchholz is a police officer in Independence. Andy Hellman is training new recruits at the military academy. Bill Stout owns his own company inspecting for mold and rot.

Shane Ward had unfinished business overseas. After recovering from his June 13 wound, he left Oregon to train Rangers. The job changed his life and he's now in special forces training and will start sniper school soon. He'll return home someday to finish school and settle down, but with America at war, his country needs him. For Shane, it is duty *always*.

I started this book project as a way to contribute to my country in time of war. Instead, it became my way of paying tribute to the finest humans I've ever known. I am loath to type the final word, for when the book is finished I know I will grieve for it. Every book is a journey. This one was an adventure. Meeting the Volunteers changed my life.

A job does not define a soul. Raised in the Silicon Valley, I was taught that the value of a man lay in his position in a corporate hierarchy. What nonsense. It lies in the content of his character. Phil Larson, Vinni, E. Z., Sergeant C, Dis, and Z—they all proved that to me. Men like these are barely noticed back home. They are clerks and deliverymen, bricklayers and landscapers who live anonymously among us. They have one thing in common: underneath their name tags beats a hero's heart.

ACKNOWLEDGMENTS

This book could not have been written without the help of the men and families of 2-162. A huge thank-you must also go to Major Warrington, Major Tanguy, and Staff Sergeant Bruns for providing as much of the documentation of the deployment as could be released.

Eric Hammel made it happen. Richard Kane suffered through its completion and remained cheerful despite the torturous hours I put him through. To my two friends, thank you for allowing me to tell the story of the Volunteers. Everyone at MBI needs a huge round of applause. They worked late hours trying to make me look good. Thank you for all that, and for making me feel at home within the MBI family.

Finishing this book strained my own family to the limit. My wife, Jennifer, was my rock, my inspiration. Without you, Jenn, I'd have nothing. Eddie and Renee, you both have been so supportive and understanding, I owe you both lots of time together. To Donna Henderson, who is now my favorite Oregon poet, the insight you provided and the epiphanies you sparked made all the difference in my life. To Dave, Billy Kay, Andy, Denice—your food fueled the book—and Volunteers. Thanks for taking care of us both.

To every family of 2nd Battalion: I wish I could have written about each one of you and your own experiences during OIF II. There just was not room within these pages. Know that the men I did write about were selected because they represented the spirt and values shared by every Volunteer.

A portion of the proceeds of this book will be given to Ben Isenberg's two sons and Eric McKinley's daughter. If you would like to donate to this fund, please contact Darcy Woodke at 541-686-0415 or wwdrc77@msn.com

For more stories of the Volunteers in Iraq and New Orleans, please visit: www.thedevilssandbox.com

APPENDICES

I

June 4 and the Iraqi Stringers

The June 4, '04, ambush brought the Volunteers face to face with the Information War in Baghdad. The Iraqi stringers supply vast amounts of images and raw story material for the Western press corps, which has been virtually imprisoned in the downtown hotels since late '03.

Some journalists are willing to embed with American units. Most do not because they believe it compromises their objectivity. Yet, Western reporters cannot move around unrestricted in Iraq. They are prime targets for kidnapping and assassination. During the Shia uprisings, their hotels were frequently under fire.

As a result, Western news outlets heavily rely on local national stringers to deliver them the news. But who are they? And because they embed with the insurgents, how is it their objectivity has not been questioned?

To date, there has been no national debate on this issue. Stringers for the Associated Press, Reuters, and other Western agencies are still out photographing attacks on American forces. As on June 4, they have advance knowledge of these attacks and work closely with the insurgents. Their photographs of dead and dying Americans have been spread throughout the world by U.S., French, and British news corporations.

In '05, Karim Kadim and Khalid Mohammad received Pulitzer Prizes for photojournalism. Kadim earned his for a picture of a dead Iraqi child who allegedy had been killed by U.S. troops. Khalid Mohammad received his for a photo of a Mahdi militiaman standing guard near the Imam Ali Shrine during the Battle of Najaf, a white dove of peace perched serenely on his shoulder.

How did these stringers gain such unfettered access to the Mahdi Militia when other journalists have been shunned, kidnapped, or killed? The question remains unanswered, but it is easy to suspect that they are sympathizers to Al Sadr's cause, if not actual operatives working for him. If the latter is the case, Al Sadr has used these stringers to wage his own propaganda campaign in American and Western news outlets. It is brilliant, and it has worked. The photos these stringers have routinely taken end up on America's front pages and cannot but help to shape public perception of the war.

The American military cannot be defeated on the battlefield in Iraq; the insurgency is too fragmented and ill-equipped to do that. But, the United States can be defeated should public opinion back home turn decisively against the war.

On that front, the information front, the United States is particularly vulnerable. To date, America has been crushed in the information war. The insurgents and their allies have proven to be quite adept at getting their message out, while the U.S. military has been very clumsy in its response. In the months to come, the information war will probably decide the fate of millions of Iraqis. Will their nascent democracy survive, or will Iraq fall into the hands of Al Sadr and his ilk? America's resolve will provide the answer.

II

The Gray-Haired Mystery Man Revealed

Two years after the events at the Ministry of Interior complex, Staff Sergeant Kevin Maries tumbled across the Gray-Haired Mystery Man's identity after encountering his photograph online. According to a *Boston Globe* article published on July 4, '04, Steven Casteel had been the American in charge of Iraq's Ministry of Interior until the changeover on June 29, '04. At that point, he became the senior American advisor to the MOI. By his own account in the *Globe* article, he arrived at the torture complex to "smooth things over" after Lieutenant Colonel Hendrickson was ordered out. Written by Anne Barnard, a *Boston Globe* staffer, the article described the events of June 29 as a "turf battle between Iraqi Interior Ministry officials and U.S. military police" that "ruffled feathers all the way to the prime minister's office."

The article, which relied on Iraqi MOI officials and Casteel as its sources, strongly suggested that the American "MPs" overreacted by bursting into the complex. Barnard wrote, "agents in plain clothes were questioning suspects from the [al] Betawain raid at a ministry outbuilding, dragging them from one place to another in the hot sun, officials said. U.S. military police thought abuse might be going on. . . . they stormed in . . . and made the police lie on their stomachs while they checked their identification."

The ridiculousness of this version is clear from one glance at the photos shot by Kevin Maries and Kurt Engle. The fact is, on June 27, '04, MOI agents, backed up by U.S. troops and American-supplied satellite imagery, raided the al Betawain district of Baghdad and netted well over a hundred suspects who were allegedly involved in criminal activity. They were beaten, electrocuted, deprived of food and water, and stuffed into a single, steaming hot room for two days. Had it not been for the snipers' alertness and Hendrickson's decision to move on the compound, who knows how many of these prisoners would have died at the hands of their captors.

Steven Casteel had been an intelligence chief for the Drug Enforcement Agency prior to going to Iraq after the '03 invasion. As head of the MOI until June 29, '04, he ultimately must bear final responsibility for the treatment of the al Betawain prisoners.

III

Reunion

In March of '05 I stood on the tarmac at McChord AFB in Washington, awaiting the arrival of the final flight of Volunteers from Iraq. Vinni Jacques anxiously paced nearby. His platoon was on the plane. I had tentatively started writing this book a few weeks before this day, but was still unsure if a non–World War II book was for me. My area of expertise as a historian is the Pacific War, a far different conflict from the one in Iraq.

The plane arrived, the door opened, and the Volunteers quietly debarked. There was no ground-kissing, no hollering or shouting. Each man (and Rebekah-mae Bruns) descended the stairs with surprising solemnity. As they reached American soil, Congresswoman Darlene Hooley greeted them. She was the only Oregon politician there that day.

As I watched the men come home, I wondered what I would know about them in a year's time. They were largely strangers to me at that moment, but when I look back I remember seeing Brunk Conley and Pete Salerno, Bruns and the BC as they paused to shake hands with Hooley. And then, Vinni's men piled on him, and one after another was engulfed in a typical Jacques bear hug. I photographed this emotional moment with singular detachment. I did not know these people, I did not know the bond they shared. I did not understand.

Then a shadow crossed in front of me. Through my camera's viewfinder, Vinni's reunion disappeared, replaced by chocolate-chip DCUs. I looked up into the eyes of a tall, handsome young soldier.

"Hi, John," he said to me. The moment caught me speechless. I was staring at my wife's favorite former student from Central High School.

Dawson Officer was a freshman when my wife first started teaching. Upon graduating in '98, Dawson went to work at our local bank. I got to know him through those four years at Central, then during visits to the bank. Intelligent, dynamic, and a total smartass, Dawson was one of those kids teachers never forget.

He fought in Iraq with Delta Company for a year and I never even knew it. As I stood with him, I realized what a fool I had been. This defining event in our generation was unfolding around me, and I was so clueless I didn't even know young men from my community were in the middle of it. The war in Iraq was remote. Up until now, it had not affected me in any way. I was so focused on the past, I was ignorant to the present.

But that moment with Dawson changed everything for me. He had fought his share of battles with Delta Company's 3rd Platoon. In Zone 22 during August '04 he'd been wounded. Dawson had been in skirmishes large and small. He did his job, was proud of his accomplishments, and had returned home to a community that had *no idea* of his service.

Overwhelmed with a myriad of emotions, I burst into tears and gave Dawson the hugging of his life. I didn't want to let go. I wanted to apologize for my ignorance, for my lack of support. I should have been there for him during his time in Iraq. I should have sent him care packages, chewing tobacco, Xbox games, porn, and papers from home. I should have been a part of this effort. It was too late for that, but I could still do something for these men. I finally let Dawson go so he could find his folks and fiancée. Across from me, Vinni's platoon had broken away from the big man's bear hugs. Vinni stood alone, watching them walk to the terminal area. Detached no more, this moment gave me clarity.

Now, I understood.

Though I wasn't able to write about Dawson in Iraq—I simply ran out of space—he is the reason why this book was written. Eighteen months, over 350 interviews, and a trip to New Orleans later, I look back now and realize that this brief encounter at McChord changed my life's direction forever. Thank you, Dawson, for showing me the way.

GLOSSARY

ACOG: advanced combat optical gunsight
AGR: Active Duty Guard and Reserve, *compare to* MDAY
AO: area of operations
AT: annual training (typically, two-week summer training session that
    supplements monthly drills)
BC: battalion commander
BFT: Blue Force Tracker
BFV: Bradley fighting vehicle
BMP: Soviet mechanized infantry vehicle (*Boyevaya Mashina Pehoti*)
CASEVAC: casualty evacuation
CCP: casualty collection point
CIB: combat infantryman's badge
CLSB: combat lifesaver bag
CPA: Coalition Provisional Authority
COTTAD: Contingency Operation Temporary Tour of Active Duty
CSC: convoy support center
CSH: combat support hospital
DAC: district advisory council
DRRF: Division Rapid Reaction Force
EOD: explosive ordnance detachment
FO: forward observer
FOB: forward operating base
FOBbits (rhymes with *hobbits*): FOB bitches, *see* POG and REMF
FSO: fire support officer
HHC: headquarters and headquarters company
HMMWV: high-mobility multipurpose wheeled vehicle (Humvee)
HUMINT: human intelligence, as opposed to signal intelligence (SIGINT),
    which refers to radio and other electromagnetic transmissions
IBA: Interceptor body armor system
IED: improvised explosive device
ING: Iraqi national guard
IO: information officer
IOBC: Infantry Officers Basic Course
IP: Iraqi police
JAG: Judge Advocate General (army lawyers)
JDAM: Joint Direct Attack Munition
JRTC: Joint Readiness Training Center
JTAC: Joint Tactical Air Controller

KBR: Kellogg, Brown and Root (Halliburton subsidiary)
LZ: landing zone
MDAY: part-time National Guard, *compare to* AGR
MEU: Marine Expeditionary Unit
MOI: Ministry of Interior (Iraqi)
MOS: military occupation specialty
MOUT: Military Operations in Urban Terrain
MSR: main supply road/route
MTOE: official, published standard
NAC: neighborhood advisory council
NOC: noncommissioned officer
NVG: night vision goggles
OBJ: objective
OC: observer controllers for field training exercises and evaluations
OIC: officer in charge
OIF: Operation Iraqi Freedom
OPFOR: opposition/opposing force
OpSec: operational security
PAO: public affairs officer
PFLI: Patriotic Front for the Liberation of Iraq
PKM: Soviet 7.62mm general purpose machine gun
POG: personnel other than grunts
POO: point of origin
PSD: personal security detail
PSYOP: psychological operation
QRF: quick reaction force
REMF: rear echelon motherfuckers
ROE: rules of engagement
RPG: rocket-propelled grenade
RPK: Soviet light machine gun (*Ruchnoi Pulemet Kalashnikov*)
RTO: radio telephone operator (radio man)
SAW: squad automatic weapon
SF: special forces
SITREP: situation report
SOCOM: Special Operations Commmand
SRM: short-range marksmanship
TAAB: Tactical Assembly Area Black
TC: truck commander/truck command
TCP: traffic control point
TOC: Tactical Operations Center
TTP: tactics, techniques, and procedures
VBIED: vehicle borne IED

MAPS

KEYS

AO Volunteer Map

A. Jamelia Power Station on Gold & Grizzlies.
B. Martyr's Monument.
C. Skeletal building used by Scouts on August 10, 2004.
D. Patrol Base Volunteer.
E. Budweiser Bridge.
F. Adhamiya District.
G. Sheik Umar District.
H. Iraqi Police Station Six on Route Gold.
I. June 4, 2004 Ambush on Route Pluto.

Jamelia Power Station

A. As Alpha advances down Route Gold, Neibert peels his squad off to the left to secure the flank between the apartments and the power station.
B. While Neibert covers the flank, Rogers, Larson and the rest of 3rd Platoon establish their first position near the end of Route Gold. They immediately make contact and are heavily engaged.
C. Neibert deploys his Humvees in this cul-de-sac, then dismounts and advances toward Grizzlies on foot.
D. Neibert, Cole, and Presler get pinned down as fire comes from E, G, and F.
E. The dirt mound, one of the key insurgent fighting positions throughout the engagement.
F. A warehouse used as an insurgent fighting position.
G. Insurgent machine gun position in an apartment building.
H. Another insurgent position in an apartment building used to deliver fire on Neibert and Terrel's Humvees.
I. The blue Opal and an insurgent stronghold opposite the Grizzlies-Gold traffic circle.
J. Larson, Brase, Pennington, and Ellifret's position amongst the construction equipment later in the fight.

Budweiser Bridge

A. IED in traffic circle.
B. Larson, Brase, Cole, and Neibert's initial position on top of the catwalk on Budweiser Bridge.
C. Iraqi Special Forces troops trapped under the far end of Budweiser Bridge.
D. The warehouse where Pink Shirt was found.
E. Two insurgents on the bank, killed by Ezelle's men.
F. Wrecked Iraqi Special Forces pick up truck full of ammunition and RPGs.
G. DeGiusti secures the flank by assaulting the three insurgents on the near bank. When finished, he gets his squad on line and kills two more across the river at position E.
H. Larson and Neibert start their dash across the bridge. Ezelle's Humvees move to the bridge's crest in support.
I. Charlie Company engages insurgent positions atop apartment buildings.
J. 1-9's Bradleys and Abrams advance into the action.
K. Furthest advance of 1-9's tanks.
L. DeGiusti's squad gets into a grenade fight around this residential block.

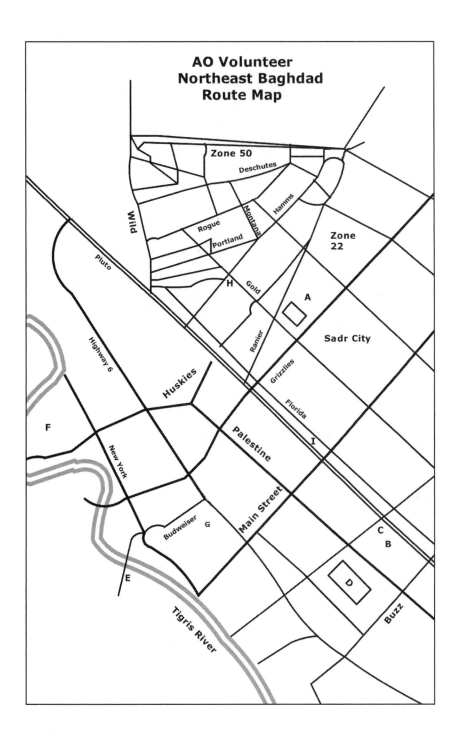

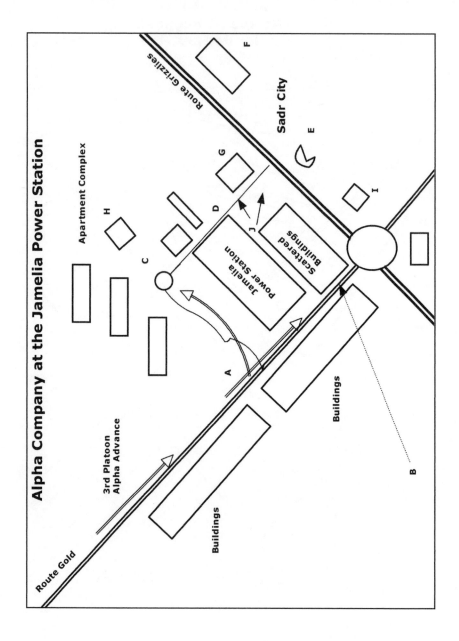

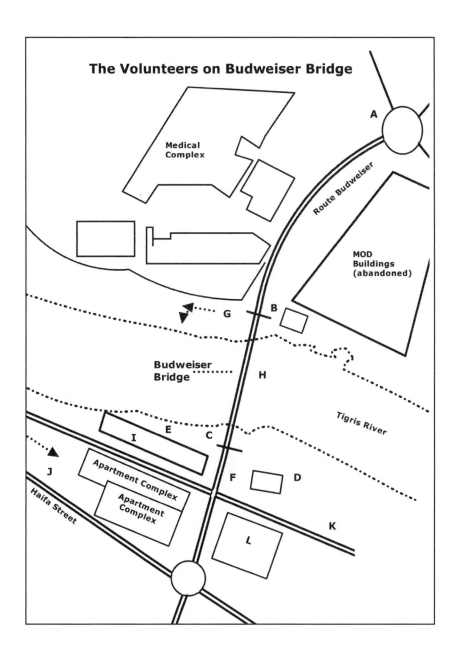

The Volunteers on Budweiser Bridge

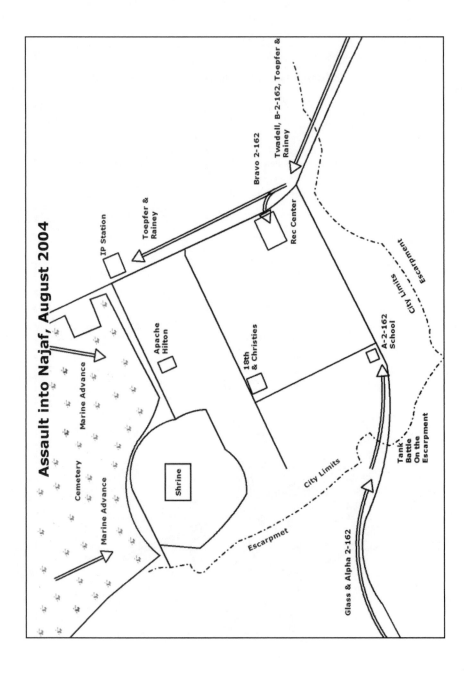

INDEX